THE
Founding Lawyers
AND
America's Quest for Justice

How American lawyers built the world's only legal system that makes the Rule of Law work for all the people

STUART M. SPEISER

POUND
CIVIL JUSTICE
INSTITUTE

The Founding Lawyers and America's Quest for Justice
Copyright ©2010 Stuart M. Speiser
All rights reserved

Published by Pound Civil Justice Institute
777 Sixth Street N.W., Suite 200
Washington DC 20001
www.poundinstitute.org

For information about special discounts for bulk purchases, please contact the Pound Civil Justice
Institute at (202) 944-2841 or info@poundinstitute.org

Cover Design by Pine Hill Graphics
Interior Design by Pine Hill Graphics

Library of Congress Cataloging-in-Publication Data
(Provided by Cassidy Cataloguing Services, Inc.)

Speiser, Stuart M.
       The founding lawyers and America's quest for justice : how
       American lawyers built the world's only legal system that makes the
       rule of law work for all the people / Stuart M. Speiser. -- 1st ed. --
       Washington, DC : Pound Civil Justice Institute, 2010.

           p. ; cm.

           ISBN: 978-0-933067-23-3
           Includes bibliographical references and index.

           1. Lawyers--United States. 2. Rule of law--United States.
       3. Practice of law--United States. 4. United States. Constitutional
       Convention (1787) 5. Constitutional law--United States. 6. United
       States--Politics and government. 7. Sociological jurisprudence--
       United States. I. Pound Civil Justice Institute. II. Title.

KF298 .S64 2010
340./1150973--dc22   1006

10 9 8 7 6 5 4 3 2 1

Printed in the United States of America.

Contents

Introduction 1
Scope and Method 2

PART ONE: The Untold History of American Lawyers

1. The Rule of Law According to Generalissimo Trujillo 7
2. A Summer in Philadelphia 15
   The Convention Begins. 21
   The Battle for Ratification 25
3. Why Call Them Founding Lawyers? 31
   Separation of Powers with Checks & Balances 33
   The Founding Lawyers' Coup d'État 36
   Lost in the Shuffle: The Bill of Rights. 48
   The Founding Lawyers' Roots in Colonial History 51
   The Constitution's Moral Deficiencies 60
4. Initiating a Government of Laws (1789-1864). 63
   The Third Branch Blossoms 70
   The Elephant in the Living Room 78
   The Great Emancipator 83
5. Restoring the Government of Laws (1865-1937). 87
   The New Deal and the Government of Laws (1933-1937) 91
6. Preserving the Government of Laws (1937-1974). 109
   Looking Jim Crow in the Eye 111
   The White House Tapes 122
7. Bush v. Gore: Testing the Government of Laws (2000-2009). 129
   What If the U.S. Supreme Court Had Not Intervened?. 134
   The Public's Reaction to the Supreme Court Decision. 146

PART TWO: Americans' Unique Access to Their Courts

8. Checks and Balances in Everyday American Life. 153
   George Washington's Vision of the National Character. 154
   The Rule of Law According to Rolls-Royce. 160
   The Effects of Fee-Shifting on Litigants Like Oliver Brown. 166
   The Official Reasons Given for Fee-Shifting 168

9. The Truth about "Frivolous" Lawsuits 171
   The Incompetence Required to Tolerate Frivolous Lawsuits 181

10. The Rule of Law According to "Lex Onassis" 191
   Terror by Writs: How Wealthy Crooks Pollute Legal Systems 199
   How Would McCusker v. Onassis
     Have Fared in Other Legal Systems? 201
   England's Failed Attempts to Provide Access to Justice 203
     English Legal Aid in the 21st Century 204
     Conditional Fee Agreements (CFAs) 206
     Legal Expense Insurance 206
     Contingency Fees Compared with CFAs 208
   The 2009 Jackson Report: Broadening Access
     Through Contingency Fees and Changes in Loser Pays 209

11. The Rule of Law for David and Goliath 211
   How Would Nader v. GM Fare in Other Legal Systems? 223

12. The Lawyers Who Provide Citizens' Checks & Balances 225
   The Non-Governmental Lawyer-Statesman 225
   The Four Legs Supporting the American Civil Justice System 231
   Role of Bar Associations in Citizens' Checks & Balances 234
   The Janitor and Philip Morris 237

PART THREE: The Pros and Cons of America's Heavy Reliance on Lawyers

13. American Lawyers in Public Office 247
   Thinking Like a Lawyer 251

14. The Myth of the Purifying Lawyer-Statesman .257
   Exhibit A: Kronman's Lost Lawyer 258
   Exhibit B: Glendon's Nation Under Lawyers 260
   Exhibit C: Linowitz's Betrayed Profession 264
   The Missing Exhibit: David Dudley Field 268
   Why the Truth Matters 271

15. Lawyer-Statesmen and the American Rule of Law 275
   Credit Mobilier 276
   Teapot Dome 278
   Senator McCarthy v. the U.S. Army 282
   Watergate 284
   The American Rule of Law Today 286
   The Bottom Line: Accountability to the People 288

16. Defining the Rule of Law 291

   Endnotes 297
   Bibliography/Sources 313
   Index 321
   About the Author 329

Introduction

On January 20, 2009, a lawyer named Barack Obama, once a teacher of constitutional law, took the oath of office as president of the United States. In his inaugural speech, he said:

> Forty-four Americans have now taken the presidential oath. The words have been spoken during rising tides of prosperity and the still waters of peace. Yet, every so often the oath is taken amidst gathering clouds and raging storms.

> At these moments, America has carried on not simply because of the skill or vision of those in high office, but because We the People have remained faithful to the ideals of our forbearers, and true to our founding documents.

> The time has come to reaffirm our enduring spirit; to choose our better history; to carry forward that precious gift, that noble idea, passed on from generation to generation: the God-given promise that all are equal, all are free, and all deserve a chance to pursue their full measure of happiness.

> Our Founding Fathers, faced with perils we can scarcely imagine, drafted a charter to assure the Rule of Law and the rights of man, a charter expanded by the blood of generations. Those ideals still light the world, and we will not give them up for expediency's sake.

This is the story of those founding documents, that charter to assure the Rule of Law and the rights of man. It is the story of the Founding Lawyers, led by James Madison and Alexander Hamilton, who used their forensic skills and daring legal strategies to give us that better history. I believe that without their use of those legal strategies, no viable nation would have emerged from the

American Revolution. Their precious gift still lights our world today, thanks largely to the succeeding generations of American lawyers who have made the United States the only nation in which all citizens have access to justice.

Scope and Method

This book is about civil justice. It does not deal with criminal justice. As important as the American criminal justice system is, it impacts the lives of comparatively few citizens on any given day. Civil justice, of course, deals with civil rights, personal rights, and property rights, subjects which affect the everyday lives of people in all nations to a much greater extent than does criminal justice.

My claim—that the work of lawyers has made the United States the only nation in which all citizens have access to (civil) justice—is a broad one. To enable you, the reader, to judge its accuracy, I felt it necessary to give this book an equally broad scope. Accordingly, it surveys the entire political and legal history of the United States, and compares that history with the experience of other nations.

Part One, *The Untold History of American Lawyers* (Chapters 1-7), documents the work of American lawyers in conceiving, initiating, and executing the plan for an entirely new form of government, which they called a Government of Laws. Chronologically it runs from the 1787 Constitutional Convention through 2009, including the controversial 2000 Supreme Court decision which awarded the presidency to George W. Bush.

Part Two, *Americans' Unique Access to Their Courts* (Chapters 8-12), examines some representative court cases which illustrate the American citizen's right of access to the courts, and goes on to explain why these cases could not have been brought to court in any other nation, even in the other developed democracies. This unique American access to justice has created what I call Citizens' Checks and Balances, which protect individual citizens from oppression by superior forces, whether governmental, business, or wealthy individuals.

This citizens' access is under constant attack from lobbyists paid by major business interests—including the auto, pharmaceutical, chemical, oil, and financial industries, consumer products manufacturers, and especially the makers of cigarettes and other destructive products. I believe that Americans need to appreciate and protect their unique access to justice, and encourage other nations to remove the artificial barriers which shut most of their citizens out of their courts.

To facilitate the comparison of American access to justice with the situation in other nations, I have chosen the English legal system as the surrogate for all the developed democracies. England is the most useful exemplar, for three reasons: (1) its government-constructed barriers to access are typical of the other developed democracies; (2) it has conducted many detailed studies of its lack of access, and has attempted (unsuccessfully) to mitigate the harmful effects of restricted access, taking great pains to avoid being accused of mimicking the American system; and (3) because the English common law is the foundation of American law, it is easier (and fairer) to compare American law with English law than with the law of other European nations whose legal systems are derived from Roman or Napoleonic roots.

This book breaks new ground in documenting the indispensable role played by lawyers in the creation, development, and preservation of the Constitution and American democracy. Standing alone, this might appear to be an attempt to deify lawyers, but that is not my purpose. Therefore, in order to present a balanced account, I felt it necessary in Part Three, *The Pros and Cons of America's Heavy Reliance on Lawyers*, to document the negative side effects of the reliance on lawyers to exercise governmental powers, and especially to debunk some myths which have grown up about the American lawyer-statesmen and the role of civic virtue as a substitute for the rules the courts have historically put in place to govern lawyers' conduct.

Since the Government of Laws created by the Founding Lawyers has evolved into what we call the Rule of Law today, I use the two terms interchangeably. President Obama's mention of the Rule of Law in his inaugural address typifies the current worldwide interest in that concept, which is universally admired, claimed by many nations to be part of their governing philosophy, but usually not clearly defined. In the final chapter I discuss the various definitions which have been proposed, and conclude by suggesting a provision which would require nations claiming to follow the Rule of Law to remove all obstacles to court access, including specified obstacles which now block access in all nations outside of the United States.

PART ONE

The Untold History of
American Lawyers

Chapter One

The Rule of Law According to Generalissimo Trujillo

On a blustery March day in 1956, Jesus Galindez came to my cramped one-man Manhattan law office at my request to discuss his acting as a paid consultant on the law of the Dominican Republic. Three days later, the *New York Times* reported that he had disappeared, arousing suspicion of foul play.

Earlier that week, I had been retained by the parents of a young New York cameraman to seek compensation for his death in a Dominican Republic plane crash. The cameraman had been hired to do aerial photography work for a documentary film about a Dominican shipyard owned by the country's dictator, Generalissimo Rafael Trujillo. The plane in which he was killed was owned and operated by Compania Dominicana de Aviacion (CDA), the national airline which also happened to be owned by Trujillo.

All the foreign aviation accident cases which I had previously handled had involved major airlines that were subject to independent government regulation. There was always an official accident investigation, and usually I was able to gain access to enough of the government investigation materials to determine the cause of the crash. But I knew this one was going to be different. One man owned the airline and the airplane—the same man who controlled the government and practically everything else of value in the Dominican Republic, including the accident investigators and the legal system. That one man was the guy I would have to haul into court in order to collect compensation for the parents of the deceased cameraman. What were the chances of getting access to any "investigation" that Trujillo permitted his aviation "authorities" to make? I pictured them as being too terrified to breathe any criticism of *el Jefe* or his relatives and cronies who ran the airline.

I had never been to the Dominican Republic, but managed to acquire a little knowledge of its recent history. President Woodrow Wilson had dispatched the U.S. Marines to occupy the country in 1916, to safeguard American interests from foreign threats. The Marines were ordered to organize and train a Dominican national police force which would replace them once it demonstrated the ability to keep the peace. Rafael Trujillo, theretofore a petty criminal, joined that police force, and quickly impressed his Marine Corps mentors with his brains, charm, and particularly his skill at pimping, consistently producing for their pleasure the most serviceable local prostitutes. These qualifications assured his rapid rise from the ranks, and by the time the Marines went home in 1926, he was the police force's chief of staff.

By 1930, the police force had morphed into the national army, with General Trujillo as its commander. He then led a military coup which toppled the government, and elected himself president by terrorizing the opposition, assigning his soldiers to count the ballots and discard those for candidates whose names did not begin with "Truj." Since that coup, he had maintained a brutal dictatorship through his command of the army, placement of relatives in key offices, and crushing of any potential opposition by terrorist tactics in which the primary procedure was torture (e.g., cattle prods applied to the genitals) followed by murder. Along the way he had discarded the name bestowed on the capital city by Christopher Columbus in the fifteenth century—Santo Domingo—in favor of the more accurate Ciudad Trujillo.

CDA did not operate any scheduled air services into the United States, nor was it registered to do business in any of the states. Those missing links, plus the fact that the accident happened abroad, meant it would be very difficult to establish that any American court had jurisdiction of my clients' damage claims. I was also concerned about the law of the Dominican Republic, which an American court would automatically apply to this case even if it were tried in the U.S. (Years later, the choice of applicable law would become more flexible, but in 1956 the rigid rule was that the *lex loci delicti*— the law of the place of the injury—would govern.) What if Trujillo simply ordered his subservient legislators to pass a law exempting CDA from liability, or limiting it to a few pesos? And if we had to sue Trujillo's CDA in the Dominican Republic, was there a lawyer in that country who would dare to put his name on such a lawsuit?

The key to answering these questions was to find someone who was an expert in the law of the Dominican Republic, preferably one who was familiar with its politics and legal profession. I phoned a friend of mine on the faculty of my alma mater, Columbia Law School, and immediately struck pay dirt. He put me in touch with Jesus Galindez, who was then a lecturer on Latin

American government at Columbia. My friend said that Galindez should fill the bill, since he had lived and worked in the Dominican Republic from 1939 to 1946 and as legal consultant to the Trujillo regime, he had actually written some of the laws that were now in effect.

So it was that the lanky, balding, fortyish scholar landed in my office. I was struck by his resemblance to the Argentine president, Juan Peron, later to gain immortality as the husband of "Evita," the First Lady played by Madonna in the film version. Galindez spoke perfect English with a trace of a Spanish accent. He was my favorite kind of academic expert: unpedantic, practical, and easy to talk with. I soon learned that he had helped to write into the Dominican law of torts (civil wrongs) the most enlightened measures available anywhere:

> Any act by which a person causes damages to another
> makes the person by whose fault the damage occurred
> liable to make reparation for such damage.
>
> Reparation shall include moral as well as material damages.

These jewels came right out of the *Code Napoleon* of 1804. While American law was derived from the English law rather than the French, our provisions for liability (responsibility, accountability) are similar to Napoleon's. But in dealing with fatal accidents, the early English law—designed to protect the nineteenth-century railroads from large awards for passenger deaths—limited damages to "pecuniary loss," meaning the loss of financial support suffered by surviving relatives. Indeed, in *Blake v. Midland Railway*, the 1852 English case which established the pecuniary loss limitation, the judges demonstrated their sensitivity by noting what a catastrophe it would be if a railroad's negligence resulted in the death of the father of eight children—a catastrophe, that is, for the railroad if it had to compensate those eight children for the emotional damage they suffered. Most American courts adopted the English pecuniary loss limitation in wrongful death cases, and so excluded damages for grief suffered by surviving relatives—the "moral damages" which French law allows in all accident cases, whether fatal or not.

This distinction was vitally important to my clients, the parents of the deceased photographer, who was unmarried. As it happened, he was not contributing any financial support to his parents or anyone else, and so the "pecuniary loss" damages were almost non-existent. The real damage was the loss of the son as a human being, not as a financial provider. At that time, the New York courts would approve damage awards of no more than $15,000 to $20,000 for the death of an unmarried child who was not supporting the parents. But in the few states which permitted damages for parental grief, much higher awards—sometimes ten times higher—were allowed.

Therefore, what Jesus Galindez told me about Dominican law was the best possible news. CDA would be liable for damages if we could prove fault (negligence), and the amount they would be ordered to pay would include moral damages for the parents' grief brought on by the loss of their son. Then we got around to discussing how I might be able to get a Dominican lawyer to work with me if the suit had to be filed in that country.

"I'm afraid I can't help you in that respect," he said. He explained that his thirst for democracy and human rights had provoked the displeasure of Trujillo, and that if he had not managed to escape to New York in 1946, he would probably no longer be above ground. He thought that using his name to find a Dominican lawyer would have a chilling effect on the whole project. I believe he mentioned "the kiss of death."

When I told him I was planning to visit the Dominican Republic to recruit a local lawyer and gather evidence about the cause of the plane crash, he advised me to take a gun along.

"Well, I don't have a gun," I replied. "But do you really think Trujillo would dare to harm an American citizen—a tort lawyer, at that?" That was a pretty cocky statement since this conversation took place decades before American tort lawyers came to be considered a force of nature.

"I wouldn't put anything past him," said Galindez. "He is a law unto himself in the Dominican Republic, and I don't think he would take kindly to a foreign lawyer poking into his conduct of the airline or any of his business affairs."

I made a mental note of this warning, and wondered whether I could get President Eisenhower to send a detachment of Marines with me. After all, Ike had moved directly to the White House from the exalted post of president of Columbia University. Surely he would extend this protection to a dues-paying alumnus.

Galindez agreed that he would keep track of his time and bill me each month for his services at the rate of $15 per hour. I said I would need a written statement from him about the provisions of Dominican law, and might need him to testify in court or by deposition if the airline's lawyers disputed his interpretation. He agreed, provided he did not have to return to Ciudad Trujillo, and we shook hands as I walked him to the door.

Having deftly solved the expert witness problem, I turned to investigating the operations of CDA. Here my luck was even better, for I found that CDA conducted enough charter flights into and out of Miami International Airport to make it likely that the Florida courts would take jurisdiction. In other words, we could probably sue CDA in Miami instead of having to file in Ciudad Trujillo.

Over the next few months, two parallel events played themselves out: the disappearance of Jesus Galindez, and the wrongful death case against CDA. Galindez's disappearance was investigated by the New York Police Department, the FBI, and later by a Congressional committee. Since none of these investigations determined what happened to him, we are left with little more than speculation about his fate. He was last seen entering a Manhattan subway station on March 12, 1956. Conjecture centered on the story that an American pilot working for CDA, Gerald Murphy, had been assigned to fly a sedated Galindez that day from a remote Long Island airport to Ciudad Trujillo by way of West Palm Beach, Florida. But this could not be verified because Murphy himself disappeared. Eventually another CDA pilot, Octavio de la Maza, was arrested in the Dominican Republic and charged with the murder of Murphy, but he too became silent forever after he was found hanging from the showerhead in his jail cell, leaving behind an unconvincing suicide note.

One theory was that Galindez was murdered because he was known to have been writing an exposé of the Trujillo regime. But he had not set foot in the Dominican Republic during the previous ten years, which would make his first-hand knowledge of the dictator's doings badly out of date. Another theory—possibly leaked by Trujillo's henchmen—was that Galindez was murdered by agents of his native country, Spain, because he had vigorously opposed the Franco regime, to the point where he was forced into exile in 1939. Again this appeared to be an unlikely reason to kidnap a little-known scholar from the streets of New York, for it was 17 years since he had left Spain.

Media stories theorized that Galindez had either been thrown alive into the boiler of a Dominican ship in New York harbor, or flown to Ciudad Trujillo to be tortured to death as a deterrent to future criticism of the dictator. I was haunted by the knowledge that he had disappeared three days after his meeting with me. What if Dominican agents had him under surveillance, or he had unwisely mentioned to a supposed friend that he was acting as a consultant in a case that might bring to public notice Trujillo's use of his CDA airliners for Florida charter flights? I later learned that Trujillo's colleagues at CDA were very much concerned about maintaining the secrecy of the nature and contents of those charter flights. I could not help feeling that Galindez's undertaking to help me in the lawsuit was more of an immediate provocation to Trujillo than the 10-year-old exposé manuscript. Half a century later, the mystery of what happened to Jesus Galindez—and why—remains unsolved.

The story of the wrongful death action against CDA had a happier ending. An American insurance company wrote the liability coverage for CDA, and their lawyers informed the airline officials that in the Florida court, the parents' attorneys would be able to force production of all of CDA's records concerning the cause of the accident. Furthermore, if CDA contested the jurisdiction of the Florida court, the parents' lawyers would be entitled to probe into the nature and extent of the charter flights which formed the basis for subjecting the airline to suit in Florida. Apparently the prospect of the all-powerful dictator

Trujillo facing the parents of the deceased photographer on equal legal footing was not an attractive one. Soon after filing suit, I was able to obtain a settlement that was very satisfactory to the cameraman's parents. It included moral damages under Dominican law for the grief they had suffered, which they would not have received if the crash had occurred in New York.

Thus in my first and only encounter with Trujillo's justice, I was able to use it to achieve a just result, for one reason: I did not have to try to enforce it in the Dominican Republic. What's more, I experienced an unusual feeling of power—power that I, as an obscure one-man law firm, was able to wield against a pompous dictator who wore gold-braided uniforms fit for a king. I even felt I had achieved a measure of retribution for the killing of Jesus Galindez, although there was no evidence that his death was connected with his work for me. It occurred to me that I was able to wield this power only because the United States honored and enforced the Rule of Law, even if the applicable legal rule came from a country which would never have enforced it against the wishes of its dictator. Once the American courts took jurisdiction of the case, its outcome was determined by the existing law, not by a dictator or any other person, no matter how powerful.

During the 50 years after that case was settled, I didn't give much thought to Trujillo's mockery of the Rule of Law, until I sat down to puzzle out just what is meant by the Rule of Law. We see the term in the news nearly every day, as one nation after another claims it follows the Rule of Law and calls upon other nations to respect it. There is no standard definition of the Rule of Law, but let's start with one of the latest and most comprehensive definitions, the one composed by the U.S. Agency for International Development (USAID):

> The Rule of Law embodies the basic principles of equal treatment of all people before the law, fairness, and both constitutional and actual guarantees of basic human rights; it is founded on a predictable, transparent legal system with fair and effective judicial institutions to protect citizens against the arbitrary use of state authority and lawless acts of both organizations and individuals.

That no-nonsense definition was drafted by AID staffers at the request of the Government Accountability Office—the GAO—as part of the process of justifying U.S. government expenditures for promotion of the Rule of Law in foreign countries. It jumps through many more hoops than the definitions that have been used throughout the world for more than a century. Most of the older definitions are content with requiring a predictable legal system with rules applicable to all litigants that are enforced by judges who are "independent" of the government which put them in office, at least to the extent of making their own decisions without consulting other government officials. More generally, the Rule of Law has been equated with the phrase first written by John Adams: "a Government of Laws, not of men." Or, in the words of the motto engraved over the entrance to the U.S. Supreme Court building, "Equal Justice Under Law."

Under any sane definition, Trujillo's Dominican Republic did not follow the Rule of Law. Although he allowed his hand-picked legislators to write laws that appear humane and fair on paper, the legal system he created and controlled did not permit the enforcement of any of those laws without the Generalissimo's permission. The same sad situation applies to much of the world's population today. In contrast, the world's developed democracies (Britain, France, Germany, Switzerland, Japan, etc.) have legal systems which purport to maintain the Rule of Law, following fixed rules which are enforced by independent judges who cannot be ordered around by the likes of Trujillo.

Yet, on closer study, a startling fact emerges:

The overwhelming majority of people living today in developed democracies which purport to follow the Rule of Law have no more power to invoke the Rule of Law by enforcing legal remedies against the rich and powerful than did the lowliest peons in Trujillo's Dominican Republic.

The reason is that the legal systems of those developed democracies are *inaccessible* to the great majority of their citizens. There is only one nation whose legal system provides access for the great majority of its citizens, regardless of their wealth/poverty and prominence/obscurity. Yes, you guessed it: the much-maligned United States of America, and its equally reviled legal system.

How did this happen?

Let's begin by considering how the United States was able to create the universal access needed to breathe life into the Rule of Law. We will focus especially on the role of American lawyers—now one million strong—in building that living, breathing Rule of Law, and in solidifying the principle of Separation of Powers with Checks and Balances which lies at the heart of a truly democratic government.

As we hike through this largely unexplored region of history and look at some actual cases demonstrating access to the American courts (and lack of it elsewhere), please keep this question in mind:

If American lawyers are responsible in any significant degree for establishing and maintaining the world's only accessible Rule of Law, and all the other developed democracies, while incorrectly claiming that they also maintain the Rule of Law, denounce the American legal system as "lawyer-dominated"—is this the ultimate lawyer joke?

Chapter Two

A Summer in Philadelphia

In 1786, "the United States of America" was as much of a misnomer as "the Democratic People's Republic of North Korea" is in 2010.

In the years since the 1781 British surrender at Yorktown, the thirteen former colonies had become independent sovereign states, nine of them having their own navies and three calling their chief executives "president" instead of "governor." They conducted their very limited relations through the Confederation Congress in New York, without anything resembling a true union or national government. (The Congress originally met in Philadelphia, but was forced to move to New York in 1785 because it left a trail of unpaid bills in the City of Brotherly Love.) The Articles of Confederation, written in 1777 but not ratified until 1781, were more like a treaty than a blueprint for effective government. Article III recited that the "said states hereby severally enter into a firm league of friendship with each other."

Each of the 13 states had one vote in the Confederation Congress, with nine votes required to pass any act. The Congress could only request the states to act. It could not compel states or their citizens to do anything, not even to pay or collect taxes. No state ever came close to meeting the financial requests made by the Congress. By 1785, the Congress had become a pathetic joke, with so little power that states frequently could not be bothered to send delegates, causing great difficulty in obtaining the quorum required to conduct what little business it undertook. John Hancock, one of the great leaders of the Revolution, put it succinctly: "The obvious imbecility of the Confederation of the United States has too long given pain to our friends and pleasure to our enemies."

There were rumblings about the need for a government stronger than the boneless Confederation, but the long suffering of the colonists under British rule left them with a strong distaste for any central authority which could impose taxes or otherwise control their lives. They had fought the war as separate states to escape taxation and domination by Britain, and now they were not interested in creating a powerful national government of their own to step into the British shoes. Such was the distrust of government that many states insisted on annual elections for important public offices.

This celebration of liberty was well-earned, but it ignored the serious threats at both borders: the empire-building British sitting in Canada, and the imperial Spaniards sunning themselves in their Florida colony, both waiting confidently for the chaotic United States of America to self-destruct so they could walk in and appropriate the riches of the New World. There were also serious internal threats, epitomized by Shays's Rebellion, an armed assault on the Massachusetts government by farmers which stopped the state's courts from carrying out foreclosures of debtors' property in the fall of 1786. Other major problems included wildly conflicting claims to the western territories; defaulted payment of public debt (including wartime soldiers' salaries), aggravating the difficulties of dealing with the serious post-war economic depression; lack of a uniform currency, as each state printed its own paper money; and lack of the authority needed to raise or maintain armed forces, conduct diplomacy, or facilitate foreign trade. As each state treated the others like foreign countries, they imposed trade and navigation restrictions on each other, causing endless turmoil because there were no federal courts or other authorities empowered to decide such disputes.

The palliative for such head-on collisions between the states was to convene a commission to conciliate the competing claims. So it was that a major dispute between Maryland and Virginia over navigation of the Potomac River resulted in those states sending delegates to meetings in Virginia in the spring of 1785. That led to the calling of a more ambitious meeting at Annapolis, Maryland, in September of 1786. Ostensibly the Annapolis Convention was designed to focus on regulation of commerce between the states, but behind the scenes two far-sighted young lawyer-statesmen—Alexander Hamilton of New York and James Madison of Virginia—saw a larger opportunity. They instigated the broadening of the Annapolis agenda to deal with the nation's structural problems, for which purpose delegations from all thirteen states were invited. Delegates from only five states attended, making any real progress impossible. But in the Hamilton-Madison master plan, Annapolis was only a stepping stone to a third convention.

Hamilton wrote the Annapolis resolution which recommended to the Confederation Congress that a convention of all 13 states meet in Philadelphia in May 1787. John Dickinson, a prominent lawyer both in Pennsylvania and

Delaware, had served as chairman of the Annapolis Convention, and he supported the Hamilton-Madison views on the need for a stronger national government. With Dickinson's help, the Confederation Congress was persuaded to adopt a resolution on February 21, 1787, calling on all the states to send delegates to a convention in Philadelphia in May for "the sole and express purpose of revising the Articles of Confederation." If the two years consumed in engineering the Philadelphia convention seems excessive, recall that it then took the better part of a week to travel from New York to Boston; it would require as much as a month of travel each way for delegates from the southern states to attend the Confederation Congress in New York; and letters, the only means of communication, moved at the same pace.

Alexander Hamilton and James Madison had very dissimilar backgrounds. Hamilton was born out of wedlock in the British West Indies in 1755, and after his father abandoned the family, he was raised by his shopkeeper-mother on St. Croix (then a Danish colony, later to become one of the U.S. Virgin Islands). Despite the odds against him, Hamilton made his way to New York and studied at King's College (later Columbia). He served with distinction as an officer in the Revolutionary War, and at the age of 22 joined General Washington's staff as a lieutenant-colonel, executing many important assignments. Even before the war ended, he began writing and speaking of the urgent need to create a strong national government capable of protecting and developing the future United States. In 1783, he began law practice in New York, becoming the prototype Wall Street lawyer by opening his office at 57 Wall Street (where he also lived). In 1786 he was elected to the lower house of the New York State legislature, and wangled the assignment as its delegate to the Annapolis Convention. In 1787, at age 32, he became one of New York's three delegates to the Philadelphia convention. He had his work cut out for him, since his state's other two delegates, Robert Yates and John Lansing, were so firmly opposed to creation of a truly national government that they departed from the convention as soon as they discovered what it was up to, leaving Hamilton without the 2-out-of-3 majority needed to commit the New York delegation to the Convention's crucial votes.

James Madison was born in Virginia in 1751, the son of a wealthy tobacco planter. He completed the four-year course at the College of New Jersey (later Princeton) in two years, but as he was frail and given to spells of poor health, the effort exhausted him. He returned to Montpelier, the family plantation, where he spent the next four years in private study of a range of subjects, including law and government. (Since there were as yet no law schools, private study was the route to becoming a lawyer.) He was uncomfortable living off the proceeds of the plantation's slave labor, and often spoke of entering law practice. But the persistence of his mysterious ailments and his inability to speak forcefully made him decide instead to become a scholar of public law, particularly the law relating to constitutions and governmental affairs. In 1776 he was elected to the Virginia legislature, where he became a friend and protégé of Thomas Jefferson. He served in the Continental (later Confederation) Congress from 1780 to 1783, and returned to the Virginia legislature in 1784. While serving in Richmond, he busied himself in the office of Virginia Attorney General Edmund Randolph, broadening his experience of public law. He was appointed chairman of the Virginia legislature's Committee on the Courts of Justice, where he headed the successful effort to reform and revitalize the chaotic Virginia court system, despite stiff opposition from judges and lawyers.

In 1787, at the age of 36, Madison returned to the Confederation Congress in New York and began serious preparation for the Philadelphia convention which he and Hamilton had stealthily plotted as the mechanism for creation of a true United States of America. By that time, his health had improved somewhat but he was still not a forceful or confident public speaker. The records of important debates in which he participated are replete with notes like "Mr. Madison spoke so very low that his meaning could not be comprehended." He had to rely on the logic and documentation of his arguments rather than his oratorical powers.

While Hamilton was forced to attend to his burgeoning New York law practice, Madison had the luxury of spending the time between the February Congressional call and the May opening of the Philadelphia convention boning up on the history and public law he would need to make his case. His friend Thomas Jefferson was then the U.S. Minister to France, but that distant posting did not prevent Jefferson from supplying dozens of books and pamphlets about European history and government, to prepare his protégé for the monumental task of turning the Philadelphia convention into the birthplace of a workable republic. By far the most important book was one by a prominent Massachusetts lawyer, John Adams, who was then resident in London as America's first minister to Great Britain.

John Adams wrote *A Defence of the Constitutions of Government of the United States of America* by hand in 1787 and had the first volume printed in London just in time to exert great influence on the Philadelphia convention. Since the early years of his law practice in the 1760s, Adams had been aware that short of an armed rebellion, the main arena for colonial America's resistance to Britain was the courts, where the British officials attempted to collect taxes and customs, and colonial lawyers could protest their oppressive tactics. With this courtroom experience he combined an extraordinary grasp of history and philosophy, which he put to work in two documents that became foundation stones of American democracy: the Declaration of Independence and the Constitution of the Commonwealth of Massachusetts.

Adams was a member of the five-man committee assigned to draft the Declaration of Independence in 1776. The other four members were Thomas Jefferson, Judge Roger Sherman of Connecticut, Judge Robert Livingston of New York, and Benjamin Franklin (the only non-lawyer). While Jefferson did most of the writing, he acknowledged that Adams contributed many of the legal theories, as we shall see.

Adams single-handedly wrote the Massachusetts Constitution of 1780, which put into practice his deeply-held conviction about the need for separation of powers. At that time "democracy" was a dirty word, not to be mentioned even once in the Declaration of Independence or the Constitution. The word "republic" was then more popular, indicating a government run by representatives elected by the people, whereas "democracy" envisioned direct rule by the people. Both those forms of self-government had given way to monarchy after their failures in ancient Athens and Rome. Adams perceived the reason for those failures: all the governmental power was given to the legislature—the Assembly in Athens, the Senate in Rome—with no independent executive or judicial bodies to provide checks and balances. As a result, both the Athenian and Roman legislatures fell into mob rule and anarchy, famous examples being the death sentence imposed on Socrates by the Athenian Assembly and the Roman Senate's descent into a tool of dictatorship for Julius Caesar and his successors.

Tom Paine's inspirational pamphlet *Common Sense* was the popular revolutionary rallying point of the day, but Adams calmly sidestepped Paine's emotional call for concentration of all governmental power in a single legislative body. Adams built the Massachusetts Constitution on the foundation of a two-house legislature, an independent executive, and an independent judiciary with lifetime tenure to serve as a check on both the other branches, just as the executive and the legislature would check and balance the judicial power. As he famously wrote, "the legislative, executive and judicial power shall be placed in separate departments, to the end that it might be a government of law, and not of men."

Adams brought these principles into even sharper focus in his 1787 *Defence*, which defended the existing state constitutions, including the one he wrote for Massachusetts. Again he cited the mob-rule examples of Athens and Rome and the absolute need for separation, checking, and balancing of powers. Without that separation and balance, the government would be corrupted "as necessarily as rust corrupts iron, or as arsenic poisons the human body."

Adams's commitment to separation of powers was rooted in his realistic appraisal of human nature, summarized in David McCulloch's prize-winning biography, *John Adams*:

> To Adams nothing had changed about human nature since
> the time of the ancients. Inequities within society were

inevitable, no matter what the political order. Human
beings were capable of great good, but also great evil. Thus
it had always been and thus it would ever be…such were
the weaknesses and folly of men, "their love of domination,
selfishness, and depravity," that none could be elevated
above others without risk of danger.

In *Defence,* Adams undertook to refute other ideologies, notably that of
the French philosopher Jacques Turgot, who was then advocating the "perfect democracy" of a one-house legislature exercising all the authority of the
nation. In Turgot's proposal for legislative powers that were neither separated
nor checked, Adams clearly foresaw the debacle of the 1789 French Revolution
which quickly morphed into the bloody rampage that became known as the
Reign of Terror, destroying France's First Republic in less than a dozen years.

Adams reiterated his vision of the ideal government, the only one that
could possibly cope with the imperfections of human nature:

…the legislative, executive, and judicial powers are carefully separated from each other…and where all these
circumstances take place, it is unnecessary to add that the
laws alone can govern.

Adams's *Defence* quoted extensively from more than fifty important works,
including those of Plato, Aristotle, Cicero, Montesquieu, and Rosseau. Here in
one book was all the ammunition James Madison needed to document the
case for separation and balancing of powers, for this was the age in which the
written word was revered.

Now Madison turned his attention to preparing a plan of action for the
Philadelphia convention. While the delegates were summoned officially to
amend the Articles of Confederation, Madison knew that task would be hopeless, for unanimous consent of all 13 states was required. Rhode Island wasn't
even going to send a delegation, and the remaining 12 states could rarely agree
on anything within the framework of the Confederation. To create a true
republic and guarantee the separation, checking and balancing of its powers, an
entirely new blueprint was needed—nothing less than a unique constitution.

Before journeying to Philadelphia, Madison made a move that demonstrated he was as shrewd a politician as he was a dedicated scholar. He decided
to recruit a particular delegate to the Philadelphia convention, one who knew
little about constitutional government, but was a priceless ally because he
was by far the most highly respected man in the United States. On the way
to his Virginia home from Annapolis, Madison stopped off to visit George
Washington, retired from army service and attending to his plantation at

Mount Vernon. There Madison persuaded a pessimistic Washington to lend his enormous prestige to the quest for a real union of the states.

Washington feared that the fledging USA was rapidly approaching anarchy, and would probably break up into two or more confederations with conflicting foreign alliances, or completely disintegrate before long. In 1786 he wrote, "From the high ground we stood upon, from the plain path which invited our footsteps, to be so fallen! so lost! It is really mortifying." He probably had some difficulty envisioning how the often sickly 100-pound five-foot-four James Madison—nearly a foot shorter than Washington and an ineffective speaker to boot—could solve these monumental problems. Washington spoke of "the monster"—the jealously-guarded sovereignty of each of the 13 states—that haunted the young country. He held out little hope of repelling that monster, but if others like Madison were willing to try, he would spend the sweltering summer in Philadelphia with them, doing all he could to support their efforts.

The Convention Begins

The meeting we have come to call the Constitutional Convention opened officially on Friday, May 25, 1787, when a quorum of seven states was obtained. It was then called "the Foederal [Federal] Convention," for good reason. Hamilton, Madison, and their co-conspirators were not about to let the cat out of the bag by labeling it "Constitutional" when the Congressional mandate was strictly limited to amending the Articles of Confederation. Historians are nearly unanimous in concluding that such a label would have scared enough of the delegates away from Philadelphia to make the Convention a non-starter.

In our age of media saturation and blogging it is difficult to contemplate, but somehow the conspirators were able to obtain and enforce a vow of complete secrecy. Despite the fact that many of the delegates were opposed to a strong national government, no word of what the Convention was up to would reach the public until its work was completed.

James Madison arrived in Philadelphia well ahead of most other delegates, and used the lead time to caucus with the other influential members of the Virginia delegation, especially Governor Edmund Randolph. In these sessions they whipped together the framework of a new Constitution: 15 points which became known as the Virginia Plan. So it was that when the Convention began to address its main business on Tuesday, May 29, 1787, the delegates were presented with the Virginia Plan, which in broad outline called for a new national government with three independent branches: a national executive, a national judiciary, and a national legislature of two houses—the representatives, to be elected by the people, and the senators, to be elected by the representatives. The Convention would continue well into September, but the broad agenda originally set by the Virginia Plan held fast all the way. There were long and heated debates about important details such as specific powers and restrictions, and other plans were proposed, but in the end the Virginia Plan was the focus of discussion and furnished the structural outline of the final document.

The main sticking point of the Virginia Plan was that it assured control of both houses of the legislature by the most populous states—Virginia, Pennsylvania, and Massachusetts—since the number of representatives and senators from each state would be determined by its population. As the debate wore on, the Convention was deadlocked on this issue, since the delegates from most of the states felt they were being asked to forfeit their precious sovereignty to a national legislature dominated by the larger states. Into this deal-breaking breach stepped the 66-year-old Judge Roger Sherman of the small state of Connecticut, with a Solomon-like solution: while the House of Representatives would be proportional to population—one representative for each 30,000 inhabitants—each state legislature would elect two senators, and the Senate would be given more prestige and power than the House, including a six-year term instead of the two years allotted to the representatives.

Sherman introduced his compromise proposal on June 11. The fate of the entire Constitution hung in the balance as this issue was debated day after day. Many delegates were disenchanted to the point of giving up the whole project at that point. They came so close to dissolving the Convention that on June 28 Benjamin Franklin made an impassioned plea for the engagement of a chaplain, since it appeared that without the intervention of God, "we shall succeed in this political building no better than the builders of Babel." The 81-year-old Franklin's appeal was received with due respect for his towering intellect and lifetime of great achievements, but as there was no money available to pay a chaplain, the delegates went back to arguing among themselves. Not only were they without divine guidance, but to make matters worse, the debate was dominated by lawyers. Since 34 of the 55 delegates were lawyers, judges, or legal scholars, it should not surprise us to learn that the legal fraternity did most of the talking. The principal speakers throughout were James Madison; two prominent Pennsylvania lawyers, James Wilson and Gouverneur Morris; and Judge Roger Sherman of Connecticut compromise fame.

With the outcome of the Convention very much in doubt on July 11, George Washington, who had been elected its president by acclamation, wrote to Alexander Hamilton (temporarily absent in New York) that he despaired of seeing a favorable conclusion "and do therefore repent having had any agency in the business." But somehow the wrangling lawyers were able to convince many of the small-state delegates that the loss of their presently unrestricted sovereignty would be compensated by the strength that all the states would gain from the formation of a real union. On July 16 came the final vote, and it could not have been closer. Only nine states were able to reach consensus within their delegations, and they divided five to four in favor of Judge Sherman's compromise. There is no doubt that if one state had gone the other way, the Convention would have ended right then and there. Luther Martin, the attorney general of Maryland and a delegate from that state, put it concisely: "We were on the verge of dissolution, scarce held together by the strength of a hair."

Once this daunting problem was solved, the Convention picked up positive momentum in dealing with other disputed provisions. There were 60 ballots taken on the method of selecting the president—many of them resulting in appointment by Congress—before the present form of popular election was agreed upon. By July 26, the delegates concluded that they had adopted enough long-winded resolutions to require clarification of what they had agreed upon and what remained to be debated. For this purpose a Committee of Detail was appointed, consisting of three judges (Oliver Ellsworth of Connecticut, Nathaniel Gorham of Massachusetts, and John Rutledge of South Carolina) and two lawyers (Edmund Randolph of Virginia and James Wilson of Pennsylvania).

The Committee of Detail finished its work on August 6, reformulating the rambling resolutions into 23 articles which roughly expressed the sense of the Convention thus far. But this was only the starting point for producing a final document, since all 23 articles were to be reargued and voted on again. Five more weeks of intensive debate followed the Committee of Detail's report, during which the delegates had great difficulty in reaching consensus on many key issues. They decided to refer the most vexing problems to a Committee on Postponed Matters, composed of one member from each of the eleven states then participating. It became known as the Committee of Eleven, or the Brearly Committee, after its chairman, New Jersey delegate David Brearly, chief justice of his state's supreme court, who had presided over the 1780 case of *Holmes v. Walton,* noted as the first decision in which an American court struck down a statute as unconstitutional.

Brearly's committee was dominated by the lawyers who had done most of the work in creating the Constitution: James Madison of Virginia, Gouverneur Morris of Pennsylvania, Roger Sherman of Connecticut, Rufus King of Massachusetts, and John Dickinson of Delaware. They were joined by Abraham Baldwin of Georgia, the seventh lawyer out of the committee's eleven members. Through their efforts the committee worked out such crucial provisions as the election and powers of the president, the powers of Congress to impose taxes and declare war, and the conduct of relations with Indian tribes.

Finally the Constitution was ready to be written, and that monumental task was entrusted to another panel, this one called the Committee of Style and Arrangement. The members were chosen by ballot, and again all five were lawyers: Judge William Johnson of Connecticut (the chairman), Alexander Hamilton, James Madison, Rufus King, and Gouverneur Morris.

Although all five members contributed to the final document, the actual draftsmanship and many of the crucial editorial decisions were the work of the 35-year-old Gouverneur Morris. He was probably the Convention's most colorful character, better known for his drawing-room wit and his indefatigable pursuit of women (despite the handicap of a highly visible state-of-the-art wooden leg) than for statesmanship. A member of the landed aristocracy, he enjoyed great success as a lawyer in New York and Pennsylvania. But his crowning achievement would come as that sultry Philadelphia summer turned toward autumn, and he began to scratch out on parchment the instrument that would make or break the United States of America.

His artistry appears immediately in the preamble. The unwieldy draft handed down by the Committee of Detail began, as did all the previous Confederation documents, with a long-winded recitation more suited to a treaty than a constitution: "We the undersigned delegates of the States of New Hampshire, Massachusetts-bay" etc., reciting all 13 states, "do ordain, declare and establish the following Constitution for the government of ourselves and our posterity." With a stroke of his quill pen, Gouverneur Morris swept away that sterile opening paragraph and captured the magic of the moment in which a new kind of nation was born:

> We, the People of the United States, in order to form a
> more perfect union, to establish justice, insure domestic
> tranquility, provide for the common defence, promote
> the general welfare, and secure the blessings of liberty to
> ourselves and our posterity, do ordain and establish this
> Constitution for the United States of America.

That was the first public usage of "We the People of the United States," a phrase that would come to epitomize both the nation and the Constitution on which it was built. Even Patrick Henry, who became the most vociferous opponent of ratification, acknowledged that "We the People" represented a sea change, a break from the principle of thirteen sovereign states.

Morris's artistry was not limited to catchy phrase-making. He and his four colleagues boiled down the twenty-three wordy articles they inherited from the Committee of Detail to just seven. Each article was designed to say just enough to create the framework of a workable government, leaving sufficient vagueness, generality, and flexibility to allow the Constitution to develop with the country. James Madison praised Morris's work for its brevity and clarity. Scholars would later laud its "genius for studied imprecision."

Its vitality today as the world's oldest functioning constitution confirms the prescience of the lawyers who created it. For reasons explained in the next chapter, we shall call them the Founding Lawyers.

The exhausting work of the Constitutional Convention was finished at last, and on Monday, September 17, the document as drafted by Morris, with minor changes, was signed by the supporting delegates in the Assembly Room of Independence Hall, where they had held all their meetings, the same room in which the Declaration of Independence had been adopted in 1776. George Washington and James Madison—neither man given to hyperbole—called the Constitution "a miracle."

Only then was the text of the draft Constitution given to the *Pennsylvania Packet & Daily Advertiser* for its first publication to an astonished nation. The lawyers who had worked so hard to create it were fully aware that it was, after all, only a proposal. Now came an even sterner test of their advocacy skills: ratification of their draft by the requisite nine states.

The Battle for Ratification

Knowing that any form of ratification would be a difficult struggle, James Madison, Gouverneur Morris, and their fellow Founding Lawyers had taken precautions to avoid three legal traps: requiring approval by the Confederation Congress, requiring ratification by vote of the state legislatures, and treating the exercise as an amendment of the Articles of Confederation (which required unanimous approval by all 13 states). Avoiding these traps was a task requiring legal finesse that approached sleight of hand, since the Congressional resolution calling the Constitutional Convention "for the sole and express purpose of revising the Articles of Confederation" added the requirement of "reporting to Congress and the several legislatures such alterations and provisions therein as shall when agreed to in Congress and confirmed by the states" render the existing Articles of Confederation adequate to govern the nation.

Imposition of any one of these three requirements would practically assure defeat. Since the new Constitution would completely displace the Confederation Congress, ratification by its members would be a vote to put themselves out of business. The state legislatures were the seats of entrenched authority, and while they would survive, they would be shorn of many of their powers and perquisites. And it was apparent that at least three states—Rhode Island, Maryland, and New York—were dead set against ratification.

To steer the ratification process away from these rocky shoals, Madison and his colleagues had to dig deeply into their bag of lawyer tricks. First, they put through a resolution taking the Confederation Congress out of the ratification process "in order to save Congress from the necessity of an act inconsistent with the Articles of Confederation under which they held their authority." They executed a similar maneuver to shut out the state legislatures, citing the doubtful legality of requiring them to rescind the authority they derived from the Articles of Confederation in a manner not permitted by those Articles. This was a bit more of a stretch, since most of the state constitutions and the Articles of Confederation—which the Congress in its extravagance called "the federal constitution"—had been ratified by the state legislatures.

Here Madison was on his best form. Borrowing from Thomas Jefferson's language in the Declaration of Independence and building on Morris's "We the People" preamble, Madison made the case for the inherent power of *the people* to cast aside inadequate or inappropriate forms of government, maintaining that ratification must be "by the supreme authority of the people themselves." He argued that a league or treaty like the Articles of Confederation was different in principle from the constitution being shaped in Philadelphia: a league/treaty was founded on the legislature, but a true constitution was founded on the people, "the fountain of all power." He also questioned whether a state legislature had the legal power to "change the Constitution under which it held its existence." He insisted that ratification by the people was necessary to establish that the Constitution was clearly paramount to the legal authority of the legislatures.

Since their opponents persisted in arguing that the Convention had no power to do anything but amend the Articles of Confederation, the Founding Lawyers wielded those battered Articles alternatively as a sword or a shield, depending on which favored their objectives. During his pre-Convention studies, Madison had adapted from international law the "breached-treaty" principle: the promises in a treaty are "perfect and reciprocal," so that if any of its provisions are breached, the entire treaty fails, absolving all parties from further duty to comply with it. Madison quoted Article III of the Articles of Confederation, "The said [sovereign and independent] states hereby enter into a firm league of friendship with each other," to demonstrate that this was the legal equivalent of a treaty. He argued that because many notorious breaches had occurred, the requirement of unanimous approval of amendments no longer applied, and certainly had no effect on the power of the people to adopt a new constitution. Madison also used the breached-treaty principle to avoid ratification by the state legislatures, arguing that such a process would create nothing more than another treaty among sovereign states in the mold of the Articles of Confederation, so that the slightest future breach would legally dissolve the union.

Following up on Madison's breached-treaty maneuver, two of the country's leading lawyers, delegates James Wilson of Pennsylvania and Rufus

King of Massachusetts, deftly disposed of the unanimity requirement. They pushed through a resolution that ratification by nine states would bring the Constitution into operation—but only between the ratifying states. The Founding Lawyers were confident that once nine or more states began functioning as a union, the stragglers would be forced to join eventually.

Thus Gouverneur Morris covered ratification in the single sentence of Article VII, the final provision of the Constitution:

> The Ratification of the Conventions of nine states shall
> be sufficient for the establishment of this Constitution
> between the states so ratifying the same.

Specifying "Conventions" meant that the people of each state would elect delegates to represent them in debating and voting on ratification. The Confederation Congress was not mentioned, but under cover of an explanatory letter drafted by Gouverneur Morris for the signature of George Washington, the proposed Constitution was sent to the Congress for forwarding to each of the state legislatures, whose only specified role was to arrange for the election, by popular vote, of the delegates to their state's ratification convention.

Washington signed that explanatory letter on September 17, and it was dispatched to the Confederation Congress in New York. Madison, a member of the Congress, rushed to New York to make sure there would be no detours in the carefully-plotted itinerary of the proposed Constitution. His foresight proved providential, for Richard Henry Lee, a fellow member of the Congress, had other ideas. Lee, a prominent Virginia lawyer who had been one of the leading lights of the Revolutionary period, opposed the Constitution mainly because he feared its adverse impact on state governments. When the proposed Constitution arrived in New York, he attempted to persuade the Congress to reconsider and amend it before sending it to the states, a process designed to talk it to death.

Along with the proposed Constitution had come Washington's letter of explanation, and a resolution signed by "G. Washington" as President of the Convention, which directed the Congress to forward the Constitution "to a Convention of Delegates, chosen in each State by the People thereof… for their Assent and Ratification." Madison, brandishing the letter and resolution signed by G. Washington, argued that the Congress lacked the legal power to change one word of the proposed Constitution, for doing so would turn it into a mere Act of Congress which would require approval by all 13 state legislatures. Lee responded that the so-called Constitution was nothing more than a report of the activities of the Philadelphia Convention, with which the Congress could do whatever it saw fit. Lee submitted a large batch of proposed amendments which would have destroyed the framework built in Philadelphia.

The fate of the fledgling Constitution again hung in the balance as the Confederation Congress debated its handling for three days. Finally Madison was able to carve out what appeared to be a compromise solution: the Congress would not take any official action on the proposed Constitution, but would merely forward it to the state legislatures as a "report" which spoke for itself. So it was that on September 28, this resolution was adopted without a dissenting vote:

> Congress, having received the report of the Convention lately assembled in Philadelphia
>
> Resolved Unanimously that the said Report with the resolutions and letter accompanying the same be transmitted to the several legislatures in order to be submitted to a convention of the Delegates chosen in each state by the people thereof in conformity to the resolves of the Convention made and provided in that case.

Thus the revolutionary Constitution was forwarded to the states disguised as a mild-mannered report, still packing the imprimatur of G. Washington. That was sufficient to enable it to arrive intact at ratifying conventions elected by the people of each state, although there were unsuccessful attempts by opponents in several states to amend or otherwise emasculate it as it made its stealthy way through the state legislatures. Washington himself was elated at this progress, and wrote to Madison that its movement through the Congress, even in disguised form, would give people the impression it was actually approved by the Congress, and that the "appearance of unanimity in that body, on this occasion, will be of great importance." Although a surveyor and planter by profession, he got caught up in the lawyerly maneuvering that was needed to make the Constitution a reality.

The public debut of the Constitution on the front page of the *Pennsylvania Packet & Daily Advertiser* on September 19, 1787, was quickly followed by publication in newspapers throughout the country. There was an immediate outcry from both sides, with an unprecedented deluge of letters of approval or denunciation. As the public discussion began, the Founding Lawyers led by Madison and Hamilton scored a coup by anointing themselves as the Federalists, foisting on their opponents the less desirable Anti-Federalist label. The opponents of ratification argued that they were the true Federalists, since they supported the confederation principle under which both the state and federal governments had important functions, whereas the proponents of the Constitution were really trying to terminate the states' functions by consolidating all the power in an octopus-like national government. But they soon found they would have to march into this battle against the Founding Lawyers carrying the unwanted Anti-Federalist banner.

The argument was waged largely in the newspapers. On October 4, the *Pennsylvania Packet & Daily Advertiser* published a long list of objections submitted by George Mason, a Virginia delegate to the Constitutional Convention who quickly became a leading Anti-Federalist. Mason's attack, and others published elsewhere across the country, charged that the rogue Philadelphia Convention, conducted in total secrecy to avoid the inevitable public outrage, was designed to destroy the state governments, and that its lack of a Bill of Rights opened the door to tyranny, which would soon be inflicted upon all the states by the power-hungry aristocrats who were bent upon seizing control of the young nation.

Explaining and defending the proposed Constitution was a monumental challenge. It was the first written national constitution, and there was no human experience with the kind of government that was hazily sketched in the document. Could anyone visualize how this three-headed monster would work, or what its words would come to mean in the lives of ordinary citizens? Even today, two centuries later, many of our best legal minds are continuously jousting to define those words one way or another. But the Anti-Federalist attacks were fomenting opposition, and they had to be countered quickly. This challenge was met mainly by Alexander Hamilton, James Madison, and John Jay, a leading New York lawyer who had drafted that state's first constitution and was then serving the Confederation Congress as its nearly powerless secretary of foreign affairs.

Writing under the joint pen name *Publius,* the trio produced 85 essays in support of ratification. Becoming known as *The Federalist Papers,* they have survived to this day as the leading body of authority on the original meaning of the Constitution. The *Publius* essays were originally published in New York newspapers, but soon found their way into print in other states, as did the 85 counter-essays produced by the Anti-Federalists.

It was a battle for the soul of the nation, fought out with legal briefs as the weapons.

We'll return to analysis of the battle for ratification in the next chapter. Here it will suffice to mark up a brief scorecard. Among the early state conventions to act were Delaware, New Jersey, and Georgia, all of which ratified the Constitution unanimously by early January 1788. Connecticut soon followed suit by a vote of better than three-to-one. Both sides had expected those results, since Georgia, menaced by Spaniards on the south and Indians on the west, was desperately in need of military assistance from a strong national government, and the other three were small states at risk of being gobbled up by larger neighbors in the absence of a union. In Pennsylvania, the first of the large states to vote, the score was closer, but the Federalists were able to win ratification by exactly two-to-one. Massachusetts was the sixth, ratifying by the narrow margin of 187 to 168 on February 6, 1788. This was followed by Maryland's 63-to-11 ratification, and then by South Carolina, where stiffer opposition was fought off (and victory by 149 to 73 was won) under the leadership of the cousins Charles Pinckney and Charles Cotesworth Pinckney, both lawyers who had made important contributions to the success at Philadelphia. On June 21, New Hampshire's ratification by 57 to 47 brought the total to the nine states required to bring the Constitution into force. Virginia ratified in June, and New York followed in July.

North Carolina first rejected ratification by more than two-to-one, but in November of 1789 it ratified by a vote of 194 to 77. Little Rhode Island refused to be hurried, and it was not until May 29, 1790, that it ratified by 34 to 32. Those actions were an anti-climax, for G. Washington, elected president without opposition, was inaugurated in New York on April 30, 1789—and the rest is history.

———

So the deed was done, and the true United States of America was born. By now you must have noticed that from the plotting of Madison and Hamilton at Annapolis which began the Constitution's tortuous odyssey, through the scorching summer in Philadelphia and the nine-month campaign for ratification, the milestones were the handiwork of lawyers. It was the fulfillment of Tom Paine's 1776 *Common Sense* thesis that "in America, THE LAW IS KING" (capitals in original).

Let's take a closer look at the Constitution. How had it come about, what did it really mean, and how did the lawyers' role in its advent affect the future course of American democracy and the Rule of Law?

Chapter Three

Why Call Them Founding Lawyers?

I n a 1985 speech, *The Lawyer-Statesman in American History,* Supreme Court Justice William H. Rehnquist paid tribute to eight leaders "who played a vital, perhaps a transcendent, role in steering the ship of state through the shoals that confronted it." He chose these exemplars from two critical eras: the Founding Period following the 1787 Constitutional Convention, and the decade preceding the Civil War (1854-1865). The four men he selected as leading lawyer-statesmen in the Founding Period were Thomas Jefferson, Alexander Hamilton, James Madison, and John Marshall. Of particular interest to us is Rehnquist's theory of how their backgrounds in law helped them to play crucial roles in the nation's founding:

> They were people who held high public office but also dealt
> easily with ideas; they left their marks not only by their acts
> but by their spoken and written words. It seems very likely
> that their legal education and practice must have contrib-
> uted to this facility with words and ideas.

Rehnquist also noted that their legal training "taught skills that were transferable in their entirely to the stump speeches and printed tracts that were the staples of Nineteenth-Century political campaigns," and that "in law, the power of clear statement is everything." He found James Madison at the Constitutional Convention to be "an extraordinarily able advocate of his political point of view."

I will presume to go further than the late chief justice and suggest that several other lawyerly attributes were useful to these statesmen (and to the fledgling USA) in creating the Constitution, getting it ratified, and making it work in the real world. As lawyers it was part of their professional study and practice to deal extensively with the defects and excesses of human nature, such as duplicity and thirst for power. This experience and insight equipped them to ferret out the vulnerabilities which might be exploited to manipulate the prospective new government into tyranny—and how those vulnerabilities might be neutralized by artfully designing the separation of powers and specific checks and balances. The lawyer-statesmen were also adept at negotiating difficult compromises, and were forensically skilled at turning their opponents' arguments against them, as Madison and his cohorts did in deploying the Articles of Confederation at Philadelphia. And they were able to convey in words—as Hamilton, Madison, and Jay did in *The Federalist Papers*—the image of this Constitution actually working well despite its reliance on so many untried concepts.

The tasks handed to the Founding Lawyers were strikingly similar to those routinely assigned to lawyers since time immemorial: *Clean up this mess*—in this case, the mess left by the dysfunctional Articles of Confederation. Take it one step at a time, building a case or an agreement by increments, making no more changes than those required to achieve the objective; hold your noses and walk around (not through) the client-created cesspools; keep the argument focused on your strongest points and ignore the inevitable attacks on your personal integrity; tread nimbly along the fine line between forensic rhetoric and Machiavellian duplicity; persuade the contending forces to accept conditions they would never have dreamed of agreeing to; and leave in place a workable structure, an *enforceable procedure* that will govern future repetitions of this problem—but whatever happens, make sure that your lawyering cleans up this mess.

Could all that have been accomplished if the founders had been predominantly merchants, farmers, clergymen, teachers, philosophers, beekeepers or bookkeepers, rather than lawyers? I don't think so, because they would not have been up to the lawyerly analysis, strategizing, and maneuvering required to create the Constitution, slip it past the entrenched powers waiting to sabotage it, and then make it work.

We'll never know the answer. But we do know that the plot to replace the Articles of Confederation with a working constitution was conceived, instigated, and executed by lawyer-statesmen; that these tasks were entrusted to them by the leading non-lawyer founders, including the American icons George Washington and Benjamin Franklin; and that the lawyer-statesmen performed their services so well that the Constitution remains today the most admired of American institutions. When Franklin signed it, tears came to his eyes, and he said to Washington, "It astonishes me, sir, to find this system approaching so near to perfection as it does." A century after it was put into operation, William Gladstone, the four-time prime minister of Great Britain, called it "the most wonderful work ever struck off at a given time by the brain and purpose of man." And Barack Obama wrote of the Constitution and the Federalist Papers in *The Audacity of Hope:*

> As we read these documents, they seem so incredibly right
> that it's easy to believe they are the result of natural law if
> not divine inspiration.

Therefore, I believe it is reasonable to conclude that without the deeds of this particular group of lawyer-statesmen, no viable nation would have been founded in the wake of the American Revolution. Hence my suggestion that it is appropriate to call them the Founding Lawyers.

Let us return to the history of the Constitution, and try to define more precisely the role of the Founding Lawyers in its creation.

Separation of Powers with Checks & Balances

We are concerned here with the methods by which James Madison and the other Founding Lawyers created Separation of Powers with Checks and Balances. How did they separate the powers, and what ingenious checks and balances did they fashion to curb the intrinsic human thirst for unrestrained power which had destroyed earlier republics?

Madison, like John Adams, took a realistic view of human nature, so that in designing the Constitution, "Ambition must be made to counteract ambition." He perceived that merely establishing three separate branches of government ("parchment barriers") would not in itself create an effective separation of powers. In *Federalist No. 48*, he wrote:

> …unless these departments be so far connected and
> blended as to give each a constitutional control over the
> others, the degree of separation which the maxim requires
> as essential to a free government can never in practice be
> duly maintained.

Madison was especially concerned about the powers of the legislature, the runaway chariot that had brought down the Athenian and Roman democracies. He and his colleagues set about to prevent such a debacle by insisting on two separate houses of Congress, each to be a check on the other, since no bill could be enacted without approval of both houses. The popular election of representatives for a two-year term created a counterbalance to the six-year term of the senators, who would be chosen by the state legislatures (a system which remained in effect until passage of the 17th Amendment in 1913 created popular election of the senators, retaining their six-year term). The terms of the senators were further staggered by electing one-third of them every two years, providing another safeguard against a tyrannical power grab.

As a further check, the states were left in charge of conducting Congressional elections. The powers of Congress were carefully defined and limited in Article I, which required as many written lines as the remaining six articles combined. Many historical abuses were specifically prohibited, such as bills of attainder (criminalization and punishment by the legislature) and suspension of habeas corpus. Beyond these internal controls, the president was empowered to veto all legislation, and the judicial branch was given powers which proved broad enough to permit court review of legislation for compliance with the Constitution.

The debate in Philadelphia over executive powers had ranged far and wide, from crowning the president as a king to making him a puppet of the legislature. In the final version of Article II, the president is to be elected for a four-year term by the people through the Electoral College, with the elections to be conducted by the states. While the president is the commander-in-chief of the armed forces, the power to raise and maintain those forces, as well as to declare war, is vested in Congress. The president's power to veto legislation is checked and balanced by the Congressional power to override vetoes by a two-thirds vote. Since the power to appropriate funds and impose taxes is given to Congress, the president cannot spend government money on his own authority. The president can make treaties, but they must be approved by two-thirds of the senators. The president appoints all federal judges, but they must be approved by the Senate. The same is true of many other high-level appointments by the president. And ultimately Congress can remove the president from office, if a majority of the House votes to impeach and two-thirds of the Senate votes to convict the chief executive "of treason, bribery, or other high crimes and misdemeanors."

The lawyers' touch is evident in the impeachment procedures specified in Article I, especially in the provision that requires the chief justice to preside over trials of presidential impeachments. As explained by Hamilton in *Federalist No. 65*, it would not be appropriate for the entire Supreme Court to be involved in impeachment trials, because the president would also be subject to criminal prosecution in the courts. In such cases, the Supreme Court would be thrust into the legally untenable position of reviewing its own prior finding of guilt.

Article III creating the judicial branch is the shortest. While the president appoints the federal judges, the Senate must approve them, and Congress is given the power to ordain and establish the federal courts other than the Supreme Court, and even to alter the number of Supreme Court justices. All federal judges are to have tenure for life, unless impeached by the House and convicted by the Senate. While the president must "take care that the laws be faithfully executed," those laws are to be made by Congress and interpreted by the courts. The President has the power to pardon those convicted of offenses against the United States. Article III limits the jurisdiction of the federal courts to specified matters of concern to the national government and to suits between citizens of different states. Congress also has power to alter the federal courts' jurisdiction. Although the Constitution does not mention judicial review—the power of the federal courts to declare acts of Congress or the president unconstitutional—this crucial safeguard is inferable from the broad language of Article III, as we shall see. Thus, as Yale Law Professor Akhil Reed Amar notes, "Separation of Powers would also embody the Rule of Law" through which "America hoped to rise above a personalized rule of men."

Article III also reflects the Founding Lawyers' concern that trumped-up treason prosecutions had been a favorite tyrant's device for suppressing dissent and covering up corruption in England. Departing from the vague generalities that occupied much of the text, they specified in Article III, Section 3:

> Treason against the United States, shall consist only in
> levying War against them, or in adhering to their Enemies,
> giving them Aid and Comfort. No Person shall be convicted
> of Treason unless on the Testimony of Two Witnesses to the
> same overt Act or on Confession in open Court.

As we have seen, one of the main points of contention at the Constitutional Convention was the sharing of power between the states and the federal government. The Separation of Powers was augmented by the principle that the federal government would have only those powers enumerated in the Constitution, with all other governmental powers to be retained by the states. This was later set in stone by the Tenth Amendment. Thus, Separation of Powers with Checks and Balances includes many layers of checks and balances at the state level. As described by Supreme Court Justice Stephen Breyer, the Constitution "avoids concentrating power in too few hands by dividing power, vertically between states and a federal government and horizontally among three federal branches."

This exquisite interweaving of powers and counter-powers, checks and balances, reminds me of *Spy vs. Spy,* the wordless comic strip published in *Mad* magazine since 1961. The two identical-looking spies, one dressed in black and the other in white, are dedicated to terminating each other. In each strip, they come up with ingenious plots of simultaneous assassination and devilish counter-measures as they sip coffee at an outdoor café or face each other on a high wire strung between the roofs of skyscrapers. In the same mode, the Founding Lawyers led by Madison called on the wisdom of Adams and Jefferson and their own experience as judges and lawyers to catalogue loopholes through which the tyrants of history usurped governmental powers. Then they set out to plug those loopholes with checks and balances, hoping that the plugs would hold fast when they were tested by the inevitable floods of power-grabbing ambition. In the process, they plugged some seemingly remote loopholes—e.g., seating the vice-president in the chair to preside over the Senate and cast the tie-breaking vote—as well as those most likely to be employed by tyrants, such as abusing Congress's power of the purse by cutting the salaries of the president and the federal judges, which the Constitution explicitly forbids.

In this process the Founding Lawyers projected themselves into the minds of would-be cheaters, a mental exercise they were accustomed to performing when they drafted agreements designed to protect clients from being swindled by crooked business associates and in conducting litigation on behalf of those who had been victimized. They gave each branch of government a little of the other branches' powers, hoping it would be just enough to mold the three-headed government into a seamless web. They tried to complicate the task of those seeking to abuse governmental power, forcing them to seize or corrupt more than one branch of the government. Whether by the distillation of their collective legal and governmental experience, or by sheer luck, or a combination thereof, finally they achieved what Alistair Cooke, the astute long-term British observer of American affairs, called "the instinct of the balance valve, which yields steam protectively first to one side, then the other."

The Founding Lawyers' Coup d'État

Columbia University Professor John W. Burgess (1844-1931) was a pioneer in the teaching of political science and constitutional law. In his authoritative textbook, he said of those who engineered the Constitutional Convention:

> What they actually did, stripped of all fiction and verbiage, was to assume constituent powers, ordain a constitution of government and of liberty, and demand a plebiscite thereon over the heads of all existing legally organized powers. Had Julius Caesar or Napoleon committed these acts they would have been pronounced *coups d'états*.

As we have seen, the Founding Lawyers did not attack the "legally organized powers" of the Articles of Confederation head-on, but deftly took them out of the picture by the lawyers' maneuver of making them irrelevant. The Articles were legally made to disappear before the eyes of the members of the Confederation Congress when the draft Constitution containing the Confederation's death warrant arrived on their desks with a directive from George Washington that—described as a "report"—it be submitted to a vote of publicly-elected state conventions (Professor Burgess's "plebiscite").

The *coup d'état* that peacefully interred the unworkable Confederation was the culmination of the legal strategy which began with the 1786 Madison-Hamilton decision at Annapolis to conjure up the Philadelphia Convention and have the Confederation Congress authorize it without stating its real purpose. The lawyers' touch can be seen in all the crucial steps taken at Philadelphia:

+ maintaining secrecy to avoid revealing the purpose, public notice of which would have aborted the Convention;
+ Judge Sherman's historic Connecticut compromise (giving the small states equal representation in the Senate) which broke the most threatening deadlock;
+ lawyers serving as the main speaking advocates (Madison, Wilson, G. Morris, and Sherman) to repel the opposition assaults which threatened to derail the Constitution from the opening day to the final signing ceremony;
+ lawyers manning seventeen of the twenty-one seats on the three committees which produced the final instrument, with Madison, Hamilton, and G. Morris in at the finish to assure the inclusion of the ingeniously-crafted checks and balances;
+ innovatively structuring the ratification process to bypass the deadly legal traps of the Confederation Congress and the state legislatures (Professor Burgess's "existing legally organized powers");
+ insisting that each state must accept or reject the Constitution as a whole, rather than empowering the states to make amendments or attach conditions;
+ presenting the plebiscite document as a directive from G. Washington, the impeccable client, instead of labeling it as the product of lawyers; and
+ seizing the initiative in the ratification process by appropriating the Federalist label, publishing monumental legal briefs like *The Federalist Papers,* and maneuvering for early ratification votes in key states to establish momentum before the Anti-Federalists could organize effective opposition.

Perhaps the most skilful legal maneuver by the Founding Lawyers was to place the Constitution on a pedestal far above any previous enactment. Stanford history professor Jack Rakove notes that the Articles of Confederation and most of the original state constitutions were adopted by the state legislatures rather than by the popularly-elected ratification conventions specified by the Founding Lawyers. He goes on to explain:

> ...the resort to popular sovereignty in 1787-88 marked
> the point where the distinction between a constitution
> and ordinary law became the fundamental doctrine of
> American political thinking. Far from being less legal than
> the other charters that had gone before it, the Constitution
> established a more profound criterion of legality itself.

Historian Joseph Ellis notes Madison's "lawyer-like thinking" at the Philadelphia Convention, where he exhibited the "mentality of a lawyer defending a client, which in this case was a fully empowered American nation-state." Ellis also writes that in turning out *The Federalist Papers* under great time pressure, Madison and Hamilton performed "like beleaguered lawyers producing briefs for a crucial client." And Ron Chernow, in his biography of Hamilton, writes that "the attorney's ability to make the best case for an imperfect client" may have helped Hamilton to overcome his skepticism about some parts of the Constitution.

The secrecy surrounding the Constitutional Convention reflects the time-honored lawyers' tactic of keeping the opponents in the dark until the time is ripe for revelation. This was well over 100 years before the introduction of "discovery" rules which forced American lawyers to reveal their hands before trial. Even so, the Anti-Federalists charged Madison & Co. with perpetrating an ambush to cover up their illegal maneuvers. To that charge the Founding Lawyers replied that at Philadelphia they were not passing a law or taking any official government action, but were merely drafting a proposal which they needed to debate vigorously for months; that they could not have conducted such a debate if there had been any outside interference or if the delegates had arrived with inflexible instructions; that they had planned from the beginning to require ratification by votes of state conventions elected by the people; and that in the end the draft Constitution was submitted to popular vote as a report of their debates, not as an act of government. A technical lawyers' argument, perhaps, but it was all part of strengthening the Union by draping its creation in the bunting of legality.

To James Madison, the secrecy of what the Founding Lawyers did at Philadelphia (and how they did it) was so important that he withheld publication of his written notes of the daily convention proceedings until the death of the last surviving delegate (which turned out to be himself). Since his notes were the only comprehensive record of the proceedings, for decades he was put under great pressure to publish them, but he steadfastly refused. When pressed for an explanation in 1821, he wrote that publication "should be delayed till the Constitution should be well settled by practice and till a knowledge of the controversial part of the proceedings of its framers could be turned to no improper account." By the time his notes were published in 1840, the Constitution had been in force for more than 50 years, and it was the acknowledged bedrock of the American republic. If he had published his notes before the state ratification conventions, or at any time during the early years following George Washington's inauguration, it would have given opponents of the Constitution ammunition to attack the entire procedure by which the Founding Lawyers pulled off their coup d'état.

The Founding Lawyers' legal handiwork shows up clearly in the state ratification conventions where the coup was completed in public. They knew that despite the Article VII provision for activating the Constitution upon the ninth ratification, there could be no viable union without ratification by four major states: Massachusetts, New York, Pennsylvania, and Virginia. Those states made up half the country's population and furnished most of its leadership during the Revolutionary period. Virginia, its tobacco much in demand in Europe, was the richest and most populous state, while the other three were leaders in shipping, finance, and trade. The Founding Lawyers were aware that if they put together a constitutional republic of nine or more states which did not include all four of the majors, there was a serious risk that the non-ratifying majors would either form their own confederation and seek a powerful European ally, or hold out and force a second constitutional convention, one which was not likely to produce nearly as strong a union as the one in hand.

Fittingly enough, the first major test came in Philadelphia, where the Pennsylvania state ratification convention opened on November 28, 1787, barely two months after the signing. The Federalists were eager to get an early ratification vote in Pennsylvania because they were armed there with a weapon which the opponents could not match: James Wilson. The eminent Philadelphia lawyer who had done so much to push the draft Constitution through now became its leading public advocate. Speaking with a pronounced burr that betrayed his Scottish birth, Wilson—known as "James the Caledonian"—was a brilliant orator with a mind that was described by his Federalist colleague, Dr. Benjamin Rush, as "one blaze of light." Wilson kicked off the ratification campaign on October 6 with a speech in the State House Yard, one so effective that it was reprinted for use at other ratification conventions. Ultimately it appeared in 34 newspapers in 12 states, receiving more coverage than *The Federalist Papers* or any other argument for either side. After illuminating the Constitution's vital features and debunking all its alleged defects, Wilson pointed out that it was natural to expect that those politicians in Pennsylvania who stood to lose some of their present powers to the national government would oppose it, regardless of the public good. He concluded:

> If there are errors, it should be remembered that the seeds of reformation are sown in the work itself and the concurrence of two-thirds of the Congress may at any time introduce alterations and amendments. Regarding it, then, in every point of view with a candid and disinterested mind, I am bold to assert that it is the best form of government which has ever been offered to the world.

The Federalists controlled the Pennsylvania legislature, and on the momentum of Wilson's landmark speech they overcame the desperate efforts of their opponents to thwart a quorum, voting by 45 to 2 to fix the November date for the ratification convention. This forced the Anti-Federalists to face Wilson without much time to organize their opposition or whip up popular support. The convention rolled on for five weeks, with Wilson on his feet hour after hour, trashing every opposing argument while hardly repeating himself. He was ably spelled by another Philadelphia lawyer-statesman, Thomas McKean, a justice of the Pennsylvania Supreme Court. Finally on December 12, the exhausted delegates, still being harangued by a buoyant Wilson, voted 46-23 to ratify. Wilson's bravura performance so enraged the Anti-Federalists that he was beaten by a mob in the street, but he rose to his feet, dusted himself off, and in 1789 took a seat on the bench of the original United States Supreme Court.

Now it was one major state down and three to go, with those three looming as much tougher contests than Pennsylvania. Next up was Massachusetts, where the convention opened on January 9, 1788, in Boston's Brattle Street Church. In that state where the armed rebellion against Britain had begun and the town meeting tradition was still vibrant, Anti-Federalist sentiment appeared dominant. To fiercely patriotic and independent leaders like Samuel Adams and Elbridge Gerry, the proposed Constitution smacked of the tyranny and aristocratic snobbery they had suffered at the hands of the British. Adams, a second cousin of John Adams, was so disinterested in business that he nearly managed to sink his father's prosperous brewery. Gerry was a more successful merchant and shipper, and (like Sam Adams) was not a lawyer. Their opposition was not based on their personal interests, for as in other states, the Constitution was largely favored by the big-city business and shipping men who hoped for expanded foreign trade and development of the West under a stable national government, and was opposed by farmers who feared that a strong central government (i.e. a counterpart of Britain) would tax them oppressively. Among the 355 delegates were 29 farmer-members of Shays's Rebellion.

The pro-ratification forces were led by a group of lawyer-statesmen: Rufus King, Caleb Strong, and Judge Nathaniel Gorham, who had played significant roles at the Philadelphia Convention; Theophilus Parsons; and Justice Francis Dana of the Massachusetts Supreme Judicial Court. Between them they answered most of the attacks on the draft Constitution during the month-long debate. Their presence was noted (sometimes derisively) by Anti-Federalist delegates, most of whom came from rural areas rather than the refinement of Boston. A farmer named Amos Singletary expressed the sentiments of many of his fellow delegates:

> These lawyers and men of learning, and moneyed men
> that talk so finely, and gloss over matters so smoothly,
> to make us poor illiterate people swallow down the pill,
> expect to get into Congress themselves. They expect to be
> the managers of this Constitution, and get all the power
> and all the money into their own hands. And then they will
> swallow up us little fellows, like the great Leviathan, Mr.
> President; yes, just as the whale swallowed up Jonah.

Amos was not quite the illiterate country bumpkin he portrayed, as he was a long-time member of the state legislature. But his description of the leading Constitutional proponents had some substance. As Judge Gorham proudly wrote to James Madison, the Federalist delegates included "three judges of the Supreme Court,…ten or twelve of the first characters at the bar, judges of probate, high sheriffs of counties." In his detailed study of the ratification process, historian Robert Allen Rutland covered the Massachusetts ratification convention in Chapter 4, which he entitled "LAWYERS vs. FARMERS—*No Contest.*"

Washington and Madison were keeping in close touch with the Massachusetts Federalists, feeding them copies of James Wilson's speeches and *The Federalist Papers* as they came off the press. A steady procession of express riders carried dozens of Washington's personal letters from Mount Vernon to convention delegates in Massachusetts and other major states.

The Federalist forces expected Sam Adams and Elbridge Gerry to lead the attack on the Constitution. The highly-respected and influential Gerry (who would later become the fourth U.S. vice-president and lend his name to the term "gerrymandering") had refused to sign the Constitution when his objections were voted down in Philadelphia. The Federalists got a big break when Gerry failed to win election as a delegate to the Massachusetts ratification convention because he had to run for a seat in his home district, which was dominated by Federalists. He tried to attend and answer questions as a consultant, but that arrangement did not work, and he departed in disgust halfway through the convention. That left Sam Adams as the leading figure among the Anti-Federalists.

Adams had the disadvantage of not being as familiar with the Constitutional Convention as were Gerry or the Federalist leaders. But whatever he lacked in detailed knowledge he made up in oratorical skills and the prestige he had gained as the driving force behind the Boston Tea Party and other key events in the Revolution. He could turn an assembly or a street crowd in his favor with a few choice sentences, such as those he had used to dismiss British sympathizers among the colonists in Revolutionary days:

> If ye love wealth greater than liberty, the tranquility of
> servitude greater than the animating contest for freedom,
> go home from us in peace. We seek not your counsel, nor
> your arms. Crouch down and lick the hand that feeds you.
> May your chains set lightly upon you, and may posterity
> forget that ye were our countrymen.

Sam Adams was opposed to the Constitution in principle, mainly because it did not contain a Bill of Rights and it appeared to give the national government unbridled power which could be used to crush the state governments and impose British-style tyranny. But he was keenly aware of the need for a stronger national government, and he listened in silence as the pro-ratification lawyers debated with the skeptical farmers and other opponents. After Amos Singletary had denounced "the lawyers, learned and moneyed men," another farmer named Jonathan Smith rose "to say a few words to my fellow plow joggers." Smith, who had served as a wartime colonel in the Massachusetts militia, began to speak about Shays's Rebellion, which had convinced him that the country was headed for anarchy because it lacked a true national government. His fellow plow joggers tried to shout him down, but Sam Adams intervened and insisted that Smith be allowed to continue. Smith said that he had read the Constitution over and over, and it came through to him as a cure for disorders like Shays's Rebellion. Facing down Amos Singletary, he said:

> I don't think worse of this Constitution because lawyers,
> and men of learning, and moneyed men, are fond of it....
> These lawyers, these moneyed men, these men of learning,
> are all embarked in the same cause with us, and we must all
> swim or sink together.

This exchange made a strong impression on Sam Adams, and he began to think in a new direction. Calling on Governor John Hancock, who had previously avoided attending and chairing the convention by claiming illness, Adams worked out a list of proposed amendments to be attached to the Massachusetts ratification, not as conditions but as recommendations. The pro-ratification lawyers, who were in touch with Washington and Madison, assured Hancock and Adams that they would put the recommended amendments before the new Congress and support their enactment. (Under Article V of the draft Constitution, Congress could propose amendments by a two-thirds vote of both houses, and the amendments would come into force when ratified by three-fourths of the state legislatures.) In this way, the Massachusetts convention was brought around to a consensus in favor of ratification. Even so, it was approved by the slim margin of 187 to 168. The Founding Lawyers had judged correctly that if they had not agreed to support the Hancock-Adams recommended amendments plan, they would have lost the ratification vote.

So it was that church bells rang and cannon boomed in Boston on February 6, 1788, celebrating the Massachusetts ratification. Its statesmen on both sides of the issue predicted—immodestly but accurately—that this would tilt the scales in favor of the Union, just as their state had led the way in the Revolution. They were confident that the innovative Hancock-Adams compromise plan, which permitted the Anti-Federalists to attach recommendations, would be adopted in the remaining states, leading to a stronger Constitution that would unify the nation.

On receiving the good news, Washington and Madison breathed sighs of relief, acknowledging that their case for the Constitution might well have been lost if the Massachusetts vote had gone the other way. Now they faced the last two hurdles, which shaped up as the most difficult challenges: Virginia and New York. In the ratification conventions up to that point, the Federalists had enjoyed the advantage of having nearly all the leading lawyer-statesmen on their side. That was about to change in Virginia, and later in New York.

In Virginia the contest was not between big-city merchants and rural farmers, since the wealthiest Virginians were tobacco planters rather than businessmen. It was more a matter of local politics, which had always been controlled by the wealthy planters. The new Constitution was seen by many of them as a threat to their power circle. It seemed especially menacing to Patrick Henry, the pugnacious lawyer-statesman whose position at the summit of Virginia politics dated back to his stunning legal victories against the Anglican Church and the British tax collectors in the 1760s. Henry was a leading force in the breakaway from British rule, delivering his famous "give me liberty or give me death" speech in 1775, and becoming the first governor of Virginia after it proclaimed an end to its colonial status on May 15, 1776, weeks before the Declaration of Independence.

Between 1776 and 1785, Henry was elected five times to one-year terms as governor of Virginia. By the force of his oratory and domineering character, he maintained tight control of the state legislature even when not serving as governor. He had refused to become a delegate to the Constitutional Convention because he "smelled a rat." When the rat arrived in Richmond for ratification, Henry perceived it as a threat to Virginia and the nation for all the reasons recited by the Anti-Federalists, and also because it endangered his personal power base. He took charge of the campaign to abort the Constitution, and in this task he had some powerful allies.

George Mason, one of Virginia's wealthiest planters, had long been a leader in the quest for constitutional protection of personal rights. He was the author of the 1776 Virginia Declaration of Rights, which was widely copied in other states and became a model for the federal Bill of Rights. He had spoken extensively in support of the Virginia Plan at the Constitutional Convention, but since the final document lacked a Bill of Rights, he refused to sign it. Now a senior statesman at age 63, he joined forces with Patrick Henry to stop the Constitution in its tracks at the Virginia ratification convention to be held in Richmond. (He was the only non-lawyer in a leadership position on either side at the Richmond convention, and even he had served as a justice of the Fairfax County Court.)

Patrick Henry was the one man most likely to succeed in blocking ratification, because of his political control of Virginia, the state which was dominant enough to provide the president for 32 of the nation's first 36 years. He was then 52, but seemed much older, perhaps because he was the father of 17 children. He had used his control of the Virginia legislature to delay the ratification convention until June of 1788, expecting that by then Massachusetts would have rejected the Constitution. The Hancock-Adams recommended-amendments compromise had taken him by surprise. When the Virginia convention began on June 2, eight states had ratified, and New Hampshire was in the midst of its convention which would ultimately produce the ninth ratification. But to Patrick Henry, who would rather fight than eat, this was hardly an obstacle. Allied with the Anti-Federalist forces in New York, Henry set out to use the power of the two remaining major states to force a second constitutional convention which would gut the document produced in Philadelphia. He believed his control of Virginia politics had produced a majority of delegates to the ratification convention who would vote to disapprove the Constitution unless it was heavily amended *before* it went into effect, unlike the Massachusetts format of amendments to be initiated later by the new Congress.

Thus the definitive ratification battle played out like a courtroom drama. It was presided over by Edmund Pendleton, Virginia's prestigious chief justice, who had been elected chairman of the convention by a unanimous vote. Henry began his assault on the Constitution with a wily legal maneuver, demanding that the Confederation Congress's resolution authorizing the Philadelphia Convention be read aloud, to show that its mandate was limited to amending the Articles of Confederation and therefore that the replacement Constitution was legally invalid. This move by Henry must have caused grave concern in the Federalist camp, since (as we have seen) that Congressional resolution of February 21, 1787 also required that the amendments to the Articles of Confederation be "agreed to in Congress and confirmed by the states," i.e., the state legislatures whose powers would be severely curtailed by the proposed Constitution.

Patrick Henry's motion was addressed to the 67-year-old Chief Justice Pendleton, who had agreed to be a delegate at the specific request of George Washington despite being in frail health. Refusing to be intimidated by Henry, Pendleton briskly ruled the motion out of order, saying of the delegates to Philadelphia:

> Although those gentlemen were only directed to consider
> the defects of the old system, and not devise a new one,
> if they found it so thoroughly defective as not to admit a
> revision, and submitted a new system to our consideration,
> which the people have deputed us to investigate, I cannot
> find any degree of propriety in reading those papers.

Here we observe the lawyerly wisdom of James Madison's decision to keep his notes of the Constitutional Convention confidential. The detailed record of what was done in Philadelphia, with the fingerprints of the Founding Lawyers on nearly every page, might well have enabled Patrick Henry to evade Chief Justice Pendleton's summary ruling, leading to an ugly and dangerous battle over the legality of the Founding Lawyers' coup d'état.

Chief Justice Pendleton's ruling forced Henry to focus on the Constitution itself. He attacked it in his customary style, using lofty rhetoric and bombastic generalities to condemn it as a whole, leaving the criticism of specific provisions to George Mason and a team of Anti-Federalist lawyer-statesmen: William Grayson, a former aide-de-camp to General Washington who would soon become a U.S. senator; John Tyler, later governor of Virginia and father of the tenth president; and the 30-year-old future fifth president, James Monroe, a hero of the Revolutionary War.

The Founding Lawyers' team defending the Constitution was headed by James Madison, who struggled through severe stomach problems ("bilious attacks") which kept him at home for nearly a third of the three-week convention. He was ably supported by a phalanx of lawyer-statesmen: Chancellor George Wythe, the "Socrates of Virginia," legendary mentor of Thomas Jefferson and many other leading lawyers; John Marshall, then 32, another hero of the war; George Nicholas, an eloquent speaker whose voice came in handy to deliver phrases crafted by the ailing Madison; James Innes, the state attorney general; and a quiet but useful ally, Bushrod Washington, the general's young nephew, later to serve as a U.S. Supreme Court justice for 30 years. But with all their experience and prestige, none of the Founding Lawyers were as crucial to the Virginia ratification as one who at first appeared to be dead set against the Constitution: Edmund Randolph, the popular 32-year-old governor.

While Randolph had worked closely with Madison in formulating the Virginia Plan at Philadelphia, and had actually introduced it there, at the end he had joined George Mason in refusing to sign. When the Virginia ratification convention began, there was every indication that he would stick with Henry and Mason in holding out for "previous amendments" instead of accepting the Sam Adams procedure. But with New Hampshire expected to bring the Constitution into force in a matter of days, he had a change of heart. A staunch patriot, he refused to become responsible for permitting the pivotal state he governed to take a step which could destroy the Union in its infancy. Like all the delegates, he left unspoken a serious concern that hovered over the convention: if Virginia did not ratify, George Washington, the Virginia resident whose service as the first president was considered essential to the safe launching of the Union, would not be eligible for that office. Despite Randolph's strong aversion to the original form of the Constitution, he took the podium and—in what many historians consider the performance of his life—he exhorted the delegates to ratify it and work for later amendments. He concluded:

> Previous amendments are but another name for rejection.
> They will throw Virginia out of the Union, and cause heart
> aches to many of those gentlemen who may vote for them.
> If, in this situation, we reject the Constitution, the Union
> will be dissolved, the dogs of war will break loose, and
> anarchy and discord will complete the ruin of this country.

Randolph's patriotic switch was the turning point of the convention. Virginia Attorney General James Innes made a crucial legal maneuver which further eroded support for Henry's "previous amendments" stance. Innes opined that the people of Virginia had sent the delegates to Richmond based on their reading of the draft Constitution produced in Philadelphia; none of the voters had seen the amendments now being proposed by Henry; therefore, the delegates could not legally bind the people to provisions that the people had never seen.

Patrick Henry tried to brush aside the speeches of Randolph and Innes, but in the end his motion to insist on previous amendments was rejected by a vote of 88 to 80, and on June 25, Virginia ratified the Constitution by a margin of 89 to 79, attaching 40 suggested amendments in the Massachusetts style.

The New York ratification convention opened at Poughkeepsie on June 17, 1788, with the Virginia convention still in session. As in Virginia, the New York contest was more about local politics than the clash of business and farming interests. Governor George Clinton, a prominent lawyer, was the chief political power, eager to maintain his control of the state. As president of the convention, Clinton masterminded the attack on the Constitution, coordinating with Patrick Henry's Virginia Anti-Federalists in the attempt to force a second constitutional convention. He was supported by a team of lawyer-statesmen, including Thomas Tredwell and the two delegates Clinton had sent to Philadelphia to outvote and hamstring Alexander Hamilton: Robert Yates and John Lansing. Carrying the Federalist banner was Alexander Hamilton, supported by fellow Founding Lawyers John Jay, Chancellor Robert Livingston, and James Duane (who was also the mayor of New York City).

Hamilton was keenly aware of the potential effects of Virginia's decision on the prospects for ratification by New York. Continuing his close cooperation with Madison, Hamilton wrote to Madison two weeks before the opening of the Virginia ratification convention:

> It will be of vast importance that an exact communication should be kept up between us at that period; and the moment *any decisive* question is taken, if favorable, I request you to dispatch an express to me with pointed orders to make all possible diligence, by changing horses etc. All expenses shall be thankfully and liberally paid.

Governor Clinton went into the meeting confident that he had the votes to force a second constitutional convention. But after it had been in session for two weeks, with Hamilton and his fellow Founding Lawyers ably defending every section of the Constitution, the news of Patrick Henry's defeat reached Poughkeepsie. Virginia's ratification was actually the tenth, as New Hampshire had sealed the Union with the ninth ratification on June 21. Since North Carolina and Rhode Island had not even begun the ratification process, Governor Clinton was left out on a limb in seeking to make his state the only one to reject the Constitution. Nevertheless he did his best, keeping the convention in session for another three weeks. Finally Hamilton and his fellow Founding Lawyers forced Clinton's hand, and on July 26, New York ratified the Constitution by a vote of 30 to 27, attaching a list of 32 recommended amendments. Thereupon the people of New York City honored Founding Lawyer Alexander Hamilton with a forerunner of the ticker tape parade, featuring a 27-foot-long miniature frigate named the "Federal Ship *Hamilton*" pulled down Broadway by ten horses.

So it didn't take the armed might of a Caesar or a Napoleon or a Trujillo to pull off this coup—just a small band of unarmed, harmless-looking lawyers. In the process the United States became the first nation whose people had chosen their own form of government. Alistair Cooke and other historians called it "inventing a nation." Historian Joseph Ellis marveled that this "provincial and wholly peripheral outpost of Western Civilization, somehow managed to establish a set of ideas and institutions that, over the stretch of time, became the blueprint for political and economic success for the nation-state in the modern world." But on one major issue, the Founding Lawyers got carried away with their roles as lawyers and neglected the statesmanship.

Lost in the Shuffle: The Bill of Rights

By now you may be wondering why the original Constitution contained no Bill of Rights, even though the authors were pretty much the same group of men who had led the fight for those principles of liberty and natural rights throughout the Revolutionary War and had written such safeguards into their state constitutions as an antidote to British-style tyranny. Inclusion of a Bill of Rights was debated briefly in Philadelphia, but it was voted down because Madison and the other Founding Lawyers in charge of the drafting thought it unnecessary and potentially counter-productive. Their reasoning, colored by their perception that they were writing what was essentially a legal document, went like this:

+ The powers of the new national government were limited to those specifically delegated to it in the Constitution itself;
+ no power to interfere with civil rights was delegated to the national government, and therefore it was unnecessary to prohibit the government from such interference (e.g., since the Constitution did not give the government any power to regulate religion, speech, or the press, it was unnecessary to prohibit the government from restricting freedom of religion, speech, or the press);
+ most of the state constitutions contained bills of rights, which were left in place by the new Constitution; and

✦ if the framers undertook to list all the things the government could *not* do, the list would be longer than the Constitution, and this would create a risk that the government could get away with tyranny by using methods which were not specifically prohibited in the Constitution.

While this argument may have had some legal merit, the public perception was that it left a gaping hole in the foundation stone of the United States government. Harvard Law Professor Archibald Cox (1912-2004), an authority on constitutional law, called it a "rather technical lawyers' argument" that was unsatisfactory to the people. Both John Adams in London and Thomas Jefferson in Paris, when told of this omission, immediately said it was a big mistake. They felt that in taking the revolutionary step of creating a new kind of nation and requiring the states to surrender their sovereignty, it was necessary to spell out safeguards against the type of tyranny which the young country had so recently shed by winning the Revolutionary War. As we have seen, it was this omission that furnished the Anti-Federalists with their main source of ammunition.

Two centuries later, it is impossible for us to imagine the Constitution without the Bill of Rights. But we owe the Founding Lawyers a sympathetic understanding of what they were up against during that humid Philadelphia summer. Many of the delegates were influential state office-holders who were being asked to forfeit or weaken their own powers. The 13 states had more disparity than unity of interests—slave vs. non-slave, farmers vs. business and financial—and many cultural and religious differences, since the white population contained various groupings of English, Scottish, Irish, Welsh, Dutch, German, French, Scandinavian, and other European heritages, as well as Anglican/Episcopalian, Congregationalist, Presbyterian, Quaker, Calvinist, Roman Catholic, Jewish, Lutheran, and other religious beliefs. Having herded that fractious group to the point of agreement on a constitutional framework after four months of nit-picking lawyerly debate, all the while straining to keep their monumental project a secret, can Madison & Co. be faulted for deciding not to take on another major controversy which would require them to reconcile the delegates' views on specific civil rights? Could they have reached agreement on basic principles of liberty without touching on the toxic slavery issue? Could they have maintained Gouverneur Morris's ingenious deployment of generalities if they had laboriously particularized the no-no's?

In any event, the inclusion of a Bill of Rights was rejected at Philadelphia by a vote of ten states to none. But as we have seen, to achieve ratification the Federalists were forced to promise they would support a Bill of Rights in the First Congress, and it fell to James Madison to deliver on that promise. When the First Congress met in New York in April 1789, he was there as a representative from Virginia. He had two strong reasons for performing: first, he had given his word (and that of George Washington) to John Hancock, Sam Adams, and other Anti-Federalist leaders, and to the Virginia constituents who elected him to Congress; and second, if he failed to produce a Bill of Rights in the first Congress, there was a good chance that this would trigger a new constitutional convention capable of tearing the fragile Union apart. Article V provided two methods of amending the Constitution: the one pursued by Madison through Congress, and an alternative which required the calling of a fresh constitutional convention on the application of two-thirds of the state legislatures. Two such applications had already been filed with Congress: one from Patrick Henry's Virginia legislature, and the other from George Clinton's New York legislature.

It took James Madison all spring and summer of 1789 to bring his proposed Bill of Rights to a vote in the House. He must have had many of his bilious attacks as he slogged through the 200 suggested amendments which were attached to the ratifications of five states. He was keenly aware that one of Patrick Henry's proposals would deprive the national government of the power to tax, reverting to the bad old days of the Articles of Confederation. He weeded out that landmine and others planted by Anti-Federalists intent upon wrecking the Union, and got his list down to 17 proposed amendments.

Even though the Federalists had a large majority in both houses, not many of the legislators shared Madison's sense of urgency about the Bill of Rights. Most felt that higher priority should be given to the many statutes needed to establish the new government from scratch. But Madison persisted, and he let it be known that President Washington was strongly in favor of immediate action. Finally on August 24 the House approved Madison's proposed amendments by the necessary two-thirds majority. (The House Clerk, new to the job, failed to record the exact voting tally.)

Madison's work was not finished, as the Senate made 26 changes in his House-approved version, reducing the number of amendments to twelve. The most significant change was elimination of Madison's proposal that the states as well as the national government be prohibited from denying basic civil rights. The Senate version was passed by an unspecified vote of more than two-thirds, and then conference committees from each house had to wrestle with reconciling the two versions. Of particular interest to us is the composition of those conference committees: for the Senate, Oliver Ellsworth of Connecticut, William Paterson of New Jersey, and Charles Carroll of Maryland; and for the House, James Madison, Roger Sherman of Connecticut, and John Vining of Delaware—all six of them being lawyers.

Finally on September 25, 1789, both houses passed an agreed version which listed 12 proposed amendments, and the following week President Washington forwarded them to the state legislatures for ratification. They sailed through half the state legislatures with little opposition, but Patrick Henry was not about to throw in the towel. Although he had vigorously advocated the measures written into the Bill of Rights, he now opposed them, knowing that if they were ratified, he would probably lose the opportunity to scuttle the Union through a second constitutional convention. He managed to stall Virginia's vote for two years, and largely because of his obstructionist moves, the Bill of Rights was not approved by the requisite total of three-quarters of the states until Virginia ratified it on December 15, 1791. Two of the proposed amendments failed to achieve the necessary majority, leaving the Bill of Rights in its final form as the first ten amendments to the Constitution.

Thus the five-year odyssey, which began with the Madison-Hamilton scheming at Annapolis, ended in Richmond with Madison's final triumph over Patrick Henry. It took that long for the Founding Lawyers to cobble together all the pieces of the Constitution which the world regards today as the seamless masterpiece of American civilization.

The Founding Lawyers' Roots in Colonial History

Some readers may wonder why the role of lawyers in the making of the Constitution is such a big deal. After all, the Constitution is a form of statutory law, and writing legal language is what lawyers do, isn't it?

The fact is that the 1787 Constitution was a sea-change of public policy rather than a mere legal document—"a set of ideas and institutions that… became the blueprint for political and economic success for the nation-state in the modern world," as historian Joseph Ellis puts it. And, as we have seen, the Founding Lawyers did not merely *write* the Constitution. The Founding Lawyers invented and then successfully advocated the political principles that gave the United States a Government of Laws, according to their unique vision of a workable representative democracy: a process of governance based on Separation of Powers with Checks and Balances and what would later be called the Rule of Law. Therefore, the unique skills of the Founding Lawyers were required throughout the process that began at Annapolis in 1786.

Others may surmise that these deeds were to be expected of lawyers because they were of the elite class of early Americans who were able to attend college and become educated in the science of government. Adams at Harvard, Jefferson at William & Mary, Hamilton at Columbia, and Madison at Princeton did acquire some knowledge of government in courses such as history and moral philosophy. But so did thousands of other pre-Constitution Americans who did not become lawyers and did not play crucial roles in the creation of the American republic.

The idea of entrusting the creation of the United States of America to lawyers did not spring out of the blue in 1787. To appreciate the crucial founding role of American lawyers, we need to revert briefly to Colonial history, especially the events leading up to the Declaration of Independence. Here our main guide will be University of Georgia History Professor Peter Charles Hoffer and his comprehensive treatise, *Law and People in Colonial America.*

Apart from fruitless petitions to London and sporadic acts of disobedience such as the famous Boston Tea Party of 1773, the colonists' efforts to obtain relief from Britain's oppressive colonial policies were centered in the colonial courts. In a section titled "Briefing the Case for Colonial Rights," Professor Hoffer writes, "By the middle 1760s lawyers representing protesters were becoming adept at using civil and criminal suits to organize and energize opposition to the crown." Hoffer provides details of illustrative cases which were litigated by lawyers such as John Adams, Thomas Jefferson, Patrick Henry, John Dickinson, and James Wilson. Hoffer explains their methods:

> The lawyers within the ranks of the revolutionaries, predisposed by training, intellectual and professional habits, and experience in the courts to think in legal terms, were willing and able to do more than give lip service to the task of legalizing the protest. Despite the variety of sources they used, American revolutionary lawyers read and debated political philosophy, history, and law as lawyers. They thought like lawyers, not like political philosophers or disinterested scholars....

> From 1763 to 1775 American lawyers ransacked common law to find evidence against parliamentary impositions.... If common law was what English authorities said it was, a coil in the cord that bound the subordinate colonies to a dominant center of power, the lawyers would fashion an American common law that was part of the longer cord but still gave Americans freedom to protest parliamentary impositions.

Professor Hoffer goes on to describe how the Founding Lawyers turned these courtroom battles into political weapons by publishing pamphlets about them:

> There followed, at first sporadically and then with greater regularity as the crisis grew, lawyers' accounts of arguments against the writs of assistance, stamp taxes, and

the Townshend duties.... The pamphlets that were to
become the staple of revolutionary propaganda featured
an extended exchange of legal ideas and functioned as a
surrogate for an American common law. Some of these
pamphlets, written in haste early in the crisis by leading
lawyers...actually looked and sounded like briefs.

One of the leaders in this movement was James Otis, Jr., a distinguished
Boston lawyer who was John Adams's mentor and role model. In 1761, Otis
represented 63 Boston merchants pro bono (free of charge) in opposing writs
of assistance (broad search warrants that gave English tax collectors power
to enter and search colonists' houses and businesses at will). Although Otis
technically lost that trial, his eloquent statement of the colonists' case and his
follow-up pamphleteering motivated other lawyers to press legal challenges
against British oppression. Otis's five-hour summation speech inspired John
Adams to write, "Then and there, the child Independence was born."

Otis continued his crusade of court actions and pamphlets for 10 years,
focusing on the argument that it was a violation of the English constitution
for Parliament to impose taxes and other coercive measures on the colonists
who had no vote in choosing its membership. It was Otis who coined the rallying cry, "Taxation without representation is tyranny." In later pamphlets,
Otis asserted that rights are not derived from human institutions, but from
nature and God, a principle that was to be written into the Declaration of
Independence.

When Parliament passed yet another set of oppressive laws in the spring
of 1774 to punish the colonists for the disturbances in Boston and other
places, leaders of the resistance branded them "the Intolerable Acts." To
organize their resistance they convened the First Continental Congress at
Philadelphia in September of 1774, a meeting which historians mark as the
first formal step toward establishing our national government. All the colonies except Georgia sent delegates. The two main objectives of that Congress
were to adopt a comprehensive boycott of imports from Britain and to send a
message to King George III asserting the legal rights of the colonists. To draft
that Declaration of Rights and Grievances the Congress appointed a committee (called the Grand Committee) which included two members from
each of the 12 participating colonies. The Grand Committee, which took
most of the eight-week meeting to complete its work, was dominated by lawyers, including John Adams, Roger Sherman, John Jay, Edmund Pendleton,
John Rutledge, and James Duane.

The first draft of the 1774 Declaration of Rights and Grievances was
written by Grand Committee member John Sullivan, a New Hampshire lawyer
who later became one of George Washington's generals and finished his career

as the first judge of the U.S. District Court of New Hampshire. The final version was largely the work of John Adams. It began the recitation of legal rights with this statement:

> That the inhabitants of the English colonies in North
> America by the immutable laws of nature, the principles
> of the English constitution, and the several charters or
> compacts, have the following RIGHTS:

By invoking English philosopher John Locke's principles of natural law and specifying many violations of the colonists' alleged legal rights, the 1774 declaration foreshadowed some basic features of the 1776 Declaration of Independence. In order to mount a valid constitutional challenge, its legal arguments alleging abuse of power were directed at Parliament rather than at the king. It proclaimed that because the colonists were not represented in the British parliament, "they are entitled to a free and exclusive power of legislation in their several provincial legislatures." It also alleged that "the respective colonies are entitled to the common law of England, and more especially to the great and inestimable privilege of being tried by their peers of the vicinage, according to the course of that law."

The 1774 Congressional debate was essentially a legal argument because the delegates and the colonists they represented were deeply divided over how to resist. Joseph Galloway, a prominent Philadelphia lawyer-delegate, proposed a compromise plan which would create a new American parliament subject to the crown. Galloway's plan attracted considerable support and was extensively debated before it was voted down. The Grand Committee's declaration that replaced it had to be solidly grounded in English constitutional law in order to satisfy the delegates' determination to make a reasoned appeal to King George III. As Professor Hoffer notes, "no experienced revolutionary lawyer would want to risk life, liberty, and sacred honor in that cause without first donning the armor of legality."

Despite the care taken by the delegates to plead a case for relief from what they perceived as an unconstitutional deprivation of their legal rights, the British government rejected the Declaration of Rights and imposed even more repressive measures designed to stifle colonial resistance. By the time the Second Continental Congress met in Philadelphia in May 1775, the Battles of Lexington and Concord had begun the Revolutionary War. The Second Continental Congress served as the de facto national government of what became the United States, until it was replaced by the Confederation Congress which came into being when the Articles of Confederation were ratified in 1781. Its 1775 session was preoccupied with mobilizing the forces needed to conduct the war, beginning with the appointment of George Washington as commanding general of the Continental Army. It was not until June 7, 1776, that Congress took up the question of declaring independence when Virginia lawyer-delegate Richard Henry Lee introduced the famous resolution:

> *Resolved:* That these United Colonies are, and of right ought to be, free and independent States, that they are absolved from all allegiance to the British Crown, and that all political connection between them and the State of Great Britain is, and ought to be, dissolved.

Despite the fact that the Revolutionary War was already in its second year, many colonists hoped that the uprising would lead to reconciliation with Britain. Historians estimate that 15 to 20 percent of the colonists remained loyal to Britain, while another 35 to 45 percent attempted to remain neutral, leaving no more than 40 to 45 percent fully supporting a war of liberation. Tom Paine's revolutionary pamphlet, *Common Sense,* published in January 1776, gained wide popularity but did not produce overwhelming support for independence. When Congress moved toward declaring independence in June of 1776, it again became necessary to create a legal foundation which would satisfy the concerns of the many colonists who questioned the grounds for permanent separation from Britain. Such prominent lawyer-delegates as John Jay, John Dickinson, James Wilson, and James Duane were not inclined to support a complete breakaway, as Professor Hoffer explains:

> The New York lawyers in the delegation to the Continental Congress, Jay and Duane, were not eager for independence. With Dickinson and Wilson of Pennsylvania, Jay and Duane researched the common law for an alternative to complete separation. Dickinson, the penman of the first two Congresses, searched particularly diligently in his law books and his memory for a way to preserve the peace. John Adams was more forward in countenancing a final breach, joining Thomas Jefferson in the drafting of a legal document declaring independence.

On July 1, 1776, Congress prepared for a crucial vote on the Lee Virginia resolution which would break the ties with Britain. John Dickinson remained adamantly opposed, and he sought to convince the other delegates that it was folly to declare independence. At that point it appeared that at least four of the delegations opposed the resolution, which had to be adopted unanimously if it was to be effective. Although Thomas Jefferson had already prepared a written declaration, it was John Adams who confronted Dickinson and spoke for those committed to independence. The stage was set for one of American history's greatest debates, as Adams biographer David McCulloch tells us:

> John Dickinson had resolved to make one last appeal
> and Adams would be obliged to answer. They would rise
> to make their cases as the great lawyers they were, each
> summoning all his powers of reason and persuasion.

Dickinson's two-hour speech expressed the concerns of many colonists that declaring independence would project them into a long war against a super-power that they could not win, and would end the chances for a reconciliation which many colonists felt was vital to development of the American economy. Dickinson argued that even a stalemate would be disastrous, as it would invite France and Spain to expand their control of portions of the continent. To declare independence now would be "to brave the storm in a skiff made of paper."

Unfortunately no transcripts or notes of Adams's response were made, but it swept away the opposition and brought approval of Lee's resolution on July 2 without a dissenting vote. As David McCulloch writes:

> That it was the most powerful and important speech heard
> in the Congress since it first convened, and the greatest
> speech of Adams's life, there is no question.

Jefferson wrote of Adams's performance that he "spoke with a power of thought and expression that moved us from our seats." Richard Stockton, a New Jersey lawyer-delegate, observed that Adams was "the Atlas" of the hour, "the man to whom the country is most indebted for the great measure of independency.... He it was who sustained the debate, and by the force of his reasoning demonstrated not only the justice but the expediency of the measure." The one-sentence July 2 Lee resolution was actually a political declaration of independence, but the lawyer-dominated Congress would not be satisfied without a strong legal and philosophical explanatory document. Jefferson presented his draft on July 2, and stood by as the delegates began to peck away at his language on July 3. Even though Jefferson had been chosen for the task because of what Adams called his "happy talent for composition," other delegates insisted on deleting or rewriting about a quarter of it before finally approving it on July 4. Fortunately they did not tamper with the second paragraph, which stands as Founding Lawyer Jefferson's master-piece, capturing the spirit of the American Revolution:

> We hold these truths to be self-evident, that all men are
> created equal, that they are endowed by their Creator with
> certain unalienable rights, that among these are life, liberty,

and the pursuit of happiness. That to secure these rights,
governments are instituted among men, deriving their just
power from the consent of the governed.

Needless to say, this was an aspirational statement in 1776, before there
was a real United States government, and it remains aspirational today, part
idealism and part hard-won reality. The Founding Lawyers used it to engineer
the ratification of the Constitution they wrote, insisting that "the consent of
the governed" be obtained in state conventions of popularly-elected delegates,
thus placing the Constitution at the highest level in the Government of Laws.

Here we encounter a little-noticed twist in the legal story of the Declaration.
In addition to his doubts about the outcome of the military struggle, the highly
respected John Dickinson opposed independence because, in Professor Hoffer's
words, he was "wedded to the common law," and could find no legally tenable
ground for breaking the contracts that bound the colonies to the king's law. To
the rescue came Thomas Jefferson, who in his law practice was a specialist in
equity, the body of Anglo-American law that furnishes "equitable" remedies in
cases where the common law falls short of achieving justice. Professor Hoffer
writes:

> Thomas Jefferson stepped forward to propose another
> line of argument. He averred that the Crown had violated
> its duties as a trustee, acting in a partial, self-serving, and
> mean-spirited manner, bringing ruin to the beneficiaries of
> the trust, the colonists.

Therefore, in drafting the Declaration, Jefferson followed the prescribed form of a bill in equity. The introductory paragraphs identified
the complainants and established their standing to complain. Then followed 28 paragraphs stating the specific grievances which cried out for an
equitable remedy, including charges that King George III "has refused his
Assent to Laws, the most wholesome and necessary for the public good;…
has obstructed the Administration of Justice, by refusing his Assent to Laws
for establishing Judiciary Powers;…and has combined with others to subject
us to a Jurisdiction foreign to our Constitution, and unacknowledged by our
Laws." (The "Constitution" Jefferson referred to was the British Constitution,
which is not a written document like ours, but rather a body of statutes, treaties, court decisions, and customs.) Professor Hoffer concludes:

> It was a lawyer's Declaration, adapting a form of pleading
> that could overcome the hurdles of common law-based
> loyalism. At the same time, it raised equitable concepts of
> trusteeship to the level of constitutional principles.

Jefferson then devoted one paragraph to reminding "our British brethren" that they too "have been deaf to the voice of justice and of consanguinity," and closed with a paragraph which proclaimed that the newly independent states "have full Power to levy War, conclude Peace, contract Alliances, establish Commerce, and to do all other Acts and Things which Independent States may of right do." This final paragraph was crucial to the success of the missions later undertaken by Benjamin Franklin to obtain aid from France and by John Adams to negotiate loans from Holland. Stanford history professor Jack Rakove explains:

> Though we now read the Declaration first and foremost as a statement of the idea of equality among individuals, the intent of this concluding passage—the whole point of the Declaration as a public document and an act of state—was to affirm a different proposition.... Having appealed to the "opinions of mankind" to understand the reasons for American resistance, the Declaration ends by asking other states to deal with the United States of America as they did with all other nations.

> ...the Declaration was meant just as much for foreign readers. In that sense, it was a statement of international law, designed to permit and encourage other nations—principally France—to provide the recognition and support the former colonies would require to assure the political independence the document proclaimed.

The pre-Constitution activities of the Founding Lawyers are summarized by NYU Law Professor Bernard Schwartz:

> In a broad sense, the struggle for American independence was a legal struggle; or, at the least, it was framed in terms of legal issues. The conflict which led to the Revolution was in large part a conflict over differing interpretations of the colonies' status under the British Constitution....

> Particularly in the generation before the Revolution, lawyers came to the fore. They were the most influential members of the colonial legislatures and the Continental Congress. They not only led the revolutionary movement, but also, perhaps more important, they translated the Revolution into institutions that gave its peculiarly legal cast to the American polity.

While the Declaration of Independence was clearly the work product of the Founding Lawyers, its adoption did not require the same level of deft legal maneuvering as did the Constitution. The movement toward independence was spear-headed by non-lawyer leaders such as Samuel Adams, Tom Paine, Benjamin Franklin, and John Hancock. Unlike the Constitution, the Declaration did not establish a governmental or legal structure, nor did it have to be guided through an obstacle course of entrenched governmental power. But the Founding Lawyers' role in the Declaration of Independence is an integral part of the history which explains the Government of Laws and the modern American Rule of Law. And since both George Washington and Benjamin Franklin served as delegates to the Continental Congress, it is not surprising that they threw their crucial support behind the efforts of the Founding Lawyers to create and install the Constitution.

As it happened, the wording of the Constitution was crucial because the future flexibility that Gouverneur Morris's calculated vagueness provided was essential to its success. But the fact that lawyer Morris was capable of writing the finished document does not detract from the policy-making done by Adams, Jefferson, Madison, Hamilton, Sherman, Wilson, and the other Founding Lawyers (including Morris himself) who created the nation's government. Their deeds have been recounted in the preceding pages, and their names are worth listing here.

The Founding Lawyers (listed alphabetically)
John Adams (Mass.)
Abraham Baldwin (Ga.)
David Brearley (N.J.)
Charles Carroll (Md.)
Francis Dana (Mass.)
John Dickinson (Del.)
James Duane (N.Y.)
Oliver Ellsworth (Conn.)
Nathaniel Gorham (Mass.)
Alexander Hamilton (N.Y.)
Patrick Henry (Va.)
James Innes (Va.)
John Jay (N.Y.)
Thomas Jefferson (Va.)
William Johnson (Conn.)
Rufus King (Mass.)
Richard Henry Lee (Va.)
Robert Livingston (N.Y.)
James Madison (Va.)
John Marshall (Va.)

Thomas McKean (Pa.)
Gouverneur Morris (Pa.)
George Nicholas (Va.)
James Otis, Jr. (Mass.)
Theophilus Parsons (Mass.)
William Paterson (N.J.)
Edmund Pendleton (Va.)
Charles Pinckney (S.C.)
Charles Cotesworth Pinckney (S.C.}
Edmund Randolph (Va.)
John Rutledge (S.C.)
Roger Sherman (Conn.)
Richard Stockton (N.J.)
Caleb Strong (Mass.)
John Vining (Del.)
Bushrod Washington (Va.)
James Wilson (Pa.)
George Wythe (Va.)

(Patrick Henry and Richard Henry Lee are included, despite their opposition to the Constitution, because of their many important contributions during the colonial and wartime periods.)

In no other nation did lawyer-statesmen play such a central role in creating the constitution or designing the form of government. That is the vital point which, as we shall see, helps to explain the uniquely important position of law and lawyers in the United States today.

The Constitution's Moral Deficiencies

We cannot leave the creation of the Constitution without mentioning its moral deficiencies. From our vantage point, the abominable image of slavery looms over Independence Hall in the summer of 1787 like an all-enveloping storm cloud. That the Constitution emerged with slavery virtually intact is best explained by Catherine Drinker Bowen in *Miracle in Philadelphia*:

> The Convention of '87 discussed America not in terms of social philosophy but in relation to the country as they saw it around them....

> That a large part of America rested upon slavery was again no part of the Convention's immediate problem; they were

met not to reform society but to create a government for society as it existed.

Gouverneur Morris, Roger Sherman, and a few other delegates denounced slavery from the floor, but they all knew that they could not possibly emerge with a union if they tried to eliminate it. Key figures like Washington, Jefferson, and Madison owned slaves. The best that the Founding Lawyers could achieve was to open the way for shutting down the importation of slaves beginning in 1808. This was part of a dehumanizing compromise: the Southern states wanted their slaves counted in the census which would determine the number of seats they would be allocated in the House of Representatives, and finally they were permitted to count each slave as three-fifths of a free white inhabitant. The hope was that once a strong, stable union was created, slavery would wither away over time. Certainly there would have been even less chance for abolition of slavery if the states had retained their sovereignty under the Articles of Confederation.

There were other features that make the Constitution appear elitist to our eyes. As part of the Checks and Balances, voting requirements for national elections were left to the states, which generally limited suffrage to white males who owned property of specified minimum values. Thus women, African-Americans, Indians, and the poor could not vote. Most of the delegates were relatively wealthy, many of them (including George Washington) profiting handsomely from speculation in the Western land which was one of the subjects under their consideration at the Convention. There was much work left to be done before the national goal matured from *liberty* (with unspecified beneficiaries) to *liberty and justice for all.* But at least the new Constitution provided the framework and flexibility which made such progress possible. As we shall see, the power of judicial review planted in Article III became a commanding force in the movement toward that lofty goal.

———

Now, thanks mainly to the Founding Lawyers with whom he had conspired, President Washington had the Constitution he had wished and worked for. But it was all a grand experiment, a document built on untested theories that might be more suitable as a doctoral thesis than as a field manual for operating a government. The earlier experiments in Athens and Rome had been designed to govern homogenous people who lived practically within shouting distance of each other. This one would have to deal with a melting-pot nation sprawled over a huge continent, with horses still providing the fastest method of communication.

How was G. Washington going to make it work?

Chapter Four

Initiating a Government of Laws
(1789-1864)

When George Washington took the oath of office on April 30, 1789, there were no rules, precedents, or manuals to guide him in governing the nation. Nearly every day he had to improvise, to invent procedures from scratch. Many of them, starting with his inaugural address on that first day, became established practices or traditions that have survived to the twenty-first century. In his words, he was seeking "to establish a national character of our own."

From the moment when the Founding Lawyers began the creation of the Constitution at Annapolis, they assumed that Washington would have to be the first president. As historian Ron Chernow puts it:

> The battle royal over the Constitution exposed such glaring rifts in the country that America needed a first president of unimpeachable integrity who would embody the rich promise of the new republic. It had to be somebody of godlike stature who would seem to levitate above partisan politics, a symbol of national unity as well as a functioning chief executive. Everybody knew that George Washington alone could manage the paradoxical feat of being a politician above politics.

Washington had such extraordinary prestige that he could have shaped the fledgling government into one of men (led by himself) rather than one of laws. Fortunately, he did just the opposite. Historian Gordon Wood measured Washington's performance in these terms:

> Not only did he have to justify and flesh out the new office
> of the presidency, but he also had to put together the new
> nation and prove to a skeptical world that America's grand
> experiment in self-government was possible. That he did all
> this in the midst of a revolutionary world at war and did it
> without sacrificing the republican character of the country
> is an astonishing achievement, one that the achievements
> of no other president, however great, can begin to match.

Historian Glenn Phelps's detailed studies of Washington's letters and papers culminated in his 1993 book, *George Washington and American Constitutionalism.* There Phelps documents the conclusion that the first president had "a passionate commitment to a fully developed idea of a constitutional republic on a continental scale." Washington saw the job of creating the government largely as the process of breathing life into the Constitution, which was purposely worded vaguely to permit flexibility and innovation. To help him in that task, he called upon the men whom he trusted to interpret the Constitution judiciously and in the best interests of the country. Nearly all were Founding Lawyers who had played important roles in conceiving the principles of Separation of Powers with Checks and Balances and planting them in the Constitution which emerged from the Philadelphia Convention over which Washington had presided.

Always a stickler for the rule book, Washington consulted the Constitution before doing anything new. There was no provision in the Constitution for a cabinet, an advisory council, presidential advisors, or assistants. The only hint about assistance was the Article II provision that the President "may require the opinion, in writing, of the principal officer in each of the executive departments, upon any subject relating to the duties of their respective offices."

John Adams, the original advocate of the Government of Laws and Separation of Powers with Checks and Balances, was a source of advice as the elected vice-president, and he was not shy about trying to shape the new government himself. Since it was against Adams's combative nature to treat his duty to preside over the Senate as merely ceremonial, he did his best to take control of the debates on the formative legislation, injecting his own strong views on how to make the Government of Laws work. He was trying, in his words, to "throw a little light on the subject." Two days before Washington's inauguration, in his first speech to the Senate, Adams said:

> It is with satisfaction that I congratulate the people of
> America on the formation of a national constitution,
> and the fair prospect of a consistent administration of a
> Government of Laws.

Washington decided to appoint four heads of executive departments to serve as his cabinet: Thomas Jefferson, secretary of state; Alexander Hamilton, secretary of the treasury; Edmund Randolph, attorney general; and Major General Henry Knox, secretary of war. All were lawyers except Knox, who had served as Washington's aide in important battles of the Revolutionary War. While Washington's initial instinct was that a military man should head the War Department, upon Knox's retirement in 1795, Washington replaced him with Massachusetts lawyer Timothy Pickering, completing a cabinet composed entirely of lawyers. To negotiate the crucial 1794 treaty with Great Britain, Washington recruited John Jay, then serving as chief justice of the Supreme Court.

In organizing the government, setting its initial policies, and making key appointments (including the cabinet), Washington relied most heavily on the advice and statesmanship of James Madison. This collaboration began early in 1789, before Washington was elected. It became so intense that during the formative stage of the government, Madison was dubbed Washington's "prime minister." In the early years, Madison spent much of his time assisting President Washington even though he held a Virginia seat in the House of Representatives and continued to spearhead legislation in that capacity.

Washington's choice of Madison (the main architect of the Constitution) as his principal advisor, backed by John Adams and the other Founding Lawyers in his cabinet, underscores the president's determination to build a Government of Laws on the Constitution's foundation of Separation of Powers with Checks and Balances. Some examples:

+ One of the first problems of the new government was to establish a tax base to finance its operations. At that time the main potential source of revenue was the tariff (the duty imposed on imports), there being no income taxes until the twentieth century. While the Confederation Congress had utterly failed to achieve the consensus required to create a viable tax system, the new government succeeded in reconciling conflicting interests, such as those of manufacturers desiring protection from foreign imports and importers seeking cheap foreign goods. By midsummer of 1789, the vital revenue stream was established, thanks mainly to the work of James Madison in his dual capacity as advisor to President Washington and shepherd of the tariff legislation in Congress.
+ Madison was chiefly responsible for Congressional approval of the Bill of Rights, as we have seen, and also for the 1789 legislation creating the executive departments, which were not defined in the Constitution. Power-hungry senators sought to establish an inappropriate measure of control over the executive departments,

including a role in the President's decisions to fire department heads. The debate on this question turned largely on interpretation of the Constitution, which required the advice and consent of the Senate as to appointments but was silent about firings. With Madison's help and a tie-breaking vote by Adams in the Senate, Washington was able to establish a balanced, workable system that left the chief executive in control of his department heads.

✦ Article III of the Constitution left the makeup and jurisdiction of the Supreme Court almost a blank slate, and limited the description of the rest of the Judicial branch to "such inferior Courts as the Congress may from time to time ordain and establish." Here Gouverneur Morris had risen to new heights of artful vagueness in order to avoid a battle-royal over the issue of usurping the established jurisdiction of the state courts, in which many of the delegates to the Constitutional Convention practiced or sat as judges. Now it was up to Congress to turn the opaque wording of Article III into a truly effective third branch of government, checking and balancing the other two. Since Madison was busy all through the first summer advising Washington and pushing the Bill of Rights through Congress, the burden of this task fell mostly on Senator Oliver Ellsworth, a Connecticut lawyer who had played an important role at the Constitutional Convention. Ellsworth, who would become the Supreme Court's second chief justice in a few years, was assisted in the Senate by William Patterson of New Jersey and Caleb Strong of Massachusetts, and in the House by the ubiquitous Roger Sherman—three more lawyer-statesmen. The job Ellsworth and his fellow lawyer-statesmen did in creating the Judiciary Act of 1789 has won praise from every generation of legal scholars, for that statute erected the framework of the present federal court system and cleared the way for solving many knotty problems of federal law and jurisdiction, especially those involving the interplay of federal and state law. In her 2003 book, *The Majesty of the Law*, Supreme Court Justice Sandra Day O'Connor said of the 1789 Judiciary Act:

> The Judiciary Act was a crucial, foundational part of that American tradition of seeking to perfect the nation through considered change in accord with the Rule of Law…. Because this one act of Congress established so many lasting, fundamental elements of the nation's judicial system, it has deservedly won much praise [and] provided the means for our nation's continuing constitutional revolution.

✦ Treasury Secretary Alexander Hamilton is credited with building the foundation for America's eventual financial and industrial pre-eminence. Washington believed Hamilton was a brilliant innovator and gladly gave him a free hand, subject only to keeping within the confines of the Constitution. Hamilton's plans were so far-sighted and complicated that few of his contemporaries could fully comprehend them. After designing and pushing through legislation to deal with the pressing problems of state and national public debts, Hamilton proposed his most radical innovation: creation of the Bank of the United States, a government financial facility to be modeled after the Bank of England. This scheme heightened the concerns of Jefferson and Madison that Hamilton was seeking to drive the country toward monarchy and an alliance with Britain, which was then the archenemy of France, the nation they favored as an ally. They tried to turn President Washington against the Bank plan, and knowing of his reverence for the Constitution, they attacked it as unconstitutional. When Congress passed the Bank legislation early in 1791, Washington faced a dilemma. He had great confidence in Hamilton's financial insight, but he was troubled by the arguments (especially those of Madison) that the Bank legislation exceeded the constitutional powers of Congress. When he ordered written opinions on the Bank's constitutionality from Secretary of State Jefferson and Attorney General Randolph, both agreed with Madison's negative views. Washington then told Hamilton that he would not sign the bill unless Hamilton wrote an opinion convincing him that the three distinguished Virginia lawyer-statesmen were wrong. At the same time, he asked Madison to prepare a veto message—an extreme step for Washington, who believed that the president should use the veto power solely to uphold the Constitution, never over policy conflicts. Hamilton was up to the challenge, quickly writing an opinion which, in Washington's eyes, justified creation of the Bank through the power of Congress under Article I, Section 8, to "make all laws which shall be necessary and proper for carrying into execution" its specific powers over commerce and the general welfare. Thus one of President Washington's most pivotal decisions during the formative days was based on a battle of legal briefs authored by the Founding Lawyers who were his chief advisors. He often took advantage of their presence in his administration to help him make collective decisions about the Constitution.

While the deification of George Washington as the Father of His Country is based mainly on his leadership of the victorious Continental Army, the importance of his post-war efforts to shape America's own "national character" should not be minimized. The main feature of the national character he began to establish with the help of the Founding Lawyers was a Government of Laws based on Separation of Powers with Checks and Balances. A few authoritative observations:

+ In *George Washington & American Constitutionalism*, Professor Glenn Phelps notes that "Washington accepted the view that a constitutional presidency was one that was subordinate to the Rule of Law" and that Washington "viewed the president as having a special guardianship of the Constitution."

+ In his 2002 book, *George Washington: Unifying a Nation*, Professor Don Higginbotham endorses the views of Professor Phelps, and adds that "Washington played his own part in the growth of the Supreme Court as a voice for the Rule of Law" by appointing judges of outstanding quality.

+ In *Founding Friendship: George Washington, James Madison and the Creation of the American Republic*, Professor Stuart Leibiger says of Washington's support for Madison's draft Bill of Rights, that "without Washington's help, Madison's crusade for what has become a constitutional cornerstone would have been hopeless."

+ Washington's farewell message, which was published throughout the country in 1796, summed up his views on government and the national character. In the final sentence, he told the nation that in retirement, he was looking forward to enjoying "the benign influence of good laws under a free government, the ever favourite subject of my heart, and the happy reward, as I trust, of our mutual cares, labours, and dangers."

+ After Washington's death, John Marshall was given access to his papers, and wrote the authorized biography. In the concluding section on Washington's "Legacy and Character," Marshall writes, "Real liberty, he thought, was to be preserved only by upholding the authority of the laws, and maintaining the energy of government."

+ In *His Excellency: George Washington*, Professor Joseph Ellis writes of Washington, "Without him to center it, the political experiment in republicanism might very well have failed."

+ In *The Great Upheaval: America and the Birth of the Modern World, 1788-1800*, historian Jay Winik writes that "ultimately it was not life among Virginia's social elite or military glory where he would make his lasting imprint. It was in leading his nation."

Washington's choice of Founding Lawyers as his chief advisors reflected his appreciation that getting the Constitution into operation by creating a

Government of Laws required considerable legal input. Near the end of his first term, he was leaning strongly toward retirement. All of his advisors opposed that idea, arguing that he was still indispensable. James Madison wrote a memorandum of his May 1792 discussion of this subject with Washington:

> He [President Washington] then entered on a more explicit disclosure of the state of his mind, observing that he could not believe or conceive himself anywise necessary to the successful administration of the Government; that on the contrary he had from the beginning found himself deficient in many of the essential qualifications, owing to his inexperience in the forms of public business, his unfitness to judge of legal questions, and questions arising out of the Constitution;...

Washington's methods of establishing the national character left the lasting impression in the political community that the effort to successfully launch a constitutional government would greatly benefit from participation by the lawyer-statesmen who had designed it. Thus it should not be a surprise that the next four presidents (John Adams, Thomas Jefferson, James Madison, and James Monroe) were lawyers of the Founding period, and that in the 18 elections between the end of George Washington's administration and the re-election of Abraham Lincoln in 1864—the crucial early decades when so many experiments in popular government self-destruct in coups or revolutions—lawyers won the presidency 16 times.

The three presidents who followed Monroe (John Quincy Adams, Andrew Jackson, and Martin Van Buren) were also lawyers. The pattern was interrupted in 1841 when William Henry Harrison took office, but he governed for only a month before he died, to be succeeded by Vice-President John Tyler, a lawyer who occupied the office until succeeded by James Polk (also a lawyer) in 1845. Polk was followed by non-lawyer Zachary Taylor in 1849, but Taylor died after serving less than 17 months, giving way to Vice-President Millard Fillmore, a lawyer. Thereafter the three presidents who served between 1853 and 1865—Franklin Pierce, James Buchanan, and Abraham Lincoln—were all lawyers.

Let us now focus on some nineteenth-century highlights of the development of America's Government of Laws. We should note that from the nation's birth through the nineteenth century, the legal profession, in addition to dominating the presidency, was by far the largest source of cabinet officers, members of both houses of Congress, state governors, and state legislators. And we should also consider the observations of Harvard Law Professor Morton Horwitz:

In a nation lacking either an established social order or an established church to produce the social cement of legitimate authority, from the beginning Americans turned the Rule of Law into a "civil religion." And in this most democratic country in the world, Americans after the Revolution obsessed about the dangers of "tyranny of the majority" and about how a "government of laws, not of men" might spare them from its ravages.

The Third Branch Blossoms

Guided by James Madison and his other lawyer-advisors, President Washington chose his Supreme Court appointees with great care, mindful that the respect they commanded would strongly influence the chances of creating a Government of Laws. Maintaining his strong commitment to constitutionalism, Washington chose lawyers who had played important roles in creating and ratifying the Constitution and the Bill of Rights. John Jay and Oliver Ellsworth (the first and second chief justices), John Rutledge of South Carolina, and James Wilson of Pennsylvania—all of them Founding Lawyers—were among the early appointees.

During Washington's two terms, the Supreme Court lacked the opportunity to become an important force in constitutional government, because it could not simply start making landmark decisions on its own. As a court of law, it had to await the arrival of litigated controversies on its docket. In those years of the federal courts' infancy, when the nation was feeling its way into the new and unprecedented governmental structure, few important cases were filed in the federal courts. Most disputes between the federal government's legislative and executive branches were settled without resorting to litigation. The Supreme Court justices spent most of their time "riding circuit" as itinerant trial judges rather than hearing appeals of precedent-making cases. It was an onerous and unattractive job, unworthy of the talents which Washington's appointees brought to it.

More significant cases began to come to the Supreme Court during the John Adams administration (1797-1801). In 1801, weeks before leaving office, Adams appointed as the third chief justice a Founding Lawyer who was destined to define the role of the Third Branch: 45-year-old John Marshall.

Marshall could well have qualified as the prototype All-American boy: eldest of 15 children, self-educated, a hero of the Revolutionary War, successful lawyer, protégé of George Washington, supporter of the Constitution in the historic Virginia ratification convention, member of Congress, John Adams's secretary of state—one of the few to attain high office in all three branches of government.

Under his leadership during the next 34 years (1801-1835) the Supreme Court fulfilled the role envisioned by Washington and his lawyer-advisors: completing the framework of a Government of Laws by providing checks on—and balances against—the legislative and executive branches. Marshall did this by establishing the Supreme Court as the final interpreter of the Constitution, with the ultimate power to decide whether statutes and other actions of federal and state government officials violate the Constitution, and to order those officials to comply with the Court's interpretation of the Constitution. In its broadest form, this power came to be called *judicial review.*

That was a gutsy step to take in 1801, since Article III, the most loosely defined part of the Constitution, did not mention judicial review. As Marshall's biographer, Jean Edward Smith, put it:

> Above all, Marshall asserted the authority of the Supreme Court to interpret the Constitution. Today that authority is taken for granted, but it was not universally recognized in 1801. Constitutions are political documents. They define the way a nation is governed. The central issue of whether they were justiciable in courts of law was problematic. The English tradition held that the great constitutional documents of British history were purely political statements that lay in the realm of Parliament to interpret, not the courts.

Historians differ as to whether the framers of the Constitution contemplated judicial review. It was discussed briefly during the Constitutional Convention debates, but it was not put to a vote since it was not mentioned in the drafts that were presented to the Convention. During the Confederation period, some of the state supreme courts had ruled on the constitutionality (under state constitutions) of state legislative acts, but those few decisions were neither popular nor authoritative. The issue was squarely raised during the ratification debates, when the Anti-Federalist No. 11 paper, *On the Power of the Judiciary* (authored by "Brutus"—probably Robert Yates, a New York lawyer-delegate to the Constitutional Convention) was published in 1788. Brutus argued:

> It is, moreover, of great importance to examine with care the nature and extent of the judicial power, because those who are to be vested with it are to be placed in a situation altogether unprecedented in a free country. They are to be rendered totally independent, both of the people and the legislature, both with respect to their offices and salaries. No errors they may commit can be corrected by any power

> above them, if any such power there be, nor can they be
> removed from office for making ever so many erroneous
> adjudications.

Brutus went on to warn that the unrestrained judges, tenured for life, would determine for themselves "the reason and spirit of the Constitution," extending their own powers in the process, giving "such meaning to the Constitution as will enlarge the sphere of their own authority." Brutus's bottom line:

> This power in the judicial will enable them to mold the
> government into almost any shape they please.

In response, Publius (alias Alexander Hamilton) wrote in Federalist Paper No. 78 that because "there is no liberty if the power of judging be not separated from the legislative and executive powers," limitations on the powers of Congress can be preserved only "through the medium of the courts of justice, whose duty it must be to declare all acts contrary to the manifest tenor of the Constitution void." To Brutus's argument that this judicial review power would raise the judiciary to a position of superiority over the elected legislature, Publius replied:

> It is far more rational to suppose that the courts were
> designed to be an intermediate body between the people
> and the legislature, in order, among other things, to keep
> the latter within the limits assigned to their authority. The
> interpretation of the laws is the proper and peculiar prov-
> ince of the courts. A Constitution is in fact—and must be
> regarded by the judges as—a fundamental law. It therefore
> belongs to them [the judges] to ascertain its meaning, as
> well as the meaning of any particular act proceeding from
> the legislative body.

Marshall's introduction of judicial review took place during the dawn of American party politics, a time of daunting political turmoil. George Washington was elected twice as a Federalist without opposition, but in the election of 1796, Thomas Jefferson ran unsuccessfully as the candidate of the Republican Party against the Federalist John Adams. The Adams administration was marked by one crisis after another, including a quasi-war with France. The democratic promise of the French Revolution had given way to anarchy which brought Napoleon Bonaparte to power as a virtual dictator, and he led his country into war against most of Europe, including Britain. France had provided crucial assistance to the American Revolution under a 1778 treaty alliance, and now the French government claimed that this treaty, still in force, obligated the United States to support France's war campaigns. The Federalists leaned more toward establishing friendly relations with Britain, and when Adams took office, he refused to involve the United States in France's military adventures. After negotiations failed to bridge the impasse, in 1798 the United States abrogated the 20-year-old treaty with France.

This stalemate resulted in France treating American merchant ships (especially those trading with Britain) as enemy property, seizing hundreds of them on the high seas and threatening to cripple America's foreign trade. Adams responded by building naval warships and putting Alexander Hamilton in charge of mobilizing a new army to fight off an expected French invasion. The fledgling U.S. Navy concentrated its small forces on driving French privateers from the American coastal waters and the West Indies. Finally Adams was able to negotiate a new peace treaty with Napoleon in 1800, and the quasi-war ended.

Adams believed that avoiding a disastrous war with France was his most important accomplishment, but his political opponents did not take such a kindly view of his performance. In 1798 he signed the Alien and Sedition Acts, for the ostensible purpose of protecting the nation against "the enemy within" in the form of more than 25,000 French émigrés who were said to pose potential security threats. But the main use the Adams administration made of these statutes was to prosecute and imprison editors of opposition (Republican) newspapers for criticizing the government—a crime under the Sedition Act. Jefferson and his Republican supporters insisted that Adams had exaggerated the French threat, and in the 1800 election he used Adams's unpopular repression of free speech as a lever to push the second president out of office after a single term. By that time, Adams's Federalists were seen by many as aristocratic champions of an all-powerful central government beholden to the commercial establishment, while Jefferson's party (renamed Democratic-Republicans) espoused a more egalitarian ideology designed to appeal to the yeoman farmer.

This conflict found expression in the legal system, where much of the litigation dealt with the confused condition of land titles. Suits between citizens of the same state were tried in state courts, but investors had become large landowners, and if they resided outside the state where the land was located, they could sue state residents in the federal courts. Many of the absentee landowners were Federalists, and they often used their clout with the central government to seek advantages from the Federalist-appointed judges in the federal courts, while the Democratic-Republicans tried to maintain the pre-eminence of the state courts, whose judges leaned more toward their interests. The federal courts were also the venue for enforcement of federal statutes like the Alien and Sedition Acts, and some overzealous federal judges (including Supreme Court Justice Samuel Chase when sitting as a trial judge on circuit) used those trials as platforms to make political speeches in favor of Adams's Federalist administration.

Against this volatile background, Jefferson's 1800 election victory threw the legal system into further disarray. President Adams, who had four more months in office, tried to prolong Federalist control of the federal judiciary, ramming through a Federalist-controlled lame duck Congress the Judiciary Act of 1801, which expanded federal court jurisdiction and empowered him to appoint many new federal judges. He made those appointments (known as the "midnight judges") during his final weeks in office, and unsurprisingly all his selections were Federalists who were hastily approved by the outgoing Federalist-controlled Senate. It was during those frantic final days in power that Adams appointed Marshall to be chief justice, hoping this would help the Federalists to retain control of the Third Branch despite the election defeat.

After Jefferson was inaugurated and his Democratic-Republicans took control of Congress, they enacted the Judiciary Act of 1802, which reversed Adams's last-minute power grab by repealing the Judiciary Act of 1801. This propelled the federal court system into further chaos, as the authority of many of its judges came into question. At that point, two cases came before the Marshall Supreme Court which immersed the justices up to their eyeballs in this anarchy-threatening political brawl: *Marbury v. Madison*, arising out of the Adams appointment of one of the midnight judges under the Judiciary Act of 1801, and *Stuart v. Laird*, involving the validity of the Jefferson administration's Judiciary Act of 1802, which purportedly repealed the 1801 Act.

Marshall and his five Supreme Court colleagues were all Federalist appointees. Thus, if the Court functioned merely as a political mechanism, the justices would be expected to uphold the Federalist-inspired 1801 Act in *Marbury* and strike down the Jeffersonian 1802 Act in *Stuart*. If they did so, they would then face some tough questions: How did this upstart court of six Federalist-appointed justices dare to challenge the will of the people which was so clearly expressed in the rejection of Adams and the Federalists in the 1800 election; and if the justices found the nerve to do that, how were they going to enforce their judgment when the Jeffersonians controlled the rest of the government and had already signaled their intention to ignore the Court by disdaining to defend their position in the *Marbury* case? On the other hand, if the justices believed the 1801 Act was constitutionally valid, but they struck it down anyway for fear that the Jefferson government would defy their ruling, what then was the use of having a "Supreme Court?" It was a confrontation worthy of *Spy vs. Spy*, 150 years before *Mad* magazine.

Rising above this partisan quagmire, Marshall and his five colleagues managed to strike a monumental blow for the Government of Laws, elevating the judiciary to a meaningful Third Branch of government by creating the concept of constitutional law and appearing to separate it from politics. Their names, not often mentioned today, bear recitation here: William Cushing of Massachusetts, William Paterson of New Jersey, Samuel Chase of Maryland, Bushrod Washington of Virginia, Alfred Moore of North Carolina, and John Marshall of Virginia. Their unanimous decisions in the *Marbury* and *Stuart* cases struck down Adams's 1801 Act as unconstitutional and upheld the 1802 Jefferson Act which repealed it. They accomplished this in a way which made it clear to the nation that they were delivering a legal interpretation of the Constitution rather than bowing to political pressure. So deftly did the justices carve out their legal holdings that the public immediately accepted and supported the principle of judicial review, and eventually both political parties embraced it.

On February 24, 1803, the date when Marshall was ready to deliver the Court's decision in *Marbury,* Justice Chase had fallen ill. Wanting to have the entire Court present, Marshall convened it in the living room of Stelle's Hotel, where all the justices resided during sessions. There he took four hours to read the 11,000 word *Marbury* decision, which is considered a masterpiece of legal reasoning. Its legal effect was to affirm the right of President Adams to appoint Marbury to a federal judgeship under the 1801 Judiciary Act, thus rebuking President Jefferson for refusing to honor the appointment. But the Court also rejected Marbury's application for a writ of mandamus (a court order directing Secretary of State James Madison to deliver Marbury's commission) on the ground that section 13 of the Judiciary Act of 1789, which purported to create the right to file mandamus applications in the Supreme Court, exceeded the "original jurisdiction" (trial court powers) of the Supreme Court as specified in Article III of the Constitution. In other words, they threw out Marbury's application by holding that under the Supreme Court's jurisdiction as spelled out in the Constitution, a writ of mandamus could only be granted by the lower federal court, not by the Supreme Court, where Marbury had filed the application. Thus the Marshall Court declared section 13 of the 1789 Judiciary Act unconstitutional, and in the process it defused an explosive political crisis, created "constitutional law" as a concept separate from politics, and established the Judiciary as a coordinate, co-equal branch of the constitutional government.

These excerpts from the *Marbury* decision are often cited in our time:

✦ To what purpose are powers limited, and to what purpose is that limitation committed to writing, if these limits may, at any time, be passed by those intended to be restrained?

✦ The Constitution is either a superior paramount law, unchangeable by ordinary means, or it is on a level with ordinary legislative acts, and, like other acts, is alterable when the legislature shall please to alter it.

✦ It is emphatically the province and duty of the Judicial
Department to say what the law is. Those who apply the
rule to particular cases, must of necessity expound and
interpret that rule. If two laws conflict with each other, the
courts must decide on the operation of each.

✦ Thus, the particular phraseology of the Constitution
of the United States confirms and strengthens the principle, supposed to be essential to all written constitutions,
that a law repugnant to the Constitution is void; and that
courts, as well as other departments, are bound by that
instrument.

In the *Stuart* decision a week later, with the constitutional groundwork
having been laid in the *Marbury* decision, it required only four paragraphs for
the Federalist-appointed Court to unanimously uphold the 1802 Judiciary
Act, which was the handiwork of the opposing Democratic-Republican party.
Marshall biographer Jean Edward Smith made this evaluation of *Marbury:*

The decision itself is one of the great constitutional documents of American history. Marshall's unadorned prose
evoked the spirit of constitutional balance: a government
of laws, not of men…. It is a primer on representative
government, a rationale for the Rule of Law.

Smith's view is confirmed by the placement of a copy of the *Marbury* decision in the national treasure room of the National Archives, where it is displayed
alongside the Declaration of Independence, the original 1787 Constitution,
and the Bill of Rights.

And so was born the power of the Third Branch to interpret and enforce
the Constitution, and to check and balance the powers of the other branches,
independently of the political pressures involved. It demonstrated that a
national political crisis could be averted and a constitutional policy could be
enunciated by a handful of judges whose only weapon was moral authority—
the Rule of Law.

NYU Law Professor William E. Nelson describes Marshall's *Marbury* breakthrough in these terms:

His creative act was to use the distinction between law and
politics to circumscribe, however imperfectly, the extent
to which the political, majoritarian style could engulf all
government, as it was threatening in 1800 to do.

Marshall's motivation is best expressed in his own words: "Nothing is more to be deprecated than the transfer of party politics to the seat of Justice." Alistair Cooke provides a snapshot of the nation at that point in its history:

> In the day-to-day turmoil of living out the Constitution,
> Americans came to see that it had set up a President to
> keep an eye on Congress, and a Congress to keep an eye on
> the President, and a Supreme Court to keep an eye on both
> of them.

As we shall see, once the people latched on to this judicial protection, they institutionalized it to the point where nobody—not even an extraordinarily popular and powerful president—dared to challenge it. Harvard Law Professor Archibald Cox captured the significance of the *Marbury* decision by describing what would have happened without it:

> The great questions…would then have been answered in
> political forums, by economic pressures, or by force of
> arms. For the genius of American constitutionalism to
> develop, the Court had first to assert, then win, the people's
> support for the Court's power of interpretation "according
> to law."

Writing in the 1830s, the French lawyer-statesman Alexis de Tocqueville marveled at the Marshall court's handiwork:

> The power vested in the American courts of justice of
> pronouncing a statute to be unconstitutional forms one
> of the most powerful barriers that have ever been devised
> against the tyranny of political assemblies.

Marshall's genius enabled the Supreme Court to use the momentum of *Marbury* to connect many of the ambiguous dots splattered on the Constitution's parchment by Gouverneur Morris & Co. Treading their way methodically through the largely unexplored territory of applied democracy, Marshall and his colleagues in their post-*Marbury* decisions laid out the main structure of the work-in-progress that was becoming the United States Government of Laws. Most of the early constitutional problems arose out of the intense rivalry between advocates of a strong central government and those who sought to maintain traditional state sovereignty.

In case after case, the Marshall Court spelled out the relationship between the federal and state governments, often using judicial review to strike down state statutes and actions that contravened the Constitution. Usually they came down in favor of strengthening and consolidating federal power, but they took great pains to maintain the image that they were doing so within the non-political framework of constitutional law. Professor Archibald Cox concluded that without the landmark decisions of the Marshall Court, "the whole plan of government might well have failed, destroyed by conflict among the many parts into which the power of government was divided." Thus, Separation of Powers with Checks and Balances was not an automatic pilot. It required hands on the controls, and many times during those make-or-break years the hands belonged to John Marshall and his fellow justices.

During the remainder of Marshall's service the Court did not again use judicial review to declare a federal statute unconstitutional. I suggest that the strong public support for the *Marbury* constitutional principles had a deterrent effect on the other two branches, causing them to consider carefully the constitutionality of their proposed actions before barreling ahead into a Supreme Court confrontation.

Tocqueville also observed, "There is virtually no political question in the United States that does not sooner or later resolve itself into a judicial question." It seems apparent that Marshall was assisted in his efforts to separate constitutional law from party politics as much by his skill and experience in politics as by his legal scholarship. Marshall also needed good luck to pull off this high-wire juggling act, since the political ideologies and loyalties of nearly all those selected for high judicial office are likely to play some role—directly or indirectly—in their deliberations.

Following John Marshall's 1835 death in office, President Andrew Jackson appointed Roger Taney as his successor. Some historians and legal scholars believe Taney was as talented a judge as Marshall—but he certainly was not as skilful a politician, nor was he as lucky.

The Elephant in the Living Room

By the early nineteenth century, the term "democracy" had shed its negative image and was respectable enough to furnish the name of a major American political party. In Jefferson's time the Republicans had phased into the Democratic-Republicans, and later the party name was shortened to Democratic, the ticket on which Andrew Jackson was elected president in 1828. The Jacksonian Democrats were dedicated to states' rights, since they feared a slide toward federal oligarchy and they viewed the national government largely as a device to promote business interests. When Jackson took office, he filled Supreme Court vacancies with Democratic judges who were expected to moderate the Marshall Court's expansion of federal power. Roger Taney had served as Jackson's attorney general (1831-1835). When he was appointed chief justice in 1836, he presided over a seven-judge court, of which five were Jackson appointees. A year later, the Democratic-controlled Congress created two more seats which were promptly filled by Jackson appointees. Thus, when the 1838 Court term began, the Jacksonian Democrats outnumbered the Federalist survivors of the Marshall Court by seven to two.

Taney took firm control of the Court, as Marshall had done before him. He was good at the job, and was able to maintain public respect for the Court as he methodically led his colleagues through cases that continued to shape the maturing nation. In the expanding field of economic development, the Taney Court reversed the Marshall Court's trend toward federal domination of commerce, without causing any constitutional problems. Although Taney served under four opposition-party presidents (then called Whigs instead of Federalists), his Court did not find it necessary to declare any acts of Congress unconstitutional until it undertook to deal with the elephant in the nation's living room: slavery.

As we have seen, slavery was swept under the rug at the Constitutional Convention, since the delegates concluded that they could not produce a union if they even tried to tackle that explosive issue. The one anti-slavery concession—the provision in Article II opening the way for Congress to prohibit importation of slaves after 1808—resulted in the outlawing of the African slave trade at that time. (Even that clause was designed to keep the elephant invisible, describing slaves as "such persons as any of the states now existing shall think proper to admit," thus avoiding any mention of slavery in the Constitution.) But the ban on importing did not produce the gradual erosion of slavery for which James Madison and his colleagues had hoped, as the Southern states' appetite for slave labor burgeoned with the advent of King Cotton. By the 1860 census the slave population had grown to 3.9 million, up from 1.2 million in 1810, and slavery remained the nation's most challenging moral issue.

A static agricultural society like that of the 1780s might have survived this dichotomy, but by the 1850s the coming of the railroads and the Industrial Revolution had made Americans much more interdependent. There were two major slavery problems which produced constant friction. As the nation expanded westward, there were monumental political struggles over the question of whether the newly admitted states (which would soon greatly outnumber the thirteen original states) would be slave or free. To keep the divided country functioning while officially ignoring the elephant, many political compromises were made, designed to keep the number of slave and free states equal so that neither would dominate the Senate. This delayed the admission of major states like Texas and California until they could be paired with a slave or free state to maintain the equal balance. A second irritant was the legal status of runaway slaves who took refuge in free states, and of those who moved with their masters from slave states to free states. The political compromises managed to hold the Union together, but it was only a matter of time before it would become unglued.

The Jacksonian Democrats' electoral success was based on their support of states' rights, which put them in the position of protecting slavery, a creature of state laws. The nine-justice Taney Court consistently had five pro-slavery Southerners and at least two pro-slavery Northerners, who were known as "doughfaces." Over the years the Supreme Court ruled on cases involving slavery issues, but managed to maintain the status quo without upsetting the delicate constitutional balance—until Chief Justice Taney led them into the train wreck that forced the nation to face up to the presence of the deadly elephant.

Taney was an unlikely candidate for this infamous role, since he was considered nearly as nimble as Marshall in the delicate balancing maneuvers required to deal with constitutional law, and he had already presided peacefully over the Supreme Court for 20 years. Taney, the son of a slave-owning Maryland planter, had educated and freed his own slaves, in contrast to Marshall, a Virginian who maintained slaves as personal servants throughout his lifetime. Yet when the uncomplicated case of *Dred Scott v. Sandford* came before his court in 1857, Taney came apart at the seams, and almost took the Constitution with him.

Dred Scott was a black slave owned by a Missouri physician, Dr. John Emerson, who had taken Scott with him to live in the free state of Illinois and other free territories before returning to the slave state of Missouri. After Emerson died, Scott sued the doctor's widow for his freedom, claiming he had become free forever when his owner took him to live in places where slavery was illegal. This claim was litigated for more than 10 years in the state and federal courts, finally reaching the Supreme Court in 1856. By that time there were legal precedents holding that slaves in Scott's situation were required to claim their freedom while living in free states or territories (which Scott had not done) and that when they returned to live in a slave state, their rights were governed by the law of that slave state, precluding any claim to freedom based on past residence.

The Taney Court could have denied Scott his freedom on those grounds, maintaining the status quo without involving the Constitution. In fact, the four Southern associate justices wanted to dispose of the case in that straightforward way. But President-elect James Buchanan, the victorious Democratic candidate who was about to take office, wanted a sweeping edict from the Court which would enable his incoming administration to avoid having to deal with slavery disputes that were becoming increasingly volatile.

Buchanan, a Pennsylvanian, was a noted constitutional lawyer and former chairman of the House Judiciary Committee. He had turned down the offer of a seat on the Supreme Court to pursue the presidency. He believed that a definitive Supreme Court constitutional ruling could end the controversy over slavery and keep the elephant invisible throughout his time in office. Instead he took a long step toward destroying the Union by influencing the Taney Court to stray far beyond its constitutional role.

Even though there was a 7-2 pro-slavery majority on the Taney Court, Buchanan apparently wanted to stifle dissent and come away with an unassailable judicial mandate. He used his heavy-handed influence on a fellow Pennsylvanian, Associate Justice Robert Grier, as well as on Chief Justice Taney, to turn the *Dred Scott* decision into a tidal wave capable of drowning the opposition to slavery. His immediate objective was to prevent Congress from ever banning slavery in the territories, and he hoped that ultimately the Taney Court's decision would convince the nation that the Constitution forbade Congress from taking any action to inhibit slavery. Indeed, knowledgeable people on the anti-slavery side believed that Buchanan and Taney conspired to open the way for slavery to flourish throughout the nation, by manipulating the Constitution to eliminate the free states' power to prohibit it even within their own borders.

Chief Justice Taney administered the oath of office to Buchanan on March 4, 1857, and listened as the incoming president gave the game away in his inauguration speech by declaring that slavery in the territories was strictly a judicial question, and proclaiming his full support for the Supreme Court's decision in the *Dred Scott* case, "whatever this may be." Two days later, Taney announced the 7-2 decision which trashed the whole concept of constitutional law. He labeled his decision "Opinion of the Court" even though there were six concurring opinions based on diverse theories, and two thunderous dissents.

Taney's rambling opinion sprawled far beyond the issues raised by Dred Scott's claim of emancipation. Writing that blacks were "so far inferior, that they had no rights which the white man was bound to respect," Taney held that even if they were freed, they could never be considered citizens of the United States and therefore did not have a right to sue in federal courts. Eager to inflate this non-landmark case into a towering edifice that would prevent Congress from playing any future role in slavery issues, Taney opined that the ban on slavery in the territories written into such legislation as the Missouri Compromise, which had prevented the slavery issue from erupting into civil war for over 35 years, was unconstitutional. He did this by redefining the term "territory" in Article IV of the Constitution (which gave Congress the power to enact laws relating to the territories) to include only the territories owned by the United States when the Constitution was written in 1787.

This was Taney's ultimate insult to the intelligence of those who eagerly awaited the decision trumpeted by Buchanan two days earlier, for it required the following mental contortions to support it: (a) the framers decided to give

Congress the power to regulate the territories owned by the United States in 1787, most of which at that time had not been accurately surveyed and therefore had indeterminable borders; but (b) the framers *silently* decided *not* to give Congress the power to regulate territories acquired after 1787 (thus creating at least two conflicting methods of regulation, for unexplained reasons) even though the United States could acquire new territories only by paying money appropriated by Congress or by defeating a foreign enemy in a war declared by Congress.

This crude piece of judicial chicanery excluded from Article IV the vast lands acquired in the 1803 Louisiana Purchase and indeed most of the area then constituting the United States, which Congress had been regulating under Article IV without challenge for over half a century. Besides obviously abusing the judicial power by politicizing the narrow legal issues presented, Taney's tortured reasoning thoroughly discredited the Supreme Court as an independent branch and final interpreter of the Constitution. It breathed new life into the warning of Brutus in Anti-Federalist paper No. 11 that the Supreme Court could not be trusted with the broad judicial powers granted by the Constitution. The decision brought forth an unprecedented wave of outrage in newspapers and pamphlets—a sustained outrage that has kept *Dred Scott* in high school and college textbooks to this day as the prototype of what the Supreme Court was *not* created to do.

The immediate result of *Dred Scott* was to hand the White House on a silver platter to the opposition party, which by then had adopted the name Republican. Abraham Lincoln, the Republican presidential candidate, made the *Dred Scott* decision a central target of his 1860 election campaign. Lincoln scholar Paul Finkelman notes:

> While many presidents have found the law a useful stepping stone to politics and the White House, none have used legal argumentation so successfully in gaining the nomination and campaigning for the presidency. Lincoln the candidate was really Lincoln the advocate, arguing against Taney's position in the only forum that mattered—the court of public opinion.

Lincoln used Taney's words to help sweep the Democrats out of power, despite the threats of the Southern states that they would secede from the Union if he were elected. They made good on that promise, beginning the process of seceding and establishing the Confederate States of America as soon as the election results were announced. The Civil War began officially with the Confederate attack on Fort Sumter in South Carolina on April 12, 1861, five weeks after Lincoln's inauguration.

Despite the shock waves that emanated from the conduct of Buchanan and Taney in the *Dred Scott* fiasco, most historians do not hold either of them (or the decision itself) directly responsible for causing the Civil War, albeit they probably hastened its outbreak. The cause was the elephant itself, the institution of slavery which made the clash of arms inevitable. In the words of John Marshall, slavery was "incurable but by compulsion."

The Great Emancipator

That the Government of Laws survived the Civil War is a miracle in itself. Equally impressive is the fact that Abraham Lincoln struggled mightily to keep the Government of Laws operating *during* the war, and largely succeeded despite the most daunting obstacles, including a hostile pro-slavery Supreme Court still led by Chief Justice Taney; a Congress riddled with conflicting ideologies; the secession of seven Southern states and the inauguration of Jefferson Davis as president of the Confederacy before Lincoln was inaugurated; and the presence of Confederate saboteurs and sympathizers (who were indistinguishable from other Americans) in the areas surrounding the beleaguered national capital.

I suggest two major reasons why Lincoln was able to preserve the Government of Laws: (1) of all our lawyer-presidents, his was the life most devoted to active law practice; and (2) his cabinet was composed almost entirely of lawyers who shared his dedication to the Constitution.

Lincoln's cabinet is the subject of *Team of Rivals,* a meticulous historical study by Doris Kearns Goodwin which relates the previously unheralded story of how Lincoln's three main rivals for the 1860 Republican nomination—"New York senator William H. Seward, Ohio governor Salmon P. Chase, and Missouri's distinguished elder statesman Edward Bates"—became respectively the secretary of state, treasury secretary, and attorney general in Lincoln's wartime cabinet. All of them were eminent lawyers, keenly aware of the permanent injuries which the Civil War threatened to inflict on American constitutional government. Of the four remaining cabinet members—Secretary of War Edwin Stanton, Secretary of the Navy Gideon Welles, Interior Secretary Caleb Smith, and Postmaster General Montgomery Blair—all were lawyers except Welles, and even he had studied law in college before becoming a newspaper editor. Goodwin and her sources document Lincoln's close consultation with his cabinet.

The first constitutional crisis facing Lincoln when he was inaugurated on March 4, 1861, was the legal status of the seceded states and their nascent Confederacy. The secessions had occurred on the watch of Lincoln's predecessor, James Buchanan, who proved unequal to the task of doing anything about them even though he considered them unconstitutional. It should be noted that while Lincoln abhorred slavery in any form or place, he believed that the Constitution required the president to respect and preserve it in the slave states. He assured the Southern leaders that he would take no steps to end slavery in their states, and would even enforce the Fugitive Slave Laws to return the runaways. But he drew the line at allowing slavery to expand into the territories and the free states, and quickly made it clear that unlike the inert Buchanan, he would use military force if necessary to protect the Union against Confederate aggression. In fact, his stated objective during the early years of the war was simply to protect and restore the Union. He did not shift to a strategy of eliminating slavery in the South until that became a legitimate military objective which fell within his constitutional war powers.

The Civil War was hardly under way before the Union faced a monumental security crisis. On April 15, 1865—the day after Fort Sumter fell to the Confederacy—Lincoln issued a proclamation ordering the Northern states to mobilize 75,000 militiamen and calling a special session of Congress for July 4. The capital itself was lightly garrisoned and in need of immediate reinforcements, which would have to come from the Northern states by way of the slave state of Maryland. While eight slave states (including Virginia) seceded quickly, Maryland was one of the "border" slave states whose status was uncertain. Maryland's pro-Union governor managed to prevent the pro-slavery state legislature from voting to secede, but street mobs took control of Baltimore and prevented the passage of Union troops to Washington, destroying railroad bridges and telegraph lines which linked Baltimore with the North. It took weeks for the reinforcing troops to circumvent Baltimore and reach Washington. To bring Maryland under control, Lincoln found it necessary to declare martial law there and authorize military officers to arrest suspected saboteurs. In order to free his understaffed forces from the diversion of producing prisoners in court and justifying their arrests, Lincoln authorized the suspension of habeas corpus anywhere between Philadelphia and Washington where it became necessary.

Article I of the Constitution, which enumerates the powers of Congress, provides in section 9 that "The privilege of the writ of habeas corpus shall not be suspended, unless when in cases of rebellion or invasion the public safety may require it." The question of whether Congress alone or the president alone (or both together) could suspend habeas corpus had not been adjudicated, but Lincoln exercised this power alone as an emergency measure when Congress was not in session—in fact, at a moment when members of Congress would not have been able to travel to Washington due to the interference of the Maryland Confederate supporters. When Congress convened for the emergency session on July 4, Lincoln and his cabinet advisors sought legislative approval of his emergency measures, which was quickly granted.

Throughout the war, habeas corpus was frequently suspended, under presidential powers authorized by Congress.

In 1862, with no end to the war's fearful toll in sight, Lincoln conceived the plan of freeing the slaves as a strategic military maneuver. If it worked, it would have two favorable military effects: (1) it would deplete the ranks of the Confederate armies, since many soldiers would need to return to the plantations as replacements for the slave labor that was producing the food and other crops required for Confederate survival; and (2) it would create a new source of military manpower for the Union forces. Lincoln and his cabinet agonized over how to achieve this, for there was no precedent.

They considered putting it through Congress, but decided it would require a constitutional amendment for which they would probably not be able to muster the required two-thirds vote. Finally Lincoln decided that under the Constitution, he could proceed by way of a presidential proclamation, which had to be very carefully worded to make certain that it came across as an exercise of emergency war powers rather than a moralistic denunciation of slavery—the slavery which was actually preserved and protected by the Constitution. The legal support for this radical move was furnished by William Whiting, a prominent Boston lawyer who was serving (without salary) as solicitor of the War Department. Whiting's treatise on the war powers of the president and Congress, first published in 1862, went through seven editions during the war. As Princeton History Professor James M. McPherson notes, "Lincoln's own legal mind grasped Whiting's argument that the laws of war 'give the President full belligerent rights' as commander in chief to seize enemy property (in this case slaves) being used to wage war against the United States."

To this end, Lincoln and the cabinet members put on their lawyers' hats and turned out the Emancipation Proclamation, a document which some historians have belittled as "having all the moral grandeur of a bill of lading." That Lincoln was capable of writing with moral grandeur is apparent from the Gettysburg address and his other timeless works. In this case, lawyer Lincoln was happy to settle for a bill of lading, which on January 1, 1863 delivered more than three million human beings from slavery, and at the same time represented a maximum legal effort to preserve the Constitution. To confirm that the proclamation was "a fit and necessary war measure for suppressing said rebellion," its scope was limited to the slaves within the Confederate states, thus permitting slavery to continue in border states like Maryland which had not seceded. Lincoln must have relished turning the tables on Chief Justice Taney by appropriating the dehumanizing *Dred Scott* decision to treat the Southern slaves as enemy "property" which the president was legally authorized—indeed, legally required—to seize under his constitutional war powers as commander in chief of the armed forces. The careful legal wording of the proclamation was designed to withstand a challenge in the Supreme Court where Roger Taney still presided over a pro-slavery majority. Its final sentence bears Lincoln's touch:

> And upon this act, sincerely believed to be an act of justice,
> warranted by the Constitution upon military necessity,
> I invoke the considerate judgment of mankind and the
> gracious favor of Almighty God.

In *Lincoln's Constitution*, University of California-Berkeley Law Professor Daniel Farber provides an evenhanded account of the Lincoln administration's painstaking efforts to wage a civil war of unprecedented ferocity without destroying the Constitution. As to secession, habeas corpus suspension, military tribunals, and other uncharted waters navigated by the Lincoln administration, including the then-controversial Emancipation Proclamation, Farber sums up the overall constitutional performance:

> As we have seen, most of what Lincoln did [at the outbreak
> of war] and later, was in fact constitutional.... Not a
> perfect record, but a creditable one, under incredibly trying
> circumstances.

> ...[Lincoln] could also keep clearly in mind that the long-
> term goal was not merely to crush the rebellion but to
> save the nation as a bastion of liberty.... In his ability to
> combine ruthless pragmatism with a deep fidelity to prin-
> ciple, he may have been unique....

> It was Lincoln's character—his ability, judgment, courage,
> and humanity—that brought the Union through the war
> with the Constitution intact.

Thus the two great icons of America's first century, George Washington and Abraham Lincoln, assisted by many lawyer-statesmen, began the process of shaping a unique national character by breathing life into the Government of Laws and keeping it afloat in the stormiest of seas.

Now let's see what their successors did to maintain it.

Chapter Five

Restoring the Government of Laws
(1865-1937)

Despite Abraham Lincoln's painstaking efforts to preserve the Constitution throughout the Civil War, he could do little about the damage inflicted on the Supreme Court by the *Dred Scott* decision. With his hands full conducting the war, the best he could manage was to make the Taney Court irrelevant by avoiding it or ignoring its obstructionist rulings. He was able to fill four vacancies in 1862-1863 which pushed Taney into the pro-slavery minority. When Taney died on October 12, 1864, Lincoln appointed Salmon Chase, his chief Republican rival for the presidency, as chief justice.

Chase took office on December 6, 1864, and remained chief justice until his death in 1873. His objective was to start the Court on the long road back to the prestige and power it had enjoyed under John Marshall. Wisely, Chase led the Court in exercising judicial restraint, very gradually moving it back toward a meaningful role in the Government of Laws. The justices made no heroic efforts to challenge the executive or legislative branches, which between them played the decisive roles in the Reconstruction era. The major constitutional developments were the adoption of three amendments that undid Taney's *Dred Scott* handiwork: the Thirteenth Amendment, which abolished slavery (1865); the Fourteenth, which defined United States citizenship to include African-Americans (1868); and the Fifteenth, which prohibited denial of the right to vote on account of race, creed, or previous slave status (1870).

The momentum toward equality created by these promising amendments was largely nullified when Reconstruction was brought to an end in

1877 through political dealings between the leaders of both major parties. In the election of 1876, the Republican presidential candidate was Rutherford B. Hayes, a Civil War major general who as a lawyer, congressman, and governor of Ohio had fought for the rights of Southern blacks. His Democratic opponent was New York Governor Samuel Tilden, formerly a crusading prosecutor credited with bringing down the corrupt Tweed ring. Although both candidates had reputations for rectitude, the campaign was marred by widespread intimidation, violence, and fraud on both sides. Tilden won a majority of the popular vote, but the Electoral College was deadlocked by disputes arising from the submission of two conflicting sets of electoral votes from Florida, Louisiana, and South Carolina. If the electoral votes of any one of those states were counted for Tilden, he would win the election; but if all three states went to Hayes, he would win by one electoral vote. Congress had the responsibility for resolving the conflicting claims, but the election remained undecided during weeks of acrimonious Congressional debate.

In John Marshall's day, this constitutional crisis could have been brought to the Supreme Court for resolution. But public confidence in the Court was so low that Congress created an Electoral Commission to decide the vote contests. The Commission consisted of five members from the Senate, five from the House, and five Supreme Court justices, selected as equally as possible from the two parties. To achieve equal balance, four Supreme Court justices were appointed (two representing each party) and they in turn selected as the 15th member the justice whom they considered the most independent of party control. Thus the supposedly independent judiciary was thrown into the pot along with Congress, its Supreme Court justices labeled according to political party roots. The Commission struggled for five more weeks before deciding by an eight to seven party-line vote to award all three disputed states (and the election) to Hayes.

Fearful that this blowout patch might not hold the government together, the leaders of both parties met secretly and worked out a compromise: the Democrats would allow Hayes to assume the presidency, provided that he promised to remove the federal troops which were struggling to enforce Reconstruction in the Southern states. This sealed the fate of Reconstruction, for as soon as the troops were withdrawn, Democrats at the state level nullified enforcement of the three new Amendments and thwarted other efforts to bring equality to the Southern blacks. "Black codes" and "Jim Crow laws" enacted by Southern state legislatures made White Supremacy the governing principle until the Civil Rights revolution of the 1960s. Southern blacks were free of slavery, they were U. S. citizens, and they had the constitutional right to vote, but these gains lost their impact after the Southern states were allowed to install qualifications which effectively prevented blacks from voting, blocked by subterfuges (literacy tests, property ownership requirements, and poll taxes) that were not officially based on race, creed, or servitude. For a great many Southern blacks, the only hope of escaping from an oppressive life was to pack up and migrate to the North.

The triumph of Jim Crow and the Southern Democrats over the Reconstruction Amendments occurred during a 44-year stretch (1869-1913) when every president except Grover Cleveland was a Republican. Even Cleveland was a New Yorker, not a Southerner. No candidate from any of the former Confederate states was elected president until Lyndon Johnson of Texas in 1964. Indeed, he was the first Southern Democrat to even be nominated for president after the Civil War. Thus the postwar Republicans—the party of Emancipation—more often than not had the Congressional majorities needed to legislate against White Supremacy, and they usually controlled the executive branch which was empowered to enforce such statutes. Republican presidents also made the great majority of appointments to all the federal courts during this period, including the Supreme Court. This presented the Chase Court and its successors with the opportunity to make the Constitution work again in the South. But those Republican-dominated courts went the other way.

In the 1873 *Slaughter-House Cases,* the Chase Court decided that the Fourteenth Amendment protected only against state action, thus exempting discriminatory practices of private citizens. Then the Court presided over by Chief Justice Morrison Waite, who was appointed by Republican President Ulysses Grant to succeed Chase in 1874, proceeded to nullify the efforts of Congress to curb White Supremacy. In a series of decisions culminating in the 1883 *Civil Rights Cases,* the Waite Court declared the Civil Rights Act of 1875 unconstitutional. University of Southern California Law Professor Howard Gillman assesses the performance of the Waite Court:

> Most tragically, they took the lead in facilitating the deconstruction of Reconstruction, making direct federal protection of blacks virtually impossible and inviting hostile state legislation, including the imposition of Jim Crow. The best that can be said for these efforts is that the Court was taking its cue from other national power holders and was playing its role as a partner in a national governing coalition.

Such a partnership in a national governing coalition would be inconsistent with the Supreme Court's constitutional role of independently riding herd on those governing at the moment, both at the federal and state levels. Obviously the Court's authority had not developed to the point where the justices could hope to dislodge Jim Crow from the Southern cities and towns where their orders would have to be enforced. Chief Justice Waite and his colleagues were probably accurate in their perception that the nation was not ready to give judges the power to order what local politics would not accept, in a conflict as fundamental as that between Southern whites and blacks.

Professor Gillman properly places the responsibility on the national governing coalition rather than solely on the Southern whites. While the North had gone to the extent of shedding the blood of its youth to eliminate the abomination of slavery, only a small minority of whites were ready to progress much further at that time. Yes, slavery had to go, but that did not mean that whites would move on from there to promote political, social, or economic equality for blacks. That was a broader idea whose time had not yet come in the United States. Thus it was no surprise that after Melville Fuller succeeded Chief Justice Waite in 1888, the Fuller Court provided Jim Crow segregation safe passage into the twentieth century by holding (notably in the 1896 *Plessy v. Ferguson* decision) that "separate but equal" was as far as the national governing coalition was required to go.

We are using the Supreme Court as the symbolic stand-in for the whole legal system, the structure of which dictates that nearly all the landmark constitutional decisions which create the public image of the Third Branch will emanate from the highest federal court. As the early twentieth-century Supreme Court continued its efforts to regain public support, the justices handed down many decisions which are of great significance to legal scholars. But we shall skip over most of them here since they don't tell us much about what we are seeking to illuminate: how the Rule of Law became accessible to most Americans. It is worth noting that during the Progressive Era (roughly 1890 to 1929) the Court aligned itself mainly with the captains of industry who were nurturing the Golden Goose of American laissez-faire capitalism. Usually the majority of justices saw it as their duty to protect the Golden Goose against the most ambitious attempts of the progressives to regulate working conditions and business practices. Under the banner of "states' rights," the Court maintained Jim Crow in control of the South, and this also served to minimize the federal government's role in business and finance. The Robber Barons and their more subtle successors had less to fear from state regulation, which they were usually able to forestall (often with the aid of bribery) without having to spend much on legal services. The Supreme Court itself, by avoiding controversial decisions, was able to emerge relatively unscathed by the muckraking journalists of the era—a fact which indicates that the public was not expecting much in the way of checks and balances from the Third Branch.

The Court gained some prestige in 1921 when former president William Howard Taft became the chief justice. Taft made it clear that he rated his new job as more desirable than the presidency. Although he had not been a very effective president, he was an excellent administrator. In his decade as chief justice he modernized and improved the entire federal judicial system and was the driving force behind construction of the imposing Supreme Court building, finally enabling the justices to move out of their cramped hand-me-down quarters in the Capitol building. But for all of Taft's enthusiastic stewardship, it remained for a much more popular president—one who was constantly engaged in combat against the Court—to restore it to its hallowed place in the Government of Laws.

The New Deal and the Government of Laws
(1933-1937)

When Franklin Delano Roosevelt took the oath of office on March 4, 1933, the nation was in the throes of its worst crisis since the Civil War. The Great Depression that began with the 1929 stock market crash had caused over 9,000 banks to close, and depositors' insurance had not yet been invented. Unemployment was at 25 percent, and millions of those who still had jobs were desperate enough to work for wages that barely put food on the table. A quarter of the farmers had lost their farms to foreclosure, and the stock market had sunk to less than 20 percent of its 1929 value. Most deadly was the lack of hope, as the outgoing Hoover administration had not taken any steps which convinced the public that government could do anything to stem the ongoing Depression. Historian Arthur M. Schlesinger Jr. describes the situation that confronted FDR on his first inauguration day:

> It was now not just a matter of staving off hunger. It was a matter of seeing whether a representative democracy could conquer economic collapse. It was a matter of staving off violence, even (at least some thought) revolution....

> Capitalism, it seemed to many, had spent its force; democracy could not rise to economic crisis. The only hope lay in governmental leadership of a power and will which representative institutions seemed impotent to produce.

Roosevelt set about to remove the clouds of despair that enveloped the nation by assuring the people that their government would help them through this crisis. His ability to project contagious self-confidence in his public speeches provided an emotional lift, which he quickly followed up with a spate of legislative and executive initiatives that came to be known as the New Deal. Since there was little precedent for the steps he envisioned, and his own law practice had not been much involved with the Constitution, he assembled a group of advisors which was heavily weighted with lawyers.

During the 1932 presidential campaign, FDR had formed a "brain trust" consisting of three Columbia University professors: Adolph Berle and Raymond Moley of the law faculty, and Rexford Tugwell of the economics department. They did much of the planning for innovative government intervention designed to lift the economy out of the Depression. Before moving into the White House, Roosevelt consulted Harvard Law Professor Felix Frankfurter, with whom he had maintained a close bond since they served together on the World War I War Labor Policies Board. Frankfurter was convinced that the nation could be saved by the creation of administrative agencies which would keep the economy running smoothly, cushioning the roller-coaster movements of laissez-faire capitalism. But he anticipated that business firms would vigorously litigate against this government intervention, and that the tradition-bound federal judges at all levels would be disinclined to perform the constitutional calisthenics required to uphold the radical-looking recovery program. The Supreme Court was dominated by "horse-and-buggy" justices. Seven of the nine had been appointed by Republican presidents.

Frankfurter counseled FDR to bring to Washington an army of bright lawyers (mostly young, and mostly former Frankfurter students) who could build into the designs of the new agencies the protective armor needed to withstand constitutional attacks, and who could step into courtrooms to defend the new programs against the legal challenges that were bound to ensue. Many of the New Deal lawyers were recruited by Frankfurter's leading protégé, Tommy ("the Cork") Corcoran, and became known as Frankfurter's "Happy Hot Dogs." Among those who served in the federal agencies or the Justice Department and later became prominent were Adlai Stevenson, Dean Acheson, Robert Jackson, William Douglas, Abe Fortas, Stanley Reed, Jerome Frank, and Thurman Arnold.

Thus the task of designing and implementing the New Deal became largely a legal initiative, with Frankfurter (commuting between Cambridge and Washington) as its mastermind. General Hugh Johnson, head of the flagship agency, the National Recovery Administration (NRA), insisted that Frankfurter was "the most influential single individual in the United States." Frankfurter's handiwork was denounced by the anti-Roosevelt journalist Westbrook Pegler, who complained of "the New Deal philosophy, which itself was derived from…Frankfurter, through his contamination of mischievous cub lawyers who, in turn, have polluted the thought of the government." In the first phase of the New Deal, this "pollution" was carried out mainly by coaxing industries to adopt NRA codes which controlled production and fixed prices, wages, and hours of work—a sort of government-sponsored cartelization of American business. On its face this was a voluntary program, but those who did not opt to participate were targeted with taxes designed to make it difficult for them to compete. The Happy Hot Dogs argued that these measures, and others which redesigned agriculture, labor, and the financial system, were constitutional when tested by an expansive construction of the Congressional power to regulate interstate commerce and to provide for the general welfare—a construction which they claimed was justified by the desperate need to pull the nation out of the catastrophic Depression.

As the New Dealers had anticipated, many businesses resisted the new programs, driving the Happy Hot Dogs into federal courts all over the country to enforce the statutes and agency regulations they had drafted. This litigation, which encompassed thousands of cases, worked its way through the federal trial and intermediate appellate courts with inconclusive results, until *Schechter Poultry Corp. v. United States* reached the Supreme Court. There on May 27, 1935, the blood was nearly drained out of the New Deal when the Court held in *Schechter* that key provisions of the legislation creating the NRA were unconstitutional.

Probably the most daunting feature of the *Schecter* decision was that it was unanimous. The Happy Hot Dogs had failed to gain a single vote from the nine justices, even though three of them (Louis Brandeis, Benjamin Cardozo, and Harlan Fiske Stone) were considered liberals. The New Dealers had expected no better from the hard-core conservative "Four Horsemen of the Apocalypse" (Willis Van Devanter, James McReynolds, George Sutherland, and Pierce Butler) who perceived almost any government regulation of business as a step toward socialism. But the hope was that the three liberals would be joined by the two moderate Republican swing voters, Chief Justice Charles Evans Hughes and Justice Owen Roberts, to clear the constitutional path for the New Deal legislation. Instead they were confronted by nine red stoplights.

Since the hyper-complicated NRA experiment had not been working very well anyway, the *Schecter* decision was not a fatal blow to the New Deal. But other Supreme Court decisions in 1935 and 1936 punched gaping holes in FDR's overall plans to revive the economy and make capitalism work for all the people. The justices struck down the Agricultural Adjustment Act, the Railroad Retirement Pension Act, the Farm Mortgage Act, the Bituminous Coal Act, the Municipal Bankruptcy Act, and the New York State minimum-wage law for women and children. When Chief Justice Hughes adjourned the Court for its 1936 summer recess, the New Deal was left in smoking ruins. The Court had invalidated 12 major statutes during FDR's first term, compared with the average of one every two years between 1790 and 1932. But then came the 1936 election.

In his campaign for a second term, FDR asked for an overwhelming Democratic vote which would send a message to those who opposed the New

Deal that the people insisted it be given a chance to succeed. He did not attack the Supreme Court directly, but his surrogates made it clear that the justices (who were appointed for life, with no mandatory retirement age) were out of touch with the needs of the American people. In his keynote speech at the Democratic Convention, Kentucky Senator Alben Barkley brought the crowd to its feet by asking rhetorically whether the Supreme Court may "be regarded as too sacred to be disagreed with." But it was the Republicans who made the Court a campaign issue, hoping to frighten dictator-wary voters by warning that because most of the Supreme Court justices were elderly, FDR in a second term would have the opportunity to replace enough of them to tip the majority over to supporting the New Dealers' zealous expansion of the federal government. The Republican platform pledged to "resist all attempts to impair the authority of the Supreme Court."

The election resulted in the biggest Democratic landslide in history, with FDR receiving 523 electoral votes to 8 for moderate Republican Alf Landon. The Democratic majorities in both houses of Congress soared near the 80 percent level. FDR had his mandate, and he soon made it clear that he would not hesitate to put it into action to fix the Supreme Court roadblock problem. There were well-founded rumors that he had Frankfurter and the Happy Hot Dogs working on constitutional amendments which would widen the scope of Congressional power under the commerce and general welfare clauses. But in the wake of the election landslide, FDR opted for something far more dramatic.

As we have seen, the Constitution gives Congress the power to fix the number of Supreme Court justices, as one of the checks and balances against the Third Branch. The number was fixed at six in the Judiciary Act of 1789, and thereafter various acts of Congress set it between five and ten until 1869, when it was leveled off at nine. By 1936, most Americans took it for granted that the number was permanently fixed at nine. But there was nothing in the Constitution to prevent FDR from using his huge Congressional majorities to change the number again. Indeed, all of the previous changes had been made for political purposes. On February 5, 1937, he announced that he was asking Congress to increase the total to as many as fifteen, by giving the president the power to name one new justice for each present justice who was over 70 and refused to retire, up to a maximum of six new justices.

The reason given by FDR for this proposed change was that the justices were overworked and unable to keep their calendar current due to their ages (which averaged 71) and the influx of larger caseloads. But when Chief Justice Hughes responded by presenting a report showing that the Court's calendar was remarkably up to date, it became obvious to Washington observers that the president's real purpose was to nullify the votes of the arch-conservative Four Horsemen (all of whom were over 70) by appointing new justices who could be relied upon to give the green light to the New Deal programs.

Quickly, members of Congress, the media, and the public rejected FDR's explanation, despite his lofty status as the most popular and credible president since George Washington. Although the New Deal lawyers titled the proposed statute the Judicial Branch Reorganization Act, it quickly became known as the "Court-packing bill."

In his Fireside Chat radio speech of March 9, 1937, FDR focused on the Court problem. He abandoned the already-discredited pretext of speeding up the Court's calendar, and recounted the damage done by elderly justices to the protection against economic disaster provided by the New Deal legislation, pointing out that the overwhelming majority of the American people "voted a mandate that the Congress and the president begin the task of providing that protection." He accused those unelected justices of "acting not as a judicial body, but as a policy-making body," substituting their own antiquated economic views for those of the representatives elected by the people. Then he explained his reasons for seeking to offset the votes of the "policy-making" justices:

> We have, therefore, reached the point as a nation where we
> must take action to save the Constitution from the Court
> and the Court from itself. We must find a way to take an
> appeal from the Supreme Court to the Constitution itself.
> We want a Supreme Court which will do justice under
> the Constitution and not over it. In our courts we want a
> Government of Laws and not of men.

Despite the obvious desires of Depression-ridden Americans that their popular president be permitted to proceed with the New Deal experiments, the Court-packing bill was slow to gain public support. Many blamed this on FDR's devious initial approach, in which he underestimated the intelligence of the public and its idealistic commitment to truth in government by giving a phony reason for the bill. Others—even some strong supporters of FDR and the New Deal—were concerned that such a radical reordering of the Separation of Powers with Checks and Balances posed an unacceptable threat to the Constitution itself, despite the fact that revered presidents like Jefferson and Lincoln had appointed additional justices authorized by Congress during their administrations. Representative Arthur Lamneck, a Democratic congressman from Ohio who had supported FDR in both his election campaigns, sounded an alarm that raised widespread fears during the era of Hitler, Mussolini, and Stalin:

> In a world given over to one-man governments, the
> President has stood out as the defender of democracy....

Can this be the same man who, controlling the legislative
branch of the government, now seeks to gain control of the
judiciary? Do we want a one-man government, no matter
how benevolent?

This conflict dominated the media during the first half of 1937, demonstrating the strong public concern for preservation of Separation of Powers
with Checks and Balances. We are left to wonder how it might have turned
out if other events had not intervened before Congress moved the Court-
packing bill to a definitive vote.

Elsie Parrish, a former chambermaid at the Cascadian Hotel in Wenatchee,
Washington, claimed she had been paid less than the Washington state min-
imum wage, and sued the hotel owner for $216 in back pay. The Supreme
Court of Washington upheld the validity of the minimum wage law under the
Washington state constitution, and ordered the hotel to make up the under-
payment of Elsie's wages. The hotel owners appealed to the United States
Supreme Court, which agreed to hear the case and scheduled it for argument
on December 16, 1936.

This news was greeted with great joy by opponents of minimum wage
laws, for it gave every indication that the Supreme Court was again using
its discretionary jurisdiction to carry on its policy of invalidating state minimum wage laws, thus leaving the nation's employers and its Elsie Parrishes
free to bargain out the terms of chambermaid employment contracts without
government interference. Only six months earlier, in the *Tipaldo* case, the
Hughes Court had invalidated a New York state minimum wage law that
was virtually identical to the Washington state law, again preserving what the
majority called the constitutional right to freedom of contract—a right ridi-
culed by Interior Secretary Harold Ickes as "the right of an immature child or
a helpless woman to drive a bargain with a great corporation."

Among those who followed the Supreme Court, the betting was nearly
unanimous that the justices would vote in *Parrish* exactly as they had six
months earlier in *Tipaldo*: the Four Horseman and the moderate Republican
Owen Roberts upholding freedom of contract, and the three liberals joined
by Chief Justice Hughes voting to uphold the Washington state minimum
wage law. That 5-to-4 margin would be sufficient to deprive Elsie Parrish
of her $216 back wages, and to force thousands of other menial workers in
Washington state and throughout the country to settle for whatever wages
their bargaining powers could gain for them without any help from state
minimum wage laws. It would also send a signal to the New Dealers that they
had better not even think about trying to enact a federal minimum wage law.

On December 19, 1936, the justices held their private weekly conference
and voted on the cases they had just finished hearing. There Owen Roberts

shocked the other justices by announcing that he was voting in favor of Elsie Parrish, upholding the constitutionality of the Washington state minimum wage law. He was joined by Hughes, Brandeis, and Cardozo, with the Four Horsemen standing by their defense of freedom of contract. The third liberal, Justice Harlan Fiske Stone, was confined to his home by illness, but they all knew he would vote as he had in *Tipaldo,* to uphold the state minimum wage law. When Stone returned to his duties in February, he recorded the fifth affirming vote. Chief Justice Hughes then assigned himself the task of writing the majority opinion, which he read from the bench on March 29, 1937.

The courtroom was packed that day, mostly with Easter-vacation visitors and other sight-seers eager for a glimpse of the splendid new Supreme Court building. Since the Court's decisions are subject to tight security until announced from the bench, the Washington press corps was not expecting anything unusual. But the white-bearded Chief Justice Hughes, whose patrician appearance and manner earned him comparisons to Jove, shocked them as he read the majority decision, delivering it so elegantly that it sounded like a pronouncement from Mount Olympus. When he came to the crux of the decision—the freedom of Elsie Parrish to contract with the hotel owners—he thundered, "What is this freedom?" He then laid to eternal rest that illusory freedom which had been a favorite prop for the Court's nurture of laissez-faire capitalism (including child labor) since the turn of the century:

> The Constitution does not speak of freedom of contract.
> It speaks of liberty and prohibits the deprivation of
> liberty without due process of law.... Liberty under the
> Constitution is thus necessarily subject to the restraints of
> due process, and regulation which is reasonable in relation
> to its subject and is adopted in the interests of the commu-
> nity is due process.

The announcement that Owen Roberts had voted with Hughes and the three liberals to form the five-vote majority set off a legal whodunit chase which continues to this day: What caused Roberts to change the views he had expressed only a few months ago in *Tipalido,* which involved the identical issue—the constitutionality of interfering with freedom of contract by legislating a minimum wage? Before the media and the legal scholars had their say, Roberts's brethren on the right wing of the Court made their feelings plain. In the dissenting opinion, the Four Horsemen proclaimed that a judge's duty to pass upon the validity of a statute "cannot be consummated justly by an automatic acceptance of the views of others which have neither convinced, nor created reasonable doubt in, his mind." They went on to condemn Roberts for his betrayal:

> If upon a question so important he thus surrender his
> deliberate judgment, he stands forsworn. He cannot subor-
> dinate his convictions to that extent and keep faith with his
> oath or retain his judicial and moral independence.

Since they did not refer to Roberts by name, these words could be passed off as an affirmation of the Four Horsemen's own duty to express their dissent. But nobody had ever questioned the right or the duty to dissent, and to Roberts and the informed spectators it was apparent that this was an attempt to impugn his integrity for yielding to the pressures of the electoral mandate and the pending Court-packing bill. Especially galling was the use of the ancient legal term "forsworn," meaning the making of a knowingly false statement, as disgraceful as an act of perjury.

The headline in the next morning's *New York Times* blared, "MINIMUM WAGE LAW CONSTITUTIONAL; SUPREME COURT SWITCH DUE TO ROBERTS." In the style of contemporary Raymond Chandler mystery novels, Roberts's startling vote in the *Parrish* case became known as "The Big Switch." While FDR and his advisors were not convinced that Roberts had switched permanently, the *Parrish* decision was enough to tilt public opinion sharply against the Court-packing bill, now seen as a drastic and dangerous change that was probably unnecessary due to the newly-formed 5-to-4 majority in favor of upholding economic regulatory legislation. This position was reinforced when on April 12, just two weeks after *Parrish*, Roberts again joined Hughes and the three liberals in upholding the constitutionality of a key New Deal statute, the National Labor Relations Act, known popularly as the Wagner Act, which greatly enhanced the bargaining power of labor unions.

The effect of upholding the Wagner Act was to declare that Congress's Constitutional power to regulate interstate commerce was no longer limited to those businesses directly and solely engaged in interstate commerce. Under that narrow construction, the Four Horsemen had characterized manufacturing, mining, and farming as "local" and therefore not sufficiently related to interstate commerce, regardless of where the products were shipped or how large the enterprises were. Now the fourth and fifth votes of Hughes and Roberts extended the Congressional power to activities which were merely part of the "stream of commerce," or merely affected interstate commerce, thereby applying the Wagner Act—and potentially other New Deal statutes—to virtually the entire spectrum of business activity. Thus the two main weapons of the Four Horsemen—freedom of contract and narrow construction of interstate commerce—had been snatched from their hands by the votes of the other five justices. That convinced Court-watchers that the Roberts switch was permanent, and they began calling this the Judicial Revolution of 1937.

A few weeks after the Wagner Act was upheld, the new Hughes Court majority rejected challenges to the constitutionality of the jewel in the New Deal's crown, the Social Security Act of 1935. And on May 18, 1937, Justice Van Devanter announced his retirement, signaling that the Four Horsemen were throwing in the towel. Nevertheless FDR persisted in pushing for passage of the Court-packing bill. Late in March, just before the Big Switch in the *Parrish* case, *Time* magazine had reported that "the staunchest foes of the President's Plan were privately conceding that, if he chose to whip it through, the necessary votes were already in his pocket." But the tide-turning *Parrish* decision—along with Roberts's continuing support of the New Deal and Van Devanter's retirement—caused the Senate Judiciary Committee to announce on May 18 that they had voted against supporting the Court-packing bill. That sent FDR back to the drawing board, and he came up with a watered-down bill authorizing the president to appoint one new justice per calendar year for each sitting justice over 75 who chose not to retire.

Roosevelt reasoned that it was the frightening spectacle of appointing six new justices at once which led to public revulsion against the Court-packing bill. He hoped that making the change more gradual and raising the age to 75 would mitigate some of the backlash. But these hopes were dashed on June 14 when the Senate Judiciary Committee published its written report rejecting the original six-justice bill. This document, remarkable in itself as the first Congressional rebuff of any legislation sponsored by the Roosevelt White House, is all the more significant because seven of the ten Senators who signed it were Democrats. It began by condemning the bill for applying force to the judiciary, which threatened to undermine the independence of the courts and remove the protection which the Constitution affords to minorities and the rights of individuals. It warned that the bill would endanger the Constitution's Separation of Powers with Checks and Balances because it "tends to expand political control over the judicial department by adding to the powers of the legislative and executive departments respecting the judiciary." The report said of the Constitution:

> For the protection of the people,…for maintaining the
> checks and balances of our dual system, the three branches
> of the government were so constituted that the indepen-
> dent expression of honest differences of opinion could
> never be restrained in the people's servants and no one
> branch could overawe or subjugate the others. That is the
> American system. It is immeasurably more important,
> immeasurably more sacred to the people of America,
> indeed, to the people of all the world than the immediate
> adoption of any legislation, however beneficial.

The report demonstrated how the bill would reduce the Supreme Court to a political football: "If we may force the hand of the Court to secure our interpretation of the Constitution, then some succeeding Congress may repeat the process to secure another and a different interpretation and one which may not sound so pleasant in our ears as that for which we now contend." It declared that if Congress is allowed to reverse the Court's rulings by enlarging the Court, "our constitutional system is overthrown!"

The report's final words delivered a ringing rebuke to President Roosevelt:

> Its ultimate operation would be to make this government
> one of men rather than one of law.... It is a measure which
> should be so emphatically rejected that its parallel will
> never again be presented to the free representatives of the
> free people of America.

When Raymond Clapper, veteran political columnist for the *Washington Post*, read this Senate report, he noted in his diary, "Bitter document, extremely rough, reads almost like a bill of impeachment." This was not a discredited or lame duck president, but the strongest leader in the Democratic party's history, in the first year of a second term to which he had been elected in an unprecedented landslide that also was responsible for many of the Democratic senators winning the most smashing victories of their careers. FDR was the consummate politician, skilled at doling out patronage to his friends and denying it to his critics. And the Court-packing bill was vigorously supported by the powerful majority leader, Senator Joe Robinson of Arkansas, to whom FDR (in Washington's worst-kept secret) had promised the appointment to the first vacant seat on the Court.

Given the intensity of public and Congressional opposition, it was no surprise that when the full Senate considered the bill (the watered-down version, at that) on July 22, the vote was 70 for the Supreme Court and 20 for Roosevelt, in a body that contained only 17 Republicans. It was the worst political defeat of FDR's extraordinarily successful career.

Thus ended the constitutional crisis and judicial revolution which historian William E. Leuchtenburg described in his 1995 book, *The Supreme Court Reborn: The Constitutional Revolution in the Age of Roosevelt* as "the most significant chapter in the two centuries of existence of the U.S. Supreme Court." Never again did the Supreme Court strike down a New Deal statute. Indeed, since 1937 the Supreme Court has not invalidated any federal or state economic regulatory legislation, leading scholars to conclude that the Court has practically abandoned judicial review in that field.

Owen Roberts's gallop away from the Four Horsemen was quickly dubbed "the switch in time that saved nine," confirming the widespread fear in 1937 that passage of the Court-packing legislation might have dislodged the Supreme Court permanently from its role in the Government of Laws. Why did Roberts switch?

The definitive answer is lost in the mists of history, largely because of the secrecy which necessarily attends the deliberations of Supreme Court justices. The most logical scenario is that he changed his position because of the pressure of the electoral landslide and the impending brawl over the Court-packing bill, which to the level-headed, patriotic Roberts must have loomed as a greater threat to the nation's future than the New Deal experiments.

After Roberts's retirement from the bench in 1945, Felix Frankfurter put the question directly to him, and he responded in a two-page memo-randum published after his death in 1955. There Roberts tried to explain that he had not really switched from his earlier legal position. He claimed that the arguments presented in the 1936 *Tipaldo* case did not call into question the freedom of contract principle, whereas those in the 1937 *Parrish* case did raise that issue. But most legal scholars consider that explanation to be dis-ingenuous since Supreme Court justices are not limited to choosing between arguments presented by the parties, and Roberts could easily have voted to uphold the New York minimum wage statute in *Tipaldo* (as did four other justices) if he had been so inclined. Roberts's memorandum points out that he had voted in favor of Elsie Parrish on December 19, 1936, several weeks before the Court-packing bill was publicly announced, and he claims that no action taken by the president "had any causal relation" to his vote in the *Parrish* case. Although Frankfurter declared himself convinced by this mem-orandum that Roberts had not switched his legal position, most historians and scholars think otherwise. They point out that it was a matter of common knowledge that FDR, emboldened by the November 1936 electoral mandate, was planning to do whatever was required to prevent any further judicial nullification of New Deal legislation.

The Four Horsemen's dissenting opinion in *Parrish* reveals their con-viction that Roberts had indeed switched his legal position. If Roberts was merely expressing a previously-held view in sympathy with state minimum wage laws enacted decades before the New Deal, that would not indicate he was about to uphold any and all New Deal legislation. I do not believe that the venerable equestrians would have read Roberts off publicly as "forsworn" if they had not been certain he was lost to them forever. The writing of the *Parrish* dissenting opinion was assigned to Justice Sutherland, the most schol-arly and moderate of the Horsemen. The harsh language that Sutherland employed makes it clear that all four believed Roberts had sold out to New Deal political pressure and would never return to the old corral.

It appears that the key role in defusing this constitutional crisis was played behind the scenes by the Jovian chief justice. Like John Marshall,

Charles Evans Hughes was not just a highly-skilled judge but also an experienced high-level statesman and politician. He was elected governor of New York in 1906, defeating William Randolph Hearst. He was first appointed to the Supreme Court in 1910, where he served as an associate justice until 1916, when he resigned to accept the Republican nomination for president. He lost a close race to the incumbent Woodrow Wilson by the margin of a few thousand California votes. He then served with great distinction as secretary of state under presidents Harding and Coolidge (1921-1925) and judge of the World Court (1928-1930) before President Hoover appointed him chief justice in 1930. Although he was ideologically unsympathetic to the New Deal, by 1936 he perceived that the Court's invalidation of emergency anti-Depression legislation enacted by a nearly unanimous Congress at the behest of an enormously popular president was propelling the justices onto a collision course with the other branches which could only end in disaster for the Court, the Constitution, and the nation.

Hughes must have realized that the *Tipaldo* decision of June 1936 was the Four Horsemen's last hurrah. Joseph Tipaldo was palpably undeserving of assistance from any court, much less the highest in the land. He was manager of the Spotlight Laundry, a Brooklyn sweatshop that employed nine women in an abandoned bottling plant at the edge of nowhere. He was paying the laundry workers $10 for a 47-hour week, despite the state law minimum of $14.88. When state inspectors ordered him to pay the difference, he forced the women to return the money to him or lose their jobs. Thereafter he issued weekly checks for the required $14.88 but made the women hand the checks back to him, and continued to pay them $10 in cash. One or more of those laundry workers had the spunk to report Tipaldo's misconduct. He was arrested and charged with forgery and conspiracy as well as violation of the minimum wage law.

Tipaldo's lawyer, assisted by lawyers for hotel and restaurant owners whose clients were eager to maintain starvation wages and seven-day work weeks for their employees, sprung him from jail and fought his case to New York's highest court, the Court of Appeals. In 1936 that court invalidated the state minimum wage law and dismissed the charges against Tipaldo, on the authority of *Adkins v. Children's Hospital*, the 1923 U.S. Supreme Court decision holding a similar statute unconstitutional because it interfered with freedom of contract. The state's lawyers then applied to the U.S. Supreme Court for a writ of certiorari which would bring the case there for final review. At the urging of Chief Justice Hughes, the writ of certiorari was granted and the Supreme Court heard the case. By a 5-to-4 margin it found the New York law unconstitutional. Hughes had tried his best to convince the others that depriving women and children of this minimal protection would be too much for the Depression-scarred public to swallow. But the majority decision by Justice Butler, which rebuked New

York for enacting such a law in the face of the well-established freedom of contract constitutional principle, was joined in by the other three Horsemen and Justice Roberts. Hughes voted with the three liberals in dissent. With that decision on June 1, 1936, the Supreme Court closed shop for the summer. But their vacation travels did not muffle the public uproar that Hughes had feared.

Most of the nation's newspapers, their editorial opinions then unashamedly controlled by their owners, were hostile to FDR, the New Deal, and government regulation of business. But the judgment freeing Joseph Tipaldo to resume exploitation of the Brooklyn laundresses was so obviously unjust that 80 percent of the newspapers denounced it. So did leading Republicans, including former president Herbert Hoover, it being politically more palatable for them to support a state statute than a New Deal measure. New York Republican Congressman Hamilton Fish, FDR's lifelong arch-enemy, called *Tipaldo* "a new Dred Scott decision condemning millions of Americans to economic slavery." The Republican campaign platform pledged to support state minimum-wage laws for women and children, even if this required a constitutional amendment. (At that time social reformers did not dare to go beyond advocating protection for women and children, in the face of the *Adkins* freedom-of-contract barrier.)

When Hughes found his Court confronted by the *Tipaldo*/Court-packing crisis, he was sitting in a position where he could do more to avert it than anyone else. He focused all his judicial prestige and powers of statecraft on Owen Roberts, the only one whose vote he could possibly change. It is not known whether Hughes made any special effort to convince Roberts to go along with him in *Tipaldo*, but in the wake of that disastrous decision, he certainly pulled out all the stops to drag Roberts across the line in *Parrish*. Behind the scenes he strove to convince Roberts that regardless of ideology, the future of the Court and perhaps of American democracy was on the line. That he finally succeeded is evidenced by the bitter language of the Four Horsemen's dissenting opinion in *Parrish*, in which they berated Roberts (and Hughes by implication) for surrendering "his deliberate judgment" by "an automatic acceptance of the views of others"—a charge that Roberts had dishonorably forfeited his judicial independence under the brow-beating of the chief justice.

In uttering this last gasp of reactionary fury, the Four Horsemen shut their eyes to the patriotism demonstrated by Owen Roberts during his long career. He was an aristocratic Philadelphia Main-Liner whose law practice was largely devoted to serving railroads and other big-business opponents of government regulation, but at a time of grave governmental crisis he had devoted years to vigorous prosecution of the crooked Republican officials responsible for the Teapot Dome oil scandal. Later he was entrusted with the official investigation of the Pearl Harbor disaster, in which he placed the blame on the military but not the Roosevelt administration.

The perfectionist Hughes did not rest on his successful recruitment of Roberts. Interior Secretary Harold Ickes, one of the most perceptive insiders of the era, recorded in his diary that his close friend and reliable informant, Tommy the Cork Corcoran, had told him that Chief Justice Hughes had engineered the resignation of Van Devanter at the crucial moment in May 1937 when it could (and probably did) tip the scales against the Court-packing bill, and that "Hughes has played a bad hand perfectly." Probably Hughes was able to convince Van Devanter that with Roberts now firmly committed to support of the New Deal legislation, he could end his distinguished career on a positive and patriotic note by striking a fatal blow against the infamous Court-packing bill—a much more harmonious and significant note than reciting "Amen" to the Horsemen's now fruitless dissents. The fact that Van Devanter sat as a trial judge in the Manhattan Federal Court from 1937 until his death in 1941 indicates that he had not intended to retire until Hughes persuaded him to step down in order to help thwart the Court-packing bill.

After retiring from government service, the blunt-speaking Harold Ickes published more details about Hughes's role in saving the Court:

> The whole world knows that, while at first it appeared that
> the president would be strong enough to carry his reform
> through Congress, he was outmaneuvered in the end,
> largely by Chief Justice Charles Evans Hughes, who fought
> determinedly, with all his great skill, to avoid the stigma
> upon the Court that the adoption of the president's plan
> would have meant.

Yet Hughes himself took great pains to deny any role in the affair, lest it appear that his Court forfeited its judicial independence by deciding cases under political pressure rather than under constitutional law. Hughes did not publish his memoirs but he left what he called Autobiographical Notes which were published after his death. There he insists that Roberts would have voted the same way "if the president's bill had never been proposed" and that "the Court acted with complete independence." Hughes's biographer, Merlo Pusey, accepts Hughes's denials at face value, and writes of the Van Devanter retirement, "The chief justice had nothing whatever to do with it." Yet Pusey also recounts an interview with Senator Burton Wheeler, the leader of the Democratic revolt against the Court-packing bill, in which Wheeler quotes Hughes as telling him that "if this bill should pass, it would destroy the Court as an institution." It is difficult to imagine that Chief Justice Hughes—who was described by Frankfurter as "radiating authority"—would stand by and let the Court be destroyed on his watch, without using all of his great prestige and statecraft skills to prevent that disaster.

To twenty-first-century eyes, the members of this divided Court seem a bit out of character. The five who helped to save the Court—Hughes, Brandeis, Stone, Cardozo, and Roberts—were sons of privilege, products of Ivy League law schools, and successful practitioners in eastern financial centers, serving many large corporate clients. The 75-year-old Hughes, in his starched wing collar and white-bearded elegance, looked more the part of the laissez-faire champion than any of the Four Horsemen. Van Devanter received a law degree from the University of Cincinnati and practiced mainly in the Wyoming Territory before becoming a judge. Sutherland, like many lawyers of his day, was admitted to the bar without a degree, and established a law practice in the Utah Territory before serving in Congress and earning a Supreme Court nomination by President Harding. Butler, who grew up on a subsistence farm in Minnesota, was also admitted to the bar after private study, and practiced in Minnesota before being nominated by President Harding. McReynolds, the son of a wealthy Tennessee plantation owner, received a law degree from the University of Virginia and practiced in Tennessee before entering politics. He served briefly as Woodrow Wilson's attorney general, but his notorious temper caused so much disruption of the cabinet that Wilson hurriedly nominated him to the first Supreme Court vacancy.

While the Four Horsemen also represented railroads and large business corporations in their private practices, their roots in rural and frontier societies led them to value "rugged individualism" above government welfare measures. This helps to explain their life-long dedication to restraining the growth of government, a philosophy that was shared by millions of Americans in an age when the principal threats to the nation's future were seen as the dictatorships which grew out of the all-powerful central governments of the Soviet Union, Germany, and Italy—each of them sporting a version of the "socialist" label. The Horsemen saw themselves as the guardians of "freedom" against what they perceived as the socialism inherent in governmental responsibility for the workings of the economy and welfare of the people.

The Horsemen's earlier life experiences taught them that depressions eventually cured themselves without government intervention. They believed that people had to play the hands that a cruel world dealt to them, with the most worthy surviving and building a stronger society. Their anti-New Deal postures were reinforced by the perception that the radical schemes of the egg-headed Ivy League professors and lawyers were not really working. The economy showed moderate improvement during FDR's first term, but unemployment was still very high, and the nation slipped into a major recession in 1937-1938 despite the Judicial Revolution which cleared the way for the New Deal agencies to function. It was not until the military buildup preceding World War II that the economy returned to its pre-1929 strength. Thus cynics gave major credit for the economic recovery to Adolf Hitler rather than to FDR.

In a 1938 book, prominent Washington journalists Joseph Alsop and Turner Catledge spotlighted two great ironies of the Big Switch: "the Court's self-salvation by self-reversal" and "the Court's destruction of the President by giving him what he wanted." In 1938 it looked as though the debacle had destroyed FDR, for he expended nearly all of his vast reservoir of political capital in the unsuccessful attempt to pack the Court. It destroyed the unity of the Democratic party and led to an anti-New Deal coalition of Republicans and conservative Democrats (mostly Southerners who chaired many of the key Congressional committees). FDR was never again able to write his own ticket on economic legislation. Henry Wallace, then a cabinet member and later FDR's vice-president, wrote that "the whole New Deal really went up in smoke as a result of the Supreme Court fight." FDR made matters worse in 1938 by unsuccessfully attempting to purge leaders of his party who had opposed him on the Court bill. It was only the outbreak of World War II on September 1, 1939, that saved FDR's presidency and propelled him to immortality in his third and fourth terms.

Obviously the politically erudite Roosevelt greatly underestimated the importance of the Supreme Court to the American people. The Big Shift was a national civics lesson: not even a super-popular president could get away with challenging the integrity of America's unique symbol of national unity. Millions of Americans who had voted for FDR—and could not name the Supreme Court justices—rebelled at the thought of tampering with this revered institution. Town meetings were held across the country to debate and ultimately to denounce the Court-packing bill. Congress was flooded with more than 10 million letters about the bill, most of them opposed to it.

The bottom line is that Alsop and Catledge were correct in their 1938 assessment that the Big Switch was the Court's salvation, and William Leuchtenburg was on the mark in titling his 1995 book *The Supreme Court Reborn*. The Supreme Court was reborn as the indispensable Third Branch of the Government of Laws—a status it had not fully achieved during its first incarnation. After the Judicial Revolution of 1937, the Supreme Court became the sacred cow whose basic function in the Separation of Powers with Checks and Balances no politician would again dare to challenge. As Leuchtenburg puts it:

> In attempting to alter the Court, Roosevelt had attacked
> one of the symbols which many believed the nation needed
> for its sense of unity as a body politic. The Court fight

evoked a strong feeling of nostalgia for the days of the Founding Fathers, when, it seemed, life was simpler and principles fixed.

As in John Marshall's day, the Supreme Court was saved from becoming a political casualty by another American lawyer-statesman, another great judge/politician who sat as the chief justice and was to be the godfather of the Court's rebirth. Charles Evans Hughes had Marshall's gift of insight which told him that although the Court, as one of the instruments of governance, performs what is ultimately a political function, it must be executed in such a way that the people see it as a *judicial* function, a unique role that is essential to the Separation of Powers with Checks and Balances which the Founding Lawyers left as their legacy to the nation.

FDR biographer Jean Edward Smith sums it up neatly:

> The victory in the Court fight of 1937 belonged not to Roosevelt but to Hughes, to the constitutional separation of powers, an independent judiciary, and the law.

Chapter Six

Preserving the Government of Laws
(1937-1974)

After suffering through his entire first term without the opportunity to appoint a Supreme Court justice, President Franklin D. Roosevelt suddenly reaped a bonanza, making eight appointments to fill vacancies caused by death or retirement during the final eight years of his tenure. When the next major constitutional crisis came before the Court in 1952, the president was FDR's successor, Harry Truman, and all nine justices had been appointed by Democratic presidents. The house-cleaning aimed at exterminating the Four Horsemen's ideology was so thorough that by 1952 the "conservative" bloc was led by the erstwhile left-winger, Felix Frankfurter, appointed to the Court by FDR in 1938.

In 1952, Harry Truman was in the last of his eight years in the White House, struggling to keep the unpopular Korean conflict from deteriorating into a fiasco. The nation's steel manufacturers were embroiled in negotiations for a new labor agreement, but were unable to reach an accord with the union officials, who gave notice that on April 9 the steelworkers would go out on strike. On April 8, President Truman, concerned that the strike might lead to steel shortages which would impair the war effort, ordered his secretary of commerce to take possession of the steel mills and keep them running under government control. Lawyers for the steel manufacturers sought an injunction against the government seizure, claiming that the president had exceeded his constitutional powers. Because it involved a national emergency, the case was speeded through the lower federal courts and the Supreme Court scheduled it for argument on May 12, 1952, barely a month after the seizure.

We have unusual access to the inside story of the Supreme Court's handling of the case because William Rehnquist, later to serve on the Court for 33 years, was then a law clerk to Justice Robert Jackson, and wrote about this experience in his book, *The Supreme Court*. Rehnquist recounts the strong Democratic Party connections of many of the justices, led by Chief Justice Fred Vinson, who had served in Congress for 14 years and was an ardent New Deal supporter. During World War II President Roosevelt recruited Vinson to serve as head of several administrative agencies. In 1945 President Truman named him treasury secretary, and in the next year appointed him chief justice, insisting that he retain his seat at the weekly White House poker game. Two other Truman appointees, Tom Clark and Sherman Minton, were long-time government colleagues and close friends of the president. Based on these connections, Rehnquist and his fellow law clerks were betting that the Court would uphold the constitutional power of the president to seize the steel mills in this emergency situation.

The case was argued for the steel companies by John W. Davis, the senior eminence of American appellate lawyers who was making his 128th appearance in the Supreme Court. Rehnquist found Davis's argument masterful, noting that the justices held him in such awe that they asked him only one question. By a vote of 6 to 3, the Court decided that neither the Constitution nor any Act of Congress gave the president the power to seize the steel mills in this situation. The Court granted an injunction against the president's seizure order and thereby returned the mills to their owners.

Despite the admiration which many of the justices felt for Harry Truman, he had three strikes against him in this argument. First, he had never called upon Congress to declare war against North Korea, choosing instead to conduct the conflict as a "police action." (Had there been a declaration of war, the president's constitutional war powers might well have provided the authority for such an emergency seizure.) Second, Truman had seized the mills by issuing an executive order without seeking the approval of Congress, which had the constitutional law-making power required in this situation. Third, Truman and the stalemated Korean police action were both at low levels of public approval at that time. Rehnquist observes that in 1952 "the tide of public opinion suddenly began to run against the government, for a number of reasons" and that "this tide of public opinion had a considerable influence on the Court." He states his view that in general the justices are not able to isolate themselves from public opinion, nor should they try. He explains:

> No honorable judge would ever cast his vote in a particular
> case simply because he thought the majority of the public
> wanted him to vote in that way, but that is quite a different
> thing from saying that no judge is ever influenced by the

great tides of public opinion that run in a country such as
ours. Judges are influenced by them, and I think that such
influence played an appreciable part in causing the Steel
Seizure Case to be decided the way it was.

The Supreme Court announced its decision at noon on June 2, 1952. That
afternoon, President Truman issued a written order to Secretary of Commerce
Charles Sawyer directing him to return custody of the mills to the owners.
Sawyer complied immediately. Thus the authority of the Supreme Court to
control the conduct of the world's most powerful official was not questioned
for a moment. The Court had come a long way since *Dred Scott* and its aftermath, aided immeasurably by the Court-packing dispute which brought on the
Judicial Revolution of 1937. But a more daunting challenge to the Government
of Laws was just over the horizon.

Looking Jim Crow in the Eye

When the Supreme Court abandoned the policing of economic regulatory
legislation in the late 1930s, it began to focus more on civil rights. This was
partly due to the Hughes Court's broadened interpretation of "interstate commerce" which included virtually all of American business, opening the way for
effective nationwide judicial intervention. It was also due to an unprecedented
legal campaign waged by a unique organization, the National Association for
the Advancement of Colored People (NAACP), which succeeded, against heavy
odds, in bringing before the Court the cases that launched the Civil Rights
Revolution.

As the nation moved into the second half of the twentieth century, Jim
Crow was still firmly in control of black life in the South. There was a modicum
of progress toward equality, but the promise of the Civil War Constitutional
amendments was a long way from being realized. Racial segregation of public
facilities (schools, buses, restaurants, theatres, hotels) remained the rule in the
South, and voting was a dangerous if not impossible undertaking for many
black people.

The NAACP was founded in New York in 1909 by a group of black intellectuals and white progressives, in response to a series of Illinois race riots. At
first its main efforts were devoted to life-saving campaigns against lynching
and kangaroo-court prosecutions. In the liberalizing atmosphere of the New
Deal era, black leaders began to dream of integration. In 1941, Walter White,
executive secretary of the NAACP, helped to persuade President Roosevelt to
issue an executive order prohibiting racial discrimination in filling defense
industry jobs. White also influenced President Truman to issue a 1948 order

desegregating the armed forces. Encouraged by this progress, White was convinced that the time was ripe to launch an all-out offensive against Jim Crow, and that the surest route to victory was through the courts. For this purpose he brought on board Charles Houston, dean of the Howard University Law School, who in turn recruited the services of other leading black lawyers. One of Houston's prize pupils at Howard, Thurgood Marshall, had joined the NAACP legal staff in 1935, and three years later he became general counsel of the Legal Defense Fund (LDF), a separate unit of the NAACP created to carry on the court campaign for desegregation.

With a shoestring budget and the seemingly impossible assignment of removing racial discrimination from American life, Marshall and his LDF colleagues took aim at some of Jim Crow's favorite playthings: restrictive housing covenants; voting restrictions; segregated transportation. During his quarter-century with the NAACP, Marshall made considerable legal progress against all of those injustices. But the jewel in the crown of the Legal Defense Fund was its campaign against segregation in the elementary and high schools, where American children were carefully taught that the nation must be racially divided.

At a national strategy conference in September 1950, Marshall decided that the LDF should launch the school desegregation campaign with the filing of class actions in four states (Kansas, South Carolina, Delaware, and Virginia) where black children were required to attend separate schools which were allegedly equal to those serving white children. This practice was protected by the 1896 Supreme Court decision in *Plessy v. Ferguson*, which held that a Louisiana statute providing "separate but equal" railway carriages for whites and blacks did not violate the Fourteenth Amendment's requirement that every state afford all persons "equal protection of the laws." The *Plessy* separate-but-equal standard had grown beyond railway cars to govern schools and many other public facilities. The NAACP had brought numerous lawsuits challenging the equality of specific black schools, with mixed results. Now Marshall decided it was time for a frontal assault on the *Plessy* standard itself, asking the courts to rule that segregated schools were inherently unequal by their very nature and could not possibly be made equal even if the buildings, teachers, and budgets were comparable.

In the trial courts, Marshall and his LDF colleagues called as expert witnesses some 30 social scientists, psychologists, and historians, to support the claim that school segregation caused black children to develop a false feeling of inferiority that lasted through their lifetimes. In one experiment, psychologists interviewed black schoolchildren one by one, presenting them with two baby dolls, identical except that one was black and the other white. The children were asked, "Which doll is nice, and which one is ugly; which is the doll you want to be like?" Overwhelmingly the children chose the black doll as ugly and the white doll as the one they wanted to be like. The law-yers defending the school boards generally did not call expert witnesses to rebut this testimony. Instead they relied on the writings of W.E.B. Du Bois, a leading black intellectual who had broken with the NAACP and maintained that racial separation was beneficial to blacks, far more so than integration with the white culture.

As expected, the four desegregation lawsuits were unsuccessful in the lower courts, but in 1952 the Supreme Court granted reviews in all four cases, grouping them under the title of the suit filed in Kansas, *Brown v. Board of Education of Topeka.* When *Brown* came on for argument in December of 1952 before the Court headed by Fred Vinson, the justices were divided and uncertain of how to handle this hot potato. Although the separate-but-equal standard was difficult to justify morally, it had been the law of the land since 1896, fortified by six post-*Plessy* school segregation decisions in which the Supreme Court had refused to overrule it. Congressional intent, usually an important factor in construing a constitutional or statutory provision, was not well documented. The LDF lawyers could not demonstrate that Congress had intended to prohibit school segregation when it proposed the Fourteenth Amendment in June 1866, because Congress (which had legislative responsi-bility for the District of Columbia and its school system) had established seg-regated schools for the District in 1865 and continued to approve and fund them year after year, even as *Brown* was being argued in 1952.

Chief Justice Vinson, a Kentuckian, did not see how the Court could now force the Southern states to abandon a vast educational system oper-ated with the continuing approval of the Court for more than half a cen-tury. Justice Tom Clark, a Texan, felt the same way. Justice Stanley Reed, also from Kentucky, had fought valiantly for liberal New Deal economic mea-sures as solicitor general (1935-1938) but was a committed segregationist who refused to attend Supreme Court Christmas parties if black workers were invited. At the other end of the spectrum, four of the Supreme Court justices—Hugo Black of Alabama, William Douglas of Washington state, Harold Burton of Ohio, and Sherman Minton of Indiana—were ready to reverse *Plessy* and consign school segregation to the scrap heap of history. That left the decision in the hands of two contentious intellectuals: Felix Frankfurter of Massachusetts and Robert Jackson of New York.

Jackson believed that segregation was shameful and should be ended immediately—but by Congress rather than the Court. He saw it as a purely political question and did not believe the Court could responsibly declare "separate-but-equal" unconstitutional. Frankfurter, always concerned that lack of judicial restraint would weaken the Court's authority, had similar misgivings, although he was more actively supportive of black equality than was Jackson. Thus it appeared that if the decision came to a vote in the customary way (on the Saturday after the argument) the Court would have divided 5-to-4 in favor of affirming the lower court decisions which upheld *Plessy*-style segregation. John W. Davis, who argued the case for the school boards, predicted to his colleagues that this would be the Court's alignment.

For the next five months, the Court struggled through six conferences without producing either a decision or a modus operandi for reaching a decision. Finally Frankfurter suggested that the cases be reargued. Since Vinson was neither an astute enough jurist nor a strong enough leader to fashion a viable consensus, he eagerly embraced Frankfurter's proposal. This required a court order specifying the points which were not covered adequately during the first argument. Frankfurter, who was actually stalling for time in the hope of finding a solution, drafted five questions which the lawyers for each side would be required to address during the second argument. The Court issued an order on June 8, 1953, incorporating Frankfurter's questions, and scheduled the reargument for December 8, exactly a year after the original argument. Little did Frankfurter dream that in the intervening months, the 63-year-old Fred Vinson would die of a heart attack on September 8, and President Eisenhower would appoint Earl Warren as the new chief justice.

On paper, the 62-year-old Warren's experience gave no hint that he would be capable of solving the legal conundrum of the school segregation cases. He spent 18 years as a prosecutor before his election as California's attorney general in 1938. He was elected governor in 1942, and was reelected in 1946. A popular and efficient governor, he was chosen by the 1948 Republican presidential candidate, Tom Dewey, as his running mate. When the Republicans lost the election to Harry Truman, Warren returned to his governor's job, and was reelected to a rare (for California) third term in 1950. Richard Kluger describes Warren in *Simple Justice*, his book about the *Brown* case:

> There was, to be sure, an admirably wholesome sort of
> Smokey-the-Bear robustness behind that broad smile of his,
> but one sensed in him a trustworthiness and a purposeful
> bustle more in keeping with a lifelong Eagle Scout than a
> dynamic statesman. [Those who underestimated Warren]
> failed to note how thoroughly the man had been steeped
> in the pressure cooker of American power politics and
> how skillfully he had managed not merely to survive but to
> emerge from it as a master pragmatist whose ideals, strange
> to say, had been tempered, not shattered, by the ordeal.

He was an attractive and successful politician, but since he had never served as a judge or a law professor or held national office, it did not appear that he had the legal gravitas to influence the likes of Frankfurter and Jackson.

Nor was it thought likely that the Republican Warren, now presiding over eight justices who had been appointed by Democratic presidents, would be able to achieve the consensus that had eluded his Democratic predecessor.

When Warren took his seat at the start of the October 1953 term, he had just a few weeks to get up to speed for the December 8th *Brown* reargument. In the interim he began to build solid professional and personal relationships with all his fellow justices, impressing them with his willingness to listen and his dedication to producing decisions that would be respected by the public as well as the law professors.

The reargument of *Brown*, again pitting Thurgood Marshall against John W. Davis, did not produce any thunderbolts that moved the justices one way or the other. But it gave Warren the opportunity to bring his unique talents to bear on the problem, and he rose to the historic occasion. In his history of the Warren Court, Jim Newton describes how the chief justice took charge at the Saturday conference following the reargument:

> There was, Warren told his brethren, no way to duck the question any longer. After more than a year of argument and contemplation, after the death of one chief justice and the arrival of another, the Court was "now down to the point of deciding the issues." And for Warren, the matter that had so vexed the Court was in fact simple. There was, he said, only one way that he could imagine for upholding segregation. *Plessy* could only stand upon the "basic premise that the Negro race is inferior."

This simple but jolting analysis cut through the intellectual posturing and confronted the other justices with the heart of the matter: Regardless of how difficult it might be for you as judges to hold that separate-but-equal segregation is unconstitutional, if you do not stand up to that challenge, there is no way you can escape branding yourselves and the Court as *white supremacists*.

Warren did not speak as though he were handing down a tablet from Mount Sinai. He went out of his way to commiserate with the justices about their valiant struggle to carry out the duty to apply legal precedents judiciously. It was easier for him as a newcomer to take a fresh look at the problem in the light of a principle more compelling than legal precedent, which he hoped they would all consider. But his words made it clear that he would supply the fifth vote needed to end segregation, and now the other justices knew it was a different ballgame. *Plessy* was on the way out, and the only remaining question was how the Court would handle this long-delayed confrontation.

Stanley Reed, who spoke after Warren, was the only justice who contested Warren's white supremacy analysis. He insisted that segregation was not based on inferiority but on racial differences and the desirability of avoiding the mixing of races. None of the other justices supported this view. When Tom Clark's turn came, he reluctantly agreed that he would probably join the new majority, provided the order was carefully drafted to permit gradual implementation tailored to local conditions in each school district. Frankfurter and Jackson remained on the fence, while the other four justices made it clear they would vote with Warren to overrule *Plessy.* Warren could have put it to a vote and come away with a 5-to-4 majority, perhaps even a 6-to-3 vote. But even before Clark spoke, Warren was aware of the monumental problems facing those who would have to enforce desegregation, and he was determined to achieve a unanimous decision. If there were any dissenting opinions, they would supply devastating ammunition to segregationists who were already preparing to sabotage any movement toward integration.

Therefore Warren asked, and the other justices agreed, that the decision be suspended pending further discussion, without the customary recording of tentative votes. That gave him the opportunity to speak one-on-one with Frankfurter, Jackson, Clark, and Reed, which he did for weeks on end in private luncheons, meetings at homes and in chambers, and walks around the block. Meanwhile at the weekly conferences, Warren turned the discussion to the form of the implementation order, so that all the justices were now focused on how—not whether—to end segregation. In March 1954, three months after the reargument, Warren decided to draft the opinion himself and use it as the lever to achieve a unanimous vote.

It took Warren more than a month to complete the draft, which he distributed informally to each of the justices on May 8. He had taken pains to make the opinion short and simple, so that newspapers could reprint it in full and the public could readily absorb it. He tried to model it on Lincoln's Gettysburg address, and while he did not rise to those poetic heights, the result he achieved was of greater historical significance, for the draft opinion swept away the remaining barriers to a unanimous decision. It satisfied the rigorous demands of Frankfurter and Jackson for judicial restraint, Jackson calling it "a master work." And by putting off the implementation order to a later argument in which the attorneys general of the affected states could participate, it mollified Reed and Clark sufficiently for them to put aside their emotions and do what was best for the country.

Earl Warren read the *Brown* opinion to a packed courtroom on May 17, 1954. He began by noting the Legal Defense Fund's contention that because segregated public schools are by their very nature unequal, they automatically deny the equal protection of the laws to black children. He pointed out that the Congressional intent, usually discernable from debates and committee reports, was inconclusive, because in 1868, when the Fourteenth Amendment was enacted, "education of Negroes was almost nonexistent." These four cases required the Court to consider for the first time "the effect of segregation itself on public education," and to look at it not as it was in 1896 when *Plessy* was decided, but as it exists today, "in the light of its full development and its present place in American life throughout the Nation." After pointing out that education is now "perhaps the most important function of state and local governments," he delivered the punch line:

> We come then to the question presented: Does segregation
> of children in public schools solely on the basis of race,
> even though the physical facilities and other "tangible"
> factors may be equal, deprive the children of the minority
> group of equal educational opportunities? We *unanimously*
> believe that it does.

As he read the opinion aloud, Warren inserted the word "unanimously," which did not appear in the formal printed version but would become apparent from the absence of dissenting opinions. The addition had the desired dramatic effect, for at that point, as Warren recorded in his memoirs, "a wave of emotion swept the room, no words or intentional movement, yet a distinct emotional manifestation that defies description."

Warren went on to recite some of the evidence demonstrating the inequality which is inherent in school segregation: that it "generates a feeling of inferiority" in a way "unlikely ever to be undone," a feeling whose "impact is greater when it has the sanction of the law, for the policy of separating the races is usually interpreted as denoting the inferiority of the Negro group." That language was broad enough to open the way for ending segregation in all walks of life, but Warren was conscious of the need to take one giant step at a time by restricting this revolutionary decision to the schools:

> We conclude that, in the field of public education, the
> doctrine of "separate but equal" has no place. Separate
> educational facilities are inherently unequal. Therefore,
> we hold that the plaintiffs and others similarly situated for
> whom the actions have been brought are, by reason of the
> segregation complained of, deprived of the equal protec-
> tion of the laws guaranteed by the Fourteenth Amendment.

Recognizing that "the formulation of decrees in these cases presents problems of considerable complexity," Warren's opinion closed with an order restoring the cases to the docket for further argument at the October 1954 term on the method of implementation, with the participation of the attorneys general of "the states requiring or permitting segregation in public education."

The fifteen-paragraph *Brown* opinion did not quite match the ingenious brevity of Lincoln's three-paragraph Gettysburg Address, but its effects were far more momentous for the country. With those few sentences the unanimous Warren Court bridged the gap that had divided the nation for 165 years. For the first time, the Court wrote into the Constitution the words of the Declaration of Independence that had been excluded from the Constitution in deference to slavery: *That all men are created equal.* This historic leap was due in no small measure to Earl Warren's starry-eyed conviction that one of the main purposes of the Constitution was to bring to life the lofty principles of the Declaration of Independence.

In his memoirs, Warren wrote that the real credit for achieving the indispensable unanimity in *Brown* should go to Hugo Black, Stanley Reed, and Tom Clark, "the three justices who were born and reared in that part of the nation where segregation was a way of life and where everyone knew the greatest emotional opposition to the decision would be forthcoming.... The others of us, while enthusiastic in our adherence to the decision and fervent in our desire for unanimity, were not in danger of being faced with animosity and harassment in our home states because of centuries-old patterns of life."

Mindful of the firestorm that was likely to greet the attempt to enforce the *Brown* decision, the justices took their time in framing the implementation order. Finally on May 31, 1955, more than a year after the decision overruling *Plessy,* Chief Justice Warren delivered another unanimous opinion. It tied the implementation order to the earlier reversal of *Plessy* by specifying that "All provisions of federal, state, or local law requiring or permitting such discrimination must yield to this principle." It then remanded the four cases to the lower courts in which they were originally heard, those courts being familiar with local conditions and the need for further hearings on methods of desegregation. The opinion recognized the need for patience in making such far-reaching changes, but charged the lower courts with requiring that the school boards "make a prompt and reasonable start toward full compliance." It directed the lower courts to take such proceedings and enter such orders "as are necessary and proper to admit [the black children] to public schools on a racially nondiscriminatory basis with all deliberate speed." The self-contradictory term "all deliberate speed" was supplied by the ever-cautious Felix Frankfurter, in the hope of dampening the explosive reaction that awaited *Brown* in the Southern states.

The resistance to school desegregation was even more virulent than the justices had anticipated. The anarchy-threatening tone was set in post-*Brown* speeches like the one delivered by U.S. Senator James Eastland of Mississippi (soon to become chairman of the Senate Judiciary Committee) to a wildly cheering crowd in his home state:

> On May 17, 1954, the Constitution of the United States
> was destroyed because the Supreme Court disregarded the
> law and decided that integration was right. You are not
> required to obey any court which passes out such a ruling.
> In fact, you are obligated to defy it.

It took decades to overcome that resistance, and along the way it required the firm support of the executive and legislative branches to turn the Supreme Court's orders into reality. The president did not have the constitutional power to initiate desegregation on his own. Congress, which had the power, was too polarized to reach the required consensus. What was needed first was something like the Bangalore torpedoes (long metal tubes stuffed with explosives) used in World War II by Allied forces to breach Hitler's Atlantic Wall and open the way for the invading troops to push off the Normandy beaches and go on to liberate France. In the *Brown* decision, the Warren Court furnished the Bangalore torpedo, but it was not powerful enough to defeat Jim Crow by itself. That required such Congressional measures as the Civil Rights Act of 1964 and the Voting Rights Act of 1965, as well as the commitment of Presidents Eisenhower, Kennedy, and Johnson, who sent in federal marshals and troops when necessary to put down rebellions led by Southern governors willing to defy the law rather than suffer integration. Those legislative and executive commitments would not have been forthcoming without the heroic efforts of the Reverend Martin Luther King Jr., Rosa Parks, and the leaders of other black protest movements, whose nonviolent demonstrations (often interrupted by law officers deploying fire hoses and attack dogs) mobilized the public support that finally doomed Jim Crow.

While the enforcement of public school desegregation usually required government intervention and sometimes even military force, it should be noted that the movement was spearheaded by the civil court actions brought by private citizens like Oliver Brown. The same was true of desegregation of universities, where the opening wedge was the civil suit filed by NAACP lawyers on behalf of James Meredith against the trustees who controlled admission to universities in Mississippi. Meredith, a Korean War veteran attending the all-black Jackson State College, was inspired by President John F. Kennedy's 1961 inaugural address to apply that day for admission to the segregated University of Mississippi. On September 30, 1962, nearly two years after Meredith's application, President Kennedy announced on nationwide television that the court orders for Meredith's admission were being carried out with the assistance of federal marshals. Noting that the admission orders were the result of a private suit brought by Meredith against the university's trustees, Kennedy said:

> Americans are free, in short, to disagree with the law but
> not to disobey it. For in a Government of Laws and not
> of men, no man, however prominent or powerful, and no
> mob however unruly or boisterous, is entitled to defy a
> court of law.

President Kennedy expressed the hope that Meredith's enrollment would be peaceful, but violence erupted immediately, requiring the intervention of several thousand U.S. Army troops. Meredith was guarded by U.S. marshals in every classroom until he graduated in 1963. Thus the Rule of Law was upheld.

The direct results of *Brown v. Board of Education of Topeka* were a mixed bag. Long-distance busing of students to achieve racially balanced schools became an unpopular and sometimes counterproductive exercise, and sending children to the schools nearest their homes led to *de facto* segregation caused by the underlying demographics—a problem by no means limited to the former slave states. But removing the authority of the law from school segregation had profound consequences throughout American society. The *Brown* decision became the springboard for the Civil Rights Revolution, which quickly spread beyond school integration to take aim at other strongholds of segregation and discrimination. There the enforced departure of Jim Crow was more dramatic, as the Government of Laws made the back-of-the-bus regime and the *White Only/Colored Only* signs in public facilities disappear overnight.

While the Civil Rights Revolution will probably need to be carried on through several more generations, considerable post-*Brown* progress has been made in eliminating racial prejudice from the public side of American life. Harvard Sociology Professor Orlando Patterson, a prominent African-American scholar, summed it up in a 2006 article, "The Last Race Problem":

> The nation stands today as a global model in the sophisti-
> cation and enforcement of its civil rights laws, the diversity
> of its elite, the participation of blacks and other minorities
> in its great corporations and its public cultural life, and in
> the embrace of blacks as an integral part of the nation and
> what it means to be an American.

Professor Patterson went on to limit this praise to "public integration" and to decry "the near complete isolation of blacks from the private life of the white majority." Since the cause of that isolation appears to be a fault of human nature which cannot be cured by the Government of Laws or any other government, it is, as lawyers often say when they want to slip out of an uncomfortable spot, "beyond the scope of the present inquiry." But before leaving that inquiry, It is worth noting the views of Harvard Law Professor Charles J. Ogletree Jr. on "the Rule and the Limits of Law":

> Blatantly racial laws are off the books, but the lingering
> effects of old laws and structural arrangements remain
> and have the same result—unequal opportunity. Personal
> racism no longer comes in the form of white southern
> sheriffs and governors blocking black children from
> schoolhouse doors. Rather, it has moved underground, so
> vaguely or passively expressed that it is utterly unassailable.

The Civil Rights Revolution has produced many heroes, but four who are of particular relevance to our examination of the Government of Laws have names unfamiliar to the general public: John Minor Wisdom of Louisiana, Elbert Tuttle of Georgia, Richard Rives of Alabama, and John Brown of Texas. All were white judges of the U.S. Court of Appeals for the Fifth Circuit (the federal appellate court then covering Alabama, Florida, Georgia, Louisiana, Mississippi, and Texas) upon which fell the major burden of turning the vague *Brown* orders into the methodical termination of white supremacy. Professor Jack Bass tells their story in his book, *Unlikely Heroes*:

> The Fifth Circuit Court of Appeals began in the late 1950s
> to flesh out *Brown's* mandate for equality and expand it
> beyond education. Fifth Circuit judges issued landmark
> decisions that struck down barriers of discrimination in
> voting, jury selection, and employment.

Bass interviewed Burke Marshall, who played an important role himself as assistant attorney general in charge of the Justice Department's Civil Rights Division during the Kennedy administration. Marshall told him, "If it hadn't been for judges like that on the Fifth Circuit, I think *Brown* would have failed in the end."

Besides being saddled with responsibility for undoing the centuries-old effects of slavery, Southern federal judges placed their lives at risk. Because of death threats which were far from idle, many needed around-the-clock shifts of U.S. Marshals to guard their personal safety. In addition to threats of harm, they and their families were often treated like pariahs, ostracized in their home communities.

This burden was not limited to the appellate judges. It also fell upon the judges of the federal district (trial-level) courts who were charged with hands-on enforcement of the radical changes required in thousands of segregated communities. One of Professor Bass's *Unlikely Heroes* is Frank Johnson Jr., who was appointed a judge of the U.S. District Court at Montgomery, Alabama in 1955, just in time to reap the whirlwind of *Brown's* return to the South. For the next 24 years, he did battle with the likes of Alabama's militant white supremacist governor, George Wallace, who had been his law school classmate. In addition to supervising the integration of the public schools throughout Alabama, Johnson ordered and completed the removal of Jim Crow from the bus system and from the state's voting and jury selection practices. He also ordered Governor Wallace to permit the history-making 1966 protest march from Selma to Montgomery led by the Reverend Martin Luther King Jr. During this period, a bomb explosion destroyed part of Johnson's mother's home, and the judge's young son was repeatedly harassed. Bass recounts Governor Wallace's personal attacks on Johnson:

> Wallace's attacks lasted almost fifteen years, a period in
> which Johnson placed Alabama's prison system, highway
> patrol, property tax assessment program, mental health
> agency, and public education system all under the federal
> court's jurisdiction. Ultimately, he exercised more influence
> over public policy in that state than did Wallace, to whose
> attacks Johnson never responded.

Overcoming the malignant heritage of slavery is the most challenging civil rights reform undertaken by any American government. It dwarfs the removal of apartheid from South Africa, which was relatively simpler because the oppressed blacks were by far the majority group. The American Civil Rights Revolution remains a work in progress, but its advances thus far are a tribute to the Government of Laws, which functioned as the Founding Lawyers hoped it would—running on all cylinders with the support of the legislative, executive, and judicial branches and the American people. It was made possible by the fortunate presence of Earl Warren, another politically-skilled chief justice, who dealt with this crisis in the tradition of his similarly gifted predecessors, John Marshall and Charles Evans Hughes.

The White House Tapes

Twenty years after Earl Warren delivered the *Brown* decision, another constitutional crisis confronted the Court presided over by his successor, Chief Justice Warren Burger. For the general public, this issue did not pack as much of an emotional wallop as did school segregation, but to those who were aware of the Constitution's fault lines—the gray areas where lie the gravest threats to Separation of Powers—it involved something even more menacing: executive privilege.

On June 17, 1972, five men engaged in burglarizing the headquarters of the Democratic National Committee in Washington's Watergate hotel and office complex bungled the job and were arrested. That was the beginning of what President Gerald Ford later described as "our long national nightmare." The burglars were soon linked to the Committee to Reelect the President (known as CREEP), the president being Richard Nixon. The White House denied any knowledge of or connection with the Watergate burglary, and Nixon went on to swamp Democratic candidate George McGovern by carrying 49 states. But early in Nixon's second term, the denial of White House involvement began to unravel, and the nation's media, as well as Congress and the Justice Department, became transfixed by the legal quagmire known simply as Watergate.

By the spring of 1973, it became apparent that Attorney General Richard Kleindienst was conducting the investigation of Watergate without great enthusiasm and that officials in the White House were attempting to cover up the facts. Kleindienst and top White House aides H. R. Haldeman and John Ehrlichman were forced to resign, and President Nixon's legal counsel, John Dean, was dismissed. Nixon then nominated Elliot Richardson as the new attorney general. As a condition of his confirmation, the Senate Judiciary Committee required Richardson to appoint a special prosecutor to independently investigate and prosecute all charges arising out of Watergate. Richardson was confirmed, and he chose as the Watergate special prosecutor Archibald Cox, a Harvard Law professor who had served as solicitor general during the Kennedy and Johnson administrations. A condition of Cox's appointment (and his acceptance) was that he would not be removed from office unless found guilty of "gross misconduct."

Meanwhile the Senate had formed a special investigating committee to look into Watergate, and its fascinating televised hearings were dominating the public's attention during the summer of 1973. Fired White House counsel John Dean gave detailed testimony to the Senate committee, claiming that President Nixon and his top aides had engaged in a cover-up to hide responsibility for the Watergate burglary—a cover-up that amounted to the felony of obstruction of justice if it could be proved. But Special Prosecutor Cox feared that Dean's testimony, coming from a man who was facing prison time which he had every incentive to minimize, was not credible enough by itself to support prosecution of those whom Dean accused—especially President Nixon. Then out of the blue appeared Alexander Butterfield, a retired Air Force colonel who had the routine White House job of keeping the president's schedule and filing his official papers. When Senate committee staff members interviewed Butterfield to determine if it was worthwhile to call this small fry office manager as a witness, he revealed that practically every word spoken in Nixon's presence—in the Oval Office, the Cabinet Room, and even the Camp David retreat—was secretly recorded on tape. Thus began the climactic battle of the two-year Watergate war: the struggle for possession of the White House tapes.

Special Prosecutor Cox quickly issued a subpoena calling on the president to produce in court nine tapes covering specific dates on which John Dean's Senate testimony indicated there had been cover-up discussions. Cox held his breath, knowing that no president had ever been forced by a court to give or produce evidence. In the past, officials of all three government branches had taken great pains to avoid a confrontation that would test the president's executive privilege—his right and his duty to maintain the confidentiality of matters of state which were committed to his exclusive possession in the public interest. What they had all sought to avoid was the irreparable damage to the Government of Laws that would follow if the president refused to comply.

Nixon responded by writing a letter to John Sirica, the trial judge overseeing the Watergate prosecutions in the U.S. District Court for the District of Columbia. The letter pointed out that the president had the constitutional duty to maintain the integrity of his office, and that he could not do so if confidential documents in his possession—especially those revealing his discussions with aides—were made available to the other branches of government. He respectfully declined to produce these presidential documents, as all of his predecessors responding to such requests had done in the past (usually without bothering to express their respect for the court).

Cox then requested Judge Sirica to issue an order directing the president to produce those nine tapes, which related directly to criminal charges being considered by a grand jury in Sirica's court. After hearing extensive arguments by Cox and the lawyers representing Nixon, Judge Sirica took the fateful step that had been studiously avoided by his predecessor judges dating all the way back to John Marshall. He ordered the president to deliver the nine specified tapes to his chambers, where he would listen to them *in camera* (privately) and determine which, if any, should be handed over to Special Prosecutor Cox and the grand jury, and which should be returned to the White House as privileged from disclosure.

Nixon appealed to the U.S. Court of Appeals for the District of Columbia Circuit, the last step below the Supreme Court. Cox and his small staff of handpicked lawyers now became concerned about hints from the White House that even if the Court of Appeals upheld the order to produce the tapes, the president might defy the order, for the appellate judges had no more power to compel presidential compliance than did Judge Sirica.

On October 12, 1973, the Court of Appeals affirmed Judge Sirica's order. The three appellate judges acknowledged that the president's conversations with his aides normally would be considered privileged, but found that

Special Prosecutor Cox had shown convincingly that the nine tapes were evidence "peculiarly necessary" to the Watergate grand jury's investigation. The Court of Appeals stayed the effectiveness of its order until October 19, giving the president a week in which to seek review by the Supreme Court. But the Nixon forces had other ideas about how to avoid producing the tapes.

Nixon's lawyers proposed a compromise to Cox. The White House would prepare an edited transcript of those portions of the tapes which the president considered relevant to the Watergate investigation. That transcript would be submitted to Senator John Stennis of Mississippi, an intermediary respected by both sides. Senator Stennis would be permitted to listen to the tapes (only once) as he read the transcript, and after he certified that the transcript was accurate, it would be turned over to Cox in lieu of the tapes which the courts had ordered to be produced. Cox found this to be a one-way compromise. It was not likely to produce an accurate transcript, and in any event its usefulness would be limited to furnishing leads for further investigation since (unlike the original tapes) it would not be admissible as evidence in a criminal trial. Cox rejected the proposal, but felt it his duty to continue to negotiate for a satisfactory compromise that would avoid a head-on clash over executive privilege. In the absence of such an offer, he insisted on compliance with the court orders for production of the tapes.

Again the Nixon forces were a step ahead of the special prosecutor. The Senate Investigating Committee had also requested production of the tapes. The White House had convinced the two senators running the hearings (Democrat Sam Ervin of North Carolina and Republican Howard Baker of Tennessee) to accept the Stennis compromise transcript in lieu of insisting on production of the actual tapes. Then the White House launched a public relations campaign, seeking to discredit Cox as a witch-hunter who was unreasonably refusing to abide by the compromise which had satisfied the patriotic Senators Ervin and Baker (now firmly established as affable and folksy stars of the leading show on television).

The clock ticked down to Friday, October 19, the last day when Nixon could delay the appellate court order by seeking review in the Supreme Court. It appeared that the White House might be setting the stage for Nixon himself to address the nation on television and announce that in the interests of national security—a subterfuge he had already used extensively—he would refuse to obey the unreasonable court order which the irresponsible, unelected, obscure (to the general public) Harvard Professor Archibald Cox had procured. The theory was that Nixon would portray this heroic refusal as the patriotic and authoritative presidential action, reasoning that the public regarded the Watergate controversy as embodied in the televised Senate hearings rather than in the arcane arguments which lawyers made in untelevised court proceedings.

But instead of a television speech, the president hunkered down and resorted to a stealth move, one that characteristically underestimated the intelligence of the public and its regard for the Government of Laws. On Saturday, October 20, Nixon ordered his attorney general, Elliot Richardson, to fire Cox as special prosecutor, which Richardson had the power to do only on grounds of "gross misconduct." Knowing the order was improper, Richardson refused to comply and simultaneously resigned his office. Nixon then gave the same order to Deputy Attorney General William Ruckleshaus, who followed Richardson's course by refusing and resigning. Next in the official batting order was Solicitor General Robert Bork, who became acting attorney general, accepted the president's order, and fired Cox.

Rather than putting the Watergate problem behind him, this travesty (which became known as the Saturday Night Massacre) brought the White House roof down on Nixon's head. His ploy might have worked in the days before saturated media coverage, but now he handed the reporters a story that really had legs: PRESIDENT CLAIMS HE'S ABOVE THE LAW—AXES HIS OWN ATTORNEY GENERAL TWICE! As Cox described the reaction, "Sunday and Monday a firestorm of public outrage overwhelmed the White House.... Cars streamed by the White House, honking for impeachment." By Tuesday, the president's lawyer was forced to tell Judge Sirica in open court that Nixon would comply with the order to produce the nine tapes, adding that "this president does not defy the law."

Nixon had succeeded in getting rid of Cox, but at the price of losing the public support which had fueled his landslide re-election. Since the nine tapes produced by his lawyers revealed only the tip of the Watergate iceberg, he grimly clung to his office and busied himself with other national problems. It fell to Cox's successor as special prosecutor, Houston lawyer Leon Jaworski, to carry on the investigation and to subpoena an additional 64 tapes which contained the secrets that would prove Nixon's deep involvement in the cover-up and destroy his presidency. Again the president's lawyers resisted the prosecutor's subpoena, and this time the dispute went all the way to the Supreme Court, which for the first time in its 185-year history was forced to rule on executive privilege. Nixon felt he had reason to expect sympathetic treatment from the Court, since he had appointed four of the justices during his first term, including Chief Justice Warren Burger, whose conservative political views were particularly close to those of the president. Nixon hoped he could count on the votes of the five justices who were Republican appointees.

On July 24, 1974, the Court announced its decision. Warren Burger was able to produce a unanimous vote, officially 8-to-0, as Justice Rehnquist recused himself due to his earlier service in the Nixon Justice Department.

Burger's opinion for the Court adopted Judge Sirica's holding that "the judiciary, not the president, was the final arbiter of a claim of executive privilege." The Court rejected the president's claim that "the separation of powers doctrine precludes judicial review of a president's claim of privilege." It quoted John Marshall's words in *Marbury v. Madison* that it "is emphatically the province and duty of the judicial department to say what the law is," adding that "any other conclusion would be contrary to the basic concept of separation of powers and checks and balances that flow from the scheme of a tripartite government."

The Burger opinion confirmed the existence and importance of executive privilege, and found that while it was presumptively applicable, it was not absolute or unqualified. Thus "this presumptive privilege must be considered in light of our historic commitment to the rule of law." Viewed in that light, the privilege must give way to the need for truthful evidence in this criminal case. In other words, the president is not above the law. With that, the justices ordered that the tapes be produced to Judge Sirica in his chambers immediately.

There was still speculation that the embattled president would defy the Supreme Court's order, or that he might have already destroyed the most incriminating tapes. But public revulsion against the president who tried to place himself above the law impelled some of Nixon's staunchest supporters in Congress to rush to the Oval Office to tell him that the game was over. That afternoon, Nixon announced that he would "comply with that decision in all respects." In two weeks, with the House Judiciary Committee having voted to impeach him for obstruction of justice, he became the first president to resign the office.

Historians are still wondering why Nixon did not destroy the tapes after Alexander Butterfield revealed their existence, especially during the 10-day hiatus between that disclosure and the issuance of the Cox subpoena which for the first time identified them as evidence in a criminal investigation. The president did announce that he was taking them into his personal custody, and he could have made a halfway palatable argument that he had destroyed them in the interests of national security, of which he was the sole judge. He would have drawn plenty of criticism, but nothing like the tornado that erupted from the firing of Cox and the other efforts to resist court-ordered production of the tapes. And in the end the incriminating evidence which caused his resignation—the nature and extent of which was known only to him—would have been obliterated. One explanation is that he was banking on the tapes as a source for his legacy-building memoirs. It also appears he was confident that if the special prosecutor dared to subpoena them, his friends on the Supreme Court would uphold executive privilege.

The 37th president bet against the Government of Laws, and he lost everything. As Archibald Cox wrote:

> By the Watergate investigations and the public response, the principle that even the highest executive officials are subject to the Constitution and laws as interpreted by an independent judiciary was confirmed and strengthened, not only in legal theory but in fact. Ultimately, their [the public's] support is the only sanction for constitutionalism and the Rule of Law.

Chapter Seven

Bush v. Gore:
Testing the Government of Laws
(2000-2009)

At 7:50 pm Eastern Standard Time on November 7, 2000, Voter News Service, a joint venture of the Associated Press and the five major television networks, reported that based on their exit polls, Vice-President Al Gore had carried Florida, giving him the remaining electoral votes he needed to defeat Texas Governor George W. Bush for the presidency. Gore also led by half a million in the national popular vote totals (about one-half of one percent of the 104 million votes cast). The network anchors immediately announced that they were projecting Gore as the winner.

The Bush forces were getting a different picture from their Republican campaign officials in Florida, and they quickly complained to the networks that their projections were premature and inaccurate. By 10 p.m. it became apparent to the networks that they had created a fiasco. They began retracting the Gore victory projection and announcing that the election was now too close to call. At 2:15 a.m. on November 8, with Bush apparently leading by 50,000 votes in Florida, the networks began projecting him as the winner. At 2:30 a.m., Gore phoned Bush to concede the election. At 3 a.m., Gore left his Nashville hotel in a motorcade to the War Memorial Plaza, where he planned to address his supporters. While enroute, Gore received a phone call from his campaign officials saying that Bush's Florida lead was down to less than a thousand votes, and that he should not concede. The motorcade reversed course and returned to the hotel, where at 3:30 a.m. Gore phoned Bush again to retract his concession. By 4:15 a.m. all the networks had retracted their Bush victory projections and reverted to "too close to call."

Later in the morning of November 8, Florida Secretary of State Katherine Harris announced that the statewide results reported to her office showed Bush ahead by 1,784 votes, which under Florida law required a machine recount of all 6 million votes cast because Bush's lead was less than one-half of one percent. That was Day One of a 36-day post-election tug-of-war which was to produce dozens of hastily-written court decisions, including two from the Florida Supreme Court and three from the United States Supreme Court. The judicial system was to live through another of its worst nightmares: a dispute that required judges to decide the presidential election.

The machine recount cut Bush's lead to 327 votes, but even that narrow margin would have won him Florida's 25 electoral votes, enabling him to nose out Gore by 271 to 266 in the Electoral College. Gore's team then requested manual recounts in four counties which were Democratic strongholds. That triggered a comic opera featuring local election officials examining punch-card ballots with magnifying glasses to determine the voters' intentions. There were thousands of ballots which were either "undervotes"—those on which the voter had not pushed the punch tool with sufficient force to make a clean hole—or "overvotes," on which holes were punched for two or more candidates for the same office. The undervotes had many variations, ranging from a very slight impression on the punch-card (a "dimpled chad") to those on which the chad was dislodged but still attached, hanging by one or more corners ("dangling chads").

As county election officials struggled with the tedious manual recounts under the watchful eyes of observers from both parties, Secretary of State Harris announced on November 13 that in the opinion of her legal advisors, she was required by Florida statute to certify the election results as final on November 14, the seventh day after the election, even if the manual recounts were not completed by then. Gore's lawyers appealed to the Florida Supreme Court, which ruled unanimously on November 21 that hand-counted votes must be accepted until November 26, the new court-decreed deadline for final certification by the secretary of state. Bush's lawyers immediately appealed that decision to the U.S. Supreme Court, claiming that it changed the statutory rules after the election by extending the certification deadline. On November 24, the U.S. Supreme Court agreed to hear Bush's appeal, setting argument for December 1. Meanwhile, on the new deadline date of November 26, with the hand recounting still incomplete, Secretary of State Harris certified that Bush, with a revised lead of 537 votes, was the winner of Florida's 25 electoral votes. But that was not the end of the game, since Gore had the legal right to contest Harris's certification in court, which he did on November 29 by filing a lawsuit in Leon County (seat of the state government) requesting inclusion of the remaining thousands of disputed votes which required hand counting.

As Gore's legal challenge worked its way through the lower state courts, the U.S. Supreme Court issued a unanimous decision on December 4, vacating (nullifying) the Florida Supreme Court's November 21 decision on the ground that it was not clear which constitution—Florida or U.S.—was the source of its rulings. Chief Justice Rehnquist and his colleagues sent the case back to the Florida Supreme Court "for further proceedings not inconsistent with this opinion," a direction to clarify its November 21st decision by dealing specifically with the state and federal constitutional provisions relating to this election.

Before the Florida Supreme Court complied with that direction, on December 7 it heard arguments on Gore's appeal from a lower court decision rejecting manual recounting and upholding the certification of Bush as the winner. On December 8, the Florida Supreme Court overruled that decision by a vote of 4 to 3, ordering an immediate manual recount of all undervotes (estimated to total 60,000) in every one of the state's 67 counties, not just the four counties requested by Gore. With his lead now reduced to 154 votes, Bush immediately appealed that decision to the U.S. Supreme Court. On Saturday, December 9, the U.S. Supreme Court in a 5-to-4 decision halted the manual recount by granting an emergency stay of the Florida Supreme Court's recount order, setting argument of the appeal for (Monday) December 11.

Meanwhile a subplot of this political/legal soap opera was playing out in Tallahassee. Leaders of the Florida state legislature, controlled by Republicans with a 25-to-15 majority in the Senate and 77 to 43 in the House, had taken advice from constitutional law experts about their potential role in selecting Florida's 25 electors. Through one of many quirks in the arcane election laws, the Electoral Count Act of 1887—the federal statute enacted to prevent repetitions of the 1876 Hayes-Tilden fiasco—empowered the state legislature to choose the electors if the popular election results were in doubt. The Republican legislative leaders called a special session to consider their options, and by December 8 they were poised to pass a resolution naming the electors, all of whom would be pledged to cast their votes for Bush. (The legislators proceeded by way of a resolution in order to avoid the embarrassment of enacting a statute which would have to be signed the governor, who happened to be Jeb Bush, George's brother.) When the U.S. Supreme Court granted an emergency stay of the recounting on December 9, the legislators held up the resolution, hoping that the U.S. Supreme Court would make further action by them unnecessary. But they remained in special session, and their commitment to pass the resolution (which might result in creation of two competing sets of Florida electors) was highly publicized, with public hearings and many television appearances by legislative leaders.

As the batteries of lawyers and campaign advisors rushed back to Washington, it was apparent that another epic game of Checks and Balances—worthy of *Spy v. Spy*—was under way. The Republicans were making full use of their control of the Florida executive and legislative branches, while the Democrats were exploiting their leverage in the Florida Supreme Court, all seven members of which had been appointed by Democratic governors. Emblematic of this no-holds-barred jousting was Katherine Harris, who was called upon to serve as the impartial secretary of state in charge of certifying the election results while also functioning as co-chair of Bush's Florida campaign.

This seemingly endless legal battle was masterminded by two eminent lawyer-statesmen, both of whom had served as U.S. secretary of state: Warren Christopher of California for the Democrats, and James Baker III of Texas for the Republicans. Both chose younger gladiators to present the oral arguments in the U.S. Supreme Court: David Boies of New York for Gore and Theodore Olson of Washington D.C. for Bush.

The 90-minute argument on December 11 produced no great surprises. Olson hammered away at the Florida Supreme Court's "revision of Florida's election code," arguing that this changed the statutory rules after the election and "authorized extensive standardless and unequal manual ballot recounts" which denied equal protection to those voters disenfranchised by stricter recounting standards in their counties. Boies countered that Article I of the U.S. Constitution left the election rules up to the state legislatures; the Florida Supreme Court's interpretation of the Florida election statutes was that they established a clear standard of determining and following the voter's intent; and that the U.S. Supreme Court had always accepted the interpretation of state statutes by the state's highest court, especially those dealing with elections.

Those who tried to guess the outcome from the justice's questions—often a highly speculative undertaking—concluded that the three conservatives (William Rehnquist, Antonin Scalia, and Clarence Thomas) would surely vote for Bush; the four more liberal justices (John Paul Stevens, David Souter, Ruth Bader Ginsburg, and Stephen Breyer) would probably vote for Gore; and the decisive votes of the moderate swing justices, Sandra Day O'Connor and Anthony Kennedy, were up in the air. During her questioning of Boies, Justice O'Connor indicated that she (and possibly other justices) considered it a demerit for Gore's side that the Florida Supreme Court had steamed ahead on December 8 to order more recounts without having complied with the higher court's unanimous December 4th order to clarify the constitutional basis of their earlier rulings: "I did not find really a response by the Florida Supreme Court to this Court's remand in the case a week ago. It just seemed to kind of bypass it and...I found that troublesome."

The guesswork ended late the following evening when the Court released its decision. Since it was 65 pages long and contained six separate opinions, the journalists covering the Supreme Court had some difficulty in reporting the result, but it soon became clear that Bush had won by the same 5-to-4 alignment which had imposed the emergency stay three days earlier. The *per curiam* (for the Court) decision gained the votes of O'Connor and Kennedy (the two swing voters) and the three conservatives (Rehnquist, Scalia, and Thomas). It concluded that the manner in which the Florida Supreme Court had ordered the manual recounts to be conducted, with standards used to determine voter intent varying widely from county to county and even within some counties, violated the equal protection clause of the 14th Amendment because it treated voters unequally. It also ruled that in the limited time available, it would be physically impossible to rewrite and standardize the recounting rules, examine and recount the thousands of disputed ballots, permit a trial judge to rule on any ballots that remained disputed, and allow final review by the appellate courts. Therefore, without saying it in so many words, the five majority justices rang the closing bell of the legal contest and effectively declared George Bush the president-elect.

Justices Rehnquist, Scalia, and Thomas joined in the *per curiam* opinion and also in a separate opinion authored by Rehnquist which ruled that in addition to the equal protection violation, the Florida Supreme Court had made post-election changes in the election laws enacted by the Florida legislature by extending recount deadlines beyond the date specified by the legislature. They found that both the Florida legislature and the Florida Supreme Court itself had adopted the deadline of six days prior to the December 18th meeting of the Electoral College (i.e., December 12) which is fixed in the federal Electoral Count Act as the date up to which states can file their certified list of electors without incurring any risk of challenge—the so-called Safe Harbor provision of the federal statute governing presidential elections. They concluded that these post-election changes by the Florida Supreme Court presented a federal constitutional question because the power to make the rules for elections is conferred on the state legislatures by Article II of the U.S. Constitution, and the Safe Harbor deadline for filing a "conclusive" list of electors is part of a federal statute.

Each of the four dissenting justices filed separate opinions. Two of the dissenters, Souter and Breyer, agreed with the majority that the divergent recount standards violated the equal protection clause, but concluded that there was still enough time for the Florida Supreme Court to rewrite them and for the recounting to be completed before the December 18th meeting of the Electoral College (although neither justice mentioned the time required for trial and appellate court review of ballots which remained under dispute). The other two dissenters, Stevens and Ginsburg, found no violation of the equal protection clause, and insisted that because the U.S. Constitution assigned the selection of presidential electors primarily to the states, the U.S. Supreme Court should not have intervened, particularly because it put the Court in the untenable position of rejecting the Florida Supreme Court's interpretation of Florida election law.

None of the majority justices mentioned the governmental crisis that was likely to occur if the Court did not step in and end the electoral deadlock: the submission by Florida of two slates of electors, one voting for Gore and the other for Bush. It was certain that there would be a slate of Bush electors, for the Florida House of Representatives passed the necessary resolution on December 12 and the Florida Senate, also controlled by the Republicans, was still in special session, poised to finalize the resolution momentarily. If the recount had gone forward and yielded enough new Gore votes for him to take the lead, the Florida Supreme Court would have ordered the governor to submit a slate pledged to Gore. That would have thrown the election into Congress, to be decided according to the Electoral Count Act of 1887—if anybody could figure out what that confusing statute meant and how it was to be implemented.

Apparently the majority justices felt it inappropriate to mention this looming crisis as a reason for their decision, since it was primarily a practical political problem rather than a legal basis for judicial intervention. But Justice Breyer's dissenting opinion reveals that it must have been seriously discussed during the justices' conferences. Breyer, one of the most incisive thinkers ever to serve on the Court, explained in Part II of his dissent (in which part Justices Stevens and Ginsburg joined) the reasons why he concluded that the Court's election-ending ruling was unnecessary and improper. Most of that Part II is devoted to the problem of dealing with two competing slates within the framework of the Electoral Count Act. Breyer gives a reassuring appraisal of the ability of Congress to break the deadlock by using the powers conferred in that act.

Our main concern here is the effect of the *Bush v. Gore* decision on public acceptance of the Supreme Court's role in the Government of Laws, rather than the merits of the case or the fitness of the two presidential candidates. But in light of the practical problems that would have resulted if the Court had not decided to intervene, consideration of views contrary to those expressed in Justice Breyer's Part II may be useful.

What If the U.S. Supreme Court Had Not Intervened?

Following is a bullet-point version of various scenarios that might have followed the Court's refusal to intervene, based loosely upon the views of three legal scholars who attempted to apply the Electoral Count Act hypothetically to the 2000 election: University of Chicago Law Professor Cass Sunstein, University of Southern California Political Science and Law Professor Howard Gillman, and U.S. Court of Appeals Judge Richard Posner. (Professors Sunstein and Gilman disagree with the Court's decision in *Bush v.* Gore, while Judge Posner praises the results of the Court's intervention.)

I apologize for dragging you through what may appear to be an excerpt from *Alice in Wonderland.* I do so only because I was unable to find a published account which walks the reader through all the steps which would have become necessary if the Supreme Court had not ended the controversy. *Here we go.*

✦ On December 8, 2000, the U.S. Supreme Court denies Bush's application for an emergency stay and declines to review the Florida Supreme Court's 4-to-3 decision ordering statewide manual recounting of undervotes to proceed. As the manual recounting continues, on December 9 the special session of the Florida legislature, voting along strict party lines, adopts a resolution appointing the slate pledged to Bush as Florida's 25 electors. On December 11, Governor Jeb Bush, complying with §6 of the Electoral Count Act of 1887 ("ECA"), sends a certificate to the Archivist of the United States identifying the 25 Bush electors named by the state legislature as the official Florida electors.

✦ On December 12, Leon County Circuit Court Judge Terry Allen, pursuant to his assignment, begins televised court hearings to review the recount reports from county election officials covering more than 60,000 undervoted ballots. Bush's lawyers now request manual recount of 110,000 overvoted ballots, claiming that many of them were discarded only because the voter punched the chad properly and also wrote in the name of the same candidate, but Judge Allen rejects this as a belated attempt to stall for time. The lawyers for both sides had recorded the objections they made to the officials recounting the undervotes in each county, and now they argue those objections to Judge Allen. Bush's lawyers present their objections to over 90 percent of the undervoted ballots counted for Gore, while Gore's lawyers limit their objections to about 40 percent of the new Bush votes, since they are concerned about missing the December 18th Electoral College meeting deadline. Judge Allen begins by examining each disputed ballot, reminding himself that he must count the Broward County ballots if there is any indication of dimpling the chad, while in other counties he has to look for detachment of one or more corners of the chad. He keeps his court in session for 18 hours a day. After two days he concludes that the December 18th deadline will prevent him from examining and hearing argument on every one of the thousands of disputed ballots. Over the objections of Bush's lawyers he devises a sampling system and applies his rulings to large groups of ballots.

✦ On Saturday, December 16, a bleary-eyed Judge Allen announces that he has upheld or rejected thousands of disputed ballots, and that the final recount shows Gore making enough net gains to nose out Bush by 27 votes. Bush's lawyers appeal immediately to the intermediate appellate court, which passes the appeal through to the Florida Supreme Court because of the December 18th Electoral College deadline. The Florida Supreme Court agrees to hear the case the next day (Sunday, December 17) with each side having 90 minutes to present their arguments. Since time is not available for the printing of the customary record on appeal, Judge Lewis's entire Leon County file is ordered to be produced immediately in the Florida Supreme Court.

✦ On December 17, the Florida Supreme Court hears the appeal, including protests by Bush's lawyers that the accelerated scheduling has not allowed sufficient time for the justices to study Judge Lewis's findings and to look at any of the thousands of contested ballots and other recount documents which are now stacked in large bins at the front of the courtroom. Later that afternoon, the Florida Supreme Court announces its decision, affirming by a 4-to-3 vote Judge Lewis's findings and declaring Gore the Florida winner by 27 votes. It issues an order to Governor Jeb Bush, directing him to vacate his December 11th certification of the Bush slate and to transmit the Gore slate to the National Archivist as the official list of Florida electors. Governor Bush announces that he has received the order and is studying it in consultation with his legal advisors. Gore's lawyers go back to the Florida Supreme Court and obtain a second order stating that unless Governor Bush transmits the Gore slate to Washington immediately, he will be held in contempt of court.

✦ At 10 p.m. on December 17, Florida Attorney General Robert Butterworth (a Democrat) holds a televised press conference, telling the public that he has officially advised Governor Bush that he must comply with the Florida Supreme Court's order immediately. Governor Bush is advised by the state's election law specialists that he need not comply with the order, as he is entitled to a full hearing if an attempt is made to hold him in contempt of court, and the Florida Supreme Court has no practical means of enforcing a contempt order against him. But his political advisors tell him that if he ignores the court order, it will appear that he is trying to steal the election for his brother. At 11 p.m., Governor Bush announces that he has complied with the court order by sending the Gore slate to the National Archivist, but on the advice of the state's election law specialists he has not withdrawn the previously-filed Bush slate. Instead he has attached a letter to the Gore slate explaining that he is submitting it only because of the court order, and that as the state officer designated in the Electoral Count Act to make the official designation of the electors, he stands by the Bush slate which he filed officially and in accordance with the ECA on December 11. He adds that he has been advised that under ECA §5, the Bush slate he submitted on December 11 is "conclusive" and cannot be challenged, and that it is his duty as Florida's chief executive to avoid the disenfranchisement of the state's law-abiding voters which might result from withdrawal of the "conclusive" December 11th slate.

✦ On December 18, the official meeting date for the Electoral College, the electors actually meet and cast their votes in their home states, as in all past presidential elections. It is now apparent that there are two slates of Florida electors, and that under ECA §15, the question of which slate will cast Florida's crucial 25 votes must be decided by Congress, both houses of which must agree on which electors' votes were "regularly given." This sends the lawyers for both sides scrambling to study the legislative history of the ECA, which was enacted in 1887 with the goal of avoiding deadlocks like the 1876 Hayes-Tilden dispute over duplicate electoral slates.

✦ The media inundates the airwaves and the Internet with expert opinions from law professors, election law

specialists, and historians, who give widely varying interpretations of the Electoral Count Act of 1887. Ignored
for the 113 years since Hayes-Tilden in which there were
no deadlocked elections, it is now seen as a monstrosity,
the end product of 11 years of political haggling between
partisan legislators, with little or no attention to workable
decision procedures. Many commentators complain that
sections 2, 5, and 15 are at war with each other, each one
appearing to allow a different slate of electors to take prece-
dence, with no effective criteria mandating a final selection.
They point out that key terms like "regularly given" are
not defined in the act or in any court decision. "Too
many cooks" says one editorial writer. Another describes
the act as the typical product of multiple authors gone
wild, likening it to the old definition of a camel: "a horse
designed by a committee."

✦ ECA §15 provides that the dispute will be submitted to
Congress when it meets in the January following the election, and therefore refers to the incoming 107th Congress
which will take office on January 3, 2001. The Republicans
controlled both houses of the outgoing 106th Congress,
and they retained control of the House by a margin of
223 to 212. But the new Senate will be evenly divided, a
flat 50-50, with the tie-breaking 51st vote held by none
other than the vice president, Al Gore, who is scheduled to
remain in that office until his term expires on January 20,
more than two weeks after the new Congress is sworn in.

✦ As provided in ECA §15, the two houses of the new
Congress meet jointly at 1 p.m. on January 6, 2001,
presided over by Vice President Al Gore, to record and
make official the results of the Electoral College voting.
When the tellers open the certificates of electoral votes sent
in by the 50 state governors, they report that there are two
sets of Florida electors. Objections are made by House and
Senate Republicans to Gore's Florida slate, and by House
and Senate Democrats to the Bush slate. This requires the
two houses to meet separately and to independently decide
which slate is "regularly given" and therefore is entitled
to cast Florida's 25 electoral votes. The joint session is
adjourned, to be reconvened after each house has voted.

The media and the public are bewildered by the prospect
that the two houses will not be able to agree on one Florida
slate, particularly because the ECA offers no hint of what
is meant by votes that are "regularly given." In a final grand
flourish, ECA §15 purports to unveil the guiding principle for settling the dispute by specifying that "if the two
Houses shall disagree in respect of the counting of such
votes, then, and in that case, the votes of the electors whose
appointment shall have been certified by the executive of
the State, under the seal thereof, shall be counted"—the
difficulty being, of course, that *both* Florida slates were
necessarily certified under seal by Governor Jeb Bush.

✦ It turns out that there is one clear, unequivocal provision
of the ECA, §17, which limits debate on the disputed electoral slates to two hours in each house, with each Senator
and Representative permitted to speak no more than
five minutes. (Some observers comment that this provision is undoubtedly the result of the legislators' appetites
for debate being satiated by the 11 years it took to enact
the ECA.) Denny Hastert, the Republican Speaker of the
House, invokes this rule and quickly brings to a floor vote
in the House a resolution declaring that the Bush slate
of electors is the one that is "regularly given" because it
was regularly adopted by the Florida state legislature in
accordance with ECA §2 when the public election failed to
determine the winner by the December 12th Safe Harbor
deadline; because the Florida governor regularly submitted
it by December 12 and it thereby became "conclusive"
pursuant to the Safe Harbor provision, ECA §5; and
because the Gore slate was not "regularly given" due to
gross irregularities in the new rules written by the Florida
Supreme Court after the election. This resolution passes
by a straight party vote of 223 to 212, and at 4:30 p.m. on
January 6 Speaker Hastert announces that the House of
Representatives has declared Bush the winner.

✦ The situation in the Senate is more complicated. Al Gore
is faced with a dilemma. At best, he can force a vote and
achieve a 51-to-50 "victory" by casting his own vote to
break the tie. But what would that accomplish? It would
leave him tied with Bush at one house apiece, with no

way of breaking the deadlock, since ECA §15 peters out
with the failure of the two houses to agree. Gore would
be blamed for using his vote to plunge the nation into the
anarchy of a vacant White House, with House Speaker
Hastert first in line to fill the vacancy on January 20. The
candidates and their parties would be right back where
they were in 1876. At least Hayes and Tilden had some
basis for reaching an agreement, albeit one which traded
the White House for removal of federal troops from the
South in order to open the way for Jim Crow segregation.
What could Gore offer Bush, or vice versa—some meaningless cabinet posts?

✦ When the Senate convenes on January 6 to proceed under
ECA §15, the Republican leaders immediately raise a point
of order. They seek a ruling that Vice-President Gore and
Senator Joe Lieberman, his running mate, be disqualified
from voting since both are candidates—a ruling that would
leave the Republicans in a position to carry the Senate
vote by 50 to 49. When Gore rules against this request, it is
presented as a resolution and voted down by 51 to 50, the
deciding votes being those of Gore and Lieberman. The
Bush forces, having achieved a public relations victory by
forcing Gore to appear to be abusing his office, let it be
known that if Gore and Lieberman do not reconsider and
disqualify themselves, they will take this apparent conflict
of interest to the body empowered to finally determine the
meaning of a federal statute (the ECA): the Supreme Court
of the United States.

✦ Meanwhile, behind the scenes, Senate leaders of both
parties thrash out a plan to appoint a select committee of
12 Senators (six from each party) to conduct hearings on
the question of which Florida slate was elected by votes
"regularly given." All the senators are aware that forcing
the issue to a vote will accomplish nothing but paralysis of
the government. They don't expect the select committee to
achieve a solution, but they savor the large audiences that
the televised hearings will draw, as well as some breathing
space in which to seek an agreement before the problem
reaches the tipping point: the mandatory change of the
presidency on January 20. Gore, still impaled on the horns

of the dilemma, goes along with the select committee plan, hoping it will preserve his aura of statesmanship and buy enough time for development of a solution.

✦ On January 8, the Senate select committee begins hearing testimony of election experts from both sides. Bush's experts claim that the original Bush slate filed on December 11th is incontestable under ECA §5, the Safe Harbor provision which was adopted to avoid recurrence of the Hayes-Tilden Electoral College deadlock by giving the states a method of eliminating challenges at the source. They say it was designed to encourage each state to file a conclusive slate six days before the meeting of the Electoral College. Gore's experts counter that §5 makes a slate submitted by December 12 conclusive only if it is the result of a "final determination of any controversy or contest." They argue that since the contest was still raging in the Florida courts on December 12, §5's "conclusive" provision could not possibly apply. Bush's experts counter with §2, which unconditionally permits the state legislature to appoint the electors if—after the election—the state "has failed to make a choice on the day prescribed by law." They insist that the "day prescribed by law" was December 12, pointing to language to that effect in the Florida Supreme Court's Bush/Gore decisions and the unequivocal adoption of that date by Gore's own Florida lawyers. They maintain that Florida's legislature and courts clearly opted for the state to take advantage of the Safe Harbor provision (requiring filing with the National Archivist by December 12) in order to assure that Florida's electoral votes would be protected from the kind of challenges that now threaten to disqualify them.

✦ The televised hearings roll on from January 8 through January 18, bewildering and exhausting the public. Many Americans are beginning to wonder whether they are living in a banana republic. It quickly becomes apparent that the senators performing on television are dealmakers rather than truth-seekers. The select committee is not a court and has no effective rules or procedures for deciding the statutory issue of which electoral votes were "regularly given," or the disputes about such legal issues as Florida's adoption of the Safe Harbor date, whether ECA §2 trumps ECA §5, and the effects of the Florida Supreme Court's orders directing Governor Bush to withdraw the previously certified Bush slate. Both sides produce witnesses who testify to intimidation or improper influencing of the local Florida election officials who examined and judged the disputed ballots. The Gore forces present testimony that paints Jeb Bush and Katherine Harris as corrupt politicians who plotted to steal the election. Bush again threatens to take the legal issues to the U.S. Supreme Court, which now clearly has sole jurisdiction because the Florida courts have completed their constitutional functions and the ongoing dispute is focused solely on the meaning of a federal statute (the ECA) enacted pursuant to the powers granted to Congress in the U.S. Constitution.

✦ Some of Gore's advisors suggest that they should attempt to have Florida's 25 electoral votes thrown out completely, which would give Gore a final margin of 266 to 246 in the Electoral College. But Gore's election lawyers advise against such a move because the 12th Amendment requires "a majority of the whole number of Electors appointed," and no court has ever ruled on what that "majority" means: would it be a majority of all 537 electors, or a majority of the 512 non-Florida electors whose votes were counted? If a majority of the entire Electoral College were required, throwing out Florida's electoral votes would result in a failure to achieve the necessary majority, which under the 12th Amendment would take the Senate out of the picture and give the House of Representatives the sole power to decide the election— i.e., a clean Bush victory. Even if the Democrats somehow managed to bring the requirement down to the lesser majority, the resultant Gore Electoral College victory would quickly wind up in the U.S. Supreme Court, with the odds against the Court construing the 12th Amendment as the Gore forces desired. The proponents of eliminating the Florida electors argue that the Supreme Court would not intercede because disputes about the workings of Congress are political rather than legal questions. They also suggest that even if it doesn't work, putting this idea on the table gives Gore a little more bargaining power if a Hayes-Tilden type of agreement is negotiated. But in the end Gore decides it is risky and hyper-technical, and the idea is dropped.

✦ A prospective Republican end-run play is leaked to the media. It goes like this: On January 20 (two days from now) the terms of President Clinton and Vice-President Gore expire, leaving a vacancy in the White House which (because there is no vice-president) must be filled according to the Presidential Succession Act of 1947. First on the succession list is the speaker of the House, Denny Hastert of Illinois, who must resign his seat in the House and his job as speaker in order to qualify. Since Illinois Governor George Ryan is a Republican and he promises to reappoint Hastert to the House when the smoke clears, Denny agrees to be sworn in as president. One of his first official acts is to exercise his powers under the 25th Amendment to appoint George W. Bush vice-president. The appointment requires approval by a majority of both houses. The House quickly approves, leaving it to the Senate, which now has only 100 votes, with no vice-president to break the tie. At that point, President Hastert is presiding over a skeleton government, without the benefit of the customary transition procedures. He is unable to fill vacant cabinet posts and other key positions because competent executives are not willing to leave their civilian jobs for what might be only a few days or weeks. The Republicans float rumors that many government services (including Social Security and Medicare payments) will soon be delayed, and there are real concerns about the continuity needed to maintain national security. The major blame for this looming crisis falls upon the 50 Democratic senators who are standing in the way of Bush's confirmation as vice-president. The Republican plotters believe that this would create irresistible pressure on the Democratic senators—particularly the dozen or more with serious future presidential ambitions—to step forward and cast the one vote needed to restore the nation to sanity. Those senators would be inundated with demands from their constituents to break the deadlock. Pressure would build for a unanimous Senate confirmation, or a Gore concession, or both. As soon as Bush is confirmed as vice-president, Hastert will resign, returning to the House speakership as a national hero when Bush takes over the White House. Bush will then appoint Dick Cheney vice-president, and both houses will quickly vote to confirm him.

✦ On January 18, an obscure lawyer working as a volunteer for the Gore campaign, who has been trying to speak with the candidate for two weeks, is finally given an audience. The young woman presents a fresh idea, reminding Gore that all his present game plans ignore the strongest point in his favor: his winning margin of 500,000 in the popular vote. She suggests that Gore file suit in the U.S. District Court for the District of Columbia, asking that court to declare the Electoral Count Act unconstitutional because of its vagueness and lack of due process, defects which can result only in thwarting the will of the voting public without producing a legally tenable election result. This would be a three-judge court, as required when the constitutionality of legislation is challenged. If the judges strike down the ECA as unconstitutional, then Gore's lawyers ask them to act as a court of equity to fashion a remedy for the emergency that threatens to destroy the election process. That remedy would be simple, effective, and eminently equitable: declare Gore the winner based on his clear victory in the popular vote. After all, the election is about which candidate the American people want to be their president. It could be a narrow decision, a one-of-a-kind remedy limited to situations like this when the Electoral College system has broken down.

✦ Gore's senior election lawyers reject this suggestion as a hare-brained scheme, a shot in the dark that has little or no chance of working even in a sympathetic lower court. Even if by some miracle the lower court bought it, the three-judge court statute makes such cases appealable directly to the Supreme Court, where Gore would have no chance of upholding such a revolutionary decision. Gore asks his senior election lawyers if they have a better idea. They admit they have nothing more promising than to press behind the scenes for a Hayes-Tilden type agreement which will either give Gore the presidency or at least maintain his viability as a future candidate.

✦ As the clock ticks on through the night of January 18, both candidates avoid public statements while their representatives continue marathon negotiations for a Hayes-Tilden compromise. Bush's advisors tell him that he should not consider any compromise that would put Gore in the White House, because the Bush team has all the leverage, with one of the two houses in the bag and the 285-pound Speaker Denny Hastert poised to run interference all the way into the Oval Office. The pressure on Gore mounts as he considers his options: Take what he can get from the negotiations and concede the election while he can still emerge looking like a patriotic statesman? Deadlock Congress by forcing the Senate to a final 51-to-50 vote, and face personal responsibility for propelling the nation into anarchy? File suit to void the Electoral Count Act, or find some other way of exploiting his nearly forgotten victory in the popular vote?…

———————

This is not the only way that these events might have played out if the Supreme Court had not made Bush the winner, but nobody has come up with a more logical or convincing scenario. If the Electoral Count Act nightmare had been allowed to unfold, a public outcry would have arisen for a swift, effective, authoritative solution by the most respected institution in our government— the U.S. Supreme Court. Many observers thought that the Court's unanimous December 4th decision vacating the Florida Supreme Court's extension of the deadline for manual recounts was designed to give the Florida justices a face-saving way to end the litigation without further federal-state confrontation. But when a 4-to-3 majority of the Florida Supreme Court chose to ignore that message and opened the gates to another Hayes-Tilden crisis, the U.S. Supreme Court's five-justice majority took on the thankless task of deciding a presidential election, knowing that whichever way they finally ruled, they would incur the displeasure of at least 50 million Americans who had taken the trouble to vote for the loser.

In doing so, the majority justices exposed the Court to the charge that the decision awarding the election to Bush was a partisan political act rather than a principled application of the Rule of Law. That charge was made by many media commentators and by the overwhelming majority of law professors who expressed their opinions. Their negative views were based largely on the apparent hypocrisy of the majority justices: although they most often championed state's rights over expansion of federal sovereignty, this time they reversed course and abandoned their principled positions on the sharing of power between the state and federal governments (Federalism) by overruling a state supreme court's interpretation of its own state's statutes. There were dire predictions that this decision, widely labeled as unprincipled and politicized, would destroy the public's faith in the Court and thereby threaten its future role in the three-branch government.

The Public's Reaction to the Supreme Court Decision

In fact, the public was little concerned with the intellectual niceties of Federalism or whether the decision was consistent with the Court's prior holdings on state/federal powers. The Florida election laws had become a national rather than a state issue to most Americans because the Florida vote count proved to be the absolute deciding point of the national election. The real life 36-day legal battle had all but exhausted the public's patience, as Al Gore sensed accurately when he made decisions to pull some of the punches his lawyers wanted him to throw. The public simply wanted a quick and authoritative ending of the protracted post-election brawling. Its reaction to the Court's December 12th decision was more like a huge sigh of relief than a denunciation of inconsistent positions on Federalism. We can only imagine how sharply the public's impatience would have escalated if the Supreme Court had not intervened and we had been forced to stagger through the Electoral Count Act's hall of mirrors in the above bullet-point scenario. The opinion polls show clearly that the Court's intervention did not diminish its high standing in the minds of the public.

For example, the Gallup News Service reported on December 22, 2000, that most Americans felt "that the Supreme Court was the best institution to make a final decision to resolve the controversy in Florida—much more so than the Florida Supreme Court, the Florida legislature, or even the U.S. Congress." The Gallup Poll series measuring the public's trust and confidence in the Supreme Court showed a 75 percent favorable view (combination of "great deal" and "fair amount" of trust and confidence) in July 2000, and a 74 percent favorable view in the September 2001 poll, the first one taken after the December 2000 decision in *Bush v. Gore*. A later Gallup poll completed in September 2009 showed that 76 percent of the American people had a great deal or a fair amount of trust in the judicial branch headed by the Supreme Court, as opposed to 61 percent for the executive branch headed by the president and 45 percent for the legislative branch consisting of the House and the Senate. Other professional polls showed similar results, and confirmed that the public consistently places much more trust and confidence in the Supreme Court than in Congress or the president.

The Court's reluctance to decide electoral disputes is reflected in the majority's opinion of December 12, where they called the case their "unsought responsibility" and concluded, "Our consideration is limited to the present circumstances, for the problem of equal protection in election processes generally presents many complexities." Yet, because the judicial branch is part of the political system governing the nation and its judges are appointed and confirmed by politicians, it is impossible to keep politics entirely out of the judicial process. Probably the best we can do to maintain judicial independence is more of what we are trying to do now: take great care in selecting federal judges; put them on the bench for life so that they are not answerable to politicians; and prohibit them from all political activities. The laborious ritual of dragging judicial nominees through FBI investigations and televised Senate hearings is an indispensable part of this process. It pays off in the inability of the politicians who appoint judges to control or even predict how they will decide future cases; e.g., Republican President Eisenhower's lament that his appointment of Republican Earl Warren as chief justice was the worst mistake of his eight years in the White House.

That is not to imply that the political source of the judge's nomination will have no effect on how he or she decides cases. Justice Stephen Breyer made this point in a 1998 speech about the Supreme Court:

> Politics in our decision-making process does not exist. By politics, I mean Republicans versus Democrats, is this a popular action or not, will it help certain individuals to be elected?…Personal ideology or philosophy is a different matter….

> Judges appointed by different presidents of different political parties may have different views about the interpretation of the law and its relation to the world…. I think the Constitution foresees such differences, and results that reflect such differences are perfectly proper.

More recently, during a 2006 lecture, Justice Breyer (one of the four dissenters in *Bush v. Gore*) recalled that President Eisenhower was forced to send U.S. Army paratroopers to Arkansas to enforce a Supreme Court desegregation order. Breyer continued:

> Many people were deeply upset with the Court's decision in *Bush v. Gore*. And though that case has spawned many assessments of the Court's decision, I have yet to read about the need for paratroopers. Following the trajectory of the Rule of Law in the United States reveals that we have now arrived at the point where people will follow decisions even if they disagree with them. In many other countries, people do not share such reverence for the law.

Because the deficiencies of the Electoral Count Act made an orderly Congressional solution impossible, the 2000 Florida deadlock required a court to decide the election. The U.S. Supreme Court majority's choice was a bitter pill for millions of Americans to swallow, but handing the choice over to a

4-to-3 majority of the Florida Supreme Court would have been even less palatable to the American people, as the public opinion polls show. The public's high regard for the U.S. Supreme Court made its decision acceptable. Al Gore himself set the tone in his gracious concession speech, pointing out that the long and difficult controversy was "resolved, as it must be resolved, through the honored institutions of our democracy." He continued:

> Now the United States Supreme Court has spoken. Let there be no doubt: while I strongly disagree with the court's decision, I accept it. I accept the finality of this outcome, which will be ratified next Monday in the Electoral College. And tonight, for the sake of our unity as a people and the strength of our democracy, I offer my concession.

In my view, the main lesson of *Bush v. Gore* is that above all, the public expects the Supreme Court to make decisions that are best for the country, especially when difficult decisions are needed to deal with divisive problems that the politically-polarized elected branches have failed to solve—problems like school segregation, abortion rights, obstruction of justice in the White House, a deadlocked presidential election, and potential curtailment of civil rights caused by overreaction to threats of terrorism. In such cases, the public will support the judicial solution even if the Court finds it necessary to depart from strict adherence to past decisions, or to get involved in politics, or to reach out creatively to fashion remedies, as in *Brown v. Board of Education of Topeka*, and even as in *Bush v. Gore*.

In the end, only the Supreme Court can decide such polarizing issues in a way that satisfies the American people's demand for the appearance of a functioning Constitution based on Separation of Powers with Checks and Balances. Pulitzer-prize-winning author Richard Kluger, a non-lawyer, puts it this way:

> It is to these insulated nine men, then, that the nation has increasingly brought its most vexing social and political problems. They come in the guise of private disputes between only the litigating parties, but everybody understands that this is a legal fiction and merely a convenient political device.... In no other way has the nation contrived to frame these problems for a definitive judgment that applies to a vast land, a varied people, a whole age.

Historian James MacGregor Burns is an implacable opponent of the extraordinary powers exercised by the nine unelected, life-tenured Supreme Court justices. In his 2009 book, *Packing the Court*, he advocates curtailment of these powers, even by presidential defiance of court orders if necessary. Yet even Professor Burns was moved to comment on the public's acceptance of the Supreme Court's intervention in *Bush v. Gore*:

> There was no explosion of court-curbing proposals as controversial decisions had provoked in the past. There were no marches on Washington. Liberal scholars assailed the decision, as did many conservatives. "Desirable result aside," wrote political scientist and Bush backer John J. Dilulio, Jr., "it is bad constitutional law," an expression of "judicial imperialism." And yet, public confidence in the Supreme Court was remarkably unshaken, even, after a dip in the immediate aftermath, among Democrats.

Speculating on the reasons for this apparent anomaly, Burns notes that some political scientists suggest it was caused by the public's unusual exposure to the "legitimizing symbols" of the court—"the marble temple, the high bench, the purple curtain, the black robes"—which was presented to the public "by a media that spoke of the justices with the greatest deference and respect."

Richard Kluger wondered aloud why "the American people, as rambunctious and criminally inclined as any on earth, have come to hold their Supreme Court in such reverential regard." Perhaps, he thought, "Americans simply wish to think that the Court, as the nation's arbiter of last resort, is composed of men both wise and incorruptible in a world where men possessing abundant deposits of either quality are rare"—or perhaps the Court's mystique is the result of lawyers having "had an extraordinary degree of power in American life from the beginning" and, as Kluger reminds us, lawyers "designed the nation and saw that it worked."

University of Georgia History Professor Peter Charles Hoffer takes an even broader view of the American public's "fascination with law." He writes:

> …we are a nation of laws that work because we expect law to perform vital functions for us at our most perilous moments. When we are in most need of solutions to critical problems, we turn to law.

Whether this public acceptance is based on wishful thinking or it confirms that Founding Lawyer John Marshall actually raised judicial review above the level of pure partisan politics, *Bush v. Gore* tells us that the judicial branch is still the cornerstone of the Government of Laws.

———

I hope this extended detour into the past has made it clear that the United States has a Government of Laws based on the Founding Lawyers' vision of Separation of Powers with Checks and Balances.

The history we have examined in these first seven chapters deals mainly with governmental actions. The Constitution's Checks and Balances protect the nation as a whole against tyranny, coups d'état, and usurpation of power by the three branches of government. But they do not protect individual citizens from oppression by superior forces, whether governmental, business, or wealthy individuals. While all Americans benefit from the Government of Laws, the average citizen has little direct contact with government, and little occasion to directly exercise constitutional rights during everyday life.

What, then, is the significance of the Government of Laws in everyday American life?

PART TWO

Americans' Unique Access to Their Courts

Chapter Eight

Checks and Balances in Everyday American Life

The twentieth-century cases which we are about to consider demonstrate that the legal system which was nurtured by the Government of Laws has evolved into the American Rule of Law, which extends beyond government to the everyday lives of private citizens. The ready access which American citizens now have to their courts provides protection against oppression by superior forces, whether governmental or private. Thus the American legal system furnishes a citizens' counterpart of the Separation of Powers with Checks and Balances upon which our Government of Laws is built—a unique, individually-exercised bundle of rights, even more effective at the personal level than the right to vote.

Here we must distinguish between criminal and civil law. Citizens of other developed democracies have access to their courts in criminal cases, since they can only be punished for crimes after being tried and found guilty in courts which are designed to follow fair procedures and are not subject to manipulation by tyrants. Qualified observers may conclude that the American criminal law system is stronger than those of some other nations in such areas as protection against self-incrimination and police coercion, access to competent legal representation, presumption of innocence, and trial by jury. Others may argue that these American practices tilt the system in favor of the accused, and point out other dysfunctions which may contribute to high crime rates and chaotic criminal courts. Still others may decry the unfair advantages gained by wealthy Americans accused of crimes in their access to more effective lawyers, investigators, and expert witnesses than those available to the non-affluent. But that's not the subject of this book. My claim of American superiority in adherence to the Rule of Law is based entirely on unique access to justice in the civil courts.

Most Americans (fortunately) live through their lives without involvement in the criminal courts. They are far more likely to require access to the civil courts, or to be directly affected by decisions in civil cases to which they were not parties themselves. Most of the landmark cases we have considered in the preceding chapters were brought in civil courts to establish or enforce individual legal rights. William Marbury hauled Secretary of State James Madison into court in a civil action, seeking to force the reluctant Jefferson administration to deliver the commission which confirmed his appointment as a judge. Dred Scott brought a civil action against the widow of his owner, seeking an adjudication that he was no longer a slave. Chambermaid Elsie Parrish sued her former employer, West Coast Hotel Co., for back wages she claimed were due to her under the state minimum wage law. Youngstown Sheet & Tube Company and the nation's other steel manufacturers filed suit against Secretary of Commerce Raymond Sawyer to regain possession of their mills, which Sawyer had seized on orders from President Truman. Oliver Brown, a railroad welder, sued his local Topeka school board, seeking to open the doors of the local white schoolhouse to his daughter. James Meredith, a college student, filed a civil suit against the trustees who were arbitrarily denying him admission to the University of Mississippi. George W. Bush filed a civil action against Al Gore to prevent the Florida courts from proceeding with vote recounts which might have deprived him of the presidency.

Thus, whether they were job-seekers, slaves, chambermaids, welders, students, presidential candidates, or steel manufacturers, they all were able to use their access to the civil courts to establish and enforce their legal rights. Each of their cases had profound effects on the lives of millions of ordinary Americans. Could they have done this in other developed democracies, or anywhere outside of the United States?

The remaining chapters will spell out the answer.

George Washington's Vision of the National Character

As we have seen, George Washington set about "to establish a national character of our own" in his first inaugural address, and he breathed life into that vision by presiding over the creation of a constitutional republic, a Government of Laws which was firmly based on Separation of Powers with Checks and Balances. The classic appraisal of how President Washington's vision played out in the nineteenth century is the remarkable book by Alexis de Tocqueville, *Democracy in America*, still widely used in American classrooms 175 years after its initial French printing of 500 copies.

Tocqueville, a young French lawyer from an aristocratic family, traveled through the United States in 1831 on a French government assignment to appraise the American penal system. During his nine-month journey, he broadened his mission to a penetrating study of the great American experiment in democracy. The resulting book has been hailed as the most perceptive commentary on American character and institutions ever written. Some of his observations help us to understand how the Rule of Law developed in America.

Tocqueville marveled at the unique judicial review power given to the Supreme Court justices, praising its effectiveness in guarding against "the tyranny of political assemblies" which had destroyed earlier experiments in democracy. He also commented that the authority which Americans bestowed on lawyers, and the lawyers' influence on government, "today constitute the most powerful barriers against the excesses of democracy." Beyond the influence of law and lawyers on government, he observed the profound effects of law ("the legal spirit") on the everyday lives of Americans:

> Thus the legal spirit, born in law schools and courtrooms, gradually spreads beyond their walls. It infiltrates all of society, as it were, filtering down to the lowest ranks, with the result that in the end all the people acquire some of the habits and tastes of the magistrates.

He perceived the law in America as the leveler between the rich and the poor, exactly the opposite of its function in European nations:

> In the United States, therefore, one does not find large numbers of perpetually agitated people who see the law as their natural enemy and whose view of it is inevitably clouded by fear and suspicion. On the contrary, it is impossible to miss the fact that all classes place great confidence in their country's laws, for which they feel a kind of paternal affection.... Because the European hierarchy of power is stood on its head in America, the rich find themselves in a position analogous to that of the poor in Europe; it is often they who distrust the law.

Tocqueville was impressed with the efficiency and importance of juries in civil (as well as criminal) trials:

> The civil jury has served the American magistracy as the primary means of imbuing even the lowermost ranks of society with what I have called the legal spirit.

Henry Steele Commager is among the leading historians who have sought to update Tocqueville's observations to the twentieth century. In his 1950 book, *The American Mind*, Professor Commager writes:

> Yet if the American displayed a cavalier disrespect for law and abiding suspicion of lawyers, he venerated Law. It was his pride that every American was equal before the Law, that no one—not even the highest official—was immune from the operation of the Law…. Certainly nowhere else in the world was law more assiduously studied; nowhere else did lawyers play so important a role in politics or in daily affairs.

Citing Tocqueville's appraisal that the "the judicial bench and bar" constitute the American aristocracy, Commager continues:

> The dignity, prosperity, and influence of the legal profession is one of the most striking phenomena of American culture. Surely in no other country have lawyers occupied a comparable position or played a comparable role.

Richard Reeves, winner of many journalism awards, undertook the definitive updating of Tocqueville by retracing the Frenchman's travels 150 years later. Working from Tocqueville's notes and interviewing hundreds of representative Americans, Reeves published his findings in the 1982 book, *American Journey*. In Cincinnati, where Tocqueville had interviewed two Ohio lawyers who would become Supreme Court justices, Reeves discussed Tocqueville's views on American law with U.S. Supreme Court Justice Potter Stewart. When Reeves asked Stewart (an Eisenhower appointee) how Tocqueville's account compared with the contemporary legal scene, Stewart replied that the courts had become even more important in everyday life:

> Now there are more rights and new laws. Poverty law and environmental law were never heard of when I began. Now they are needed to provide the economic opportunity that the frontier [used to provide]…. The courts became strong because of a default of the other branches of government.

Reeves interviewed many others who agreed with Stewart, and concluded that Tocqueville's "legal spirit" was stronger than ever in America, providing "forced fairness" through equality of access to the courts. Reeves quoted Michigan Supreme Court Justice G. Mennen Williams, a former Democratic governor, on the proliferation of lawsuits that was "overloading the courts":

We should be proud of that overload. Americans are exercising rights they never had before. Americans are freer. America is more democratic.

In the opening paragraph of *The American Mind*, the book in which he seeks to define the American character, Professor Commager tells us that the American character "all but eludes description." That did not prevent him from valiantly trying for another 400 pages, but for purposes of our examination of the Rule of Law, we need not take on so demanding a task. We can probably agree on a few American characteristics (noted by Tocqueville, Commager, Reeves, and other historians) which help to explain the unique position of law in our society.

1. We are argumentative

There's an old story about Talmudic scholars, who in some versions become Jesuit priests or Buddhist monks. An argument is raging within their community about the rules of religious intermarriage, giving rise to widely differing interpretations of Scripture and tradition. The scripture is clear enough as far as it goes, but there is no consensus on how the scripture was traditionally applied in the past. Finally a committee of scholars is appointed to call upon the oldest and wisest scholar, the modern equivalent of the Oracle of Delphi. Treating him with great respect, they explain their differences and ask him, "What is the tradition?"

"The tradition," replies the wise man, "is that we argue about it!"

So it has gone with Americans, from the time of the Constitutional Convention through the war in Iraq. Historian Joseph Ellis notes that the Constitution "enshrined an argumentative process in which no such thing as a last word would ever be uttered." We were the first nation to guarantee freedom of speech, press, and assembly, and remain the most vigilant in preserving those freedoms today. Barack Obama expressed a similar idea in his 2006 book, *The Audacity of Hope*:

> ...the genius of Madison's design is not that it provides us with a fixed blueprint for action, the way a draftsman plots a building's construction. It provides us with a framework and with rules, but fidelity to these rules will not guarantee a just society or assure agreement on what's right.... What the framework of our Constitution can do is organize the way by which we argue about our future.

This contentious spirit finds expression in the ever-expanding use of civil courts to settle our major arguments peacefully and fairly. We are sometimes derided as the Litigious Society, but the critics rarely undertake to explain how these arguments could be decided peacefully and fairly without access to the courts.

2. *We are distrustful of governmental authority*

The United States is a nation of immigrants, most of whom were refugees from oppression by governmental or religious authorities. We come by our distrust of authority naturally, as reflected in the very short terms (usually one year) of elected officials in our early years, and the exquisite care taken to construct and maintain Separation of Powers with Checks and Balances throughout our history.

This accounts in part for our individualism—our reluctance to depend upon government to provide for our welfare unless there is no other solution. In my view, this traditional distrust played a major role in the failure of socialism—government ownership of the means of production—to take root in the United States, despite its many electoral victories in other democracies during the Depression-riddled twentieth century. It also helps to explain the American preference for individual remedies enforced in the courts rather than through blanket legislation or by administrative agencies which are likely to operate at the level of the lowest common denominator. In a 1999 Supreme Court decision, Justice Souter reminded us of "our deep-rooted historic tradition that everyone should have his own day in court."

Our national character also rebels against granting extensive power to large companies and wealthy people. Their money can often help them to obtain unfair advantages from legislators and government officials, and while it puts them in a better position to cope with legal problems than those less well off, it usually does not afford them the power to escape justice in the American courts.

3. *We are relatively optimistic*

Perhaps because of our youthfulness as a nation, our abundant natural resources, and our geographic position which makes military invasion unlikely, we are considered more optimistic than other developed democracies. We tend to think that bad situations can be fixed or at least improved. Witness the self-sealing rubber fuel tank, an American invention which gave early World War II U.S. fighter planes a crucial advantage over the faster, more maneuverable Japanese Zeros. A bullet in the fuel tank would usually cause the Zero to burn and explode in the air, whereas the American fuel tanks were designed to survive bullets by sealing off the damaged areas without igniting the fuel.

This philosophy was expressed by Chief Justice Earl Warren in a 1974 speech at Morehouse College: "The great virtue of our government is that the people can do something about it."

4. We pull for the underdog

We began our history as underdogs with a ragtag army of civilians which appeared incapable of seriously engaging the forces of the military and naval superpower, Great Britain. Much of the Constitution's Bill of Rights was specifically designed to protect the underdog against the majority and the power elite. Then came boatloads of immigrants carrying little but their humble clothing, their underdog status later symbolized by Ellis Island. The underdog was always an icon of American culture, lionized in writings like the dime novels of Horatio Alger which inspired millions of poor young boys with the vision that they could succeed if they worked hard.

This culture thrives today, reflected in the success of television programs like "American Idol" and Donald Trump's "The Apprentice," as well as Sylvester Stallone's endless film saga of the quintessential underdog, prize-fighter Rocky Balboa. In sports, teams like the Boston Red Sox and Chicago Cubs are perennial national favorites despite—or indeed because of—decades of exasperating failure. In politics, there is the enduring image of the underdog Harry Truman smiling broadly as he points to the premature headline of the *Chicago Daily Tribune*: "Dewey Defeats Truman."

In the legal system, the right to trial by jury assures the underdog that his case is likely to be judged fairly no matter how powerful the opponent is.

No doubt the people of other nations share some of these characteristics, but nowhere else are they embedded in the legal system to the extent that there is broad access to the courts to enforce individual legal remedies. Columbia Law Professor John Fabian Witt explains that "In the community of nation-states, the United States stands out as distinctively organized around law." Another leading legal historian, NYU Law Professor Bernard Schwartz, summarized the first two centuries of American law in these terms:

> The true American contribution to human progress has
> not been technology, economics, or culture; it has been
> the development of the notion of law as a check on power.
> American society has been dominated by law as has no
> other society in history. Struggles over power that in other
> countries have called forth regiments of troops in this
> country call forth battalions of lawyers.

To demonstrate this, let's take a familiar case, *Brown v. Board of Education of Topeka,* and see how Oliver Brown and his fellow plaintiffs would have fared in the courts of other developed democracies.

The Rule of Law According to Rolls-Royce

The Rolls-Royce dealership at 15 Berkeley Square in London is open to the public Monday through Friday, 9 a.m. to 6:30 p.m., and on Saturday by appointment. If you look like you can afford one of their cars, they will "arrange a test drive in our famously registered RRR 1 demonstrator." If you fancy the blue Phantom 4-door saloon (sedan) in the front of the showroom, and you don't need any custom-fitted extras, you can buy it for £219,950 (about $350,000) plus tax and delivery charges. Or if you prefer the red Phantom drophead coupe (convertible) you can drive it away for a minimum of £260,000 (about $420,000). Since Rolls-Royce is an equal opportunity purveyor, everyone in England has full access to its showrooms and its excellent products. All you need is the money to pay the price-tag. And so it is with the English Rule of Law.

English civil justice is a finely crafted product, deservedly admired as a great national tradition, and it works well for those who can afford it. But most English people—especially the millions in the middle class—cannot afford it and therefore are denied access to it.

It is unaffordable primarily because of the "Loser Pays" rule in effect since the 1607 Statute of Westminster: the losing party in civil litigation must pay the "costs"—legal fees and other expenses—of the winning party, as well as his own. (England will serve as our surrogate for the developed democracies, since all of them except the United States follow the Loser Pays rule.)

In the beginning, Loser Pays was a benign rule aimed at achieving complete justice by making whole the party found to be in the right, reimbursing the winner for all financial losses including the expenses of bringing or defending the suit. At that time civil litigation was largely confined to the wealthy, and was usually a short and not unduly expensive process which did not result in costs that were out of proportion to the amounts involved. But by the late decades of the nineteenth century, with the maturing of the Industrial Revolution, the railroads, and the trade unions, Loser Pays became a formidable obstacle to justice in England. For the middle-class wage earner or business owner, undertaking a lawsuit became a huge gamble. Even when you felt you were clearly in the right, if you lost the case, the combined burden of paying your own lawyers and those of the defendant would put everything you owned at risk—your savings, your business, even your home. You would literally be betting the farm on winning, in a game where the outcome is never a certainty.

Disputes that are serious enough to reach the stage of litigation usually have two sides to them, with some uncertainty as to exactly what evidence will be produced in court and how convincing it will be. Even cases which appear to be "open and shut" can be lost for unforeseeable reasons, such as a witness's faulty recollection or unimpressive demeanor, or a legal technicality arising from a forgotten document. By the late years of the twentieth century, the cost of litigation in England was so high that it often dwarfed the amount in controversy. Only the wealthy could readily afford to pay their own legal expenses, without considering the prospect of having to pay double that amount under Loser Pays. In fact, even the affluent are affected, as noted by Edward Solomons, director of legal services for London's Metropolitan Police:

> About halfway through many big damages cases, the litiga-
> tion becomes about the costs, not about the original issue,
> because neither party feels able (or may be able to afford)
> to withdraw, since this would mean paying both sides'
> costs, often more than was in dispute in the first place.

Companies and wealthy individuals involved in English litigation typically retain a prominent firm of solicitors (lawyers), at fees running between £500 and £1,000 ($800 to $1,600) per solicitor's hour. A team of two or three solicitors is assigned to investigate and prepare the case for trial by an equally pricey team of barristers (trial lawyers), headed by a leading barrister with the title of QC (for Queen's Counsel). The QC must always be assisted by a "junior" barrister who may well be fifty or sixty years old and is also quite expensive. In total, these legal teams often run up fees of £10,000 ($16,000) or more *per day*. In 2006, the *London Times* reported that the legal fees of the teams representing Sir Paul McCartney and his estranged wife Heather Mills in their divorce case were running at the rate of £15,000 ($24,000) per day for each side. A dramatic but not unusual example is the 2006 London trial of the "Da Vinci Code case."

Michael Baigent and Richard Leigh, two of the three authors of *The Holy Blood and the Holy Grail* (which came to be called "HBHG") sued Random House, publisher of Dan Brown's phenomenally successful novel, *The Da Vinci Code*, for copyright infringement. They claimed that Brown unlawfully appropriated the HBHG theory that Jesus and Mary Magdalene married and produced a child, with a secret society protecting their heirs against conspiratorial Catholic Church officials. Brown admitted that HBHG was one of the sources of his novel, but his lawyers argued that only HBHG's specific expression of the ideas, rather than the ideas themselves, are protected by copyright. The case was relatively simple, involving comparison of passages in the two books, and the fairly well-established legal boundaries of idea protection. The evidence was not nearly as complicated as that in thousands of cases which arise every year from disputes about shareholders' financial losses, environmental damage, or defective products. Yet, after the trial judge ruled that the ideas in HBHG were not protected by copyright law, and the Court of Appeal agreed, Baigent and Leigh were stuck with legal costs of $5,890,000—roughly half owed to their own lawyers and the rest to the lawyers for the winner, Random House.

Baigent and Leigh were able to assume the risk of paying those huge costs only because the publicity created by the trial propelled their 24-year-old book to the best-seller list. In fact, the trial judge mentioned in his decision that because both books were published by Random House, there were "suggestions that this action is nothing more than a collaborative exercise designed to maximize publicity for both books," noting that the sales of both books soared during the trial, with HBHG scoring a tenfold increase. Without the safety net of their greatly enhanced royalty payments, it would have made no financial sense for Baigent and Leigh to undertake such a lawsuit.

The ultimate Loser Pays horror story is the suit brought in London by supermodel Naomi Campbell against the *Daily Mirror*, alleging that the newspaper breached her confidentiality by publishing pictures of her leaving a drug treatment facility in 2001. The trial judge awarded her £3,500 in damages. The *Mirror* appealed to the Court of Appeal, which ruled in its favor, but Ms. Campbell appealed to the House of Lords (England's highest court until 2009), which reinstated the £3,500 damage award in 2004 by a vote of three to two. This left the *Mirror* responsible for all of Ms. Campbell's costs, which—when added to the fees of their own legal team—brought the newspaper's total legal bill to over £1 million. That costs/damages ratio of more than 285 to 1 is an aberration, but it is a routine matter in the English courts for the costs paid by the loser to far exceed the amount in controversy.

People in England who did not have the financial resources of the *Daily Mirror* have suffered financial ruin because of the Loser Pays rule, resulting in an inevitable middle-class revulsion against use of the courts to remedy grievances. The definitive statement on access to English civil justice was pronounced by Lord Patrick Devlin, a renowned twentieth-century barrister and legal philosopher who sat on England's highest court, the House of Lords. In 1979, when legal costs were considerably lower than in 2009 even after adjustment for inflation, Lord Devlin wrote:

> Lawsuits between ordinary citizens of limited means are so
> uncommon that it is difficult to find out anything about
> them. The main reason why they are uncommon is, I think,
> because the cost would be prohibitive.... Everyone knows,
> every lawyer particularly knows, that for the ordinary
> citizen…a lawsuit is quite out of the question.

Lord Devlin was referring to two aspects of costs: the fees of the claimant's own lawyers, and those of her opponents, which she would also have to pay if she did not win the case. In later chapters we shall consider the English efforts to deal with the costs of the claimant's own legal team through such devices as Legal Aid, conditional fees, and legal expense insurance. Here we focus on Loser Pays, which in itself constitutes an insurmountable barrier to justice for most English people, undiminished by such devices or by recent legislation aimed at reducing overall legal costs.

It is not surprising that in England the threat of ruinous costs is used to discourage the filing of lawsuits, regardless of how meritorious they might be. Tony Blair's Labour Party government was guilty of an egregious example of this in 2006, when an estimated 125,000 retired workers lost their life savings in failed pension schemes which the government had represented to the workers to be safe. Even though the Parliamentary Ombudsman found the government guilty of maladministration, the *London Times* reported:

LEGAL COSTS THREAT TO
PENSIONERS IN OMBUDSMAN CASE
The Government has threatened to pursue impoverished pensioners for massive legal costs if they challenge its decision to ignore the Parliamentary Ombudsman's ruling on pensions compensation.

Britain's constitution gives sovereignty—virtually unchecked governmental power—to Parliament. Here is how Parliament's official website explains it:

> Parliamentary sovereignty is a principle of the UK constitution. It makes Parliament the supreme legal authority in the UK, which can create or end any law. Generally, the courts cannot overrule its legislation and no Parliament can pass laws that future Parliaments cannot change. Parliamentary sovereignty is the most important part of the UK constitution.

In addition to its basic legislative power, the British Parliament exercises the executive power through cabinet ministers appointed by the party in control of Parliament. Although Britain supports separation of governmental powers in principle, for centuries the position of the Lord Chancellor challenged the credibility of that stance. Until the Constitutional Reform Act 2005 changed his functions, the Lord Chancellor served in all three branches of government. He was a member of the cabinet; he was the speaker of the House of Lords; and he was the nation's chief judicial officer, even appointing judges. The 2005 changes were enacted at least partially because of a need to demonstrate a more visible commitment to judicial independence and separation of powers.

Although the English courts are separate from Parliament, until October 2009 the highest court was one of the two houses of Parliament, the House of Lords. This judicial function was not exercised by the entire House of Lords, but by an Appellate Committee of 12 Lords of Appeal in Ordinary ("Law Lords") who usually sat in panels of five judges. Britain's Constitutional Reform Act 2005 established a new Supreme Court of the United Kingdom to replace the House of Lords as the highest court, effective in October of 2009. This removed the supreme judicial power from Parliament, but there is nothing in the statute creating the new Supreme Court which is designed to supply the type of judicial review power vested in the U.S. Supreme Court. Neither the new Supreme Court nor any other British court has the power to provide anything like the checks and balances against the legislative and executive branches exercised by the U.S. Supreme Court through judicial review.

This deficiency in checks and balances has a long history, noted by that keenest of observers, Alexis de Tocqueville, during his two trips to Britain in 1835 which followed his famous tour of the United States. He remarked upon the extraordinary concentration of power in Parliament, which alone has "the absolute right of government." His overall appraisal of the English legal system was nearly the polar opposite of his view that the American courts were the great levelers:

> There is not a country in the world where justice, that first
> need of peoples, is more the privilege of the rich.... The
> English have left the poor but two rights: that of obeying
> the same laws as the rich, and that of standing on an
> equality with them if they can obtain equal wealth.

Tocqueville's views echoed those of the renowned English philosopher Jeremy Bentham, a member of the English bar, who wrote in 1808 that the English civil justice system was closed to "all but a favored few, to whom a golden ticket opens the way," and that the "right to justice depends upon opulence."

In other words, the Rule of Law according to Rolls-Royce.

Britain relies heavily on welfare-state administrative agencies created by Parliament to furnish checks and balances in everyday life. The paucity of Separation of Powers with Checks and Balances in the British governmental structure is reflected in the traditional lack of broad citizen access to the civil courts, which has never been highly prized in Britain.

In the English legal system, Loser Pays is called "cost-shifting." In the United States, in the few instances in which it is applied, it is known as "fee-shifting." Its main function in England today is to restrict legal remedies to the privileged and the powerful, protecting the establishment against the financially-challenged underdog. It remains a staple of British justice regardless of which party is in power. As we shall see, the official reasons given for maintaining Loser Pays do not address the need for access to justice.

The U.S. Supreme Court rejected fee-shifting in one of its earliest decisions. In 1796, when the Court was meeting in Philadelphia's City Hall, it unanimously denied an attempt by the winning party in *Arcambel v. Wiseman* to collect $1,600 in "counsel fees." The Court held that "the general practice of the United States is in opposition" to the Loser Pays rule, thus enshrining what has become known as "the American Rule."

The American courts refer to fee-shifting as the English Rule, because it first arose in the courts of England (and Wales, which officially became part of England in 1746). Throughout this book, I use "English" when discussing a specific provision of English law, and "British" when referring to matters that apply throughout the United Kingdom, which consists of England, Wales, Scotland, and Northern Ireland. Fee-shifting could be called the British Rule, since it also prevails in the courts of Northern Ireland and Scotland, but to avoid confusion we'll stick to the conventional English Rule terminology.

According to University of Minnesota Law Professor Herbert Kritzer, editor of the *Legal Systems of the World* encyclopedia and a leading international authority on legal fees, "Outside the United States, some form of the English Rule is the norm." Thus it is appropriate for us to use English law as the surrogate for the other developed democracies.

Only in the United States are people free to make decisions about starting litigation without having to be concerned about paying the fees of the other side. In my view, a major reason for this dichotomy is that only in the United States was the principle of Separation of Powers with Checks and Balances anchored in a Government of Laws and carried over into everyday life through broad citizen access to the civil courts.

Every now and then, a winning American litigant tries to change the law by seeking to apply the English Rule of fee-shifting. It happened in 1967, when the Supreme Court reaffirmed the American Rule. Chief Justice Warren wrote in the opinion of the Court:

> In support of the American rule, it has been argued that
> since litigation is uncertain, one should not be penalized
> for merely defending or prosecuting a lawsuit, and that
> the poor might be unjustly discouraged from instituting
> actions to vindicate their rights if the penalty for losing
> included the fees of their opponents' counsel.

By "poor" the Supreme Court meant those not wealthy enough to risk having to pay the opponents' fees, i.e., the middle class. The truly poor are not concerned about that risk because assessment of such fees against them would be uncollectible and therefore meaningless. There are some exceptions to the American Rule, but they occur mostly in statutes designed to encourage private litigation thought to be in the public interest, casting claimant's lawyers in a role similar to that of bounty hunters without exposing claimants to fee-shifting. Examples of this one-way fee-shifting are the Civil Rights Act of 1964, the Clean Air Act, and the Americans with Disabilities Act.

The Effects of Fee-Shifting on Litigants Like Oliver Brown

If the United States had adopted the English fee-shifting rule, would we have ever heard of the case called *Brown v. Board of Education of Topeka?*

The only litigants who can ignore the financial impact of fee-shifting are those too rich or too poor to be concerned about paying the winner's legal fees. Neither Oliver Brown nor any of the other plaintiffs in the five school segregation cases decided under the consolidated title of *Brown v. Board of Education of Topeka* were too rich or too poor to care. In fact, Thurgood Marshall and his colleagues at the NAACP Legal Defense Fund (LDF) were determined to recruit African-American plaintiffs who were upstanding citizens—jobholders, taxpayers, and home owners. It would be an uphill battle even for such ideal plaintiffs to attack school segregation in the courts. If they were jobless, penniless, or homeless, with no demonstrable interest in the education of children, the courts could brush them aside as lacking legal standing to sue the local school boards.

Oliver Brown was a 32-year-old World War II veteran holding down a good job as a welder in the Santa Fe Railroad's Topeka repair depot. He served as an assistant pastor and sexton at St. John A.M.E., the leading black church in Topeka. He was married to the African-American beauty queen of his high school days, who lived with him and their three daughters in a five-room stone house which they owned. He was not a member of the NAACP, which the white community looked upon as a trouble-making organization of agitators. But he wanted to enroll his seven-year-old daughter Linda in the Sumner School for white children, which she could reach by walking three blocks through a peaceful neighborhood. She had been attending the all-black Monroe School, which required her to walk between train tracks for six blocks to catch the school bus. When the Sumner School refused to enroll her, Oliver Brown turned to local NAACP officials, who recruited him as the lead plaintiff in the Topeka segregation challenge.

The Legal Defense Fund's strategy for the attack on *Plessy v. Ferguson* called for them to recruit a total of at least a hundred Oliver Browns as plaintiffs in the suits to be brought in Kansas, South Carolina, Virginia, Delaware, and the District of Columbia. The LDF lawyers could not promise success, and indeed candor required them to inform all the plaintiffs that they had practically no chance to win in the lower courts. Their only hope was to get one or more cases to the U.S. Supreme Court (then headed by Chief Justice Fred Vinson, a Kentuckian) and pray for a miracle. The LDF could not point to any track record of success in the courts, and its total 1950 budget for desegregation cases throughout the country was $150,000. If the United States had adopted the fee-shifting rule, Thurgood Marshall would have been forced to tell Oliver Brown, "By the way, if we lose this case, you will be called upon to pay the legal fees and expenses of the school board, since the NAACP does not have the money to pay those fees for you." The amounts involved would have been high enough to convince all the responsible Oliver Browns that they could not afford to gamble their homes and life savings on this highly speculative lawsuit.

The LDF was able to recruit more than 150 plaintiffs for the school desegregation cases that reached the Supreme Court under the *Brown* title. Even without an American Loser Pays rule to keep them out of court, the school cases severely strained the LDF's meager resources. Marshall and the other LDF lawyers were working out of a cramped New York office in a seedy building near Times Square where they were constantly threatened with shutdowns of their telephone and electrical services due to nonpayment. They were helped by unpaid volunteer lawyers and scholars, but when those volunteers suggested that their voluminous research be computerized, the LDF was unable to come up with the $3,000 cost. Thus it is obvious that the chilling effects of fee-shifting would have stopped the school desegregation cases in their tracks, eliminating a glorious chapter in the history of the Rule of Law. Abner J. Mikva, former congressman, White House counsel, and federal appellate judge, puts it even more dramatically: "If the English Rule had been in effect here, none of the civil rights cases would have been brought. If they had lost, a single lawsuit would have wiped out their treasuries."

The American Rule against fee-shifting is consistent with our national character and the crucial role of the Rule of Law in our government and everyday life. Fee-shifting would eliminate as "quite out of the question" many lawsuits which seek to enforce legal remedies against powerful wrongdoers, or to establish new legal remedies which are even slightly outside the historical framework.

Brown was a remarkable piece of litigation, but there are legions of other landmark American civil cases which could never have been pursued in Britain or any other nation outside of the United States. We'll look at some examples in upcoming chapters. Here it will suffice to note that if the United States had adopted fee-shifting, millions of Americans would probably still be suffering from such scourges as the poisonous effects of tobacco, the sexual abuse of children by clergymen, the exploitation of elderly residents of nursing homes, and myriad forms of discrimination based on gender, age, ethnic origin, sexual orientation, or lack of wealth.

The Official Reasons Given for Fee-Shifting

The definitive statement of the reasons for retaining the centuries-old English Rule of fee-shifting (called "cost-shifting" there) was made by Lord Harry Woolf, then England's senior civil judge, when he conducted an intensive official review of the civil justice system beginning in 1994. Lord Woolf produced an interim report in 1995 and a final report in 1996, which paved the way for an extensive revamping of the civil justice system, culminating in the Access to Justice Act 1999. In his 1995 interim report, Lord Woolf wrote:

> The problem of cost is the most serious problem besetting our litigation system. It is directly related to access to justice. If litigation is too expensive, claimants will not proceed or will use alternative means of resolving disputes.

He recited the two main arguments for maintaining cost-shifting: it is fairer for the winner to be reimbursed, and "the rule deters unmeritorious litigation and encourages earlier settlement." He listed the arguments against the Loser Pays rule:

> ✦ It may deter meritorious as well as unmeritorious claims....

> ✦ It favours the wealthy litigant over the less wealthy....

> ✦ It can so increase the costs at stake that parties feel impelled to go on, thus making it impossible to reach a settlement.

Lord Woolf concluded that the arguments in favor of cost-shifting were stronger, noting "the phenomenon of the nuisance action" which in England was "probably less prevalent than in the United States" where there is no cost-shifting rule.

In his 1996 final report, he found that the majority of the public could not afford litigation; that the costs were out of proportion to the issues involved; and costs are so uncertain that the parties have difficulty in predicting their ultimate liability. He concluded:

> The adverse consequences which flow from the problems in
> relation to costs contaminate the whole civil justice system.
> Fear of costs deters some litigants from litigating when they
> would otherwise be entitled to do so and compels other
> litigants to settle their claims when they have no wish to
> do so. It enables the more powerful litigant to take unfair
> advantage of the weaker litigant.

Despite the obviously negative effects of these findings on access to justice, Lord Woolf stood by the cost-shifting rule, confining his major reform recommendations to expansion of smaller claims categories (where costs are minimal) to include cases involving up to £10,000 ($16,000), and efforts to streamline litigation so as to reduce the overall costs. The resultant Access to Justice Act 1999 continued to deny that crucial access to the great majority of the English people, especially the middle-class, as thoroughly as in 1979, when Lord Devlin wrote that "for the ordinary citizen, a lawsuit is quite out of the question."

In the same paper, Lord Devlin wrote that "the obligation on a State to provide justice is not discharged by devising a single and inflexible mode of trial whose cost is beyond the reach of the ordinary citizen." Yet that is what Lord Woolf's reforms have left to the ordinary people of England, despite all his good intentions. In opting to retain fee-shifting, Lord Woolf paid lip service to the myth that litigation in America, largely because of the absence of fee-shifting, is pervaded by claims variously described as *frivolous, unmeritorious,* and *nuisance.* For the sake of simplicity, we'll use "frivolous" as the blanket term for cases which do not belong in court.

Britain and the other fee-shifting nations defend this practice by claiming that it is a necessary safeguard against frivolous lawsuits which would otherwise inundate their courts. Fee-shifting supporters argue that this has happened in the United States, mainly because plaintiffs have everything to gain and nothing to lose by filing claims (usually against large companies or wealthy people) which have no merit in fact or law and are therefore frivolous lawsuits.

Let's examine that claim. We begin our inquiry in the quiet splendor of a gaslight-era mansion in Gramercy Park, once the Manhattan home of a famous actor.

Chapter Nine

The Truth About "Frivolous" Lawsuits

The Players club, officially named The Players, was formed in 1888 to serve as a New York meeting place for professional actors and others connected with the theater. The founder was Edwin Booth, the leading American actor of his time, whose 100-night run of *Hamlet* in 1864 was not equaled until John Barrymore's 101-performance run in 1921. Edwin Booth was the brother of Lincoln's assassin, John Wilkes Booth, a fact that interfered only temporarily with Edwin's career. As soon as it was learned that Edwin had no connection with the assassination, he returned to the stage and went on to even greater prominence. He served as the first president of The Players, and upon his death in 1893, his five-storey brownstone townhouse on Gramercy Park passed to The Players under his will. It became the official clubhouse, and has been preserved in its 1890s décor. In 1913, Actors Equity, the performers' union, was founded in Edwin Booth's study overlooking Gramercy Park.

Our story is set in the early 1980's, by which time most of the great names of the American theatre were members, or as they call themselves, Players. On any given day one could expect to see people like James Cagney, Jason Robards, John Gielgud, and Alfred Lunt dining or having a drink there. I lunched there occasionally as the guest of my long-time close friend, John Connell, who for many years played the starring role of Dr. David Malone in the NBC television soap opera *Young Doctor Malone* and later became a leader in voice-over television commercials. While its food was even less distinguished than most New York clubs (which is to say that it was pretty awful), I always enjoyed visiting The Players. It is a museum of the early American theatre and a musty relic of the gaslight era. That charm plus the prospect of seeing (and perhaps even meeting) legendary actors was irresistible to a show-business buff like me. Therefore, I was saddened when John told me that we wouldn't be eating lunch at The Players any more. I was even more distressed when he explained the reasons.

John Connell is a very unusual person, something on the order of Ralph Nader in his sense of moral indignation. He is not one to blink at any injustice, no matter how remote from his personal life, and he will not hesitate to get involved in trying to right wrongs that most people would shrug off as inevitable defects in our permissive society. A long-time vice-president and member of the board of directors of the Screen Actors Guild, he fought relentlessly to have that organization place some limits on the portrayal of violence in films and on television. This campaign resulted in a unanimous resolution by the SAG board condemning excessive violence in television programming. Then he proposed that the Guild get some of its famous actor-members to do something about lack of health insurance, on behalf of the thousands of SAG members who work too infrequently to get coverage, as well as the many millions of other Americans who are not insured. For this effort, which got many star entertainers involved in seeking solutions to the national health insurance problems, he was honored by the SAG with a special award.

Knowing John's background, it did not surprise me that he became estranged from The Players because he refused—as a matter of principle—to ignore charges of possible corruption. On a January morning, John participated in a SAG negotiating session with television management at a midtown Manhattan hotel. After the meeting concluded, John was walking toward the subway to take the train to The Players for lunch, when The Players' former doorman tapped him on the shoulder. The doorman, who knew John's reputation for probity, unfolded detailed charges of corruption that he said he had witnessed while working at the club.

The most serious of these charges related to The Players' then manager, a full-time professional, whom we'll call Mr. Laurel, and the then chairman of the club's management committee, whom we'll call Mr. Hardy. (The reason for using stage names will become apparent.) Hardy was a member of The Players elected by the club's board of directors to chair the management committee. While this voluntary position carried no salary, Hardy was paid for acting as a security official at club parties, and also did some maintenance and construction contracting work at the club, for which he was paid. The arrangements for these payments to Hardy were approved by the club's executive committee, and so they would be perfectly proper if Hardy rendered accurate bills. But the former doorman told John that he had witnessed the passing of money from manager Laurel to club official Hardy, under circumstances which led the doorman to believe that the payments were kickbacks or bribes. The doorman also charged that outside organizations, which were permitted to rent the club's facilities for their own functions, paid gratuities that amounted to about 15 or 20 percent of the total bill. The doorman understood that these gratuities were supposed to be paid to the waiters, bartenders, and doormen who worked at these functions, and he questioned whether these employees ever received the full amounts due to them.

The former doorman's charges rang a bell with John, since he had previously heard similar allegations of financial irregularities from the treasurer of The Players, who resigned from the club after its executive committee refused to take remedial action which he regarded as necessary to maintain the club's integrity. John had met with the executive committee to ask them to reconsider the treasurer's requests, but they had rejected that suggestion.

On the day of his encounter with the ex-doorman, John had dinner with his close friend and fellow Player, Richard Kiley, another public-spirited citizen who was unwilling to shut his eyes to allegations of corruption even if the charges involved only stealing tips from waiters and doormen. Kiley, a bright star of stage, screen, and television, was most famous for his performance in the title role of *Man of La Mancha*. John told Richard about the disturbing charges made by the ex-doorman, and both agreed that they should seek legal advice on what to do about these allegations. John made an appointment to meet with his personal attorney, an entertainment-law specialist named Nahum Bernstein, who, like several other prominent show-business lawyers, was also a member of The Players. Richard Kiley came along.

Nahum Bernstein, in addition to being a senior eminence of the New York bar, had special qualifications for determining the credibility of the doorman's charges. Nahum served as a U. S. Army intelligence officer during World War II. After distinguished field service for which he was decorated, he was made an instructor at a secret Office of Strategic Services (OSS) school in California. Returning to civilian life, he was recruited in 1947 by the fledgling state of Israel (then still called Palestine) to head up the training of its intelligence personnel, known as the Shoo-Shoo Boys (the Hebrew slang for secret agents). During the critical years of 1947-1949, he was the trusted lawyer and troubleshooter for Israel in the United States, in which position he helped that nation to raise funds, recruit volunteers, and obtain supplies needed in the conflict with its Arab neighbors.

Nahum had no way of determining whether the doorman was telling the truth, but he concluded that the charges were serious enough to warrant investigation by The Players. As a lawyer, he was mindful of the fact that the acts reported by the doorman, if they happened, amounted to felonies. This required him and his clients to report these charges to the club, for the failure to do so might leave them open to charges of compounding a felony. He advised John Connell and Richard Kiley that it would be best to write a confidential letter to the club's president, detailing the charges made by the doorman. John and Richard agreed, and so Nahum wrote a three-page letter, as a Player himself and as lawyer for John and Richard, to Players president Roland Winters, who had played detective Charlie Chan in films.

Nahum Bernstein's letter was not cordially received. Pressure was put on him to drop the request for an investigation as being unworthy of a Player, and it was suggested that he consider resigning from the club. But he and John Connell and Richard Kiley felt strongly that the charges should be investigated, especially since they were still dissatisfied with the executive committee's handling of the changes previously requested by the club's departed treasurer. Bernstein, Connell, and Kiley refused to withdraw the request for an investigation. They told Players president Winters that the issue would be raised from the floor at the upcoming annual membership meeting if he did not act. Only then did Winters agree to appoint a select committee of seven Players to look into the charges and report its findings to the board of directors. Throughout this entire hassle, Bernstein, Connell and Kiley took no position on the truth or falsity of the doorman's charges, but merely sought to have them properly investigated.

The select committee took five months to do its job. While it insisted on sworn statements from Bernstein, Connell, and the doorman, its questioning of manager Laurel and Management Committee chairman Hardy was not conducted under oath. They were questioned only about the charge that Laurel had passed kickback money to Hardy, which both men denied. They were not even asked about the alleged siphoning of gratuities that were intended for the waiters, bartenders, and doormen.

Finally, based on this skimpy investigation, the select committee unanimously concluded that there was no substance to the doorman's charges. They sent the club's board of directors a report to that effect, at the end of which they went on to castigate Bernstein and Connell for bringing up such groundless charges without verifying their truth. The report did not explain how Bernstein or Connell could have conducted such an investigation when they had no authority over Laurel, Hardy, or other prospective witnesses. It did not mention the fact that the doorman offered to take a lie detector test, or that he had gone on to fill a managerial position with a fast-food chain. The report closed with the pronouncement that any member who did not accept the select committee's conclusions had "a very simple and honorable alternative—to submit his resignation."

Two weeks after the select committee filed its report, Bernstein and Connell were summoned to a private meeting with Players' officials. Richard Kiley decided to come along. They were told that the board of directors demanded that Bernstein and Connell resign from the club immediately or face expulsion. They refused to resign.

Four days later, Bernstein and Connell each received a letter of suspension from membership pending a hearing before the board of directors on a motion to expel them from the club. No suspension letter was sent to Richard Kiley. Apparently The Players were not interested in taking on Don Quixote.

Finally Bernstein and Connell were summoned to appear before the board of directors for the hearing on their expulsion. The main ground for expulsion was the charge that the doorman's allegations which Bernstein recounted in his letter to Player's President Roland Winters were false and were *known* by Bernstein and Connell to be false. This was also cited as a violation of House Rule 11 which proclaimed that everything seen or heard in the clubhouse was confidential, and no report of any such actions or conversations could be published or circulated by any member.

As the hearing got under way it became apparent that the "evidence" supporting expulsion would consist solely of Bernstein's letter to Winters and the report of the select committee. There would be no witnesses testifying against Bernstein or Connell to substantiate the charges that they had known the doorman's allegations to be false—no accusers whom they could confront, nor anybody whom they could cross-examine. They were given the courtesy of addressing the meeting, but that was to be the extent of their "hearing" on charges that they had behaved so dishonorably as to warrant expulsion.

In his statement, Nahum Bernstein said that he had advised Connell and Kiley that as loyal Players, they had no choice but to submit the allegations of serious wrongdoing to the club president. All three of them had hoped that the charges were unfounded, but they had no way of determining that, and no authority to do anything but call the charges to the president's attention. They all accepted the select committee's finding that the charges were unfounded, as they had agreed to do when the committee was appointed. Nahum then read the charge that he and Connell had known the doorman's allegations to be false, and asked Winters to present proof of this, so that he could refute it. Winters's response was, "Just proceed, sir." Every time Nahum asked what the evidence or proof was, he was simply told to keep talking until he had completed his statement. Nobody was going to submit any proof. The expulsion vote was going to be decided on the charges, not on the evidence.

In his statement, John Connell read aloud a letter that had been sent to the board of directors:

> I believe there are three types of behavior in this world.
> One, to see the wrong and do what you feel is right. Two, to
> see the wrong and do nothing. Three, to see the wrong and
> attempt to cover it up. I believe John Connell and Nahum

Bernstein have adhered to the first rule and I continue to
stand squarely with them. If they are expelled, my resignation from The Players will be in the first mail.
Sincerely,
Richard Kiley.

The hearing ended as it had begun. The directors listened in silence as
Bernstein and Connell attempted to defend themselves against invisible witnesses and nonexistent evidence. They were called upon to prove their innocence without a word being spoken against them to their faces.

As soon as Bernstein and Connell left the meeting room, the board voted
to expel them permanently. Thus, in the stately Gramercy Park home of
Edwin Booth, new meaning was given to the terms *Star Chamber, kangaroo
court,* and *Kafkaesque.*

When the expulsions were announced to the membership of The Players,
Richard Kiley promptly resigned in protest. He was followed by other prominent Players who could not stomach the board's actions, including Jason
Robards and Gordon Parks, the pioneering African-American photographer,
producer-director, and composer whom John Connell had originally nominated for membership. In his letter, Robards expressed his shame in being
associated with those "who would attempt to destroy and malign the character and reputation of these two exemplary human beings." He signed off
with "Gentlemen, adieu."

This was not the end of the unpleasantness at The Players club. After their
expulsion, Nahum and John were served with legal papers informing them
that Laurel and Hardy were suing each of them for defamation, based on their
having published false charges by repeating the allegations of the doorman to
Players president Winters and to other Players. Laurel and Hardy each claimed
$5 million in compensatory damages and $5 million punitive damages, making
a total of $10 million each, amounting to $20 million overall.

Since Nahum was being sued himself, he was not in a position to act as
John Connell's lawyer. In fact, because Nahum was being sued for having
written a letter as a lawyer, his malpractice insurance company retained a law
firm to defend him. That firm could not defend John, and so he asked me to
look at the complaint and advise him how he should proceed.

As I read the complaint, the whole lawsuit smelled very fishy to me. One
of the main purposes of legitimate defamation suits is to stop the circulation
of false statements, even if the defendant cannot afford to pay substantial damages. Yet Laurel and Hardy did not even bother to sue the very person who was
actually performing the alleged defamation—the doorman—leaving him free
to keep repeating the charge that they had engaged in financial shenanigans.
While claiming that these charges damaged their reputations to the tune of

$20 million, they sued only Bernstein and Connell, who had never made such charges but had merely asked that The Players investigate the doorman's allegations.

Furthermore, the lawyers for Laurel and Hardy were Holtzmann, Wise & Shepard, a prominent corporate firm with such clients as Aristotle Onassis and the investment banking firm of Allen & Co. Holtzmann Wise would not normally be representing people like Laurel and Hardy, who could not afford to pay the firm's steep hourly rates. It didn't seem likely that H W & S had taken the case on a contingent fee basis (fees which are dependent on the outcome of a case, usually expressed as a percentage of the amount of damages recovered through a verdict or settlement), because it was not the type of firm to do so ordinarily, and this case was hardly a potential bonanza that would justify an exception. When I discussed my feelings with John, we both concluded that the lawsuit was probably another step by The Players' ruling clique to send a message that the management of their fiefdom was not to be questioned by the members. Thus it was apparent that John was being sued by nominal parties who were fronting for The Players' power elite.

It didn't take much sleuthing to identify the puppet-master behind this lawsuit. Roger Bryant Hunting was a partner in the prestigious Manhattan law firm of Greenbaum, Wolff & Ernst, and a protégé of Edward Greenbaum, its senior partner. Hunting showed a lot of promise early in his career but never achieved much visible success in the practice. Now in his later years he continued practicing with the Greenbaum firm, but spent much of his time at The Players, where some of the members became his clients. He had settled into a comfortable niche at The Players, where officially he was the club's secretary but behind the scenes he was the Master of the Universe. He had his own printed letterhead, complete with the venerable Player's logo featuring the masks of comedy and tragedy. The actor-dominated board of directors was happy to leave to him the formalities of club governance, and when Nahum Bernstein's unwelcome letter reached Roland Winters, The Players' president gingerly handed it off to Hunting. It was Hunting who orchestrated the sham select committee hearings and the expulsion of the two members who dared to request an investigation of the thievery reported by a former employee in a position to observe it. To John Connell and to me, it was clear that Hunting was now sending an even more ominous message: don't mess with Roger Bryant Hunting's control of The Players, or you'll face a financially ruinous lawsuit.

Regardless of who was behind the lawsuit, I had to treat it as a serious attempt to bankrupt John Connell for caring enough about his club to report to the president charges of serious misconduct by two management officials. Technically, defamation suits can be brought against those who merely repeat or pass along a false statement originally made by someone else. But as a member of The Players, John had the right and the duty to report the doorman's charges to the club's president in order to protect the club and his interest in it. This gave him what the law calls a "qualified privilege," meaning that he could not be sued for defamation (libel or slander) unless he repeated the statements in bad faith, or with malice. To overcome this qualified privilege, the plaintiffs would have to prove that John knew the doorman's statements were false, and that he spread these false charges with the intention of injuring Laurel and Hardy.

To meet this malice requirement, the complaint alleged that John caused the doorman's charges to be sent to the club president for "selfish, self-aggrandizing purposes," as part of an attempt to gain influence, office, or standing in The Players. To anyone who knew John Connell this charge would be patently ridiculous, since he had actually turned down an earlier invitation to be named to The Players' board of directors. All the actions he took as a member of The Players were clearly designed to benefit the club rather than himself. But Hunting and his puppets, Laurel and Hardy, fabricated John's quest for power as a prop to keep their phony lawsuit afloat. Without it, they would not have been able to explain what John had to gain by seeking an investigation of the doorman's charges.

I told John that I would be happy to defend him. In fact, I thought the suit was so outrageous that I offered to represent him free of charge, but he insisted on paying. This was a new experience for me, since virtually my entire career had been devoted to representing plaintiffs rather than defendants. I had always thought that defending against legal claims must be an unfulfilling task. It didn't appear that there was much room for creativity or a lot to feel good about when it was over. But I was wrong, at least about defending against phony claims. Now I found myself looking forward to every step, eager to unmask and confound the villains behind this travesty of a lawsuit.

The complaint that began the lawsuit was 52 pages long, reciting as evidence of defamation all the statements which Bernstein and Connell had passed along to The Players for investigation, including long affidavits which they had submitted only because Roger Bryant Hunting had requested them. It was time to take the offensive, where I felt more at home. The central irony of this case was that while John was being sued for $20 million for having done his duty by asking his lawyer to write a confidential letter to one person—Players president Roland Winters—the club itself and its all-powerful secretary, Roger Bryant Hunting, and the seven-man select committee which he had carefully selected, had actually spread the allegedly false charges throughout much of the membership. If John was to pay damages for informing one person, then The Players itself, along with Hunting, Winters, and the select committee should be in the same boat—only more so. There is a legal device, called a third-party complaint, to deal with situations like this where the person being sued was a conduit rather than a direct perpetrator.

I filed a third-party complaint against the club, Hunting, Winters, and the seven members of the select committee, which brought them into the case masterminded by Hunting, so that they could share the fun of getting sued for $20 million for having done their duty. They did not take kindly to this maneuver. They had to retain lawyers, who immediately moved to dismiss the third-party complaint. But the court denied their motion, and so the club, along with Hunting and his colleagues, remained aboard as third-party defendants, facing our claim that if John Connell were held liable, they should be required to pay whatever damages were assessed, for it was *they* who had broadly spread the allegedly false charges against Laurel and Hardy.

Now it was time for *discovery*, the process by which American litigants are required to disclose their evidence before the trial. I served notices for taking the depositions (oral testimony) of Laurel and Hardy, and listed the documents they were to produce. Laurel and Hardy each alleged in the complaint that he "has been greatly injured in his business, employment, and status, and...has suffered grave impairment of his good name, business reputation and social standing, has lost or may lose the esteem and respect of his friends, acquaintances, and business associates, has suffered great pain and mental anguish, and is in danger of being further seriously injured in his business and employment opportunities, all to his damage in the sum of $5 million." These standard allegations in defamation cases leave the plaintiffs open to searching examination. If their good names and reputations were so badly damaged, what were their reputations before the defamatory remarks were made? Were they spotless, as the allegation of $5 million worth of compensatory damages would imply? Or did they already have shady reputations, which therefore could not be badly damaged even if defamatory statements were made with malice? To answer these questions, one would have to know much of the life stories of Laurel and Hardy. That was what I set out to discover.

The deposition of Laurel, the club manager, came first. He had to bring with him all his income tax returns, bank statements, cancelled checks, and records of securities accounts for the preceding ten years. These documents would help me to determine whether he had received any money on the side which was not part of his agreed salary from The Players. Receipts of under-the-table income would tend to support the doorman's charges. Since truth is a complete defense to charges of defamation under American law, Laurel's income was a crucial issue in the case.

With so much ground to cover, we set aside three days for Laurel's deposition. On the first day he produced tax and bank records going back about six years. I made copies of them for study that night, and proceeded to question him about his entire career, going back to his high school days. At every stage I asked for the names and addresses of people whom he had encountered and who would be familiar with his reputation and community standing. When his lawyer objected, I reminded him that $5 million worth of compensatory damage to that reputation was being alleged. As the day wore on, I got the feeling that Laurel had been talked into bringing this suit without fully understanding its implications for him, and that his enthusiasm for the contest was waning. We adjourned for the day, with the agreement that he would return for continued questioning the next morning.

The following morning, about ten minutes before the scheduled resumption of Laurel's deposition, his lawyer phoned. "I have some startling news," he said. "My client just now reported to me by phone that he is unable to carry on with the deposition because of—in his words—uncontrollable diarrhea!" That was a first for me. Since the deposition was being conducted in my office, I quickly agreed to postpone it until Laurel got the problem under control. In the meantime, I requested that we go ahead with Hardy's deposition. The lawyer said he would see what he could do about producing Hardy.

I was looking forward with great anticipation to questioning Mr. Hardy. You will recall that he served as chairman of the club's management committee without compensation other than the agreed payments for construction jobs and for acting as a security operative at club parties. Prior to the depositions, both plaintiffs were required to submit written bills of particulars—detailed statements under oath explaining and quantifying their claims. One of the particulars they had to submit dealt with the amounts and sources of their incomes. Laurel had answered this question straightforwardly, listing his weekly salary and other agreed payments from the club. But Hardy's reply was rather vague, to put it mildly. He claimed to have been self-employed for the past 15 years, but did not name any job title, business, or profession as the source of income, nor did he supply any income figures. He too would have to produce his tax returns and all financial records for the past 10 years, including the records of all construction and maintenance work done for The Players, and the club's approvals of payment for that work. I planned to take the deposition of other Players' officials later, and require them to produce all the club's records of payments to Hardy.

A few days after the interruption of Laurel's deposition, his lawyer phoned back to tell me that Hardy was spending the entire summer in St. Louis and so would not be available until the fall (it then being early June). I have always thought that St. Louis is a fine city, but its climate does not commend it as a likely summer resort. When I pressed for resumption of Laurel's deposition and said that I would seek a court order if necessary to force Hardy to interrupt his St. Louis summer, the lawyer told me that there was a good chance that his clients would be disposed to drop the case. He did not ask whether John Connell would pay anything to get rid of the case, because I had made it clear at the outset that not a cent would ever be offered in settlement. A few days later, the lawyer confirmed that his clients wished to drop the case without any payment by Connell or the Bernstein estate (Nahum having died of cancer at age 76 soon after the defamation action was started).

Thus ended a frivolous lawsuit, a totally phony claim concocted for an improper purpose—and easily thwarted by rudimentary application of the safeguards against litigation abuse.

John Connell went on with his exemplary career and continued his public service work in retirement. Among the many decorations he received for his 43 Air Force combat missions in the European Theatre during World War II was the Purple Heart. The Hunting clique at The Players did their best to add an Oak Leaf Cluster to that Purple Heart, but they did not come close to succeeding. John's bitter experience at their hands has not caused him to shy away from speaking out against injustice or stupidity on the part of those in authority. John had been both a master of ceremonies and an honored presidential guest at the White House. But when President Ronald Reagan saw fit to salute Hitler's SS troops by making an official visit to the SS cemetery at Bitburg, West Germany, John was a leader in the public protest.

I have used the stage names of Laurel and Hardy for the two misguided plaintiffs because I think it would be unfair to connect their real names to the doorman's charges, which—thanks to Hunting's devious maneuvers—remain unresolved because they were never given a proper hearing. The use of Stan and Ollie is also appropriate because, as world-class buffoons, they serve as fitting symbols of the cast of characters who support the myth that the American courts are flooded with frivolous lawsuits.

The Incompetence Required to Tolerate Frivolous Lawsuits

The credibility of the frivolous lawsuit myth depends upon the existence of a mind-boggling array of highly-compensated professionals who are totally incompetent at their jobs.

The largest troupe of incompetents in the imaginary world of the successful frivolous lawsuit would be the lawyers representing large companies (including insurers) and wealthy individuals who would be the natural targets of phony claims. In successful frivolous suits against companies, there would be two layers of incompetents: the in-house legal departments, often comprising hundreds of lawyers headed by a general counsel likely to be receiving an annual salary of at least a million dollars, and outside law firms, the powerhouses of the American legal system, which compete vigorously for pieces of the companies' lucrative business. In the scenario adopted by Lord Woolf and legal officials of all the developed democracies save one, these highly experienced lawyers would have to be unable to recognize a phony lawsuit, or be so terrified of their inability to expose its phoniness that they advise the client to settle for a substantial sum, thus assuring that (a) there will be many more such phony lawsuits filed against the client, or (b) they will be fired for gross incompetence. If this has ever happened in the United States, it has been carefully concealed because there is no record of any such fiasco.

In the real world, both in-house counsel and outside lawyers are vigilant to spot phony lawsuits, and take great pleasure in blowing them out of the water. They are far more proficient and experienced in that task than I was as John Connell's lawyer. Defending against frivolous claims is a welcome relief from the many complex problems arising from government regulation and financial transactions which companies dump in the laps of their lawyers. Usually frivolous lawsuits are easy to defeat because most of them are brought by claimants who are unable to obtain a lawyer, or are represented by lawyers who are short on experience and resources (including brains).

But Lord Woolf did not conjure up his frivolous-lawsuit scenario out of thin air, and he cannot fairly be blamed for perceiving such suits as a "phenomenon" of American justice. Those who would profit from restricted access to American courts play a bait-and-switch game in the effort to portray legitimate lawsuits as frivolous, including many which were found to be meritorious by appellate courts. The prototype was *Stella Liebeck v. McDonald's*, which became notorious as the case in which a New Mexico jury awarded nearly $3 million to a little old lady who bought a cup of coffee at a McDonald's and spilled it in her own lap. The facts of the case were distorted by some journalists, assisted by paid professionals whose function it is to convince legislators and potential jurors that the legal system is in total disarray because of frivolous claims.

Mrs. Liebeck, 79, riding in a car driven by her grandson, bought a cup of coffee at a McDonald's drive-through. The grandson pulled to a stop at the curb so she could add cream and sugar. (Contrary to some media versions, she was not driving and the car was not moving.) Since the car did not have a cup-holder, she put the cup between her legs to remove the lid. The cup then tipped over and spilled the entire contents into her lap. Although temperatures above 150 degrees Fahrenheit were certain to cause serious burns, McDonald's served their coffee at temperatures between 180 and 190 degrees. Mrs. Liebeck sustained third-degree burns over six percent of her body, mostly on her thighs and genital areas. She was hospitalized for more than a week, undergoing painful skin grafts and debridement. She suffered terribly, wasting away to 86 pounds, and was partially disabled for about two years.

Mrs. Liebeck had never filed a lawsuit before. She contacted McDonald's herself and sought a settlement of $20,000. McDonald's offered her $800, which caused her to consult a lawyer. Since McDonald's still refused to make a settlement offer she considered reasonable, the case went to trial before an Albuquerque jury in 1994. Her lawyer presented evidence that coffee made at home and in other restaurants was usually served at 135 to 140 degrees, at which temperature it was far less likely to cause serious burns. The jury awarded Mrs Liebeck $200,000 in compensatory damages, which was reduced to $160,000 because they found her 20 percent responsible for the injuries. They also awarded her $2.7 million in punitive damages, which the trial judge reduced to $480,000, a sum equal to three times the compensatory damages—a commonly-used yardstick for fixing punitive damages. Post-trial interviews of the jurors conducted by the *Wall Street Journal* indicated that they were moved to add punitive damages because of the "callous disregard for the safety of the people" (including cavalier treatment of over 700 earlier coffee-burn victims) demonstrated by the McDonald's witnesses. The company's safety consultant testified that because McDonald's served billions of cups annually, burn injuries to less than a thousand customers over a decade were "statistically insignificant" and thus made corrective measures unnecessary.

In his decision upholding the reduced award of punitive damages, the trial judge (who happened to be a Republican) wrote, "This is all evidence of culpable corporate mental state and I conclude that the award of punitive damages is and was appropriate to punish and deter the Defendant for their wanton conduct and to send a clear message to this Defendant that corrective measures are appropriate."

Although the total verdict was reduced to $640,000, McDonald's lawyers served notice they were appealing. This led to a settlement for an undisclosed figure, which presumably was something less than $640,000. Had McDonald's lawyers been convinced that this case was frivolous, unmeritorious, or a mere nuisance, they would have insisted on proceeding with the appeal, the expense of which was negligible, because allowing the verdict to stand would invite further lawsuits if they continued serving such hot coffee.

Thus the media's quintessential frivolous lawsuit was judicially determined NOT to be frivolous, unmeritorious, or a nuisance. Reasonable people hearing all the evidence might reach different conclusions about whether Mrs. Liebeck should be compensated, and if so, the amount of compensatory damages. They might also differ as to whether there was sufficient evidence of willful, reckless, malicious, or wanton conduct to justify punitive damages. That is why the Liebeck case was submitted to an impartial jury and finally ruled upon by an impartial judge. But by definition, it was not a frivolous lawsuit. The final result, as determined by the trial judge, was to compensate Mrs. Liebeck fairly, and to send a legally appropriate message to McDonald's which caused them to reduce the temperature of their coffee to a level which provided more reasonable protection to their millions of customers, some of whom would inevitably spill coffee on themselves. They also (for the first time) printed a clear warning on the lids of their coffee cups that the contents were "HOT! HOT! HOT!"

The truth about Mrs. Liebeck's claims was revealed in a 2004 strategic study published by the British government's Better Regulation Task Force— too late, unfortunately, to be available to Lord Woolf during his studies of the "phenomena" of American justice. That study, *Better Routes to Redress,* documented the Liebeck facts in a section entitled "Media creates a storm in a coffee cup," concluding with the statement that "Under these circumstances, few would object to the injured woman having a right to claim for damages." It went on to reveal other fabrications which the media had published as the truth in efforts to alarm the public about a so-called "compensation culture."

The feature of the McDonald's coffee case that causes many people to have a knee-jerk "frivolous" reaction is that the coffee was spilled by Mrs. Liebeck herself rather than by a McDonald's employee. Legally her spill amounted to "contributory negligence," which under the English common law was a total bar to collecting damages, even if someone else was 99 percent responsible for the injuries. This restrictive rule was also adopted in the United States, letting a lot of careless people entirely off the hook because there was some fault on the part of the victim. It was first discarded by England, which in 1945 adopted a more humane rule, allowing apportionment of damages based on the degree of fault on both sides, resulting in a reduction of damages equal to the percentage of fault ascribed to the injured person. It was not until the 1970s that American courts changed the old rule by moving to what is now called "comparative negligence," the standard under which the Albuquerque jury reduced Mrs. Liebeck's compensatory damages by 20 percent. Thus, under both American and English law, a suit to recover damages for injuries where the victim was partially at fault is not frivolous if there is some fault on the part of the person or company being sued which caused or contributed to the injury.

It should be noted here that such claims involving contributory negligence are at the outer fringe of non-frivolous lawsuits. Their total impact on the American legal system is so insignificant that no studies have ever been undertaken to quantify it.

There are dozens of other American lawsuits which have been reported in the media as hilarious examples of frivolous claims: the Texas woman who won $780,000 from a store owner on a claim that she broke her ankle tripping over a rampaging child (her own); the Los Angeles man who was awarded $74,000 for injuries suffered at the hands of a driver while he was stealing the car's hubcaps; the Philadelphia woman awarded $113,500 for injuries sustained in a restaurant when she slipped on a spilled soft drink which she had thrown at her boyfriend during an argument. These stories have one thing in common: they never happened, except in the imagination of those who fabricated them. As Stanford Law Professor Deborah Rhode puts it, the media-hyped stories of frivolous lawsuits tend to be "long on folklore and short on facts."

"Frivolous lawsuits" was a favorite expression of President George W. Bush, guaranteed by pollsters to generate cheers of approval from his political supporters. In his speech accepting the 2004 Republican presidential nomination, he drew strong applause for denouncing "the explosion of frivolous lawsuits that threaten jobs across America." He did not identify any of those frivolous lawsuits because there are none which have enough impact to destroy jobs.

President Bush was playing the bait-and-switch game with the buzzword "frivolous." It is defined in *Webster's Dictionary* as "silly, not serious." The authoritative *Black's Law Dictionary* states the legal definition of a frivolous suit as "a lawsuit having no legal basis, often filed to harass or extort money from defendants." Bush was using the fabricated media image of the frivolous lawsuit—e.g., the media-distorted version of the McDonald's coffee case, and the imaginary Los Angeles hubcap thief, as the bait to attract support for limiting access to the courts. He knew that "frivolous lawsuit" is a hot-button term that conjures up images of opportunistic lawyers leading crank claimants into court, trying to turn trivial incidents into cash cows. That's exactly the image he wanted to convey, but it masked his true goal. He quickly switched to his real targets, the lawsuits that actually cause some people to lose their jobs, but only as a natural consequence of putting an end to corporate thievery by the likes of the crooked Enron management, or reducing the carnage from concealment of the deadly nature of products like cigarettes and asbestos. Those job-threatening lawsuits are undoubtedly annoying to the wrongdoers they bring to account, but they are not frivolous in either the colloquial or legal sense.

Bush and his speechwriters were untroubled by the reality that the truly frivolous lawsuits are too inconsequential to destroy any jobs, and that the anonymous job-threatening lawsuits he was brandishing, far from being frivolous, were deadly serious and were found by the courts to be legally meritorious. The lawsuits that actually threaten jobs are not the fodder of the late-night comedy shows, but often are the objects of interest to politicians advocating restrictions on damage awards, usually at the bidding of large business contributors (such as cigarette manufacturers) who have non-frivolous legal problems arising from the lethal nature of their products. Often such efforts are trumpeted as "tort reform," which is aimed at restricting access to the courts rather than reforming the conduct of those who cause injuries. Consumer advocate Ralph Nader denounces this campaign as "tort deform," for these reasons:

> Tort law produced decades of slow but steady progress in
> state after state respecting the physical integrity of human
> beings against harm and recognition that even the weak
> and defenseless deserve justice. Instead of seeing this evolu-
> tion as a source of national and global pride, a coalition
> of insurance companies, corporate defendants' lobbies,
> and craven politicians, led by George W. Bush, depict it as
> a source of shame and instability that must be stopped....
> Tort deform means less deterrence, which means more
> injuries, more uncompensated victims, and tremendous
> overall cost to society.

Whenever I see stories about the pervasiveness of frivolous lawsuits in the American courts, I search them carefully for names of the plaintiffs' lawyers. Who are the kingpins of the frivolous lawsuit racket—those raking in big money by suing for nonexistent damages? Is there a Ponzi or a Ken Lay in their ranks? Which lawyers are making their fortunes by duping gullible corporate legal departments and judges with frivolous claims? And which judges are betraying their oaths of office by failing to perform their duty to dismiss frivolous lawsuits? So far, I haven't found any names to go with these media-hyped images, other than the names of those who fabricate them— e.g., Philip Morris and George W. Bush.

Putting aside these distortions by media and politicians, there really are some frivolous lawsuits filed every year, both in the United States and England. In seeking to evaluate their impact on the legal system, these are the pertinent questions:

> (1) How do the American and English courts cope with
> frivolous lawsuits?

> (2) What would be the impact on frivolous lawsuits if
> the U.S.A. adopted the Loser Pays rule, or if the nations
> following Loser Pays eliminated it?

Both the American and English legal systems are amply equipped to dispose of frivolous lawsuits without the expense of a trial. In both systems, judges are charged with the duty of dismissing all lawsuits which are shown to be legally frivolous, unmeritorious, or brought only for nuisance purposes. In the United States, Rule 12 of the Federal Rules of Civil Procedure (and similar state rules) require the judge to dismiss any action in which the plaintiff's complaint fails "to state a claim upon which relief can be granted." English judges have even broader powers under Civil Procedure Rule 3.4 to strike out the complaint (called the "statement of case") if it "discloses no reasonable grounds for bringing the claim." For purposes of such rulings, the judges must assume that all the claimant's allegations of fact are true. Their dismissal rulings say, in effect, that even if everything happened as alleged by the claimant, those facts do not add up to a legally sustainable claim.

For example, in the Players case, even if Laurel and Hardy's allegations about John Connell having defamed them were true, they would not have added up to a meritorious legal claim if it had not been alleged that he acted out of malice in order to further his own ambitions for "influence, office, or standing" in the club. Without that allegation, the complaint would have been thrown out for failure to state a claim upon which relief can be granted.

If the lawsuit does state a claim upon which relief can be granted, but it hinges on allegations which are demonstrably false, American and English judges have the duty to dismiss it without a trial by the process known in both systems as "summary judgment." In the Players case, I planned to make a motion for summary judgment after completing the pre-trial discovery, submitting excerpts from the depositions and documents which would demonstrate to any competent judge that there was no credible evidence to support the claims of Laurel and Hardy. John Connell was ready to help me get sworn statements from long-time club members confirming that he had turned down a directorship offer and had no ambition to hold office in the club. To counter that proof and fend off summary judgment, Laurel and Hardy would have had to find other club members willing to stick their necks out by making false affidavits. Thus, claimants seeking to slip a frivolous lawsuit through the court process face formidable legal obstacles.

In the United States, there are additional judicial remedies for phony claims, known as "sanctions." The most frequently used sanctions are contained in Federal Rule 11, which has counterparts in the state legal systems. Rule 11 is aimed primarily at lawyers. It provides that the signature of a lawyer on every paper filed in court (including the complaint which commences the action) is a certification by the lawyer that the paper "is not being presented for any improper purpose," that the "legal contentions therein are warranted by existing law or by a nonfrivolous argument" for the modification of existing law, and that "the allegations and other factual contentions have evidentiary support." Among the sanctions available to judges for violation of Rule 11 are outright dismissal (or a judgment by default for the claimant in cases where the defendant violates Rule 11), monetary fines, and orders requiring the offending party to pay the other party's legal fees—a form of fee-shifting designed to punish abusive or bad-faith litigation tactics. Thus the United States enforces a Loser Pays rule for frivolous lawsuits, but without creating a barrier to court access for legitimate cases.

An example of the use of sanctions in a frivolous lawsuit is one which undoubtedly would have been titled *The Case of the Pre-Dated Panties* if it had arisen in Perry Mason's practice. Nelson Peltz, a billionaire business tycoon, was sued by his former maid, who alleged that he had sexually harassed her by presenting her with a pair of panties and asking her to pose for him in the panties. At her deposition, she produced the panties in question and fixed the time of this incident as September 1992. Peltz's lawyers, working from the serial number of the panties produced by the plaintiff, discovered that they could not have been manufactured before November 1993 (more than a year after the date when she claimed the harassment-by-panties occurred). Peltz's lawyers then made a motion to dismiss the case without a trial as a sanction for presenting false claims. The trial court judge granted the motion, dismissing the lawsuit because of litigation abuse and fraud on the court.

Peltz could have ended the case through a summary judgment, but he opted for the sanctions approach in order to judicially brand this frivolous lawsuit as a fraud on the court, a more definitive dismissal which would serve to deter other efforts to extort money from him.

Peltz's lawyers had also sought a further sanction—an order requiring the plaintiff to pay Peltz's legal fees—but they did not pursue it in view of the obvious inability of the maid to pay any such sums. Nevertheless it is clear that American courts have the power to order fee-shifting in a frivolous lawsuit like this one, both under Rule 11 and the inherent power of judges to protect the legal system. It is equally apparent that fee-shifting is rarely of any use in deterring frivolous lawsuits since most of them are brought by people who cannot afford to pay any significant legal fees.

The Peltz panties case thus underscores the reality of American frivolous lawsuits:

(1) Because American judges and corporate lawyers are reasonably competent at their jobs, such claims have no appreciable chance of succeeding;

(2) frivolous claimants would not be deterred by fee-shifting, because (like Peltz's maid) usually they do not have the money to pay the fees, costs, or sanctions; and

(3) in total, frivolous lawsuits make no discernable impact on the American legal system or economy, their major result being a juicy news story for the media and a few days' television fodder for the late-night comedy shows.

American judges are not reticent about using fee-shifting and fines to deter frivolous lawsuits or litigation abuse. In the leading textbook, *Sanctions: The Federal Law of Litigation Abuse,* author Gregory Joseph presents a chart of the Top Ten monetary sanctions, in which the lowest assessment is $5 million and the highest is over $114 million. Again, those assessments are only effective against the few litigants who can afford to pay for abusing the system. But they make it clear that there is no need to abandon cost-shifting in English cases which judges find to be frivolous. The English rule of Loser Pays can and should be retained for frivolous cases. Therefore, when Lord Woolf's misguided premise about the impact of frivolous lawsuits in the United States is removed, there is no valid reason to bar meritorious cases from the English courts, a travesty which Lord Woolf himself lamented in *Access to Justice.*

In 2009, England's highest civil judge, Master of the Rolls Lord Anthony Clarke, assigned Court of Appeal Lord Justice Rupert Jackson to review "the costs of civil litigation and to make recommendations in order to promote access to justice at proportionate cost." Lord Justice Jackson devoted all of 2009 to this exhaustive review, receiving thousands of pages of submissions from all interested organizations and holding many open meetings and seminars. In his 557-page final report, submitted in December 2009, he recommended many far-reaching changes, including adoption of contingency fees and substantial curtailment of Loser Pays cost-shifting. We shall consider those recommendations in the next chapter. Here we focus on Jackson's conclusions about the ability of the English courts to "deter frivolous or fraudulent claims."

Lord Justice Jackson found that section 11(1) of the Access to Justice Act 1999 contained a provision which already empowered judges to award costs against claimants based on "their conduct in connection with the dispute to which the proceedings relate." He adapted that language so as to apply that sanction to the new costs regime he recommended, and concluded that it would be perfectly adequate to deter frivolous or fraudulent claims even if contingency fees were permitted and Loser Pays was no longer the general rule.

Obviously, in keeping with Lord Justice Jackson's findings, it would make much more sense to impose fee-shifting selectively on those who foment frivolous lawsuits, rather than punishing the entire middle class for seeking to uphold the Rule of Law by enforcing their legal rights. The proprietors of the present English legal system, petrified by the specter of the non-existent American frivolous lawsuit phenomenon, throw out virtually the entire maternity ward with the bathwater.

All of this assumes that American and English judges are reasonably competent; that they are able to recognize a frivolous lawsuit when presented with the evidence; and that they are capable of exercising their well-defined powers to purge such contaminants from the legal system. Even in jury trials, judges have the power and the duty to override the jury's verdict if it is contrary to law or against the weight of the evidence. Because trial judges are not infallible, there are appellate courts (not usually staffed by incompetents) charged with the duty of correcting their mistakes. Thus the chances of a significant number of frivolous lawsuits making their way through the American or English systems— or any system that is staffed by reasonably competent judges—are miniscule.

Again, there are no empirical studies, but the actual number of frivolous lawsuits that even reach trial in the United States could not possibly add up to a respectable fraction of one percent of the many thousands of meritorious cases which would be denied access under Loser Pays each year. Nor are there any studies quantifying the annual expenses incurred by defendants and the court system in disposing of frivolous lawsuits. Given the many millions of dollars which have been poured into the effort by business supporters such as the U.S. Chamber of Commerce to perpetuate the frivolous-lawsuit myth, you can bet that those expenses would have been quantified if they added up to more than a pittance. In fact, a 2005 Federal Judicial Center survey of the federal district judges who administer Rule 11 sanctions found that only 3 percent of the responding judges considered groundless litigation to be a significant problem, and more than 80 percent concluded that no changes were required to make Rule 11 more effective in deterring groundless litigation.

———————

Our sole concern in this chapter is access to the courts for all the people as an essential element of the Rule of Law. We are not discussing here the relative merits of devices used in various countries to try cases—devices such as class or group actions, judge or jury trials, punitive damages, or the methods of quantifying damage awards. Those are matters about which the people in each country can argue and legislate. Their suitability will vary from culture to culture, depending on such factors as the values deemed most important locally and the existence of social safety nets outside the court systems. But nations whose courtroom doors are shut to their Oliver Browns and Elsie Parrishes cannot validly claim to be following the Rule of Law.

Now let's take a look at some of the habitual abusers of litigation who actually make an impact on the legal system. They are not people given to frivolity or seeking to become nuisances. And they have three things in common: (1) they are far too wealthy to be deterred in the slightest degree by the threat of fee-shifting; (2) they have no use or need for contingency fees; and (3) they are much more successful in the English courts (and other foreign courts) than the litigation abusers who customarily represent themselves in frivolous American cases.

Chapter Ten

The Rule of Law According to "Lex Onassis"

Aristotle Socrates Onassis, best known as the quintessential Greek shipping tycoon who founded the Jet Set and married Jackie Kennedy, was in truth the twentieth century's premier con man. He was able to hide his deceitfulness and maintain an aura of invincibility by charming journalists who were eager to report his every glamorous excess. He was also protected by his private legal system, known mockingly as "Lex Onassis," which was based on his personal motto: "The only rule is that there are no rules—there is no right or wrong, there is only what is possible."

Ari's Argentine scams in tobacco, insurance claims, and black market currency dealings while he was still in his twenties netted him a small fortune, which he used to buy his first ships in 1932. Then came bigger and bolder frauds: illegal acquisition of American war-surplus merchant ships by falsifying ownership records; pioneering the "flag of convenience" in Panama and Liberia to evade taxes and shipping safety regulations; bribing Saudi Arabian officials to obtain fabulous oil concessions; slaughtering thousands of whales in violation of international conventions; hiring Howard Hughes's hatchet man, Johnny Meyer, for use in wiretapping, intimidation, and other strong-arm tactics against business rivals and even members of his own family; and buying control of the Principality of Monaco so he could manipulate it as his own country, to evade taxes and thwart government regulation globally.

Journalists first applied the *Lex Onassis* label to the caper by which Ari tried to cheat Jackie Kennedy out of her lawful share of his $500 million estate. Greek law specified that the widow was entitled to at least 12.5 percent of the estate, and that this provision could not be waived. This technicality did not trouble Ari, who proceeded to insert a waiver in the pre-nuptial agreement, and then got the corrupt colonels who were then running the Greek government to enact a special statute validating such a waiver agreement between a husband and wife signed outside of Greece, when one of the signatories (i.e. Jackie) was of non-Greek nationality. As it turned out, when Ari died, Jackie's American lawyers advised her that the American courts would not enforce the Greek waiver statute, and they were able to negotiate a $26 million settlement in place of the miserly provisions in the pre-nuptial agreement. But *Lex Onassis* was more effective in shielding Ari from accountability in Europe, where his phony legal devices were not likely to be challenged in court.

I learned this first hand in 1970, when Nicholas Onassis, Ari's first cousin, retained me to seek compensation for being muscled out of the shipping business by Olympic Maritime, Ari's Monaco-based shipping company. We needed a lawyer in Monaco who would file the suit there against Olympic Maritime. I contacted all the law offices in Monaco, but found that every one was under retainer by Olympic. Therefore, the Rule of Law in Monaco had been supplanted by *Lex Onassis*, for Ari and his companies could not be hauled into court there. No wonder Howard Hughes enviously described Ari's control of Monaco as "the perfect setup."

Fortunately, my next case against Ari did not require a Monaco lawyer, but I still had to deal with *Lex Onassis*, this time in Greece. At the pinnacle of his success, having achieved virtual freedom from taxation, government regulation, and the Rule of Law, Ari's evasion of accountability suddenly backfired. His downfall sprang from the myth he had propagated about his personal airplane, a Piaggio that he carried aboard his mega-yacht *Christina*. The Piaggio was an amphibian, meaning that it could operate from land airports, and with its wheels retracted it became a flying boat which could take off and land on water. He boasted that it could depart from the yacht in mid-ocean to fly him anywhere. In truth it could not be operated safely on the high seas, but displaying it on the deck of the *Christina* reinforced his image of invincibility, warning his rivals that he was capable of materializing anywhere his presence was needed.

Ari's only son, Alexander, a pilot himself, was the head of Olympic Aviation, a subsidiary of the Onassis-owned Olympic Airways that operated a fleet of small aircraft like the Piaggio in air taxi and charter service to the smaller Greek Islands. Donald McGregor, a former BOAC flying boat captain, was the regular pilot for Ari's personal Piaggio. In January 1973, McGregor developed eye trouble and was temporarily grounded. This was most inconvenient for Ari since he was planning a February cruise aboard the *Christina* from Greece to the Caribbean. He ordered Alexander to recruit another Piaggio pilot in time for the cruise.

Alexander, then 25 and still dominated by his iron-handed father, had been trying for years to convince Ari to replace the outmoded Piaggio with a helicopter. Finally Ari agreed, but the Piaggio would be used one last time for the February 1973 Caribbean cruise. Finding no suitable Piaggio pilot in Greece, Alexander advertised for one in America. His ad was answered by Donald McCusker, a decorated World War II U.S. Navy pilot and former test pilot for major American aircraft manufacturers. Besides those excellent credentials, McCusker had considerable flying time in amphibians. Alexander arranged his passage on Olympic Airways to Athens, where he would be checked out on the Piaggio and if satisfactory, would be hired as Aristotle's pilot.

After sitting up all night on the Olympic flight from New York, Don McCusker arrived at Athens International Airport on Monday morning, January 22, 1973. He had not been told that his checkout flight would take place that same day. But Alexander Onassis was in a hurry because he was under pressure from his father to hire the replacement pilot. He was also eager to get away to London that afternoon to be with his 41-year-old girlfriend, the Baroness Thyssen-Bornemisza, daughter of a British admiral and formerly a famous fashion model under the name of Fiona Campbell. Married and then divorced from Baron Thyssen, she had an ongoing five-year affair with Alexander, and was helping him to plot his breakaway from Ari's dominance.

The Piaggio had been undergoing an overhaul which was performed by the maintenance department of Aristotle's airline, Olympic Airways. Since a post-overhaul test flight was required before the plane was returned to passenger service, Alexander decided to combine the test flight with the orientation and checkout of McCusker. Alexander took the right seat where the instructor/ check pilot usually sat. McCusker was in the left seat, normal for the pilot being checked out. Donald McGregor, Aristotle's former pilot, sat in a rear seat. The plan was for Alexander to talk McCusker through a few takeoffs and landings at the Athens airport, and then have McCusker do some water landings and take-offs at the nearby islands of Aegina and Poros. Then, when they all agreed McCusker was ready, Alexander would take the afternoon airline flight to London, leaving the rest of McCusker's orientation to Captain McGregor.

Under instructions from Alexander, McCusker taxied the Piaggio to the takeoff runway. When they received takeoff clearance, McCusker opened the throttles, and as the plane reached the takeoff speed of 100 miles per hour, he eased the stick back and the plane left the ground normally. But almost immediately after takeoff, the plane banked sharply to the right. Suddenly its right wing tip struck the ground. Then the plane cart-wheeled in a circle for more than 400 feet, smashing its nose, its tail, and both its wings as it crashed to the right of the runway.

The airport emergency rescue trucks sped to the crash scene. The three pilots were pulled from the wreckage, unconscious and bleeding heavily. They were rushed to a hospital, where it was determined that McCusker and the former Onassis pilot McGregor had been lucky and would survive without permanent disabilities. But Alexander was not so fortunate. Sitting in the right seat at the point of the most severe ground impact, he had suffered crushing head injuries. He underwent a three-hour operation to remove blood clots and relieve the pressure on his brain.

At the time of the accident, Aristotle Onassis and his wife Jacqueline were in New York. They flew to Athens immediately, bringing along a Boston neurosurgeon and a Texas heart specialist. But by the early afternoon of the day following the crash, all the doctors agreed that there was no hope. They kept Alexander alive until his sister Christina arrived from Brazil. Then they removed him from life support and he died that evening.

Aristotle Onassis was at once inconsolable in his grief and irrational with rage. He convinced himself that the Piaggio had crashed because of sabotage, and that the saboteurs had meant to kill him rather than his son because he was the plane's most frequent user.

Greece was then governed by the dictatorship of the colonels (1967-1974), and Onassis, as the sole owner of Olympic Airways and the nation's most visible business icon, could have his way with the Greek authorities. The official accident investigation was conducted by a court-appointed team, most of whom were Greek Air Force officers. Their report was kept secret, because it reached. conclusions that did not please Onassis.

The cause of the fatal accident quickly became apparent to the investigators. During its overhaul by Olympic mechanics (who worked for Onassis) the Piaggio's ailerons were re-rigged—i.e., the controls that made the wings bank during turns were removed and replaced. Unfortunately they were installed backwards, so that when the pilot turned his wheel to the right to put the right wing down in a bank for a right turn, the plane would actually turn to the left. And when the wind caused the Piaggio to drift to the right on its final takeoff with McCusker at the controls, his normal corrective action—turning the wheel slightly to the left to counteract the wind and stop the drift to the right—would cause the plane to turn even further to the right, because of the reversed aileron controls. At that point, any experienced pilot would turn the control wheel even more sharply to the left. Given the slow airspeed and low altitude at the time of takeoff, the right wing would dig into the ground and the crash sequence would follow exactly as it did at Athens.

The primary cause of the accident was the negligence of Olympic's mechanics in rigging the ailerons backwards, and a contributing cause was Alexander's failure to follow the checklist that required a walk-around inspection of the controls and then a test flight, both of which would have revealed the faulty rigging. McCusker did not know that the Piaggio had just come out of overhaul, and in any event he was being instructed by Alexander rather than the other way around.

Aristotle Onassis himself featured prominently in causing the accident, for he put pressure on Alexander and the entire Olympic organization to complete the Piaggio overhaul in time for his yacht cruise. The regular job of the Olympic mechanics was routine maintenance of large airliners. They were not trained or equipped for the more demanding task of overhaul, and none of them had ever worked on the overhaul of a Piaggio, the manuals for which were written in Italian. The only way to assure a proper overhaul was to send the plane to the Piaggio factory in Italy, but Ari had made the choice to save time and money by having his government-subsidized Olympic mechanics overhaul the Piaggio at no cost to him. These daunting facts led the ego-centric Onassis to put the blame on someone else rather than shoulder the burden of admitting that he was the major factor in the avoidable crash that killed his son. Accordingly, he called on *Lex Onassis* to have McCusker and three Olympic mechanics indicted for manslaughter, and through the media he offered a $1 million reward for evidence of sabotage—a reward which, as in the later O.J. Simpson case, was never expected to be paid.

When the indictments were announced in the media, McCusker was flat on his back in a Greek hospital, leveled by hepatitis which had set in during his post-accident treatment. His passport was confiscated, and during the six months of his slow recuperation from hepatitis he was too weak to do anything about defending against the criminal charges. There was little he could do anyway, for although he was certain that he had not been at fault in the accident, he could not remember anything about it, nor was he told about the deadly aileron control rigging found by the Greek Air Force investigators. Finally, through the intercession of the American ambassador to Greece, McCusker regained his passport and was allowed to return to America in July of 1973. But he was still under indictment for manslaughter, as were the three Olympic mechanics who had worked on the overhaul.

On his return to his wife and seven school-age children in Ohio, McCusker found that his distinguished flying career, which had brought him the prestigious Octave Chanute Award for flight-testing the Gemini space capsule, was in ruins. Now he was known throughout the world as the pilot who had been at the controls of the plane that killed the son of Aristotle Onassis, and he was still being charged with manslaughter. He used up most of his savings before he finally found a job in South Dakota, flying a 40-year-old World War II surplus Beechcraft in aerial mapping work, at a salary lower than that of a truck driver.

Don McCusker and his wife Helena were to endure their nightmare for another five years. They kept corresponding with a Greek lawyer whom they had hired to seek compensation for Don's injuries and expenses, but the lawyer was not able to make any progress during Aristotle Onassis's lifetime. Filing a lawsuit in Greece was out of the question, for McCusker did not have the necessary funds, and the chances of overcoming *Lex Onassis* there were non-existent. Onassis went to his grave in March of 1975 without ever having relented in his determination to cover up his own guilt. On his deathbed in Paris, he ordered his daughter Christina never to permit the manslaughter indictment to be lifted—"you owe that to the memory of your brother."

It was not until November of 1977—three years after the corrupt Greek colonels were replaced by a democratic government—that the indictment was finally dismissed. Even then McCusker's name was not cleared because the indictment was merely dropped for lack of proof. He remained at his low-paying job in South Dakota, and continued to seek compensation through negotiations in Greece. But Don had no leverage, for he still lacked the funds to sue there, and even with Ari and the colonels gone, *Lex Onassis* had enough vitality to deprive Don of his legal right to compensation.

Finally in 1978 Olympic Airways authorized an American lawyer to negotiate a settlement with McCusker. Since his Greek medical bills had been paid, all that McCusker sought was reimbursement of his financial losses, which he calculated at about $175,000. The American lawyer for Olympic made a final offer of $65,000. Don was about to accept the $65,000 offer, when his brother-in-law, Herb Mehlhorn—who happened to be a rocket scientist—suggested that he seek my advice about settling for that amount.

After meeting with Don and his wife Helena and studying the documents they left with me, I thought there was a reasonable chance of collecting a lot more than $65,000. While Don had recovered his health to the point where he could pass the stringent commercial pilot physical examination, he had been robbed of his good name and the ability to earn his living as a pilot at the accustomed level. Clearly, he should recover more than $65,000 if he could prove that someone other than the Greek government was responsible for the harsh treatment he received as an innocent victim of the Piaggio crash. While it was common knowledge in the Greek legal community that Aristotle Onassis was the instigator of the phony indictment, proving this in court would be extremely difficult since he was now dead and it was unlikely that we would find either witnesses or documents attesting to his complicity. There was also the hazard that if McCusker brought suit in America, the $65,000 offer that emanated from Greece might well be withdrawn, leaving him even worse off than before. Despite all these obstacles, I had a strong feeling that if we could sue the estate of Aristotle Onassis in America, the technical problems of our case would quickly be solved.

I checked the court records and found that no estate of Aristotle Onassis existed in New York or anyplace else in the United States. This was not surprising since Aristotle was averse to paying taxes of any kind, and had arranged his affairs so that his property would be passed on to his heirs without using the courts. Although he owned the Olympic Tower on

Fifth Avenue and other property in New York, officially he was a citizen of Argentina, and he used *Lex Onassis* to hide his ownership behind a maze of foreign trusts and corporations. When he was prosecuted for fraudulently obtaining American war-surplus ships, the New York FBI office complained to Director Hoover that no less than forty of its agents were engaged for more than two years in the effort to merely identify the nationality of the owner of those ships. As things stood in 1978, three years after his death, neither the Internal Revenue Service nor the New York State authorities had tried to collect any taxes on his estate.

There is a provision in New York law under which you can have an administrator appointed for the estate of a deceased person whom you wish to sue, even if that person's heirs have taken no steps to administer the estate. Upon a showing that the deceased left property in New York, the Surrogate's Court may appoint an administrator. Usually this is done in cases where the deceased did not leave enough property to warrant expenditures by the surviving relatives for administration through the regular court procedures. There is a county official called the Public Administrator who usually is appointed to administer such estates. Therefore, at the time I filed suit for the McCuskers in June of 1978, I also filed a petition in the Surrogate's Court for the County of New York, asking that the Public Administrator be appointed as administrator of the estate of Aristotle Onassis. This procedure always reminded me of the old Marx brothers gag in which Groucho says to the heavily-accented Chico, "I'll get you an interpreter so I can insult you properly."

When the Public Administrator's lawyer received a copy of the petition, he thought it was a practical joke. Most of the estates he administered were of paupers, and now he was a candidate to handle the property of one of the world's richest men. The petition was also served on the two people who would have the right to act as administrators themselves: Jacqueline Kennedy Onassis, the widow, and Christina Onassis, the only surviving child. A hearing was set for August 16, 1978, in the New York County Surrogate's Court to determine who should be the administrator of the estate of Aristotle Onassis.

The Onassis forces could oppose our petition on two grounds: they could argue that it should be dismissed because Onassis left no property to administer in New York, or they could exercise Christina's right to be appointed administrator instead of the Public Administrator. The no-property claim could have led to a jury trial in the Surrogate's Court to determine whether Ari had an ownership interest in the Olympic Tower and other properties, a public event which was bound to attract the attention of federal and state tax collectors. Even Christina's appointment as administrator would create a presumption that Ari had indeed left property in New

York. This led me to believe that I might get a phone call from a lawyer prior to the hearing, and I was not disappointed.

A hastily-arranged conference took place at my office, attended by three Wall Street lawyers officially representing Olympic Airways. Each was equipped with the standard legal-size yellow pad. As I spelled out the details of Don McCusker's injuries and financial losses, I noticed that the lawyers were not writing anything on their pads. The same thing happened when I summarized the proof I had assembled on the cause of the accident, including photographs showing the faulty rigging of the aileron controls by Ari's Olympic mechanics. It was only when they broached the subject of settling the case out of court prior to the appointment of an administrator for Aristotle's estate that they wrote down the figure I demanded: one million dollars. They said that they were authorized to offer $500,000, but would recommend to their clients that they pay $600,000. I told them that I would report the offer to the McCuskers but would recommend that they reject it.

After the meeting ended, I phoned Don McCusker. He could hardly believe his ears when I told him that there was now an offer of $600,000 for the claim that he had been willing to settle for $65,000 just a few weeks earlier. I said that I thought they might pay more than $600,000, and he authorized me to settle for anything over that amount.

I called the Olympic lawyers and within a few minutes the case was settled for $800,000. That same day a cashier's check for $800,000 was hand-delivered to me, even before the McCuskers had signed a release or settlement agreement. Apparently the Olympic lawyers wanted to be certain that the case was officially settled before the date of the hearing scheduled in the Surrogate's Court. Thus did the Public Administrator of New York County miss out on the golden opportunity to become the administrator of the estate of Aristotle Onassis.

News of the settlement sent a strong message to the aviation community that Don McCusker could not have been at fault. The $800,000 payment—equal to more than $2.5 million in 2010 dollars—was tantamount to a public admission that Don had been framed by a fraudulent manslaughter indictment, since the settlement was several times the amount of financial and physical damages he had suffered. It confirmed that Don was the victim of Aristotle Onassis's overbearing ego which precluded the tycoon from accepting any blame for his son's death, and it brought Don offers of employment at a salary commensurate with his splendid flying record.

I was proud to represent Don and Helena McCusker. Their five-year Greek nightmare had a happy ending because the American Rule of Law gave them the firepower they needed to overcome the arrogance of a tyrant who was able to manipulate the legal systems of other nations to the point of impunity. The legacy of the Founding Lawyers had trumped the Rule of Men which Aristotle Onassis enjoyed during his lifetime.

Terror by Writs:
How Wealthy Crooks Pollute Legal Systems

Largely through bribery, Aristotle Onassis kept himself immune from lawsuits in nations like Monaco, Panama, Liberia, and the Greece of the crooked colonels. That bribery was unlikely to happen in developed democracies like Great Britain, but such crude tactics were not necessary to shield Britons whose business principles resembled those of Onassis. All they needed was the fee-shifting rule which deprived their victims of access to the civil courts. To thwart the Rule of Law and suppress the truth, they were (and are) able to use the English legal system as both a shield and a sword. A shining example is Robert Maxwell, an English tycoon who patterned himself after Aristotle Onassis in some important respects.

Bob Maxwell was a London publishing and printing mogul who (like Onassis) constructed a web of Lichtenstein trusts to camouflage the ownership of his major business holdings. He tapped the telephones of his own associates and employees. His yacht, the *Lady Ghislaine*, named after his daughter, was more than a hundred feet longer than Onassis's *Christina*, and was elaborately equipped for use as his floating office. He verbally bullied and publicly humiliated his children, especially the three who were unfortunate enough to work in his businesses.

Unlike Ari, Maxwell generally did not create new jobs or profit-making enterprises. His usual game was to take over a losing company with bank financing, and then fire a lot of employees and manipulate the books to make the company appear profitable. He also illegally controlled his companies' employee pension funds, which were legally required to be administered by independent trustees. This enabled him to secretly plunder the pension funds, using that money (which belonged to his employees) to shore up his unprofitable and ego-feeding ventures. He was a world-class swindler who eventually stole hundreds of millions of pounds from his employees' pension funds in the desperate effort to keep his fraudulent empire of 400 companies afloat.

This thievery was not exposed until Maxwell disappeared from his yacht in 1991 and his body was found floating in the Atlantic Ocean off the Canary Islands. Then the roof caved in, and in the process his employees' pension funds were virtually wiped out. Yet as far back as 1971, the U.K.'s Department of Trade and Industry had issued a report branding him as "a person who cannot be relied on to exercise proper stewardship of a publicly quoted company." For the next 20 years, Maxwell managed to avoid being closed down by government regulators because he used Ponzi-like tactics to keep insolvent companies afloat and to pay pension benefits as they accrued.

Many of Britain's highly-skilled investigative reporters were aware of Maxwell's larcenous tactics, but when they wrote their stories, the editors killed them on the advice of their libel lawyers. As Roy Greenslade, a former Maxwell newspaper editor, wrote in his 1992 biography *Maxwell*:

> There can be little doubt that Maxwell did successfully
> intimidate the press, launching (and usually abandoning)
> more court actions than any other individual in newspaper
> history. While this added to the public perception of him as
> a malevolent business mogul, probably with something to
> hide, it did largely prevent the truth from coming out.

The investigative reports which would have exposed Maxwell much earlier were not published because of the intimidating specter of legal costs. If the lawsuits contained the slightest mistake or imprecision, Maxwell, aided by Britain's lack of constitutionally-guaranteed freedom of speech or the press, could use the English courts to collect nominal damages plus millions of pounds for his own legal costs under the fee-shifting rule. That was enough to silence even the largest English newspapers, because in English libel actions the defendant must prove the truth of every statement. (The opposite is true in American courts, where the claimant must prove the falsity of the statements in question, and often has to go further and prove that the defendant knew they were false.)

Furthermore, "truth" under English libel law means the literal and complete truth. Floyd Abrams, the renowned American First Amendment lawyer and scholar, explains that proving "truth" in the English courts "means this *really* happened; it really happened just the way you say it happened." It is not sufficient to prove that "you interviewed people who said it happened" or that "you have reliable sources, scholars, eyewitnesses." The staggering cost of reconstructing the story to demonstrate "truth" in such painstaking detail, and the chances of being unable to verify every sentence, when added to the doubling of expense under fee-shifting, were sufficient to discourage publication of the truth about Maxwell—especially after he made it clear that he would abuse the courts by litigating any unflattering statement about him or his companies. Many times English newspapers found it more expedient to retract basically accurate statements than to risk a huge bill for Maxwell's legal expenses.

Maxwell was not unique in filing abusive lawsuits to prevent revelation of crooked business practices. He was following a long British tradition of such legal atrocities, dating back at least as far as Charles Dickens's reality-inspired nineteenth-century novels. English journalists have named this tactic "terror by writs." Maxwell's contemporary, Roland (Tiny) Rowland, was another master of litigation abuse, using it to protect the financial empire he had built largely through fraudulent bookkeeping. During his nine-year attempt to gain control of the company that owned Harrod's department store, he flooded the English courts with groundless lawsuits against business rivals, government officials, and anyone who dared to utter a truthful statement about his unfitness to own that British institution.

Thus it is apparent that the filing of frivolous lawsuits which seriously impact the legal system is not deterred by the English fee-shifting rule, since abusive litigants like Onassis, Maxwell, and Rowland could not care less about the trivial expense of hiring lawyers to protect their fiefdoms—an expense which they are usually able to pass along to their own ill-treated shareholders, customers, or employees.

How Would McCusker v. Onassis Have Fared in Other Legal Systems?

The settlement that secured the financial future of the McCusker family and helped to clear Don's name could not have been achieved anywhere but in the United States. In all other countries, wealthy crooks like Aristotle Onassis were virtually immune from lawsuits by ordinary people like the McCuskers in 1978, and unfortunately that is still the situation in 2010.

The McCuskers were able to bring Ari to justice because the American Rule of Law gave them access to the legal system on a footing equal to that of an Onassis. My firm undertook their case on a contingency fee basis, under which we would receive nothing unless we won or settled the case. If we obtained a settlement or won the case at trial, we would be paid one-third of the amount recovered for them above $65,000. (We waived the fee on the first $65,000 because the McCuskers had already been offered that amount before we took on the case.) Since we would be filing the case in an American court, there would be no fee-shifting even if their case were dismissed or lost at trial. And our firm would pay all the expenses of investigation, preparation, and trial, subject to reimbursement if we were successful. Therefore, the McCuskers took no financial risks in electing to sue the Onassis estate in New York.

Even this risk-free access to the American courts would not have been meaningful unless the legal services available to the McCuskers were comparable to those which wealthy litigants like Onassis customarily used: the biggest and most powerful law firms in the country. By 1978, I had been in practice for 30 years and had successfully represented claimants in most of the major postwar airline crashes, as well as in some other relatively complicated tort cases. While our 20-lawyer firm was less than a tenth the size of those that represented the airlines and other large companies, size did not really matter in that situation. The big firms could only use three or four of their lawyers for each case, so the hundreds of their other lawyers who were busy with taxes, estates, and other specialties had no impact on the McCuskers' claims. The key point was that we had the resources and the specialized experience to put our clients on equal footing with their much wealthier opponents. Our resources included the thousands of dollars—sometimes the hundreds of thousands of dollars—needed to investigate, prepare, and try complicated cases against highly skilled opponents. (The McCusker case was especially expensive because all the physical evidence and most of the witnesses were in Europe.) Without those resources, we could not have survived on contingency-fee cases, because one-third of a zero recovery equals zero. Nor could we have attracted cases involving potentially large damages if we did not have the money to bring them to court against the well-financed opposition.

Having heaped this praise on myself, I am forced to point out that in 1978, ours was one of hundreds of American law firms which could have done the job for the McCuskers, providing them with the opportunity to neutralize the Onassis financial advantage on a risk-free contingent basis. In 2010 there are thousands of such firms in the United States, not only for personal injury cases, but for all manner of claims—investment losses, civil rights violations, unfair competition, environmental damage, employment discrimination—including those pitting a poor or middle-class individual claimant against a giant company or a billionaire. This ability to level the playing field was developed during the twentieth century because the American Rule of Law required equality of access—not only the right to sue but the opportunity to be represented by lawyers who had the experience and resources to present the claim effectively, to make the system work for clients who don't have the money to pay the fees that their lawyers' training and experience would bring in the legal marketplace. This meaningful access could not have been developed if fee-shifting blocked access to the courts, or if American lawyers were prohibited from undertaking cases on contingency fees.

Apart from the United States, Britain comes closer to providing such access than any other nation. So let's use Britain again as the surrogate for the legal systems of all the other developed democracies. We'll assume that Don and Helena McCusker were residents of England in 1978, and that the English courts had jurisdiction over Olympic Airways and the estate of Aristotle Onassis. What would have happened to the McCuskers' claims?

In 1978, no English lawyer would have been permitted to take Don McCusker's case on a contingent basis, i.e., charging no fee unless the case was won or settled. Historically, those who controlled the English legal system were aware that contingency fees would expose members of the establishment to troublesome lawsuits brought by people who could not afford to pay lawyers. Also, many English lawyers at that time thought it was beneath their professional dignity to make their services available without assurance of payment, especially in a culture which placed a low value on broad access to justice. Therefore, Don McCusker would have been required to pay fixed hourly fees to a solicitor and a barrister, a luxury which he could not have come close to affording even at the height of his storied career as a test pilot.

Attempting to bridge this gap, England provided Legal Aid in both civil and criminal cases, unlike the system in the United States, where governmental Legal Aid does not usually involve extensive litigation in the courts, and clients with meritorious cases can engage competent lawyers on contingency fees without any cash outlay. But the McCuskers would not have met English Legal Aid's financial qualifications in 1978, because Don's pilot salary, demeaning as it was to him, was above the poverty-level income ceiling, and they owned their house, which would have put the value of their assets above the very low Legal Aid disqualification threshold. Even if they had passed these means tests, their claim would have been pre-screened for prospects of success by England's Legal Aid Board, which probably would have denied them assistance because of lack of documented proof that Aristotle Onassis was behind the fraudulent manslaughter indictment, and the fact that this was a non-routine case which would require many more hours of legal work than a road accident claim.

Apart from these insurmountable obstacles, the bottom line for Don would have been the risk of getting socked with the Onassis legal fees if he lost the case. Those fees certainly would have run into hundreds of thousands of pounds, far beyond any sum that Don could have earned during the rest of his life. Therefore, suing in England was, in the words of Lord Devlin, quite out of the question. Don would have had no sane choice but to accept the $65,000 settlement offer, if indeed he'd been fortunate enough to get such an offer absent the ability to pursue the case in the United States.

That was the situation in 1978. Now, 32 years later, would Don McCusker's chances of bringing Onassis to justice in England be any better?

England's Failed Attempts to Provide Access to Justice

In recent years, England has paid considerable attention to the need for broader access to justice. As we have seen, Lord Woolf's 1995-1996 reports concluded that cost problems block access to the courts and "contaminate the whole civil justice system." But instead of permitting contingency fees and abandoning the ruinous Loser Pays rule, English legal officials have continued to look for access to justice through the wrong end of the telescope, using England's tradition of restricted access as the default position. They staunchly maintained the centuries-old obstacles they had created to block the courthouse doors, and then engaged in futile searches for magical keys that might somehow open those doors for most of their citizens. Their efforts have focused on three potential keys: Legal Aid, Conditional Fee Agreements, and Legal Expense Insurance. Here's how they have played out.

English Legal Aid in the 21st Century

The Legal Aid Act 1949 was part of the welfare state installed by Clement Attlee's postwar Labour government. In its early years it was limited to civil cases, and it was estimated that 70 percent of the population could meet the means tests. However, when Legal Aid was extended to criminal cases, they soon absorbed most of the budget, putting a fatal squeeze on many civil claims. While the total 2009 Legal Aid budget is over £2 billion, the portion devoted to civil cases consists of the money that is left after all criminal defendants have been given access to government-paid legal assistance.

As a result, civil Legal Aid in England has become a service for the indigent only. The means tests fixed in 2009 ruled out all claimants whose families' gross monthly income was more than £2,530 ($4,048). Those who cleared that hurdle would be disqualified if they had disposable capital of more than £8,000 ($12,800), including all the family's savings and the value of their homes above £100,000 ($160,000). Thus in 2010, based on their home ownership and Don's salary as a mapping pilot, the McCuskers would have been even farther removed from financial eligibility for Legal Aid than in 1978.

Even if the McCuskers had been poor enough to meet the 2010 financial qualifications, it is highly unlikely that they would have been given Legal Aid because their case was far from routine and would entail high legal expenses. Claims that are likely to require more than £25,000 ($40,000) of legal services are referred to a Special Cases Unit. Because civil Legal Aid is heavily dependent on recovering, through the Loser Pays rule, the money advanced by the government, that unit is under great pressure to fund only the cases that are most likely to be won or settled—what Americans would call "slam-dunks." As crime and terrorism continue their upward spiral, the "leftover" pool for civil Legal Aid can only get smaller. Furthermore, budget pressures have forced the government to reduce the fees of Legal Aid lawyers, to the point where the clients who qualify often have to settle for inexperienced or incompetent lawyers. Frances Gibb, Legal Editor of the *London Times*, wrote in 2007:

> In truth, the Legal Aid scheme is colloquially "on its
> uppers," and those lawyers still in the business scrape a

modest living…. Because of the low rates of pay, there is also a dearth of new entrants.

In 2009, English District Judge David Oldham, president of the Association of District Judges, concluded that "civil Legal Aid has virtually disappeared, and the numbers of people acting for [representing] themselves have soared."

Despite these shortcomings, Britain is the world leader in per capita expenditure on Legal Aid. The low level of Legal Aid funding in other developed democracies is evidenced by the assistance to needy litigants provided by the European Court of Human Rights, which pays a flat fee of 850 Euros (about $1,250) for conducting the entire case, including the cost of appearing at hearings at the court's seat in Strasbourg, France. Some lawyers handling such cases reported that this flat fee netted them less than one Euro an hour. And Melbourne Law School Professor Christine Parker writes in *Just Lawyers: Regulation and Access to Justice*:

> In all countries the merits tests (a determination of how likely the applicant's legal action is to succeed), matter tests (a determination of whether the issue falls into a priority area for funding), and means tests are becoming increasingly restrictive.

Even in English cases where Legal Aid is approved, the claimant can face a very rocky road, since the assistance can be cut off at any time, especially when the case turns out to be more difficult or expensive than it appeared at the outset. A dramatic example is the experience of Lord Spens, who sued the Bank of England for allegedly abusing its powers by causing him to be removed from the position of managing director of another bank. Having fallen on hard times, he qualified for Legal Aid, which paid his solicitors' and barristers' fees up to the eve of trial in 1999. But at that point the Legal Aid Board terminated its support because "a reasonably prudent fee-paying client would not proceed further." This forced Lord Spens to drop the case, since he could not afford to pay the lawyers himself.

Pro bono—providing voluntary legal services free of charge—has been growing in England, but it only adds up to a token force. It is largely focused on short-term services such as giving office advice, and so it is usually not available for civil cases which require significant commitments of time and resources.

Thus it is apparent that the McCuskers would not have the wherewithal to finance a viable lawsuit against the Onassis estate in England today. Had Don been a union member injured during employment, his union probably would have provided him with lawyers. But like most people in Britain and elsewhere, Don was not a union member.

Conditional Fee Agreements (CFAs)

With the introduction of Conditional Fee Agreements (CFAs) in 1990, English lawyers were permitted for the first time to take civil cases on a no-win, no-fee basis. If the case is won or settled, the lawyer does not get a percentage of the amount recovered as in the United States, but instead is allowed to add a "success fee" which raises the hourly fee that he would have charged a paying client by as much as 100 percent, thereby doubling the usual hourly rate. Theoretically this would make it possible for the McCuskers to get an English lawyer today, provided they could find one who was willing to assume the risks of investigating, preparing, and trying such a challenging case without receiving any cash payments or a percentage of the recovery. Since most of the skilled English litigators are happy to collect handsome fees without taking such risks, the McCuskers would have no real chance of suing Onassis under a CFA.

Even if the McCuskers convinced an English lawyer to take their case on a conditional fee in 2010, they would still be liable for the defendants' legal fees and other expenses if they lost the case, since CFAs have no effect on the Loser Pays rule. For the McCuskers, fee-shifting would be a double whammy, since they would have to sue both Olympic Airways (owner and operator of the Piaggio) and the estate of Aristotle Onassis, as we did in New York. If they left either one out, the opposing lawyers would be able to point to "the empty chair" and put the blame on the missing party. This is another vice of fee-shifting, since claimants rarely have all the facts at their disposal before starting suit, and often have to sue two or more defendants to discover the entire causal sequence. That multiplies the risks of fee-shifting, for a losing claimant has to pay the legal fees of all the defendants who are not held liable. If the claimant wins against one defendant but loses against another, the exonerated defendants' costs might wipe out much or all of what was gained by the winning part of the judgment.

Thus fee-shifting continues to contaminate the entire English legal process. In an effort to counteract this contamination, new forms of insurance have been created.

Legal Expense Insurance

The main product designed to mitigate the financial risks of fee-shifting is called ATE, for "after the event" insurance—the event being the filing of a lawsuit. For a fee (called the "premium") British underwriters will provide claimants with insurance against specified amounts of costs they would have to pay if they lost the case.

In 2000, with the civil Legal Aid fund running dry, England eliminated Legal Aid for all personal injury claims except clinical negligence (medical malpractice) and made CFAs the standard fee arrangement in such cases. This provided a big boost to the ATE market, since the CFAs left the claimants exposed to Loser Pays costs which could be covered by the ATE insurance. For the routine road accident claims which carry a 95 percent success rate, the ATE premium is negligible since the expected costs are not very high even in losing cases. Furthermore, the amount of the insurance premium is recoverable by the claimant under the Loser Pays rule, and thus becomes part of the settlement process which disposes of the great majority of such cases.

But legal expense insurance, even in the sophisticated ATE (after the event) form, would be worthless to the McCuskers because they could not possibly afford it. The premiums are based on two factors: (1) How much insurance is needed to cover the probable legal expenses of the defendants, and (2) Whether this is a routine road accident claim with a 95 percent success rate, or a more speculative claim that is likely to be defended to the hilt by high-powered lawyers. A rough estimate of the premium costs for a non-routine civil claim is at least 10 percent of the coverage sought, with premiums reported as high as 65 percent in more speculative cases. Again the hapless Lord Spens provides the example. When the Legal Aid Board pulled the plug on him, he sought ATE insurance to cover the defendant Bank of England's anticipated costs of £750,000. He was quoted a premium cost of £100,000, which equaled 13.3 percent of the coverage he required. His inability to pay that premium caused his solicitors to withdraw from the case for fear of being stuck for the winner's costs as "maintainers" of the lawsuit.

The McCuskers would find themselves in the same boat as Lord Spens. Clearly the Onassis interests would retain prominent solicitors and barristers to defend vigorously, and the chances of the McCuskers winning this non-routine case (to be tried by a judge without a jury) could not be rated higher than 50-50, if that high. To protect themselves, the McCuskers would have to buy well over £1 million worth of ATE insurance, bearing in mind that they would be at risk for the fees of the solicitors for both Olympic Airways and the Onassis estate, as well as QC barristers (and their "junior" assistants) for both defendants. If the case went to trial in 2010, the likely legal costs of the two defendants would run well over £1 million ($1.6 million), possibly double that figure. But we need go no further than £1 million, because the premium for that coverage would be at least £100,000 ($160,000), a sum far beyond the McCuskers' resources.

Therefore, fee-shifting remains an insurmountable obstacle for claimants like Elsie Parrish, Oliver Brown, James Meredith, the McCuskers, and the entire British middle class, who are beyond the aid of the ATE insurance market except in routine road accident cases. The combination of CFAs and ATE insurance has created a Rube Goldberg device, defined as "a deliberately over-engineered machine that performs a very simple task in a very complex

fashion, usually including a chain reaction." Instead of beginning at the logical starting point of automatically permitting full access—limited only by
special treatment for actual problem (e.g. frivolous) cases—those in charge
of the English legal system persist in the Rube Goldberg approach of shutting
out the entire middle class and then devising intricate schemes that struggle
to regain fragments of the lost access.

The chain reaction caused by the CFA-ATE machine was a principal reason
why England's chief civil judge assigned Lord Justice Jackson to spend all of
2009 reviewing civil litigation costs. CFA-ATE proved to be a runaway engine
that often raises costs to three or four times the amount in controversy, even in
uncomplicated cases. Without delving into the inevitably bewildering details
of Lord Justice Jackson's 557-page report, here is his concise appraisal of the
CFA-ATE system:

> The present system for achieving costs protection for
> claimants is, in my view, the most bizarre and expensive
> system that it is possible to devise.

Contingency Fees Compared with CFAs

By the end of the millennium it was beginning to dawn on English legal
officials that the contingency fee was a much simpler device for broadening
access than the bizarre and expensive CFA-ATE system—and much easier
for clients to understand than the "fiendishly complicated" CFAs. In a 1997
report to the Lord Chancellor, Sir Peter Middleton writes:

> There is no essential difference in principle between condi-
> tional and contingency fees. Indeed in some ways the latter
> may be preferable. Contingency fees create an incentive
> to achieve the best possible result for the client, not just a
> simple win. And they reward a cost-effective approach in a
> way that conditional fees, where the lawyers' remuneration
> is still based on an hourly bill, do not.

The leading English authority on costs (legal fees), Judge Michael Cook,
writes in his definitive 2001 textbook:

> Contingency [percentage] fees were still an abhorrence, but
> conditional fees were given cautious [English] approval. It
> was a distinction without a difference.

In 2008, as a prelude to consideration of lifting the ban on contingency
fees, England's impartial Civil Justice Council commissioned a study of the

operation of contingency fees (fees which are dependent on the outcome of a case, usually expressed as a percentage of the amount of damages recovered through a verdict or settlement) in the United States. Conducted by Cardiff University Professor Richard Moorhead and Senior Costs Judge Peter Hurst, it documented several important conclusions about American contingency fees:

(1) There is no evidence that contingency fees provide improper disincentives to settle;

(2) Contingency fees do not necessarily promote high rates of litigation, frivolous claims, or a litigation culture; and

(3) A new regime eliminating Loser Pays and permitting contingency fees in England "would operate satisfactorily and without the satellite litigation [about costs] which bedevils the current system."

Thus the Civil Justice Council study paved the way for serious consideration of contingency fees, recognizing that such a change would do little to broaden access to justice unless accompanied by retirement of the Loser Pays rule.

The most vociferous critics of American contingency fees purport to be champions of the free market system. This is ironic because American contingency fees are squarely based on a free market for legal services. They range from about 20 percent to as high as 40 percent, or rarely 50 percent of the amount recovered. The percentages are driven by market considerations such as the perceived difficulty and expense of the case, the potential amount of damages, the experience and reputation of the lawyer, and the competitiveness of the local legal community. The failed English experiment with CFAs is the laboratory study that demonstrates the cause-and-effect relationship between market-based contingency fees and the availability of such services to those who need them to achieve access to justice.

The 2009 Jackson Report: Broadening Access Through Contingency Fees and Changes in Loser Pays

Lord Justice Jackson's comprehensive final report shines as a beacon of hope that England at last may be on the right track to providing access to justice for all its citizens. It is a testament to Katz's Law (a corollary of Murphy's Law), i.e., that people and nations will act rationally when all other possibilities have been exhausted.

First Jackson tackled contingency fees, and used the voluminous evidence generated by his review to dispel many of the myths which have been used to denigrate them. He concluded: "Both solicitors and counsel [barristers] should be permitted to enter into contingency fee agreements with their clients."

Aware that contingency fees alone could not overcome the main barrier to access, he moved on to Loser Pays. While he did not recommend complete abrogation of the Loser Pays rule, he took a novel approach to personal injury cases, which constitute the largest group of civil claims: "I recommend that a regime of qualified one way costs shifting be introduced for personal injury cases." The qualifications relate to the continued empowerment of judges to assess costs in order to deter "bringing a frivolous or fraudulent claim," which we discussed in the preceding chapter. If this recommendation is followed, claimants who lose personal injury cases will not face cost-shifting, but losing defendants will have to pay the claimants' costs.

Aware that these contingency fee and cost-shifting recommendations would be seen as revolutionizing English civil practice, Lord Justice Jackson thus counseled a toe-in-the-water experiment with personal injury cases. He recommended the same approach to defamation cases, and prophetically noted: "There may be other categories of civil litigation where qualified one way costs shifting would be beneficial."

The Jackson report is only a recommendation, and will require parliamentary legislation for implementation. But the even-handed and exhaustive manner in which the review was conducted, and the well-reasoned, heavily documented 557-page report itself, give hope that it will not be ignored. One commentator who is likely to keep it in the public arena is Frances Gibb, legal editor of the *London Times*. In her column, "Let's be civil and stop Loser Pays," commenting on the May 2009 Jackson preliminary report, she reminded readers that the "civil justice system has priced itself out of the reach of ordinary people" who "face financial ruin if they venture into court and lose."

For Americans, the message of the Jackson report is that the broad access to civil courts we enjoy—thanks to the work of the Founding Lawyers and their successors—is an indispensable element of democracy and the Rule of Law, a prize that the rest of the world is beginning to recognize and to seek.

Chapter Eleven

The Rule of Law
for David and Goliath

"Why don't you go back to Connecticut, buddy-boy!" The man's voice on the other end of the phone sounded snide and threatening. Like the dozens of similar calls during the past two weeks, it came about 3:30 in the morning, and the caller hung up before Ralph Nader could say anything.

The words spoken by some of the callers seemed more harassing than threatening: "Mr. Nader, please pick up a parcel at Railway Express...(click)." "Is this Mr. Nader? Can you hear me? Can you hear me? Cut it out. You're going to cut me off (click)." But Nader felt every call as a threat, because he didn't know who was calling, or whom the callers were working for, or how far they would go to silence him. The calls had begun early in February 1966, when Senator Abraham Ribicoff announced that Nader was going to testify in support of auto safety legislation and that he was going to expose manufacturing and design defects that threatened highway safety.

As governor of Connecticut from 1955 to 1961, Ribicoff had become known as "Mr. Auto Safety," largely because of his tough enforcement of state speeding and reckless driving laws. Yet, even though suspensions of Connecticut driver's licenses rose from 400 to more than 10,000 per year, there was no significant drop in the accident rate. This convinced Ribicoff that something more than strict enforcement of speed limits was needed. In 1964, Ribicoff, then chairman of the Senate Subcommittee on Executive Reorganization, decided to hold hearings on auto safety problems, hoping to focus attention on the role of the automobile itself in road accidents and thereby open the way for auto design safety legislation.

Meanwhile, Ralph Nader made his way through Princeton, graduating magna cum laude in 1955 and going on to the Harvard Law School. In his senior year at Harvard, where he was the editor of the *Harvard Law Record*, he wrote a term paper on auto safety for the seminar in medico-legal problems. His paper concentrated on auto design defects, which Ralph felt were causing millions of injuries annually. After private practice in Hartford (1960-1964), he moved to a rooming house in Washington D.C., where he did freelance writing on auto safety for the *Christian Science Monitor.* He became a researcher and consultant for Daniel Patrick Moynihan, then assistant secretary of labor in the Johnson administration. Moynihan was one of the earliest advocates of federal auto design legislation.

Nader's work for Moynihan brought him to Ribicoff's attention. Late in 1964, Ralph, then 30 years old, became a voluntary, unpaid advisor to the Ribicoff subcommittee staff, helping them prepare searching questions for auto executives who testified in the 1965 hearings. At the same time, Ralph was polishing the manuscript of his first book, *Unsafe at Any Speed*, which focused on GM's Chevrolet Corvair as an example of irresponsible and dangerous auto design. Published in November 1965, the book charged that the 1960-1963 Corvair, a sporty rear-engine compact that was one of GM's best sellers, was a menace to life and limb. Nader charged that the Corvair had a known tendency to deprive the driver of control because the outside rear wheel would "tuck under" the chassis during turns. He claimed that GM's management concealed these known defects from the public and did not correct them until the 1964 model year.

Unsafe at Any Speed received some good reviews, but initially it didn't make much of a splash in the bookstores. It was published by a small house with little marketing clout, and Ralph himself was virtually unknown to the public. On February 10, 1966, three months after its publication, Ralph first appeared as a witness before the Ribicoff subcommittee. Sleepless the night before because of the threatening phone calls, Ralph testified for nearly three hours, supporting the case for auto design legislation.

The next day produced an historic comedy of errors which contained striking parallels to the Watergate burglary that occurred six years later. At 1:30 p.m., Ralph went to the Dirksen Senate Office Building to record a television interview. He stayed in the ground-floor television studio for about half an hour. When he left the studio, he took the elevator, intending to go down to the basement to eat in the cafeteria, but he pushed the wrong button and the elevator took him upstairs instead. Realizing his mistake, he quickly pressed the down button and took the elevator to the basement. Unknown to Ralph, he was being followed at the time by two private detectives from New York. But his rapid reversal of direction shook off the bloodhounds.

Having lost their quarry, they asked a building guard where Nader had gone. The guard became suspicious and called in a Capitol Police lieutenant, who promptly told the private eyes that they were not allowed to shadow people in the Senate Office Building and that they had better leave at once. Then the guard saw Ralph leaving the building, and told him that he had been followed by two private detectives.

Ralph then learned that investigators had interviewed some of his friends and past associates under the pretext of checking his qualifications for an important job. He noticed that men seemed to be following him, and he was accosted in a drug store and a supermarket by attractive young women who asked him to accompany them back to their apartments. Ralph related these facts to journalist friends, some of whom wrote articles seeking to smoke out the people behind this intimidation campaign. On March 6, the *New York Times* published Ralph's charges that the auto industry was attempting to harass him as part of a campaign to discredit his book and his testimony before the Ribicoff subcommittee.

Now Senator Ribicoff took a hand, announcing that he was asking the Department of Justice to investigate a possible criminal attempt to intimidate a witness before a Congressional committee. This brought statements from Ford, Chrysler, and American Motors denying any involvement. From General Motors came a "no comment," followed by a late-night press release which admitted they had launched an investigation of Nader. But they claimed it was only "a routine investigation through a reputable law firm to determine whether Ralph Nader was acting on behalf of litigants or their attorneys in Corvair design cases pending against General Motors." They denied involvement in "any of the alleged harassment recently reported in the press." Thus it was the press accounts which forced GM to admit—however evasively—that the "investigation" was theirs.

The next day Senator Ribicoff announced that he was requesting Nader, the president of General Motors, and the "detective agencies" to appear before his subcommittee on March 22, 1966, for a public explanation of the alleged harassment of a Senate witness. Senators Robert Kennedy and Gaylord Nelson joined in the request. Senator Nelson said:

> If great corporations can engage in this kind of intimidation, it is an assault upon freedom in America. No average citizen can face up to a corporation the size of General Motors which sets out to destroy him.

But the Senate and millions of people around the world watching on television were soon to learn that General Motors had not selected an average citizen to intimidate.

On the appointed day, GM President James Roche appeared before the Ribicoff subcommittee, flanked by his lawyer, Theodore Sorensen, who had been John F. Kennedy's speechwriter and was a long-time friend of Ribicoff. Roche read a prepared statement that seemed to accept responsibility for the Nader fiasco, but if you read it carefully it was that old reliable public relations ploy: an apology for doing nothing wrong. Mr. Roche wanted to apologize to the senators and Mr. Nader—"to the extent that General Motors bears responsibility." Then he proceeded to deny that the GM investigation—which he said was for legitimate Corvair litigation purposes—had employed detectives using false names, or had Nader under surveillance on the day he testified before the subcommittee, or made threatening phone calls. Roche portrayed it as a routine litigation check that had gone awry because of the overzealousness of the main private eye, ex-FBI agent Vincent Gillen of New York. He assured the senators that if he had been told that the detectives were going to prowl around Nader's home town in Connecticut and interview more than 60 people who had known him from childhood through the other phases of his life, asking searching personal questions that had nothing to do with the Corvair litigation, he would have terminated the investigation immediately.

Roche, who came across like a kindly small-town high school principal, was permitted to get away with this whitewash. The senators were satisfied that they had summoned the president of GM before the nation and that he had humbly apologized. It was a fine bit of lawyering by Sorenson.

The star witness was Vincent Gillen, the great detective himself. He was a Runyonesque character who sensed that he was being set up as the fall guy, and he wasn't about to accept that role graciously. He insisted that everything he had done, including the interviewing of 60 people under the pretext of a pre-employment check, had been approved by GM. But he had been cast as the villain of this TV show, and Senators Ribicoff and Robert Kennedy denounced him heatedly. To counteract the Gillen testimony, Roche was recalled to repeat his statement that the frolicsome detective's tactics were not within GM's instructions.

Satisfied that bringing GM's president to heel had given a strong impetus to passage of the first federal auto safety legislation, Senator Ribicoff adjourned the six-hour hearing. At the close, he waved Gillen's voluminous investigation report toward the camera, and said to Ralph:

> And I may say to you, Mr. Nader, that I have read these
> reports very carefully, and you and your family can be
> proud, because they put you through the mill and they
> haven't found out a damn thing against you.

Ralph was now a national hero, thanks to the magic of television, with an assist from Vincent Gillen's gumshoes who bungled the surveillance in the Senate Office Building. But when Ralph tried to get a copy of the Gillen investigation report, he was informed by the subcommittee staff that it had been sent to the National Archives for safekeeping and would not be available to the public or even to him.

Ralph was ambivalent about suing GM at first. He consulted me, since we had known each other earlier when I helped him in a small way with his efforts to use aviation safety regulation as a precedent for a federal role in auto design safety. Some of his journalist friends warned him that his crusader image might be tarnished by suing, and that his future auto safety activities would be branded as support tactics for his lawsuit. I tried to convince him that he could protect his image by announcing at the start of the lawsuit that the proceeds would be dedicated to his pubic interest work, since he told me that was what he planned to do. In the end, Ralph came up with his own convincing reason to sue. He wanted all the facts brought out, so the whole world would know the true extent of GM's involvement; and he wanted to broaden the law's protection against corporate harassment so that future consumer advocates would not have to rely upon acts of personal courage for survival.

Just before the one-year statute of limitations ran out, Ralph gave me the green light to sue. A few weeks earlier, he and Senator Ribicoff had been honored guests at the White House, looking on as President Lyndon Johnson signed into law the National Traffic and Motor Vehicle Safety Act, the first statute to impose safety standards on auto manufacturers.

I'd been working on a draft complaint, along with my partners Al Gans and Paul Rheingold, who were to play important roles throughout the litigation. My natural optimism and my appetite for a prestigious case led me to assume that there must be an established legal remedy for what GM/Gillen had done to Ralph. But now that we were down to writing the complaint, the remedy was not so clear.

Since GM had not published any of its investigation data, Ralph could not sue for defamation (libel or slander). His main claim against GM would have to be brought under the label of "invasion of privacy." Although it appeared in the textbooks as a well-established form of tort (civil wrong), it had proven to be a relatively undeveloped remedy, more of a plaything for legal scholars than a means of collecting damages. In all the state and federal courts there had been only twelve reported cases in which damages had been awarded for invasion of privacy. The awards ranged from $250 to a high of only $12,500, and in some states (including New York) the protection of privacy was very narrow. Ralph himself pointed out that while GM had the worst of motives, they had unwittingly increased the sales of his book (his major source of income at the time) and had helped him to become a national hero, much in demand as a lecturer and television show guest.

Ralph was properly concerned that if he sued GM, they might counter-claim or sue him, alleging that his book or other statements libeled or slandered GM's products. I agreed that we would defend him against any such claims without any charges other than the contingency fee, which we fixed at one-third of the amount collected from GM up to $300,000, and 30 percent of anything over $300,000.

Our main legal problem, apart from the fuzziness of the right to privacy and the low damage awards, was that GM had taken the precaution of erecting a Maginot Line of attorney-client privilege to shield all records of the Nader investigation. GM's legal department in Detroit had initiated the investigation, under cover of the false claim that it was part of their defense of the Corvair product liability suits. Attorney-client privilege protected communications of the client (GM) with its own house counsel, even though they were employees rather than independent lawyers. Not content with that protection, the legal department had avoided hiring Gillen directly. Instead they went to the trouble of paying a fee to a Washington lawyer, Richard Danner, for the sole purpose of having him hire Gillen, who was himself a lawyer as well as a private investigator. We had to figure out a way to circumvent those privilege barriers or we would never get our hands on the evidence needed to establish the responsibility of GM for the actions of Gillen. If we were stymied by privilege, all we could hope for would be a judgment against Gillen and his agency, which was not what Ralph wanted even if it could be collected. He was determined to hold General Motors itself accountable.

The law gives strong protection to the attorney-client relationship in order to encourage clients to confide completely in their lawyers without fear that such confidences will ever be used as evidence in court. Since the attorney-client privilege belongs to the client, GM could prevent Danner, Gillen, and the lawyers in GM's legal department from testifying if the claim of privilege was upheld. The privilege might be forfeited by public disclosure, which explains why the Gillen investigation report, which was seen from a distance by millions of viewers as Senator Ribicoff waved it to the cameras, quickly found its way into the National Archives. If that report had become a public document, the attorney-client privilege protection might well have been lost.

Once again fate took a hand, as it had when Ralph accidentally shook off Vincent Gillen's operatives by pushing the wrong button in the Senate Office Building elevator. On the day Gillen was served with the suit papers, he gave an interview to the *Detroit Free Press* in which he said of Ralph, among other things, "I would refer him to a psychiatrist." Gillen was enjoying the media interest in his role, appearing on TV talk shows and giving expansive interviews all over the country. Ralph was in the early stages of establishing his reputation and did not want to suffer any further smears. We decided to start a separate lawsuit against Gillen, seeking damages for libel based on the *Detroit Free Press* interview. We hoped this would deter Gillen from using the media to discredit Ralph.

From the beginning, Gillen's legal position in the GM investigation had fascinated me. Clearly, GM's lawyers were facing a delicate balancing act in their dealings with him. Using him as the fall guy at the Ribicoff hearings had served GM well, but Ralph's invasion of privacy lawsuit would raise tougher questions. Normally GM would provide the money for Gillen's defense and agree to pick up the tab for any damages assessed against him. But if we were able to tell the jurors that GM was backing Gillen in the lawsuit, they might decide that GM must have authorized his activities, or at least that they were ratifying his "frolic" and thereby made themselves responsible for what he had done. On the other hand, if they cut him adrift and required him to defend himself, they would give him a strong incentive to come forward with whatever evidence he might have that GM had instructed him to go as far as he did. If he did not prove he was acting under GM directions, he might have to pay a jury's award all by himself, and his detective agency was profitable enough to put substantial assets at risk.

Since Gillen was now an adverse party, I could not discuss these questions with him. But having started the separate libel suit against him, I decided to take his deposition immediately. I could do this without GM's lawyers being present since GM was not a party to the libel suit. Indeed, they didn't even know it existed because New York practice did not require it to be filed in court until a later stage.

Vincent Gillen arrived at my office for his deposition with his lawyer/brother-in-law, Francis Maguire, who had been a member of Thomas E. Dewey's crack young prosecuting team in the New York of the 1930s. Gillen's appearance and his gravelly voice reminded me of Paul Douglas, the New York radio sportscaster who had become a popular comedy film star in the 1950s. I began by asking questions that enabled him to talk about his favorite subjects: himself, and the importance of his detective agency. Then, since his statement about referring Nader to a psychiatrist was based upon what happened during the Gillen-GM investigation, I started asking him about that investigation. I was delighted to find that Gillen was willing to respond at length on that subject, as on most any other. What was even more important was that his knowledgeable lawyer was letting him answer detailed questions about the investigation. That told me that GM had probably refused to indemnify him, and so he was being forced into the position of disgorging the truth to protect himself from a ruinous judgment.

The deposition stretched out over five days. Each day I encouraged him to produce more investigation documents, which were pure gold for our side since GM probably could have prevented their production by pleading the attorney-client privilege. From the five days of testimony and the hundreds of pages of documents Gillen produced, a sordid picture of corporate power abuse emerged.

GM's own documents demonstrated that from its inception, their investigation of Ralph Nader was designed solely to "get something on Nader" that GM could use to shut him up, to discredit his auto safety work and "get him out of GM's hair." In all the communications and instructions to Gillen, there was not a single mention of the Corvair litigation, the false cover story provided to the Senate. At GM's specific request, Gillen conducted wide-ranging interviews with more than 60 people who knew Nader, from his grade school teachers to his legal associates.

Gillen's operatives questioned these people about drug use, sexual practices, and financial manipulations, making it appear that others had given such information to them about Nader. Gillen reported these interviews immediately to Washington lawyer Richard Danner for transmittal to GM's legal department, whose response—far from the revulsion exhibited to the Senate by GM President Roche—was that Gillen was not digging deeply enough and was not coming up with the dirt that they wanted. Gillen and all the GM people involved knew that Nader was scheduled to be a witness at the Ribicoff hearings, but they put him under surveillance anyway, and GM paid an extra fee for this extraordinary service. Gillen had done 26 previous jobs for GM, and each time he had dealt directly with GM instead of going through a lawyer-intermediary such as Danner. After Senator Ribicoff summoned GM to explain the Nader investigation, Gillen was flown to Detroit to participate in a session with GM's legal department that was designed to cover up the true purpose of the investigation, and he was ordered to alter or destroy some key documents.

But Vincent Gillen, who was rapidly emerging as the smartest person involved on the GM side of the investigation, kept copies of all the documents he was ordered to destroy, since they proved that he was acting within GM's instructions at all times. He produced those documents at the deposition—69 exhibits in all, some of them running into dozens of pages of notes, instructions, and records of intimidating interviews, including the detailed Gillen report that had been entombed in the National Archives after the Ribicoff hearings. The most revealing document was a letter from Eileen Murphy of GM's legal department in Detroit. While this letter was sent by Murphy to the lawyer-intermediary Richard Danner for forwarding to Gillen, it did not show any addressee. It was typed on plain white paper rather than on GM's letterhead, and since it began with "Dear Dick," it became known as the Dear Dick letter.

Written about midway through the investigation, it complained about the lack of dirt in Gillen's reports. GM's frustration came through in this sentence: "It also strikes me that everyone is going overboard to impress us with what a great, charming intellectual this human being is—Eagle-Scout type." Eileen went on to complain that numerous personal questions she had ordered the investigators to ask about Nader had not produced any useful information. She gave further detailed instructions, listing questions about Ralph's private life to be checked out by the detectives. And of course, she did not mention the Corvair litigation, which GM President Roche had claimed to be the reason for investigating Nader. She signed off with "Well friend, have fun. Sincerely, Eileen." Writing about the Dear Dick letter in his *New York Post* column, Murray Kempton titled his article, "Have Fun, Friend."

Richard (Dick) Danner was an interesting character. An FBI agent who had headed the Miami FBI office during World II, he later left the Bureau and became campaign manager for George Smathers in his notorious 1950 Senate race against the Florida incumbent, Claude Pepper. According to Pepper, Dick Danner played an important role in producing faked and composite photographs that purported to link Pepper with prominent Communists, which helped Smathers to defeat Pepper. Later, Danner went to work for the Howard Hughes organization in Las Vegas, during which tenure he delivered $100,000 in cash taken from the Silver Slipper gambling casino to President Nixon's close friend, Bebe Rebozo. When this transaction was revealed, Danner told the press that the money was a contribution to President Nixon's reelection campaign.

When the details of the Gillen deposition were made public, GM was put on the defensive. The headline for the *Washington Post* front-page story by Morton Mintz was, "DETECTIVE ADMITS GM INSTRUCTIONS TO MUZZLE NADER—Auto Executives Lied at Hearing, Gillen Swears." Since the deposition was evidence only in the libel suit against Gillen, GM's lawyers quickly moved to prevent its use in the invasion of privacy suit against GM and Gillen. They asked the court to suppress the Gillen deposition, charging that the libel case against Gillen was a "sweetheart suit" which must have involved collusion between Nader and Gillen or their lawyers.

The court found that there were serious questions of fact about the nature of the Gillen deposition, and ordered a mini-trial on the issue of collusion. But during that three-day trial, GM was not able to produce any evidence of collusion, even after subpoenaing the lawyers' diaries, because there was none. I had never spoken to Gillen or his lawyer before we started the libel action or began his deposition. The judge decided the collusion issue in our favor. GM appealed that decision, but the appellate court affirmed the lower court's finding that there had been no collusion in obtaining the Gillen evidence. The vote was five to zero in our favor.

All this legal maneuvering, including the trial hearing on the collusion issue, took nearly two years. But now we knew that we had hurdled the attorney-client privilege barrier and were armed with overwhelming evidence that GM's investigation of Nader had been designed solely to intimidate him and stop his crusade for auto safety. Prudence dictated that GM's lawyers would then try to negotiate an out-of-court settlement rather than giving Gillen the chance to display GM's dirty linen in front of a jury. But GM did not roll over so easily. Their lawyers still had some legal games left to play.

As noted, we could not sue GM for libel or slander because they had not published anything about Ralph. We could only sue for invasion of privacy. There are two types of privacy invasion: *appropriation*, which usually involves unauthorized publication or other use of the plaintiff's name or picture; and *intrusion*, which covers the harassment, surveillance, and other indignities involved in the Nader case. New York had enacted a statute which limited invasion of privacy claims to those involving appropriation. Fortunately for us, most of the harassment took place in Washington, and District of Columbia law had no such restrictions. While it did not clearly grant the right to sue for intrusion, it did not rule out such claims. GM tried to get out of the case by asking the court to rule that Ralph had no right to sue for intrusion under either New York or District of Columbia law.

GM's legal team filed a 52-page brief in support of their motion to dismiss the case "for failure to state a cause of action," meaning that even if everything Ralph alleged in his complaint was true, he could not recover any damages because he had no right to sue for intrusion and there had been no appropriation or publication. The motion was argued before Justice Joseph A. Brust in the Supreme Court for New York County (a trial level court), and it turned out to be a smashing success for our side. Not only did Justice Brust uphold our position that District of Columbia law allowed Ralph to sue for invasion of privacy by intrusion, but he went further and agreed with our contention that Ralph had the same right to sue even under New York law, since the federal constitution established a constitutional right of privacy that overrides New York's narrow limitation of that right to appropriation cases. In upholding Ralph's right to sue "on constitutional grounds," Justice Brust wrote:

> However, there is presented a constitutional right of plain-
> tiff to privacy—a right to be left alone. The right of privacy
> stands on high ground, cognate to the values and concerns
> protected by constitutional guarantees (see 4th, 5th, and
> 14th Amendments, Federal Constitution).

GM's lawyers weren't about to accept that defeat lying down. They quickly appealed Justice Brust's decision. Two months later we learned that the intermediate appellate court had decided in our favor by a three-to-two margin. The majority decision noted that while the District of Columbia had never expressly allowed a privacy action based on intrusion, neither had it ever barred such an action. Citing the leading textbook, *Prosser on Torts*, which said that the law in most jurisdictions was moving toward allowing suits for intrusion, the majority, led by Justice Owen McGivern, concluded that the District of Columbia would allow it in the Nader case. As Justice McGivern wrote:

> And since we are not dealing with the laws of the Medes
> and the Persians, the lack of an exact precedent is no reason
> for turning the plaintiff out of court when receiving his
> action will further the bringing of the law into harmony
> with the known practices of our modern society.

The last hurdle was New York's highest court, the Court of Appeals in Albany, which heard GM's appeal on October 28, 1969. This time we won by a more comfortable margin, all seven judges voting in our favor. They held that District of Columbia law should apply, and that it permitted actions for invasion of privacy by intrusion. Their decision came on January 8, 1970, a little more than three years after we had filed suit. We had been through the entire three-layer court system twice and had won every contested issue. Now it was time for GM to pay.

In addition to all the devastating Gillen evidence which was now officially admissible at the trial, GM had other incentives to settle. The public relations battle, which was as important to Ralph as collecting money in the lawsuit, had been going against GM since the day suit was filed. Every major development in the case was covered nationally by the media, with front-page stories in the *New York Times,* the *Washington Post,* and other papers. The Dear Dick letter and other Gillen disclosures kept turning up like bad pennies for GM, a company whose sales were highly dependent on a positive public image. The Gillen evidence obliterated the portrait of GM as the victim of the detective's overzealousness that President Roche had painted at the Ribicoff hearings. Now the media stories about the lawsuit, compressed for popular consumption, were saying that Roche had apologized for hiring detectives to smear Nader's reputation. By 1970, there was a new GM president, and the people in the legal department who had masterminded the anti-Nader campaign were gone. Their replacements had no incentive to sully themselves by carrying on the losing public relations battle to blame detectives gone wild.

After prolonged negotiations, GM made a final settlement offer of $425,000, which was more than 30 times the size of the highest court award for invasion of privacy, even in cases where there had been loss of income or destruction of an entire business. While Ralph would have preferred bringing the case to trial so we could play out the shocking harassment scenario for the public, he realized that most of the facts we would ever learn were divulged in the Gillen deposition. He also knew that it would be years more before we could ever get to trial if GM used all its delaying power. His small staff of Nader's Raiders were working almost on a volunteer basis, and could accomplish a lot more if he had the money to hire more consumer advocates. With this in mind, on August 13, 1970, Ralph agreed to settle for $425,000 (equal to $2.3 million in 2010 dollars).

The settlement was a front-page media story throughout the country. The *New York Times* carried an editorial which concluded:

> The settlement is significant in ways that go beyond Mr. Nader's own case. It gives added legal standing to the developing notion that an individual's private life must be safeguarded from intrusion and snooping by various institutions. And it provides further recognition to the problems of automobile-caused hazards without making these vital matters appear to be merely the concern of one bold consumer gadfly.

But it remained for Ralph himself to supply the final punch line, as quoted in *Newsweek* magazine:

> The $425,000 settlement will be General Motors' contri-bution to the consumer movement. They are going to be financing their own ombudsman.

The importance of Ralph's case as a legal precedent was highlighted by what Professor William Prosser wrote about it in the 4th edition of his classic textbook on torts:

> The most significant American decision on invasion of privacy was the trial court's finding in the Nader case that there was a constitutional right of privacy.

True to Prosser's evaluation, Justice Brust's constitutional ruling has been cited often by federal judges. For example, it was relied upon in the decision upholding Dr. Benjamin Spock's right to claim damages for interception of his mail by government snoopers, and in the decision upholding Jacqueline Kennedy Onassis's right to sue a photographer for harassing her in New York.

Few corporate executives or legal advisors would dare to launch a Gillen-type smear investigation against a critic today. But the most important effect of the case was that Ralph Nader used the settlement proceeds to build the world's first effective consumer movement, saving lives by the hundreds of thousands and uplifting American government, business, and society as no private individual had ever done before. One of the consumer organizations he founded—Public Citizen—became a potent force for Citizens' Checks and Balances, its staff lawyers arguing an astounding total of 56 cases before the U.S. Supreme Court between 1971 and 2008. The economist John Kenneth Galbraith observed that most human progress is achieved through "the kicking in of rotten doors." If there was a scoreboard recording the kicking in of rotten doors, Ralph Nader would stand alone at the top.

Nader v. General Motors helped to reinforce the Rule of Law, affirming the rights of individuals and small companies to wield power in the American courts—power that once was reserved for corporate giants like General Motors and tycoons like Aristotle Onassis. It showed that access to the civil courts could expose the entire truth which General Motors had been able to obscure during a highly publicized Senate investigation. It fortified the resolve of other underdogs to criticize, to challenge, to sue if necessary, in order to hold the establishment accountable. And it demonstrated that in the country molded by George Washington and the Founding Lawyers, the Rule of Law was the same for David as it was for Goliath.

How Would Nader v. GM Fare in Other Legal Systems?

Whether it arose in 1966 or 2010, Ralph Nader's case could not have reached a successful conclusion anywhere but in the United States. Taking Britain again as the prime foreign exemplar, if Ralph had to sue GM there, he could not have afforded the hourly legal fees generated by this long-running case; he could not have qualified financially for Legal Aid; and he would have encountered great difficulty in convincing any solicitors or barristers to take this case on the type of Conditional Fee Agreement which has been permitted since 1990. Even if he overcame those obstacles, he could not have afforded the risk of being saddled with GM's huge legal costs under Loser Pays, nor the expensive ATE (after-the-event) insurance against those costs. He would have been in the same boat as the Onassis pilot Don McCusker, lacking both access to the courts and the leverage to compel a settlement.

We have seen that these basic disabilities continue to deny court access to most middle-class claimants in Britain and the other developed democracies. There are other elements in the Nader case which contrast those nations' concepts of the Rule of Law with that of the United States. From the moment Ralph's claim arose in the Senate Office Building, right through to the Gillen disclosure of 69 incriminating GM documents and the courtroom battles over their admissibility, the media covered the story in depth. This could not have happened in Britain or in most other countries, where GM would have been able to obtain gag orders shutting down public access until the trial. If GM had been able to force us to fight this battle silently while their public relations flacks hammered away at Ralph's credibility (which he considered his entire working capital), we could not have sustained this long-running lawsuit or mustered the leverage to bring GM to the settlement table.

I believe that a major reason for permitting such media gag orders is the lack of a national policy making access to the courts a part of Separation of Powers with Checks and Balances. If Britain and the other developed democracies considered access to the courts a vital element of the Rule of Law, they would insist that the public have ongoing access to all court proceedings except those involving sensitive matters like national security or the welfare of minors.

Another distinctively American element of the Nader case is the way in which Ralph's lawyers were forced to make fresh tracks in the snow, breathing life into the right to sue for invasion of privacy and erecting its constitutional foundation. That was a task we took on with relish, despite the absence of a paying client. There was nothing heroic about such a pioneering effort, which happens often in the American legal system. Apart from the professional satisfaction, it creates publicity within the legal community which is valuable to litigation specialists whose practice depends on referrals from other lawyers. Some legal pioneering happens in Britain and other developed democracies too, but usually it requires a suit brought by a large organization, a wealthy individual, or the government. Because of the restricted access to justice described in previous chapters, Ralph Nader's pioneering campaign for legal protection of consumer advocacy would never have gotten off the ground outside of the United States.

Chapter Twelve

The Lawyers Who Provide Citizens' Checks & Balances

We have seen that broad access to the American courts for civil claimants has produced a unique system of Separation of Powers with Checks and Balances available to ordinary Americans like Elsie Parrish (against a coalition of oppressive employers supported by a reactionary U.S. Supreme Court majority); Oliver Brown (against white-dominated local school boards, state-supported segregation, and federal government inaction); Don McCusker (against Aristotle Onassis' attempt to shift the blame to him for the death of Alexander Onassis); and Ralph Nader (against General Motors' attempts to discredit and sabotage his consumer advocacy). Now let us explore the role of American lawyers in that Citizens' Checks and Balances process.

The Non-Governmental Lawyer-Statesman

The term *lawyer-statesman* is generally used to describe attorneys who take time out from law practice to perform high-level government services. Abraham Lincoln and Founding Lawyers like Hamilton, Jefferson, and John Adams quickly come to mind. In our times, lawyers like James Baker, Warren Christopher, Sol Linowitz, George Mitchell, and Cyrus Vance typify those who move readily in and out of private practice to serve in prominent government posts when the need arises. But there is another concept of the lawyer-as-statesman which deserves our attention. It harkens back to the ringing nineteenth-century rhetoric of Rufus Choate, himself a prototypical lawyer-statesman as a leader of the Massachusetts bar who also served his state as U.S. senator (1841-1845), in between terms of fellow lawyer-statesman Daniel Webster.

Rufus, a renowned orator, delivered an address at the Harvard Law School in 1845 which is remembered for this punch line:

> While lawyers, and because we are lawyers, we are
> statesmen. We are by profession statesmen.

The rest of Choate's speech makes it clear that he was not referring to those few lawyers like himself who actually held high government office. His point was that simply by practicing the profession, the ordinary lawyer was playing a vital role in the Government of Laws—a role which raised legal practice "from being a mere calling by which bread, fame, and social place may be earned, to a function by which the republic may be served...to the dignity of almost a department of government."

Choate's biographer, Jean V. Matthews, writes that he "had an exalted conception of the legal profession as almost an order of chivalry in the service of the state." Such grandiose visions are unfashionable in our times, but the "department of government" analogy persists. We have noted Professor John Fabian Witt's observation that the United States stands out against the other nations "as distinctively organized around law" and Professor Bernard Schwartz's conclusion that "American society has been dominated by law as has no other society in history." Boalt Hall Professor Robert A. Kagan writes that the American legal system "is best viewed not merely as a method of solving legal disputes but as a mode of governance, embedded in the political culture and political structure of the United States." Kagan, an authority on comparative law, concludes:

> It is only a slight over-simplification to say that in the United
> States, lawyers, legal rights, judges, and lawsuits are the
> functional equivalent of the large central bureaucracies that
> dominate governance in high-tax, activist welfare states.

Thus in their everyday practice, American lawyers serving all levels of society are called upon to make the Government of Laws work—often in an aggressive and irritating manner which does not comport with the stately image of a department of government. The courts must do important work of government because the legislative and executive branches—their authority fragmentized by Separation of Powers with Checks and Balances—are often incapable of reaching the required consensus. Thus many of the toughest issues on which Congress is deadlocked (e.g., abortion, treatment of foreign prisoners accused of terrorism, illegal immigration) are dropped in the laps of lawyers, to be fought out in the courts with the certain knowledge that regardless of the difficulty of reaching a decision, *there will be a decision.* And even when Congress or a state legislature manages to enact a statute, often its scope and meaning are not established until it is tested in court.

It would require volumes to fully describe the range of problems entrusted to the courts for resolution. U.S. Court of Appeals Judge Richard Posner compiled a partial list of issues arising in the limited field of federal constitutional law:

> Among the subjects that law regulates are public welfare, homosexual rights, discrimination against women, racial discrimination (including affirmative action), tenure contracts of civil servants, political patronage, pornography, education, hate speech, police conduct, election districting, advertising, judicial and administrative procedure, abortion, public officials' immunities from federal suits, term limits of public officials, roadblocks, school discipline, drug testing of public employees, taxation of interstate commerce, standing to sue in federal court, loitering and panhandling, public support of religion, medical treatment of prison inmates, book purchases by public libraries, immigrants' rights, legal representation of indigent criminal defendants, defamation, zoning, eminent domain, indecent Web sites, and nude dancing.

In addition to the many legal issues arising under the United States Constitution, every state has a constitution, and it has become almost automatic that the constitutionality of any statute—federal or state—making significant changes will be challenged in court before it has a chance to work for long. Likewise, many executive actions by presidents and governors, and myriad decisions of administrative agencies, are likely to be reviewed by the courts. And below the constitutional level, where most everyday litigation occurs, the traffic in the federal and state courts is even heavier. Professor Robert Kagan has coined the term *adversarial legalism* to describe this process. His book, *Adversarial Legalism: The American Way of Law,* provides an evenhanded comparison between America's "litigious society" and the legal systems of other nations. He writes:

> Compared to other economically advanced democracies, American civic life is more deeply pervaded by legal conflict and by controversy about legal processes. The United States more often relies on lawyers, legal threats, and legal

contestation in implementing public policies, compensating accident victims, striving to hold governmental officials accountable, and resolving business disputes....

Viewed in cross-national comparison, the legal system of the United States is especially open to new kinds of justice claims and political movements. American judiciaries are particularly flexible and creative. American lawyers, litigation, and courts serve as powerful checks against official corruption and arbitrariness, as protectors of essential individual rights, and as deterrents to corporate heedlessness. In so doing, they also enhance the political legitimacy of capitalism and of the system of government as a whole....

Many, perhaps most, American lawyers, judges, legal scholars, and politicians (many of whom are lawyers) see adversarial litigation as a vital tool for righting wrongs, curtailing governmental and corporate arbitrariness, and achieving a just society.

Duke University Law Professor Paul D. Carrington further explains this American reliance on the civil courts:

...we have since about 1950 acted on the belief that if individuals of modest standing and resources are to be secured protection from predation by those possessing the means of exploitation, private civil litigation is the best means available to them. Congress and the state legislatures have therefore been disinclined to create new regulatory bureaucracies and have generally expressed regulatory purposes by imposing civil liability on predatory conduct they mean to deter.

University of Georgia History Professor Peter Charles Hoffer describes this American phenomenon as a personal choice:

Americans are legal actors on a scale unparalleled in history. Much of American law is made by the people themselves when they choose to litigate for their rights. The law belongs in a very personal way to all Americans.

Thus the Founding Lawyers' basic distrust of legislative and executive power, and their emphasis on individual rights, is reflected in the American propensity to rely heavily on the courts. A fundamental aspect of the unique national character which George Washington sought to build with the help of his cabinet of Founding Lawyers (and which Abraham Lincoln and his cabinet of lawyer-statesmen sought to preserve) survives in the American Rule of Law, which requires broad access to the courts in order to fulfill the requirements of democracy. Not all foreign observers regard the resulting "litigious society" with disdain. For example, the British magazine *The Economist* said in an editorial in its edition of August 10, 1991:

> Americans spend much time suing each other partly
> because their society, more than others, emphasizes indi-
> vidual rights and allows its citizens to test them in courts;
> people in many countries would die for the chance to be so
> litigious.

Yet litigation itself is emotionally and financially onerous for most Americans. The saving grace is that our adversarial legalism creates principles, precedents, and long-term effects which apply beyond the confines of the case at hand; e.g., the decision in Oliver Brown's case eventually applied to millions of school children. The general awareness of broad access to the courts has a coercive and deterrent effect on those who might otherwise flout the law. Thus, more than 90 percent of civil cases filed in American courts are settled before trial, and millions of other disputes are settled without formal litigation due to the leverage created by broad access to the courts. To mitigate the harsh side-effects of litigation, less onerous forms of dispute resolution—arbitration, mediation, and conciliation—have been developed and are now widely available.

A lawsuit is a crude, sometimes brutal method of settling a dispute. Yet the American people are accustomed to having major disputes end up in court. To a large degree, this unwieldy procedure is accepted because of the likelihood—if not the assurance—that both sides will be represented by equally skilled and adequately prepared advocates, and that the decisions will be made by disinterested jurors or by judges who are as impartial as the politically-charged Checks-and-Balances process can produce.

Would the United States be a better, more just nation if human nature had advanced to the stage where all promises are kept and everyone obeys the law, thus making lawyers (and the coercion which they administer) unnecessary? Of course. But as George Washington noted in 1786, "men will not adopt & carry into execution, measures the best calculated for their own good without the intervention of a coercive power." Since human nature has not changed in that respect, some form of coercion is often required to make people act fairly and responsibly. Americans have accepted legal coercion as the best option available.

Given the Government of Laws' inherent dependence on the courts, it is no wonder that the United States now has a million lawyers. This is not the result of public funding, since all lawyers are paid from private sources except those prosecuting or defending criminal cases and the minority of lawyers employed by government agencies. Lawyers are not guaranteed education or employment. The market for lawyers' services is as free as a market can be. Most American lawyers would be starved out of practice if clients—individuals and companies—did not need their services.

Thus American judges and lawyers broadened access to justice by becoming the most powerful force for Separation of Powers with Checks and Balances, both in government and in everyday life. This wasn't always the case. In fact, despite Tocqueville's starry-eyed perception of earlier American lawyers, most of this power developed long after the Frenchman's 1831 visit. Gerard W. Gawalt, historical specialist in the Manuscript Division of the Library of Congress, traced this history in his 1984 book, *The New High Priests: Lawyers in Post-Civil War America.* He writes that lawyers, once often distrusted and occasionally even outlawed, were "the new high priests of an increasingly legalistic, industrial society," having accomplished this change during the post-Civil War period, "when law replaced religion as the controlling element in American society."

Despite the accolades of "high priest" and "statesman" bestowed upon American lawyers from their own ranks, the public has rarely demonstrated such admiration or affection. (It is worth recalling that the effusive Tocqueville was himself a lawyer.) Lawyers are invariably the bearers of disturbing news to persons receiving the unwanted title of "defendant," and on those occasions when lawyers are able to vindicate their clients' rights, the price of simple justice is often considered exorbitant. Shays's Rebellion, which nearly tore the fledgling nation apart in 1786, was basically an attack on lawyers and the mortgage foreclosures they procured in the courts—"a large swarm of lawyers... who have been more damage to the people at large, especially the common farmers, than the savage beasts of prey." Daniel Shays's "kill the messenger" vigilantism has been replaced by thousands of lawyer jokes, some of which are semantically as deadly as Shays's riflemen. Forcing long-suffering farmers off their land is not likely to win popularity contests, any more than is the defense of people accused of heinous crimes, especially those who appear to be guilty and stand mute, calling on their lawyers to explain the inexplicable.

While I applaud the efforts of bar associations to improve the public image of lawyers, I am convinced that the very nature of the lawyer's work makes achievement of that goal problematic. Lawyers, especially those conducting litigation, are called upon to deal with the downside of life: the broken promises, the myriad forms of cheating and stealing, the most venal and violent aspects of human nature. If it is unreasonable to expect lawyers to turn this effluent into perfume, it is equally unrealistic to hope that lawyers will often emerge from these encounters smelling like roses.

The Four Legs Supporting the American Civil Justice System

Given the broad responsibility for deciding civil disputes, the American legal system has developed several unique features, building its Rule of Law for civil cases on this four-legged foundation:

1. Contingency (percentage) fees, payable only if the claimant wins.
2. Protection of losers against fee-shifting (having to pay the winner's legal fees) unless the loser engages in litigation abuse.
3. Specialist lawyers (*litigators*) who provide legal services equal in quality to those enjoyed by the affluent, without any cash outlay by the clients.
4. Jury trials available in all civil (as well as criminal) cases.

The first two legs (contingency fees and protection against fee-shifting) have combined to nurture development of the indispensable third leg: the availability of competent lawyers for the great majority of meritorious claimants, regardless of their ability to pay legal fees. This lawyer availability itself produces true access to justice in the American civil courts—and, as we have seen, the lack of such lawyer availability in Britain and the other developed democracies reduces access to the pathetic level of Trujillo's banana republic.

Contingent percentage fees were never banned in the United States, even in Colonial days, despite the inheritance of many other features of English practice. Thomas Jefferson's Colonial-era law practice was built largely on contingency fees, sometimes payable in land or horses. But as the legal system developed in the nineteenth and early twentieth centuries, contingency fees were used mainly in the debt collection and personal injury cases taken on by the less affluent stratum of the bar, while the lawyers for big business and the wealthy disdained such speculation, usually insisting on fixed fees which were not dependent upon the results achieved.

Since the 1950s, the use of such contingency fees has spread to all segments of the bar, so that even the mega-firms with 1,000 to 2,000 lawyers representing the largest businesses handle some cases in which the fees are dependent upon the results achieved, whether for a claimant or a defendant. The pioneering work of Thurgood Marshall and his NAACP colleagues, as well as the nationwide litigation activities of the American Civil Liberties Union, combined with the momentum produced by broad public acceptance of contingency fees, created another potent force for widening access to justice: public interest law practice, or "cause lawyering." Today nearly all significant social causes—human rights, womens' rights, right-to-life, environmental rights, property rights, to name a few—are served by some form of organization providing free legal services to assist the cause or its beneficiaries through litigation. Usually the cause lawyers' salaries are paid by contributions from foundations or the public. Although originally confined to causes espoused by the under-privileged, they now cover the political spectrum from left to right. A pair of non-profit examples (from thousands of choices) illustrate the breadth of this development.

✦ The *Southern Poverty Law Center*, organized in 1971 by Morris Dees and Joe Levin, two civil rights lawyers from Montgomery, Alabama, uses contributions to fund litigation against hate groups like the Ku Klux Klan. Among other major accomplishments, its civil lawsuits have put prominent neo-Nazi and white supremacist organizations across the country out of business with crippling damage judgments.

✦ The *Washington Legal Foundation,* founded in 1977, pursues the policy of "keeping free enterprise free." Through its staff of lawyers, it "shapes public policy and fights activist lawyers, regulators, and intrusive government agencies at the federal and state levels, in the courts and regulatory agencies across the country." It "brings original lawsuits, files *amicus* briefs, intervenes in court cases, and petitions agencies for rulings." From its inception through March 2010, it litigated more than 1,000 court cases and participated in 710 administrative and regulatory proceedings.

For causes lacking their own litigation arm, the vast *pro bono publico* movement provides the free services of litigators, mostly from the large law firms. Its original impetus was the desire of outstanding law-student recruitment prospects to do some good while doing well. Much credit is also given to Ralph Nader for inspiring and pioneering new forms of cause lawyering and pro bono services. In his 1973 book on large law firms, Paul Hoffman writes, "In the argot of Wall Street and Park Avenue, all do-gooding activities are now lumped together under the title *Naderism*." Now nearly all sizeable American law firms have organized pro bono programs, with broad commitment to the goal of requiring every lawyer to contribute at least 100 hours per year of unbilled time (roughly five percent of total working hours) to clients who cannot afford to pay for legal services. It is not unusual for major firms to contribute several thousand hours of free time to a single pro bono case. The pro bono principle has spread to other nations, notably Britain, but the other restrictions on access to justice there reduce the impact of pro bono to only a token force.

Another important resource is the Legal Services Corporation (LSC), created by Congress in 1974 "to provide high-quality civil legal assistance to low-income Americans." Through its 900 offices, LSC handles nearly a million legal problems annually. Funded by Congress and assisted by pro bono services donated by law firms, LSC's staff lawyers assist poor people with legal problems like housing and family disputes, mostly with legal advice short of going to court.

That is not to say that the United States is close to achieving the "liberty and justice for all" promised in the pledge of allegiance. Stanford Law Professor Deborah L. Rhode's 2004 book, *Access to Justice,* while noting some important progress, points out many deficiencies in our criminal and civil justice systems, and calls for increased government funding and private pro bono efforts to provide broader access to competent legal services.

Even in the United States, despite the commendable growth of cause lawyering and pro bono, free legal services could not produce the broad access to justice required to breathe life into the Rule of Law. Energizing Citizens' Checks and Balances by meeting the everyday litigation needs of millions of ordinary Americans, including the services of lawyers equal in competence to those retained by the affluent, requires contingency fees, protection against fee-shifting, and the sturdy third leg of specialist private-practice litigators which the first two legs helped to create. Those specialists have built the resources needed to take calculated risks on speculative suits, with the winning cases paying for the inevitable losers. They also serve as the most effective gatekeepers against frivolous lawsuits, because their business model requires them to avoid such losers like the plague if they hope to remain in practice.

The American legal system also provides thousands of highly qualified litigation specialists for those clients who can afford to pay their fees, but this is not unique since such services are available in all the developed democracies. Indeed, many of the large American law firms now have branch offices providing such services in foreign countries. Their services are essential to the overall scheme of the American Rule of Law, and would qualify them for Rufus Choate's title of lawyer-statesmen since they are an integral part of the process by which the everyday legal system functions as "almost a department of government." They help to make the Citizens' Checks and Balances process work, even when the result of their efforts is to curtail government regulation or reduce tax revenues. So too do the thousands of unheralded lawyers who take on whatever legal business comes their way—those who appear to be doing no more than making a living through routine cases that do not call for expensive or extraordinary efforts.

The fourth leg of the foundation, civil jury trial, which is guaranteed by the federal and state constitutions, reflects the Founding Lawyers' distrust of governmental power and their commitment to individual rights. Thomas Jefferson considered the 7th Amendment's guarantee of jury trials in civil cases to be the most important provision of the Bill of Rights, and he wrote that jury trial was "the only anchor ever yet imagined by which a government can be held to the principles of its constitution." The Declaration of Independence specified deprivation of "the Benefits of Trial by Jury" as one of King George's abuses which brought on the Revolution.

The United States adopted jury trial from the English practice. England was forced to curtail jury trial in civil cases during the manpower shortages of World War II, and it was not restored except in defamation (libel and slander) cases. In most other nations, civil trials are conducted by judges without juries. In my opinion, nations seeking to gain the full benefits of the Rule of Law should experiment with civil jury trials as a valuable component of participative democracy. But the right to trial by jury would not be meaningful unless broad access were assured by adoption of the first three features—hardly more meaningful than Trujillo's elegantly written laws which were accessible only with his permission.

If it is considered too radical a change for other nations, experimentation with jury trial could be postponed until broad access has been achieved by measures similar to the first three features described above, assuring most citizens the ability to retain lawyers whose skills and resources equal those representing wealthy people and large companies. Jury trial is part of the structural foundation of American government and culture, and is not expendable here. But other nations seeking to provide broader access could take important strides toward a fully developed Rule of Law without adopting trial by jury, leaving trials in the hands of judges.

There seems little doubt that if availability of contingency fees and termination of Loser Pays were put to a popular vote in the developed democracies, they would be adopted quickly—provided they were not labeled as imports from America. They do not displace existing forms of legal services, but only increase the options available to the great majority of people. In foreign countries, the opposition to such freedom of choice usually is led by the legal profession, which jealously guards the excellent income produced for skilled litigators under the present arrangements, and therefore staunchly supports such proven methods of blocking access to justice as fee-shifting and prohibition of workable contingency fees.

Role of Bar Associations in Citizens' Checks & Balances

The American Bar Association was founded at the resort spa of Saratoga Springs, New York, in 1878. In keeping with the site, it was conceived as an elite group of "the best men at the bar." Beginning with 75 members out of the country's 60,000 lawyers, in its early years it functioned mainly as a vehicle for fraternizing, making no pretense of speaking for the bar as a whole or of working for significant changes in the legal system. Its role broadened in the early years of the twentieth century, although it remained a somewhat elitist group dominated by successful corporation lawyers until the years following World War II. In the first half of the twentieth century, the ABA's policy positions largely supported the interests of the member lawyers' big business clients, as epitomized by the ABA's vehement opposition during the 1920s to the constitutional amendment that would have outlawed child labor.

After World War II the ABA became much more egalitarian, expanding its membership outreach to all licensed lawyers and taking more mainstream policy positions. By 1991, ABA policies had moved so far away from the values of the old robber baron clients that the conservative *National Review* complained:

> Over the past 25 years, the American Bar Association has taken liberal and left-wing stands on a host of issues, especially privacy rights, civil rights, and criminal procedures—all issues that have been the focus of Supreme Court deliberations.

In 2001, President George W. Bush, persuaded that the ABA was biased in favor of liberal judges, eliminated the historic role of the ABA in assessing the qualifications of potential federal judicial candidates. But in a display of the effectiveness of Separation of Powers with Checks and Balances, the Senate Judiciary Committee, which passes on all federal judicial nominations, retained the ABA's traditional screening role in their confirmation proceedings.

In 2010, the ABA is a major force supporting the American Rule of Law. While the ABA promotes the interests of its lawyer-members, it also serves the overall legal system in many important ways. With more than 400,000 members out of America's 1.1 million lawyers, it is the world's largest voluntary professional association. While its membership is still dominated by lawyers who represent business and financial interests, its many publications and post-admission educational seminars are generally even-handed, designed to help lawyers do their jobs. It has nurtured many projects to improve access to justice, including strong support for pro bono and the federal government's Legal Services Corporation, and safeguarding the independence of judges. It has reached out to spread the Rule of Law concept to all corners of the globe, training judges and lawyers in more than 40 nations, But the diverse nature of its membership has prevented it from taking partisan positions such as those which favor the legal interests of consumers or workers who have claims against businesses. That left a gap into which sprang a new bar association, destined to play a unique role in Citizens' Checks and Balances.

In 1946, workers' compensation lawyers perceived the need for a national association of attorneys who represented injured workers, to sharpen their skills, exchange information, and overcome some of the legal advantages which large employers enjoyed. That organization, first named the National Association of Claimants' Compensation Attorneys (NACCA), expanded beyond workers' compensation in the 1950s to include lawyers for all kinds of claimants, especially those injured in accidents. It went through several name changes until it became the American Association for Justice (AAJ) in 2007, reflecting its outreach to lawyers for people suffering any and all kinds of wrongs.

AAJ did for Citizens' Checks and Balances what the ABA could not possibly do: it took a partisan stance in favor of achieving justice for people who had always been the underdogs in the legal system. It began by educating claimants' lawyers to improve their forensic skills. It then developed networking systems which enabled claimants' lawyers (typically practicing solo or in small firms) to pool their resources and thus equalize the natural advantages which large corporations and business associations enjoyed in the courts. It organized litigation groups focused on specific types of cases (e.g., asbestos in schools, abuses in nursing homes) to supply its members with computerized support services which would cost millions of dollars to duplicate.

AAJ's litigation groups supply members with copies of technical literature, scientific expert opinions, trial transcripts, settlement data, and other materials that are priceless to claimants' lawyers, putting them on a level playing field with the large law firms representing corporate giants who are their opponents in litigation. In addition to helping victims recover compensation, these AAJ services have led to improved product warnings, more thorough investigations by regulatory agencies, and more responsible business practices, all of which have saved countless lives and limbs.

Beyond helping its lawyer-members to better serve their clients, AAJ has gone into the courts itself in the continuing battle to achieve justice for the underdog. In its early days AAJ filed *amicus curiae* briefs in appellate cases which helped to achieve important breakthroughs in the governing law. At first this was a volunteer effort, but by the 1980s, as the organized "tort reform" lobby attempted to narrow the public's access to justice, AAJ employed staff lawyers to launch an offensive in the courts, challenging the validity of state "tort reform" statutes under state constitutions. This began under the direction of an internal AAJ committee, which successfully challenged the constitutionality of many restrictive state statutes. In 2001 the AAJ in-house lawyers who were conducting these challenges were organized into a public interest law firm, the Center for Constitutional Litigation PC, which is carrying on this work with a high degree of success in the courts.

In 1982, leaders of AAJ formed Trial Lawyers for Public Justice (later renamed Public Justice), a separate organization that serves as a national public interest law firm, taking on groundbreaking cases that private lawyers and other public interest organizations cannot pursue because of the financial burdens. This unique task force, which draws upon the contributed services of leading trial lawyers, has compiled an enviable record in difficult environmental, civil rights, and consumer rights cases.

The concerted efforts of cigarette manufacturers and the U.S. Chamber of Commerce to restrict access to the courts and limit trial by jury under the guise of federal "tort reform" legislation forced AAJ to become a Washington lobbyist for the consumers and other victims whose rights were threatened. There were several close calls during the Bush I and Bush II administrations, but thus far AAJ, in cooperation with Ralph Nader's organization and other consumer groups, has been able to fight off these attempts to dislodge the hard-won Citizens' Checks and Balances.

AAJ's efforts to make these Citizens' Checks and Balances effective required it to create a new legal literature, since most of the legal publications existing in 1946 were dominated by interests adverse to claimants. Here AAJ scored a coup by enlisting Roscoe Pound, dean emeritus of the Harvard Law School, to become editor of AAJ's Law Journal. Dean Pound was renowned as the chief American advocate of sociological jurisprudence, which required old precedents to be adjusted to contemporary social conditions. Pound's enormous prestige and scholarship established AAJ's publications as a respected professional resource which judges throughout the country read and cited. After Dean Pound's death in 1964, this tradition has been carried on by the Washington-based Pound Civil Justice Institute, organized by AAJ leaders to produce seminars, publications, and research grants focused on the judges and law professors whose work influences development of the law.

Thus AAJ, through its Washington headquarters staff, its affiliates in every state and chapters in many law schools, serves as the command post in the continuing battle to preserve the Citizens' Checks and Balances provided by America's civil justice system. The emergence of the third leg supporting Citizens' Checks and Balances—specialist litigators who provide legal services equal in quality to those enjoyed by the affluent without any cash outlay by the clients—coincides precisely with the rise of AAJ at the midpoint of the twentieth century. AAJ and its thousands of trial lawyer members were able to play this crucial role in balancing the scales of justice because the Founding Lawyers left them the bedrock—the Government of Laws—from which to carry on that legacy.

The Janitor and Philip Morris

Since Ralph Nader's groundbreaking litigation in the 1960s, private citizens have continued to obtain better protection of their personal interests in health, safety, and financial security through the courts, aided by the growing numbers and resources of the lawyers who provide Citizens' Checks and Balances. This progress is always hotly resisted by the business interests on the other side.

Achieving this progress has required great dedication, the investment of large sums of money by the lawyers involved, and sometimes good luck.

There are many examples of the beneficial effects of this litigation: improved auto safety, the elimination of most human contact with asbestos, better warnings for prescription drugs, and improved medical procedures, to cite just a few. A striking example of the hard work, risks, and determination involved can be found in the litigation against the tobacco industry, addressing the worst public health disaster in American history: the nationwide epidemic of smoking-related disease.

Claimants' lawyers began taking on the tobacco companies in the 1960s, bringing contingency-fee lawsuits on behalf of smokers who had developed a variety of diseases (including lung cancer) and the families of smokers who had died from them. But even after the federal government joined the battle against smoking-related illness by issuing the famous 1964 Surgeon General's Report on Smoking and Health, the victims' lawyers ran up against the daunting problem of proving in court what the scientific community had already accepted for its purposes—that tobacco smoking directly caused cancer and a number of other deadly diseases.

Proof that would stand up in court was elusive, because the tobacco companies created a political and public relations campaign (run out of their front organization called the Tobacco Institute) to suppress the relevant scientific evidence and create doubt as to the true extent of tobacco's impact on human health. The tobacco giants also lobbied heavily against every government attempt to regulate tobacco, and they fiercely contested every lawsuit, refusing to offer settlements, and throwing their huge resources into wearing down the victims who sued and the contingency-fee lawyers who represented them. These obstructions by one of America's richest and most powerful industries kept Americans smoking decades after the scientific community had concluded that the habit carried deadly risks. Millions of Americans became ill or died as a result, and even now, hundreds of thousands die every year from this scourge.

Progress in the battle to recover compensation for sick smokers and the families of those who had succumbed, as well as funds for medical expenses and support for smoking cessation programs, came in fits and starts. With the federal and state legislatures showing very little political will to stem the deadly public health effects of smoking, the lawyers who carried the ball for their clients and for the larger public had to be every bit as well-organized, creative, resourceful and determined as Thurgood Marhall and his NAACP Legal Defense Fund had been in the 1950s. They educated themselves, formed consortia of lawyers who organized and shared resources to try to offset the manufacturers' enormous economic advantages, and invested large amounts of their own money in preparing the scientific evidence needed at trial—all the while operating on contingency fees which would yield them no money unless and until they won.

A major victory was won in 1998, when the attorneys general of 46 states, represented by private contingency-fee lawyers, concluded a Master Settlement Agreement with the four largest tobacco manufacturers under which the companies agreed to pay the state governments a minimum of $206 billion over a 25-year period to provide health care for smokers. The agreement also required the tobacco giants to dissolve the Tobacco Institute and related fraudulent front organizations, and to cease promoting smoking by young people. But the master settlement did little for those who had already lost the most through the death of loved ones. Getting justice for them required further heroic efforts. A case in point is the story of Jesse and Mayola Williams.

Jesse Williams was a school janitor in Oregon. He started smoking when he was stationed in Korea with the U.S. Army in the early 1950s. The Army provided cigarettes, and other GIs told him that smoking would help to keep mosquitoes away. He began smoking Philip Morris's "male-oriented" Marlboro brand in the mid-1950s and continued for the rest of his life, unaware that the tobacco manufacturers were purposefully manipulating the nicotine content of cigarettes to "hook" smokers. Eventually Jesse was smoking three packs a day—as the Oregon Court of Appeals later noted, "he was spending half of his waking hours smoking."

Jesse's wife Mayola and his children encouraged him to stop smoking, but he was convinced that the tobacco companies would not sell cigarettes if they were dangerous, and he frequently said that he had read, and heard on television and elsewhere, that cigarettes were not harmful to health. He did make several attempts to stop smoking, trying different methods, including "cold turkey," but like millions of others he was not successful. An expert witness later testified in court that Jesse was highly addicted to cigarettes, both physiologically and psychologically.

In late 1995 Jesse developed a cough and began to spit up blood. After he began losing weight, medical tests revealed that he had inoperable lung cancer. When Jesse received the diagnosis, he said, "Those darn cigarette people were lying all the time." Despite radiation and chemotherapy treatment, he died in March 1997.

Mayola Williams wanted justice for herself and her children, but she also wanted to expose the lies which Philip Morris had told to millions of other tobacco victims. Her lawyers filed a lawsuit in an Oregon state court, alleging not only negligence by Philip Morris but also fraud, based on the company's deliberate deceptions by which they manipulated cigarette ingredients to addict smokers and lied to smokers about the health risks of smoking. She demanded compensatory damages for the loss of her husband and the support he had provided to the family, plus $100 million in punitive damages to punish Philip Morris and deter other manufacturers from engaging in such deadly deceptions.

The case went to trial in 1999. Mayola's lawyers had assembled a mountain of evidence proving that Philip Morris, along with other tobacco companies, had carried on a decades-long public relations campaign to convince Americans that there was a legitimate controversy over the health effects of smoking, and to create doubt about the connection between smoking and disease so that potential and actual smokers would have a psychological "crutch" to justify beginning or continuing to smoke. The Williams's lawyers showed that Philip Morris's fraudulent message reached large numbers of Oregonians and led to thousands of incidents of disease and death in Oregon alone.

This indisputable proof of Philip Morris's deadly disinformation campaign was later summarized by the Supreme Court of Oregon:

> At first, the industry publicly denied that there was a problem; for example, in the 1950s and early 1960s, Philip Morris's officials told the public that Philip Morris would "stop business tomorrow" if it believed that its products were harmful. For most of that period, however, the industry did not attempt to refute scientific evidence directly; rather, it tried to find ways to create doubt about it. The industry's goal was to create the impression that scientists disagreed about whether cigarette smoking was dangerous, that the industry was vigorously conducting research into the issue, and that a definitive answer would not be possible until that research was complete....
>
> Despite the industry's nominal emphasis on the need for further research, the Council on Tobacco Research designed its research program to avoid studying the biological effects of tobacco use, the very question that, according to the industry's statement, required more research....
>
> They issued press releases, influenced the content of apparently neutral articles, cultivated opinion leaders, attempted to use their advertising power to get favorable treatment from the print media, and appeared on commercial and public television to put forth that message....
>
> Although a tobacco industry survey indicated that 85 percent of smokers wished that they had never started smoking, Philip Morris concealed information that the

addictive effects of nicotine made it difficult for them to stop
without significant assistance. The fraudulent statements
from Philip Morris and the rest of the industry reinforced
those addictive effects by giving smokers a reason not to
make the necessary effort to break the addiction.

After five weeks of trial, the jury found for Mayola Williams. They awarded
her modest economic damages of $21,485.80 and noneconomic compensa-
tory damages of $800,000 on her claims of negligence and fraud. On the neg-
ligence claim, they found that Jesse was 50 percent responsible for the harm he
suffered and reduced the award accordingly. They declined to award punitive
damages on the negligence claim, but on the fraud claim they awarded punitive damages of $79.5 million. The punitive award was 97 times as large as
the compensatory damages, but it represented less than three weeks of Philip
Morris's profits in the year in which Jesse died. The trial judge initially reduced
the damage awards, but they were reinstated by the Oregon Court of Appeals
(the intermediate appellate court) in 2002.

At that point, Mayola Williams's case became a major battleground
in the corporate campaign to limit all awards of punitive damages by per-
suading the U.S. Supreme Court that some awards were so high that they
violated defendants' rights to due process of law under the U.S. Constitution.
The campaign began in the late 1980s, with corporate defendants appealing
virtually every significant punitive damage award in hopes of getting the
Supreme Court to reverse them on constitutional grounds. By 2002 the
campaign had produced several Supreme Court decisions which provided
guidelines on how high punitive awards might be—including suggestions
that punitive-to-compensatory ratios of 10-to-1 or higher might be struck
down—but no hard-and-fast limits.

Faced with the $79.5 million punitive award in the *Williams* case, Philip
Morris requested that the U.S. Supreme Court review the 2002 decision of the
Oregon Court of Appeals. The Supreme Court granted review, but it did not
rule on the question of whether the 97-to-1 ratio violated due process. Instead,
it vacated the Oregon decision and sent the case back to the state courts for
reconsideration in light of the high court's most recent punitive damage decision. Whereupon the Oregon appellate courts reinstated the full punitive
damage award, holding that the award was justified because Mayola's lawyers
had proved that Philip Morris's conduct was extraordinarily reprehensible to
a degree never seen before in Oregon. Philip Morris's lawyers persuaded the
U.S. Supreme Court to review the case again in 2007, and the justices held,
for the first time, that punitive damages may not be used to punish conduct
harming those beyond the immediate parties to the litigation, i.e., the Williams
family. However, the U.S. Supreme Court re-affirmed the use of such evidence

of widespread harm to show how reprehensible the misconduct was. It again sent the case back to Oregon for reconsideration. Again the Oregon Supreme Court reinstated the punitive damage award, taking care to consider the factors mentioned in the U.S. Supreme Court decision.

The U.S. Supreme Court receives more than 10,000 petitions to review lower court decisions every year, and it grants that review in approximately one percent of such cases. The odds against the Supreme Court reviewing a state court decision twice are astronomical. But as the widow and children of the deceased janitor Jesse Williams and their lawyers entered the tenth year of their court battle against Philip Morris, the tobacco company's lawyers successfully petitioned the U.S. Supreme Court for review a third time.

This time the U.S. Supreme Court declined to review Philip Morris's claim that the amount of the punitive damage award was excessive and disproportionate to the harm caused to Jesse Williams. The justices limited the review to the question of whether the Oregon Supreme Court had flaunted the instructions of the U.S. Supreme Court on the previous remand. Finally, after yet another round of briefing and a December 2008 oral argument, on March 31, 2009, the U.S. Supreme Court issued a one-sentence ruling that dismissed its writ of certiorari (leave to appeal) as "improvidently granted." Twelve years after Jesse Williams died, Mayola and her lawyers had outlasted and beaten the tobacco giant.

Oregon law requires that 60 percent of punitive damage awards be paid to a state crime victims' fund. At the time of this writing, Philip Morris partially satisfied the Oregon judgment by paying 40 percent of the judgment and accrued interest to Mayola Williams, but has challenged its obligation to pay the balance, arguing that its participation in the 1998 Master Settlement Agreement fulfilled all of its obligations to state governments. Litigation between the State of Oregon, Philip Morris, and the Williams estate continues.

Over the course of the twelve-plus years that her case has been in litigation, Mayola Williams and her family have been represented by a group of small Oregon law firms and individual lawyers working on a contingency-fee basis. Four of these lawyers represented the plaintiff from the beginning investigations through the jury verdict. They were from three small firms (including one solo lawyer) with a combined strength of ten lawyers. During trial, two additional lawyers with national tobacco advocacy backgrounds lent support with research and witness contacts. Once post-trial motions and appeals began, the Williams team added two solo Oregon appellate specialists and a national appellate specialist from Washington D.C. At its peak strength, the Williams legal team had the benefit of fewer than ten actively involved or consulting lawyers, although a variety of advocacy groups with their own legal talent contributed friend-of-the-court briefs at various stages of the appeals.

Philip Morris, on the other hand, brought at least 23 different lawyers from two multi-national mega-law firms to the courtroom during the trial alone.

Several additional multi-national law firms were added to the defense cadre as the endless appeals wore on. Certainly the Philip Morris legal fees added up to tens of millions of dollars. Yet it was Mayola Williams who had the burden of proof throughout this litigation. In other legal systems, she would have had to find some way of obtaining tens of millions of dollars worth of highly skilled legal services without being able to pay the bill—an impossible task.

Because of America's unique civil justice system—with its broad access to the courts, its contingency fee tradition, and the talent and motivations of the lawyers who are therefore able to devote their careers to representing ordinary people rather than powerful corporations—Mayola Williams, the widow of a retired school janitor, was able to secure skilled representation without paying legal fees up front, without risking her own limited resources for the huge expenses of the 12-year litigation, and without fear of having to pay the other side's legal fees if she lost her case.

The history of the *Williams* case contains several other important lessons. It is the type of case that George W. Bush and the lobbyists working to restrict access to justice would brand as frivolous. Their argument goes something like this:

> Here we have a janitor who inflicted deadly damage on himself by smoking for decades during which published scientific studies showed that it could cause lung cancer (shades of the McDonald's coffee case).

> Then we have a jury of ordinary people chosen at random, without any inquiry into their qualifications to decide scientific issues or their ability to appraise the economic consequences of a punitive damage award. The jurors are then manipulated by plaintiffs' lawyers whose contingency fees give them a financial interest in the result. No wonder the jurors wound up awarding punitive damages that were 97 times larger than the actual damage suffered by the Williams family.

> The punitive damage award constitutes a windfall which is harmful to American business and destroys American jobs.

The record of the Williams case refutes these distortions. The Oregon jurors demonstrated thoughtful deliberation in reaching their verdict, to the extent of reducing the compensatory damages by 50 percent to account for Jesse's own negligence in smoking, and refusing to award punitive damages for negligence, rendering the punitive verdict solely on the fraud claim. The

Oregon punitive damage statute, typical of those throughout the nation, required the Williams lawyers to prove by clear and convincing evidence (an extraordinarily heavy burden of proof—much heavier than the "more probable than not" standard used in ordinary negligence cases) that Philip Morris "acted with malice or has shown a reckless or outrageous indifference to a highly unreasonable risk of harm and has acted with a conscious indifference to the health, safety and welfare of others." In all large punitive damage awards, the justification for the punishment and the appropriateness of the amount awarded are the final work product of appellate judges rather than jurors. In the Williams case, this included multiple reviews by three judges of the Court of Appeals of Oregon, five justices of the Supreme Court of Oregon, and the nine justices of the Supreme Court of the United States.

As to the "windfall" argument, without the coercive and therapeutic effects of the punitive damage threat, tobacco companies would not be deterred from their deadly deceptions. Their business is so profitable that they could easily write off the insurance costs of compensatory damages as an insignificant operating expense. And without the chance of recovering punitive damages, claimants' lawyers would not have the financial incentive needed to carry them through long-running obstacle courses like lawsuits against tobacco giants.

In addition to Oregon's 60 percent share of the punitive damages, the broader public reaped another huge benefit from the Williams case. Shortly after the jury's 1999 verdict in favor of Mayola Williams, Philip Morris publicly admitted for the first time that cigarettes cause lung cancer and that nicotine is addictive. This removed the crutch that had thwarted the efforts of Jesse Williams—and millions of other victims of tobacco companies' fraud—to quit smoking.

So we add *Mayola Williams v. Philip Morris* to the long list of meritorious, non-frivolous cases which could get to court only in America, and Mayola Williams takes her place alongside other courageous Americans who brought positive change to the nation by taking their disputes to the courts, including Elsie Parrish, Oliver Brown, James Meredith, and Ralph Nader.

PART THREE

The Pros and Cons of America's Heavy Reliance on Lawyers

Chapter Thirteen

American Lawyers in Public Office

We noted earlier that in the 18 elections between the end of George Washington's administration and the re-election of Abraham Lincoln in 1864, lawyers won the presidency 16 times. As the republic matured, the preponderance of lawyer-presidents lessened somewhat. Fifteen of the 28 presidents after Lincoln were lawyers, bringing the grand total to 64 percent lawyer-presidents (28 out of 44) through the 2008 election of Barack Obama.

This frequent choice of lawyers as chief of state is strictly an American phenomenon. In Britain, for example, of the 52 prime ministers chosen since the office began in 1721, ten were lawyers, but only five since 1841: solicitor David Lloyd George (1916-1922), and barristers Herbert Asquith (1908-1916), Clement Attlee (1945-1951), Margaret Thatcher (1979-1990), and Tony Blair (1997-2007).

Modern presidents have carried on George Washington's practice of using lawyers as his principal advisors. Soon after President Barack Obama's 2009 inauguration, the *Washington Post* ran a story entitled "Obama Stocks White House with Prominent Lawyers," mentioning dozens of lawyers in prominent advisory posts.

The predominance of lawyers extends to all levels of American public office. In his definitive 1995 study, *The High Priests of American Politics: The Role of Lawyers in American Political Institutions,* Clark University Professor Mark Miller concludes:

> In effect, the legal profession has colonized the political
> domain in this country. Lawyers play a nearly ubiquitous
> part in American political life, and the legal profession has
> come to dominate American political decision making....

> Lawyers dominate the judicial, legislative, and executive
> branches of our government, and when they are not part
> of the government, they are often in a position to influ-
> ence their fellow lawyers who do hold official government
> positions.

According to Professor Miller's detailed research, usually about 50 percent of members of Congress and state governors are lawyers, down from about 60 percent in the 1950s. In state legislatures, historically the lawyer component has been between 25 and 40 percent. In contrast with the American experience, lawyers (barristers and solicitors combined) comprised less than 17 percent of the British House of Commons in 2007—a level maintained fairly consistently as far back as reliable statistics are available. The percentage of lawyer-legisla-tors in other developed democracies typically is lower than the British level, closer to 10 percent.

This raises a question: If American lawyers are really as unpopular and widely distrusted as would appear from the media's lawyer jokes and the mes-sages propagated by lawyer-bashing organizations, why are they the over-whelming choice for high public office, regardless of their party affiliations? This anomaly dates back at least to 1850, when 41-year-old lawyer Abraham Lincoln wrote in his notes for a lecture:

> There is a vague popular belief that lawyers are necessarily
> dishonest. I say vague, because when we consider to what
> extent confidence and honors are reposed in, and conferred
> upon lawyers by the people, it appears improbable that
> their impression of dishonesty is very distinct and vivid. Yet
> the expression is common—almost universal.

I have not been able to find a convincing explanation of this love-hate relationship. Lawyer-candidates are not in the habit of running as lawyers or touting their legal accomplishments as qualifications for office. Perhaps some of the respect which Americans have for the law as an institution—and its unique role in our constitutional democracy—rubs off on lawyers. Perhaps many voters feel that lawyers have a professional insight into the machinery of government, and therefore are likely to make it run well. Certainly that was a factor during the nation's first century, when voters could logically be expected to call upon lawyers to put the lawyer-created Constitution into operation. But that does not explain the ongoing American preference for lawyer-candidates in the twenty-first century, when millions of non-lawyers are schooled in political science and other subjects relevant to government.

Perhaps it is partly the result of so many lawyers inserting themselves into politics. Thomas Jefferson noted, "Study of law…is the most certain stepping stone to preferment in the political line." Woodrow Wilson said, "The profession I chose was politics; the profession I entered was the law. I entered one because I thought it would lead to the other." Stanford Law Professor Lawrence M. Friedman, a leading legal historian, takes this view:

> It was not so much the case that public office required legal skill; rather, the lawyers were skillful at getting and holding these offices. They were by instinct political; political animals gravitated toward the practice of law. A public career was helpful to private practice, which cannot be easily said for doctors, bankers, or farmers.

But if lawyers are as universally disrespected as would appear from the media accounts, the voters would hardly count their aggressive pursuit of office as a positive factor.

Perhaps deep down in the American psyche there is admiration for the work lawyers do—or at least for the work the public expects them to do. When the American Film Institute compiled a list of the top 100 all-time movie heroes in 2003, the number one selection was Atticus Finch, the idealistic southern lawyer played by Gregory Peck in Harper Lee's *To Kill a Mockingbird.* Nowadays television lawyer-characters have replaced the movie cowboys of the horse-opera era as America's favorite fictional heroes, beginning with *L.A. Law* in the 1980s. Huge chunks of television time are devoted to fictional-lawyer series, as well as televised coverage of real trials, and the daily reality-TV courtrooms presided over by Judge Judy Scheindlin and her many imitators.

Lawyers also dominate policy-making positions in American administrative agencies, and are the largest professional group performing unpaid volunteer services on local election and school boards. Whether they serve because of self-interest in obtaining public notice to increase their influence and clientele, or out of civic virtue, or a combination of both, lawyers have proven to be the most reliable source of skilled technicians needed to keep the wheels of American democracy turning.

Professor Miller believes that an important reason for this dominant role is the foundation on which the nation was built: the Government of Laws. He concludes that American law and politics "have converged, not merely because the lawyer's skills are valued in American politics, but because the lawyer's world has come to dominate American political institutions" to the extent that "so many lawyers are making key decisions in our political system, the governmental institutions in which they serve often adopt very lawyerlike decision-making processes." Thus the drafting of legislation is left largely to lawyers, not because of any special facility with words, but because knowledge of existing law is essential to avoid conflicts which can destroy the effectiveness of a statute.

James Bryce, the noted British jurist, historian, and statesman who served as ambassador to the United States from 1907 to 1913, wrote in his classic study, *The American Commonwealth:*

> The bar has usually been very powerful in America, not only as being the only class of educated men who are at once men of affairs and skilled speakers, but also because there has been no nobility or territorial aristocracy to overshadow it. Politics have been largely in its hands, and must remain so as long as political questions continue to be involved with the interpretation of constitutions.

The pivotal position of the law in American democracy is epitomized by the public's unique role in the selection of judges. All federal judges (including the Supreme Court justices) are nominated by the president and must be confirmed (approved) by the Senate. Nowadays this process is accompanied by a flood of public scrutiny, with the FBI and staffers of the Senate Judiciary Committee digging into minute details of each nominee's career and private life. Then come public Senate Judiciary Committee hearings, which are often accompanied by expensive public relations and advertising campaigns for and against the nominee, designed to bring public opinion to bear on the confirmation process. This months-long scrutiny is now automatic for Supreme Court nominees, and often it is applied with only slightly less vigor to lower federal court nominees.

At the state level, there is even more public participation, since the judges are elected directly by the voters in 20 states. Even in the other states, where the judges are appointed by the governor or the legislature, most of them must face the electorate in a "retention election," in which sitting judges run against their own records after a specific number of years on the bench. Many states have procedures for evaluating the performance of sitting judges, including some scrutiny by non-lawyer appointees.

In England, the judges are appointed by a process which involves little or no public participation. Until creation of the Judicial Appointments Commission in 2006, judges were selected secretly by the Lord Chancellor.

The new procedure provides slightly more transparency, but nothing like the Senate hearings, media scrutiny, or public participation that accompany the appointment of American judges. In other developed democracies, typically the judiciary is organized like a civil service hierarchy, with the public playing no part in the selection process.

These cultural differences point up the much greater importance of the law in America, tracing back to Colonial times and the work of the Founding Lawyers.

Thinking Like a Lawyer

Law professors pride themselves on making their students "think like a lawyer." This process is described generally as digging into a vast amount of complicated material, analyzing it logically, identifying the crucial points which will determine the outcome, isolating the irrelevant, and formulating logical arguments from which a final decision can be made. The study of law is designed to inspire development of the analytical and decision-making skills which lawyers will need in dealing with the puzzling morass of facts, claims, opinions, and speculations presented by their clients' problems. Felix Frankfurter described the trained lawyer as an "expert in relevance." Obviously such skills, sharpened by the skepticism which years of law practice are likely to produce, are also potentially useful in solving many problems of government. It is these skills which I believe helped the Founding Lawyers to deal with the problems of turning the "imbecilic" Articles of Confederation into history's most admired governmental structure. Certainly these skills were a crucial factor in convincing the likes of George Washington and Benjamin Franklin to place the fate of the fledgling nation in the hands of lawyers.

In a 1958 law review article, lawyer-statesman John J. McCloy undertook a detailed evaluation of the legally-trained mind in government service. In between stints with his Wall Street law firm, McCloy served as assistant secretary of war (1941-1945), president of the World Bank (1947-1949), and U.S. military governor of Germany (1949-1952). He placed a high value on the lawyer's "ability to deal with large and complicated bodies of fact" and take on widely varying problems in rapid succession; to spend long hours analyzing problems; to read documents patiently, and ferret out the portions which are relevant; to present conclusions clearly in oral and written forms; and to find common ground, "locating the fruitful bases of cooperation" leading to the compromises which are so important in the work of government. He points out that while most wise and capable people try to employ these tools, they are "apt to be kept better sharpened by the lawyer" because his professional practice has demanded their sharpness. As noted in our discussion of the 1787 Constitutional Convention, the Founding Lawyers who drafted the Constitution drew upon their experience in practice to anticipate how duplicity and the thirst for power could threaten the new government, against which threats they created the appropriate Checks and Balances.

This confidence in the legally-trained mind accounts for the frequent (almost unanimous) selection of lawyers as top advisors to presidents from Washington to Lincoln. The story of how this preference was continued into the twentieth century is told by retired career diplomat Warren Zimmerman in his book, *First Great Triumph: How Five Americans Made Their Country a World Power,* in which the author chronicles America's first steps into global prominence in the wake of the Spanish-American war. One of Zimmerman's five key players is Elihu Root, "the hard-edged corporate lawyer turned colonial administrator" whom President William McKinley chose as his secretary of war. Root was given the task of overseeing the installation of civilian governments in America's first colonial outposts, Cuba and the Philippines, in 1898-1903. McKinley, an Ohio lawyer himself, insisted on putting a skilled lawyer in that job.

Root's protégé and junior law partner, Henry Stimson, carried on this tradition by serving five presidents as an influential cabinet member, including secretary of state under Herbert Hoover (1929-1933) and secretary of war (1940-1945) under Franklin D. Roosevelt. As noted by McCloy, the need for negotiating skills has played a key role in selection of many other lawyers as secretary of state, including John Jay, Thomas Jefferson, John Marshall, James Madison, James Monroe, John Quincy Adams, Daniel Webster, William Jennings Bryan, Charles Evans Hughes, James Byrnes, Dean Acheson, John Foster Dulles, Cyrus Vance, James Baker, Warren Christopher, and Hilary Rodham Clinton.

As we have seen, President Franklin Roosevelt's New Deal enlisted an army of lawyers (many recruited by Felix Frankfurter) in the effort to pull the nation out of the Depression, and their work is credited with helping to save capitalism. FDR also used a team of lawyer-advisors to open the way for aid to beleaguered Britain in 1940-1941, delivering vitally needed military equipment without which the British might not have survived the Nazi onslaught. The crisis came to a head in the summer of 1940, after the fall of France left Britain on her own to face the threat of Nazi invasion. Prime Minister Winston Churchill was concerned that the Royal Navy's devastating destroyer losses left his island nation exposed to Nazi U-boat attacks which threatened to starve Britain of the food and military supplies that could be delivered only by merchant ships. Churchill urgently requested transfer of 50 World War I vintage American destroyers to Britain, and in exchange offered 99-year leases on British possessions in the Western Hemisphere where American military bases could be established.

The prevailing legal opinion was that such an exchange would require an act of Congress, a procedure which was unattractive in view of FDR's desire to avoid bucking the widespread isolationist sentiment on the eve of the 1940 presidential election. Even if successful, the Congressional route would consume precious time and reveal more of Britain's vulnerability than was strategically desirable. Since the White House staff was then miniscule compared to today, FDR often used private-practice lawyers as unofficial advisors. To solve the destroyer-for-bases problem, he turned to one of them, "Wild Bill" Donovan, an old political opponent, who came up with the solution: broad emergency executive powers conferred upon Presidents Jefferson and Madison by Congress during the wars against the Barbary pirates in 1804-1815, which had never been repealed. Proceeding under the authority of those ancient statutes, FDR transferred the 50 destroyers to Britain by executive order, which did not require Congressional approval.

After winning a third term in the 1940 election, FDR was in a position to provide Britain (as well as the Soviet Union and China) with comprehensive military aid through a more sympathetic Congress. He came up with the Lend-Lease concept, and to put this unprecedented expansion of presidential authority into palatable legislation, he recruited Felix Frankfurter, who drafted the Lend-Lease Act despite the fact that he was then sitting as a Supreme Court justice.

When the United States entered the war in 1941, FDR turned again to Wild Bill Donovan, to create and command the Office of Strategic Services (OSS), the innovative intelligence unit which became the predecessor of the Central Intelligence Agency (CIA). Donovan recruited dozens of his fellow Wall Street lawyers for key positions in the OSS. On the same theory that lawyers are skilled at tackling tough problems by discarding the irrelevant and focusing on the solution, the U.S. Army Air Forces recruited Harvard Law Professor W. Barton Leach for the task of improving bombing accuracy at a time when less than five percent of American bombs were landing within 500 feet of their targets. Leach in turn recruited many lawyers for this work, choosing John Marshall Harlan (later to become a U.S. Supreme Court justice) for the chief position in the European theatre. Although neither Leach nor Harlan had any experience with flying, bombardment, or scientific research, their unit is credited with helping to increase the bombing accuracy rate to over 65 percent.

President John F. Kennedy was criticized for selecting his brother Bobby as attorney general, but during the 1962 Cuban missile crisis, this choice was vindicated by Bobby's advice under pressure, which was credited with dampening the apocalyptical mood that threatened to trigger nuclear warfare. The White House had received back-to-back messages from Soviet leader Nikita Krushchev, the first containing proposals which could possibly form the basis for negotiation, and the second leaving no room for rational discussion. Bobby Kennedy suggested that they respond to the first message with reasonable counter-offers, and that they make the second message irrelevant by treating it as if it had not been received. A non-lawyer might have come up with the same solution, but the task was entrusted to a lawyer; his advice was followed even though it was contrary to the views of the military commanders; and the world's first nuclear exchange was averted.

In a later time of crisis following the 2001 attack on the World Trade Center, Congress and the president created the National Commission on Terrorist Attacks Upon the United States. Of the commission's ten members, six were lawyers. In 2006, a similar commission, the Iraq Study Group, was created, with seven of its ten members being lawyers.

Professor Miller points out some negative aspects of making governmental decisions based on the lawyers' way of thinking: that lawyers often are preoccupied with technicalities—with procedure rather than substance—and therefore are prone to missing the big picture. The most striking example of this proclivity is the failure to include the Bill of Rights in the original Constitution drafted by the Founding Lawyers at Philadelphia—a blunder that nearly aborted the birth of the nation. Another case in point is the bewildering maze of Depression-era NRA (National Recovery Administration) codes, designed to control wages, prices, production, and virtually the entire business cycle. The codes' procedures were so convoluted that only a few of the New Deal lawyers who drafted them claimed to understand how they were supposed to work, and in practice they did not work well.

On the other hand, the genius of the lawyer-designed Constitution is that it established a procedure, a process for achieving consensus while curbing tyranny, which has enabled the United States to survive longer than any other democracy in history.

Professor Miller observes that lawyers in government "prefer an incrementalist approach to decision making, and they abhor radical change in society." Historian Joseph Ellis traces this minimal-change approach—"an evolutionary rather than a revolutionary version of political and social change"—to its origins during the Confederation period (1781-1787) which preceded the Constitution. Ellis finds that "this deferral strategy, far from being a moral failure, was in fact a profound insight rooted in a realistic appraisal of how enduring social change best happens." His Exhibit A is the implosion which followed the French Revolution. Here we should note that during the Confederation period, the Confederation Congress and the state legislatures were dominated by lawyers, and the governors of major states were lawyers: e.g., Thomas Jefferson (Virginia), John Dickinson (Pennsylvania), and George Clinton (New York). Likewise, the main authors of state constitutions adopted during the Confederation period were lawyers: e.g., John Adams in Massachusetts, John Jay in New York, and Thomas Jefferson in Virginia.

Edward H. Levi (1911-2000), who served as law professor and dean of the University of Chicago Law School and later as U.S. Attorney General, wrote *An Introduction to Legal Reasoning* in 1949. It is still in academic use today. Levi focused on the methods of legal reasoning used in court decisions, statutes, and constitutional interpretation. He did not deal specifically with the creation of the Constitution or the work of the founders. However, I believe that the following excerpts from his final paragraph are relevant to our consideration of the Founding Lawyers and the role that thinking like a lawyer plays in public affairs today:

> The emphasis should be on the process....
>
> Legal reasoning has a logic of its own....
>
> This is the only kind of system which will work when people do not agree completely. The loyalty of the community is directed toward the institution in which it participates. The words change to receive the content which the community gives to them. The effort to find complete agreement before the institution goes to work is meaningless. It is to forget the very purpose for which the institution of legal reasoning has been fashioned. This should be remembered as a world community suffers in the absence of law.

Despite the limitations of the legal mind-set, American lawyers have convinced most of the voting public that they are the best choices to perform many governmental functions, particularly legislation. In everyday private life, obviously lawyers are needed to conduct the litigation which is at the heart of Citizens' Checks and Balances. Given this broad (if sometimes reluctant) public acceptance, perhaps we lawyers should not be touchy about lawyer jokes. After all, the holders of our highest public offices, as well as our most popular entertainers, have always been fair game for ridicule, sometimes more harsh than that directed against lawyers. It appears that in a free society, it is the destiny of those considered most powerful or interesting to become the butt of many jokes—something like a badge of honor.

There is no comparable genre of derogatory jokes about those who earn their living as engineers or exterminators. An overly sensitive reaction to lawyer jokes implies that lawyers believe the public actually considers the practice of law to be inherently evil, despite the enormous public respect for lawyers like

St. Thomas More, Thomas Jefferson, Abraham Lincoln, Mohandas Ghandi, Franklin Roosevelt, Felix Frankfurter, Wild Bill Donovan, Thurgood Marshall, Archibald Cox, Nelson Mandela, Robert Kennedy, and Sandra Day O'Connor.

––––––––––

The exemplary government service of many American lawyers has given the rest of us lawyers much to be proud of. But we need to be careful not to get carried away with this imagery. It has inspired some eminent legal scholars to mythologize the American lawyer-statesman in ways that I consider inaccurate—and dangerous.

Chapter Fourteen

The Myth of the Purifying
Lawyer-Statesman

Wouldn't it be great if lawyer-statesmen like Thomas Jefferson, Alexander Hamilton, Daniel Webster, Elihu Root, Henry Stimson, and John W. Davis were still around? As they did in their own times, today they would shuttle between the highest echelons of government and their private law offices. After distinguished service in public office (usually at a considerable financial sacrifice), they would return to their private practices, where they would use their immense prestige to talk crooked clients like the savings-and-loan swindlers and the corrupt executives of Enron and WorldCom out of their nefarious schemes, and along the way they would inspire ordinary lawyers to *purify* their clients by inducing them to put the public interest ahead of the clients' selfish interests. They would, in the words attributed to Elihu Root—a leading lawyer-statesman of the gilded age—spend half their time telling would-be clients that they are damned fools and should stop acting against the public interest.

So goes the legend of the purifying American lawyer-statesman, as recounted by several influential commentators. It's a beautiful story. But is it true? Is there, in fact, as much as a grain of truth in it? Did any of our revered lawyer-statesmen ever lift a finger in an attempt to purify a client by insisting that the client stop acting against the public interest? If not—if it is only a myth—does its continued propagation pose an obstacle to the rules and reforms needed to promote not only the public interest, but the independence and integrity of the legal profession? Will its use to resist "rule-based ethics" deceive the public and play into the hands of lawyer-bashing organizations by brandishing a dysfunctional fig-leaf that can be manipulated to cover up lawyer dishonesty? And will it stymie our efforts to accurately evaluate the pros and cons of America's heavy reliance on lawyers, both in public service and private practice?

To answer these questions, we need to do something never before attempted. We must put the law practices of the American lawyer-statesmen under a microscope to see what they actually did for their clients. (Note that here we are talking about lawyers who held high public office, not the everyday non-governmental lawyer-statesman of the Rufus Choate vision.) Fortunately, there is plenty of evidence to be discovered. But first, let us examine the claims made for the "purifying" activities of the lawyer-statesmen, as recounted in prominent books authored in the 1990s by Anthony T. Kronman, Mary Ann Glendon, and Sol M. Linowitz, and as partially echoed in a 2004 article by U.S. District Judge Jed S. Rakoff.

Exhibit A: Kronman's Lost Lawyer

In 1993 Anthony Kronman, then the dean of Yale Law School, published his fourth book, *The Lost Lawyer: Failing Ideals of the Legal Profession,* which the *New York Law Journal* hailed as "a major document in the history of American law." It remains highly influential and widely quoted.

The introduction to *The Lost Lawyer* describes the crisis that Kronman calls a threat to the soul of the legal profession—a crisis which "has been brought about by the demise of an older set of values that until quite recently played a vital role in defining the aspirations of American lawyers."

He says that at the center of that older set of values was an ideal:

> I have given this ideal an old-fashioned name to stress
> its roots in the past and the air of obsolescence that now
> surrounds it. I call it the ideal of the lawyer-statesman. It is
> an ideal that has had distinguished representatives in every
> age of American law.

Among the forces that have caused the decline of this ideal, he lists:

> ...the explosive growth of the country's leading law firms,
> which has changed forever the practice of the lawyers in them
> and created a new, more openly commercial culture in which
> the lawyer-statesman ideal has only a marginal place;...

Here we should note that Kronman does not claim the "commercial culture" is a completely new phenomenon, but only that it manifests itself "more openly." He continues:

> Thus for the early nineteenth-century bar, whose leaders
> still viewed their work and social functions in classically
> republican terms, the idealized figure of the lawyer-
> statesman was the embodiment of professional excellence.
> In him, lawyers of the period could see gathered the entire
> range of qualities they valued most.

This begins Kronman's broadening of the lawyer-statesman ideal to include the classical republican (with a small "r") visions of *civic virtue, prudence,* and *practical wisdom,* drawn from Kronman's first love: philosophy. He goes on to display a dazzling command of Aristotle, Kant, and Max Weber, reflecting his pre-law school doctorate in philosophy and his authorship of the widely-praised 1983 book, *Max Weber.* From that philosophical platform, Kronman embarks on a definition of what the lawyer-statesman is, or should be:

> He is distinguished, too, by his special talent for discov-
> ering where the public good lies and for fashioning those
> arrangements needed to secure it. The lawyer-statesman is
> a leader in the realm of public life, and other citizens look
> to him for guidance and advice, as do his private clients....
>
> Whether acting as the representative of private interests or
> as a counselor in matters of state, one important part of
> what he does is to offer advice about ends.

By citing the lawyer-statesman's special talent for discovering the public good and securing it by advising his clients about "ends," Kronman introduces client purification as an important element of the lawyer-statesman's private legal work. Again calling on his scholarship in philosophy, Kronman further defines this special talent:

> The lawyer-statesman is a paragon of judgment, and others
> look to him for leadership on account of his extraordinary
> deliberative power. This power is more than a clever knack
> or skill. It is, most fundamentally, a trait of character.

Kronman concedes that "lawyers in the past were not giants with extraordinary gifts that dwarfed our own, and on the whole had no more success in living up to their ideals than their counterparts do today."

But, unlike ordinary lawyers, Kronman portrays the lawyer-statesmen as "models to be copied and admired," "the embodiment of professional excellence," prepared "to sacrifice their own well-being" for the public good, persistently offering "advice about ends" to convince their clients to serve the public good. This clearly implies that he is writing about historical figures rather than fictitious or idealized symbols of rectitude. Not surprisingly, *Lost Lawyer* has been interpreted broadly by the legal community as a call to return to the deeds and practices—not merely the ideals and aspirations—of the pre-1960 lawyer-statesmen.

We are seeking here the historical facts: Did any of the lawyer-statesmen actually attempt to purify their clients by insisting that they stop acting against the public interest, and if so, did this inspire their fellow private practitioners to emulate those efforts? The above Kronman quotations suggest that he believes the answer is a double "yes," but in the end, he submits no evidence. Indeed, the reader scans Kronman's book in vain for a single example of client purification in the practices of the lawyer-statesmen.

Exhibit B: Glendon's Nation Under Lawyers

Mary Ann Glendon, Learned Hand Professor of Law at the Harvard Law School, is recognized as a leading authority on constitutional law, human rights, and the legal profession. Her 1994 book, *A Nation Under Lawyers: How the Crisis in the Legal Profession is Transforming American Society,* received glowing reviews. The *New York Times Book Review* called it "One of the most accessible and best-written books about the legal profession in the last few years."

Glendon's *Nation* was published the year after Kronman's *Lost Lawyer,* which she quotes several times. She identifies the "crisis" of her subtitle in nostalgic terms similar to those of Kronman, declaring that lawyers, judges, and teachers are "rapidly shedding the habits and restraints that once made the bench and bar pillars of the democratic experiment," leading to a "far-reaching transformation of lawyers' beliefs and attitudes that has been quietly under way since the mid-1960s." Among radical propositions that "have achieved respectability and prominence, if not dominance, in mainstream legal culture," she lists the notions "that law is a business like any other; and that business is just the unrestrained pursuit of self-interest."

She agrees with Kronman that the large corporate law firms set a shining example for the profession before the 1960s, but she limits that praise to the period between 1920 and the mid-1960s, which period she calls "the golden age." She claims that in those good old days, the "wise counselor" (Kronman's lawyer-statesman) was able to restrain the forces that brought on the post-1960 crisis:

> With hindsight, what seems remarkable about the
> American legal profession from the 1920s to the 1960s is

not that lawyers often failed to live up to the ideals their leaders publicly professed, but that lawyers were so widely oriented for so long to a common set of ideals. Even more remarkable is the evidence that lawyers' ideals had important effects on their habits and practices—effects that could and sometimes did override a variety of personal and economic considerations....

The old "wise counselor" ideals were part of the idea of professionalism articulated by bar leaders in the earlier part of this [the twentieth] century.

Here Glendon refers the reader to Kronman: "For an eloquent plea for reviving the 'lawyer-statesman' and 'wise counselor' roles, see Anthony Kronman, *The Lost Lawyer*..." Her use of "reviving" and "roles" appears to indicate that she believes the lawyer-statesmen (or wise counselors) actually practiced client purification during the golden age. By mentioning "evidence" of such "practices," she is more explicit than Kronman, most of whose statements about purification are couched in terms of ideals rather than practices.

She offers this justification for her choice of the Wall Street (or large corporate) law firms as the standard-bearers of the golden age virtues:

The lawyers who gained ascendancy in the profession from the 1920s onward were more skilled and better educated than American lawyers, as a group, had ever been. They were university-trained, genteel, and eager to distinguish themselves from the buccaneer lawyers of the gilded age.... They seemed concerned not only to distinguish themselves from the lawyer sidekicks of robber barons but also to make clear they were no mere tools of their own clients.

Glendon goes on to explain why she felt it necessary to lop more than 100 years off the time span during which Kronman's lawyer-statesman ideal allegedly held sway:

Still, if one's benchmark for corporate firms is the palmy days at the turn of the century when lawyers were using every tactic in the book (and many that were not) to help clients bust unions, consolidate monopolies, drive competitors out of business, and obtain favorable treatment from judges and legislators, it would be hard to demonstrate a marked ethical decline. Many among the founders of

today's grand Wall Street firms were no strangers to the
kind of behavior that again became rampant in the 1980s.
Men whose portraits now adorn the walls of paneled law
libraries were often up to their sideburns in Tammany
Hall-style corruption. Many collaborated with and covered
up dealings of railroad builders, oil pioneers, and utility
magnates that included bribery and violence.

Paradoxically, those buccaneer lawyers, the "lawyer sidekicks of the robber
barons," were for the most part "university trained" and "genteel"—graduates of the leading schools, prominent in society. And of all the generations
of American lawyers, they were the most dedicated to assisting business clients to evade the law, to the point (as Glendon specifies) of using bribery and
violence when the clients so desired. Thus the buccaneers also possessed the
unique qualifications by which Glendon distinguishes her golden-age Wall
Street lawyers. But according to her view of history, the 1920-1960 golden-
agers broke with their firms' traditions by making it clear that "they were no
mere tools of their own clients."

Having mentioned the "remarkable evidence" that ideals had important
effects on the practices of the golden-age Wall Street lawyers, what evidence
does Glendon cite? Here she marches in step with Kronman, presenting not
a single instance of client purification. Instead she serves up a time-worn and
totally inaccurate play on the words of Elihu Root:

"About half the practice of a decent lawyer," lawyer-statesman
Elihu Root is supposed to have said, "consists in telling
would-be clients that they are damned fools and should
stop." Indeed, it was once considered to be a lawyer's duty to
persuade the client to attend to the spirit as well as the letter
of the law…. When house counsel began switching business
from one firm to another [in the 1960s], how many lawyers
told erring clients they were "damned fools"?

By transposing the Root legend to the more competitive legal market of
the 1960s, Glendon implies that the leading lawyers of her golden age actually
would have told crooked clients they were damned fools. The Root saga originated in the two-volume authorized Root biography written by Columbia
Law Professor Philip Jessup, in which the author laid out the full story that is
invariably downsized and distorted when repeated:

He [Root] was still pre-eminently a trial lawyer, but he was
already wise in consultation and constantly adhered to the

principle which he expressed years afterward in private
conversation, as he had suggested it to the Havemeyer
Sugar Refining Company in 1882, that "of course a lawyer's
chief business is to keep his clients out of litigation." Or, as
he phrased it on another occasion: "About half the practice
of a decent lawyer consists in telling would-be clients that
they are damned fools and should stop."

Thus it is clear from the unedited Jessup account that Root was talking
about the need to keep big business clients (like the Havemeyers, known to
their contemporaries as "lords of the sugar trust") out of litigation whenever
possible, not because it was in the public interest, but because it was in the
clients' interest to avoid the exposure of their internal affairs that was a frequent side effect of litigation. Root practiced in an era when virtually no corporate disclosure was required—whether to government, media, or even the
shareholders—and therefore the private interests of the corporate insiders
were best served by avoiding litigation whenever possible. Root never mentioned to Jessup or anyone else the high-minded concept of lecturing a client
on the public interest. He told his clients they "should stop" when they were
headed for the transparency of litigation, not when he felt they were acting
against the public interest.

Another difficulty with Glendon's use of the distorted Root anecdote is
that Root was the lawyer of choice for the likes of John D. Rockefeller, Boss
Tweed, Jay Gould, and Jim Fiske, a veritable poster boy for Glendon's "lawyer
sidekicks of the robber barons" whose ready collaboration with the worst of
the business scoundrels caused Glendon to exclude them en masse from her
golden age. In fact, Glendon herself pulls poor old Elihu out of the client-
purification game with this later passage:

> The motto of the day [in the 1980s] seemed to be another
> old saying attributed to Elihu Root: "The client never wants
> to be told he can't do what he wants to do; he wants to be
> told how to do it, and it is the lawyer's business to tell him
> how."

Root is the only exemplar of the purifying lawyer offered by Glendon. She
devotes nine laudatory pages to John W. Davis, the 1924 Democratic presidential candidate, but she focuses on his renowned courtliness, courtesy, and skill
as an appellate advocate, without mentioning any instances of client purification. She mentions Davis's view that it was his duty "to discourage litigation
whenever possible," quoting William H. Harbaugh's acclaimed biography of
Davis, *Lawyer's Lawyer*. As in Root's time, the Wall Street law firms of Davis's

era were so dedicated to keeping their big business clients' affairs confidential that their partners were overwhelmingly counselors rather than litigators. In the Harbaugh passage cited by Glendon, the biographer mentions that Davis' "corporate practice was making him more and more tolerant of the concentration of wealth and power in America" and goes on to say that Davis limited his advice to questions of law:

> This indifference to management and corporate policy strengthened Davis' conviction that he was a free moral agent, that his legal counsel had no relation to his social and political conscience. On Wall Street, no less than in Washington a decade earlier, he adhered absolutely to the principle that the lawyer's duty was to represent his client's interest to the limit of the law, not to moralize on the social and economic implications of the client's lawful actions.

Exhibit C: Linowitz's Betrayed Profession

The story of Sol Linowitz's life reads like a Frank Capra script for the American Dream, culminating in the awards of the Presidential Medal of Freedom and more than 40 honorary degrees from universities as diverse as Notre Dame and Yeshiva, in recognition of his illustrious public service which included key roles in negotiation of the Camp David Egyptian-Israeli accords and the Panama Canal treaties.

In his 1994 book, *The Betrayed Profession: Lawyering at the End of the Twentieth Century*, Linowitz opines that the profession he loves has changed "drastically and disappointingly in the past half century." Therefore his golden age runs from the beginning of our nation until the 1950s, roughly equivalent to Kronman's good old days. Linowitz proclaims his admiration for the lawyer-statesmen who were leaders of their communities and of the country—Adams, Jefferson, Madison, Jay, Marshall—"how many of our founding fathers were lawyers!"

Much of what Linowitz misses about the old days has to do with the collegiality of practice in firms composed largely of friends and with the close personal relationships that developed between lawyers and their long-standing clients, which he describes generally as "the nonpecuniary satisfactions that lawyers once sought and found in the law." What concerns us here is Linowitz's major goal: "to create the possibility of a legal profession that is once again independent," thus indicating his belief that it was "independent" in the good old days before 1960.

When we look for evidence of independence as demonstrated by client purification, we find none. There is only a re-run of the distorted Elihu Root "damned fools" aphorism, and this lament:

> Today there are too few lawyers who see it as part of their function to tell clients (especially new clients) that they are damned fools and should stop: Any such statement would interfere with the marketing program.

Here Linowitz (like Glendon) overlooks the portion of the quotation in the Jessup biography which makes it clear that Root was referring to avoidance of litigation rather than client purification. And by condemning today's lawyers for putting the "marketing program" ahead of the public interest, he joins Kronman and Glendon in assuring us that the legal giants of the past saw it as "part of their function" to purify clients who were seeking ends which conflicted with the public good.

The Root distortion is doubly misleading because Elihu was describing not merely his own law practice, but "half the practice of a decent lawyer," thus emboldening the proponents of virtue-based ethics to claim all the golden age's decent lawyers—not just one lawyer—as their historical source. Root may well have been accurate in what he actually said: that in his day, most of the lawyers for large businesses spent a great deal of time talking their clients out of litigation, in order to maintain the shroud of secrecy which shielded their conduct from the prying eyes of shareholders, tax collectors, and prosecutors.

Thus Linowitz, like Kronman and Glendon, leaves us with an image of the pre-1960s Wall Street lawyer as the lawyer-statesman or wise counselor whose elite standing and unselfish behavior were independent forces for civic virtue, at least in part by purifying business clients whose conduct threatened the public good. And like the other two authors, Linowitz leaves us without a valid example of this lawyer-administered injection of the public interest.

This reliance on non-existent evidence is all the more remarkable because these three books are otherwise characterized by erudite scholarship and laudable goals. Their failure to present any evidence of client purification by the lawyer-statesmen led me to suspect that none existed, particularly in view of the vast scholarly resources available to these eminent authors and the specific disclaimers of such a duty by legal giants like Elihu Root and John W. Davis.

To investigate this suspicion, I examined the biographies and the collected papers of prominent lawyer-statesmen spanning all versions of the golden age, from Alexander Hamilton (1755-1804) to John W. Davis (1873-1955), including those of John Adams, Thomas Jefferson, Gouverneur Morris, Daniel Webster, William Henry Seward, Rufus Choate, Salmon Chase, Hamilton Fish, Abraham

Lincoln, Stephen Douglas, Samuel Tilden, James Garfield, Elihu Root, William Jennings Bryan, Franklin D. Roosevelt, Henry Stimson, Felix Frankfurter, Dean Acheson, and John Foster Dulles.

I found no mention of client purification as a lawyer's duty, or even as an aspirational ideal.

Technically, Louis D. Brandeis (1856-1941) does not fit our definition of a lawyer-statesman since he never held public office prior to his appointment to the U.S. Supreme Court in 1916. However, his remarkable career and the opposition which greeted his nomination by President Woodrow Wilson make it crystal clear that no ethic of client purification existed in the minds of lawyer-statesmen even in the alleged golden-age days of 1916.

Beginning in 1879, Brandeis built a highly successful private practice based in Boston, representing many business clients both in litigation and in providing legal advice. During the next 37 years, he became nationally famous for his ability to serve the public interest while representing business clients. He gained a reputation for rejecting representation of well-paying clients whose causes he believed were unjust, and for attempting to persuade clients to refrain from anti-social behavior. Along the way he volunteered his services free of charge to underdogs whom he believed were being exploited by big business. Sometimes these underdogs were entire communities, such as the customers of overreaching utilities, banks, and insurers. This earned him the title of "the people's attorney," and he became the great pioneering role model for today's public interest and pro bono lawyers.

Had there been even a hint of a client-purifying ethic among lawyer-statesmen, they would have lined up to testify before the Senate Judiciary Committee in support of the Brandeis nomination. Instead they closed ranks to block the nomination, denouncing Brandeis's efforts to protect the public interest at the expense of business clients as conflicts of interest demonstrating a lack of sensitivity to professional ethics. The crowning blow was a letter to the Senate Judiciary Committee signed by seven former presidents of the American Bar Association, performing their "painful duty" to oppose the Brandeis nomination because of the nominee's "reputation, character, and professional career." Their criticism was based squarely on what they regarded as Brandeis's "shady reputation" for letting the public interest get in the way of "undivided fidelity" to his business clients.

Among the seven ABA signatories were two eminent lawyer-statesmen: former president William Howard Taft, and—yes, you guessed it—the ubiquitous Elihu Root, once again demonstrating (when accurately quoted) how revolting he found the idea of client purification. Their opposition helped to prolong the confirmation hearings for a record-breaking four months, after which the Senate Judiciary Committee approved the Brandeis nomination by the narrowest of margins, a straight party-line vote of 10 to 8. If Elihu Root and the other lawyer-statesmen had gotten their way, the Supreme Court and the nation would have been deprived of the services of one of its greatest justices from 1916 to 1939.

Typical of the real-life lawyer-statesmens' legal practice was the case of *Le Guen v. Gouverneur*, a commercial *cause celebre* involving the then-princely sum of $100,000, which was litigated in the New York courts during the late 1790s. The case involved allegations of wholesale fraud on both sides of a large shipment of cotton and indigo from Mauritius to New York. LeGuen, the claimant, retained Alexander Hamilton, and the defendant chose Gouverneur Morris as his counsel. If these lawyer-statesmen had ever practiced client purification, here was the occasion for them to independently investigate the facts about the alleged fraud, and for at least one of them to try to talk the client out of proceeding with a fraudulent claim or defense. But the extensive documentary history of the case (complete with lawyers' notes and opinion letters to the clients) contains no mention of any consideration of the public interest on either side. Thus it is safe to assume that Messrs. Le Guen and Gouverneur sought the services of these lawyer-statesmen only for their legal skills, not for moral advice or judgment. And so it has gone throughout the history of the American lawyer-statesman.

I also scoured the published histories of leading law firms and found no trace of any firm policy or procedure for conducting any kind of client purification at any time. Indeed, this subject was so far from the minds of the golden-age lawyers that there was no word or phrase describing any such ideal or activity, so that I was required to invent the term "client purification."

The most comprehensive firm history is Robert T. Swaine's three-volume work, *The Cravath Firm and its Predecessors, 1819-1947.* Besides detailed accounts of the firm's partners and clients, it contains the much-admired operating manual of the *Cravath System,* which Swaine describes as Paul Cravath's "definite philosophy about the organization of his law firm, its partners, its practice and its relation to its associates." Cravath, a partner from 1899 to 1940, went into great detail in describing how the firm should be operated, but made no mention of client purification. The only place in Swaine's three volumes where he touches on the subject is in his discussion of the moral climate of American business when Teddy Roosevelt became president in 1901. There Swaine defends the corporate executives and bankers against charges that they deliberately flouted the law, and adds:

> As to the lawyers, they did not regard the social and economic problems as theirs. The story has often been told that Elihu Root said: "The client never wants to be told he can't do what he wants to do; he wants to be told how to do it, and it is the lawyer's business to tell him how."

Therefore, from all the available evidence it is apparent that client purification by the lawyer-statesmen of any era is a pure myth.

Perhaps the most perceptive comment about the independence of the golden-age lawyers in these volumes is Felix Frankfurter's portrayal of his encounter, as a young government lawyer, with railroad baron E.H. Harriman and his retinue of lawyers when Harriman was called to appear before the Interstate Commerce Commission:

> The way Mr. Harriman spoke to his lawyers, and the boot-
> licking deference they paid to him! My observation of this
> interplay between the great man, the really powerful domi-
> nating tycoon, Harriman, and his servitors, the lawyers, led
> me to say to myself, "If it means that you should be that
> kind of a subservient creature to have the most desirable
> clients, the biggest clients in the country, if that's what it
> means to be a leader of the bar, I never want to be a leader
> of the bar. The price of admission is too high."

Frankfurter's experience accords with that of Judge Elbert Gary, the Chicago lawyer who served as the top legal advisor to J.P. Morgan in the quest to monopolize the steel industry. Early in their relationship, when Gary had the temerity to question the legality of a proposed business plan, Morgan replied, "Well, I don't know as I want a lawyer to tell me what I cannot do. I hire him to tell me how to do what I want to do." From that point on, Gary told Morgan how to do what he wanted to do.

To find a declaration that it was considered the golden-age lawyer's duty to purify clients, I had to look at the works of a major legal scholar whose name does not appear in the Kronman, Glendon, or Linowitz books.

The Missing Exhibit: David Dudley Field

David Dudley Field Jr. (1805-1894) was America's most vociferous advocate of client purification, and a pioneering reformer who made more contributions to improvement of the legal system than any other lawyer or statesman of the nineteenth century. By the time of the Civil War, Field was a very successful New York lawyer, much in demand for important business litigation. During his 66-year career, he argued several important cases in the U.S. Supreme Court, including *Ex parte Milligan* and *Ex parte McCardle*, two landmark constitutional decisions of the Reconstruction era.

Field's statesmanship took a novel form. Instead of seeking elective office, he launched a private crusade to improve the administration of the law. At his own expense, in 1837 he undertook the prodigious task of reducing the morass of civil and criminal procedures to well-organized codes. At that time the American courts used "common-law pleading," a hyper-technical procedure that made litigation a word-game in which the misplacement of a noun or verb could result in the dismissal of a meritorious claim or defense. In 1848, New York adopted Field's Code of Procedure, which became the model for simplification of court procedure throughout the nation, and was partially adopted in England and some of the British Commonwealth nations.

Field never publicly accepted the principle that a lawyer should be totally dedicated to the client's cause, as then proclaimed most famously by Lord Brougham. In a widely circulated 1844 article, Field wrote:

> Lord Brougham has even gone so far as to say, in a speech in the English House of Lords, within a year or two, that the advocate is bound to carry his zeal for his client so far, as to forget there is any other person in the world beside him, and to lose sight of every other consideration than the one of his success.

> Now to our view a more revolting doctrine scarcely ever fell from any man's lips. We think it unsound in theory and pernicious in practice....

> "Forget that there is any other person in the world than his client." What a monstrous declaration! Sacrifice everything, every relation, every consideration, to save his client! Forget that there is a society whose welfare the advocate is bound by the highest sanctions to promote; that there are other parties, whose interests are at stake, that there are duties to society, to every member of it, as well as to the one who has retained him! How *can* a man forget these, and retain his conscience or his memory?

Five years later, Field wrote:

> Lawyers should not be indifferent to the moral aspects of the causes they advocate. It is error to believe that a lawyer may properly advocate a bad cause. Any lawyer asked to advocate the bad scheme of an unjust client should refrain from pursuing an unjust object.

This lusty rhetoric reflects the discomfort Field suffered when he was branded as a mercenary, the nineteenth-century equivalent of a "hired gun."

But Field never provided any examples of such a triumph of public interest over duty to serve the client, either from his own practice or any other. Indeed, he practiced the polar opposite of his sanctimonious preaching.

One of Field's most important early clients was Jacob Sharp, who strove for a monopoly of New York City transit by engaging in wholesale bribery of the New York Board of Aldermen. The Aldermen handed out lucrative franchises to Sharp, sometimes through secret meetings of which no public notice was given. Field devoted his extraordinary legal talents to keeping Sharp's illicit business thriving. Yet Jacob Sharp emerges as a paragon of civic virtue alongside the three clients for whom David Dudley Field is most famous: Jim Fisk, Jay Gould, and William Marcy ("Boss") Tweed. Field's lasting reputation and much of his fortune was made in providing legal cover for the most outrageous capers of that trio, which went down in history as the Erie Wars. As historian Arthur Schlesinger Jr. noted, Field's complicity in the larcenous activities of Fisk, Gould, and Tweed did "almost as much to retard legal reform as his writings [did] to encourage it."

The Erie Wars erupted in 1868, when Commodore Cornelius Vanderbilt sought to put his New York Central Railroad in a monopoly position by acquiring control of his only competitor, the Erie Railroad. The ensuing litigation became a comic opera fit for Gilbert and Sullivan, involving open bribery of judges and legislators, with the going rates published in newspapers like horse-racing results. Many of these bribes were passed through lawyers and accounted for as "legal expenses," thus moving the lawyers far outside their legitimate functions of giving legal advice and defending clients against criminal charges. At the center of this perfect storm of corruption was David Dudley Field, the reliable hired gun for the leading business brigands of his time. Before the Erie wars ended with Vanderbilt's capitulation, more than 40 lawyers—the cream of the New York bar—performed services on the side of Fisk, Gould, and Tweed, most of them brought in by Field. The Erie truce did not mark the end of Field's services to the larcenous trio, for they kept Field and his colleagues busy masterminding other legal atrocities over many more years.

But in a perverse way, Field's generalship of the Erie Wars led to some law reform. The public outcry at the spectacle of prominent lawyers buying judges and legislators on behalf of the robber barons finally brought a sense of shame to those who considered themselves leaders of the New York bar. The result was a petition to form a new body, the Association of the Bar of the City of New York (ABCNY), which in 1870 became the first bar association organized to "promote the due administration of justice." It was dogged at first by the inconvenient fact that the very scandals which called it into being were aided and abetted by Field and other members of the legal elite, the "decent part" of the New York bar.

During its first three years (1870-1872), zealots in the ABCNY engaged in a running battle with Field to denounce his Erie tactics as unethical, even though no code of legal ethics existed as yet. This story is told at length in *Causes and Conflicts: The Centennial History of the Association of the Bar of the City of New York, 1870-1970*, in which the author, George Martin, concludes that the Field/Erie conflict was "about to split the Association irreparably when it was only in its third year and its work of reform only just begun."

The moment of truth came for Field on January 10, 1872, during a meeting of the ABCNY at which some of his fellow leaders of the New York bar renewed the call for an investigation into his conduct of the Erie litigation. Field presented letters from 12 prominent judges and lawyers who found nothing wrong with his actions. In a long, impassioned speech, he disavowed the propriety of inquiring into the motives or morality of his clients. In fact, he trashed the very notion of client purification in these biting terms:

> Now, whether it was proper for me to try the characters of
> my clients before trying their causes is a question I leave to
> those members of the association who have refused such
> retainers or taken only the retainers of saints.

With his unerring eye for the vital point, Field took the occasion of his impending censure to nullify his unequivocal denunciation of Lord Brougham's credo by making it clear that American lawyers had never assumed the duty of questioning or purifying the character of their clients. Had that judging been the lawyer's function, no doubt Field would have dashed off a code laying out exactly what questions should be put to the client before taking on the case.

Why the Truth Matters

Does it really matter whether Kronman, Glendon, and Linowitz (KG&L) paint an accurate picture of the role of pre-1960s lawyer-statesmen in client purification? Or is the search for evidence of what those lawyer-statesmen actually did for their clients an exercise of interest only to history buffs?

I think it is vital to determine the true role of the lawyer-statesman in client purification, mainly because KG&L's reading of history is coupled with eloquent pleas for reform. KG&L—along with many other leading legal scholars and much of the general public—see the legal system in deep crisis, with lawyers openly dedicated to making big money by doing whatever their clients demand. If KG&L's client-purification claims are accepted at face value, their quest for reform will continue to be directed toward restoration of self-regulation of the bar by the elite Wall Street lawyers, described by

Glendon as highly skilled, well educated, "genteel, and eager to distinguish themselves from the buccaneer lawyers of the gilded age." If the thrust of KG&L's proposed reforms is to turn the clock back to the elite bar's pre-1960 level of independence from business clients, we must know whether that independence was real or an illusion. If (as demonstrated here) their legendary independence is a myth, we must look elsewhere for the changes needed to alleviate the crisis, and not waste any precious reformist energy on a self-serving fairy tale.

This need for the truth is pointed up by other influential legal scholars' acceptance and extension of KG&L's views. For example, Pepperdine Law School Professor Robert F. Cochran, Jr., who has made important contributions to legal ethics scholarship, authored a 23-page essay review of the Glendon and Kronman books in the 1996 Notre Dame Law Review. After noting that Kronman and Glendon had rejected "the rule-based ethics that the legal profession focuses on today," Cochran aligns himself with their call for "a return to an older, more subtle moral tradition—the exercise of virtues."

Cochran recounts the lawyer-statesman philosophy of Kronman and Glendon in some detail, and writes that both "provide thoughtful histories of the leaders of the legal profession." Cochran claims that these past leaders established the tradition of giving clients "independent judgment, moral as well as legal." But he recites only one alleged example of such client purification by those leaders: the incredibly shrunken Elihu Root "damned fools" pronouncement which we have examined in its full-grown (and vastly different) version. Cochran concludes:

> Kronman and Glendon do not suggest solutions to the problems of the legal profession. They provide thoughtful pictures of the history and the current status of the profession. These books can help us to attain a virtue which Alasdair MacIntyre identifies as "having an adequate sense of the traditions to which one belongs or which confront one."…
>
> Kronman and Glendon provide the sort of insight into our legal tradition that may enable us to see the possibilities that are available to us. I commend their books to lawyers and to professional responsibility classes. With their focus on character and virtues, they point us in the right direction.

Cochran's efforts to teach virtue and character to law students are commendable, but they become counterproductive when they are hitched to mythology and erroneous history like the Elihu Root distortion. The Kronman/Glendon "thoughtful pictures" of our legal history and traditions include the image of the elite business lawyer playing a vital role in client purification before 1960. Since these pictures are merely wishful thinking and there never was such an operating tradition, evoking them will serve only to seduce legal reformers away from their pursuit of the more effective rules that may be required to prevent lawyer complicity in atrocities like Enron.

Cochran's mention of "professional responsibility classes" indicates that he and other law professors are teaching their students that the virtues extolled by Kronman and Glendon may take the place of rules designed to enforce accountability. Indeed, a large section of Cochran's article is entitled "Virtues More Important Than Rules." From that position it is not a long journey to the Rule of Law according to Aristotle Onassis: "The only rule is that there are no rules—there is no right or wrong, there is only what is possible." Paradoxically, "no right or wrong" clearly is the polar opposite of the civic virtue which is visualized and sought by Kronman, Glendon, Linowitz, and Cochran.

In 2004, U.S. District Judge Jed S. Rakoff called for vigorous enforcement of existing ethical standards, and new legislation along the lines of the 2002 Sarbanes-Oxley Act, the federal investor protection statute which "in effect empowers the in-house lawyer to act as a corporation's conscience" and requires corporate lawyers to take some affirmative steps toward client purification. In his article, "Is the Ethical Lawyer an Endangered Species?" Judge Rakoff cites the Kronman and Glendon books for documentation of the post-1960 erosion in standards of professionalism. While he mentions their descriptions of client purification as practiced by earlier lawyer-statesmen, he is not blinded by that vision. He recognizes the need for the "rule-based ethics" rejected by Cochran, in the form of new legislation and stricter enforcement of existing rules relating to lawyers' accountability. The point here is that contemporary ethicists like Judge Rakoff should not have to detour into mythologized ground and pay homage to the Rule of Law according to Elihu Root, when Root himself would have laughed at the interpretation placed on his words by those who seek to substitute virtue for rule-based accountability.

Since I have been extolling the public-service deeds of America's lawyer-statesmen throughout this book, I felt a duty to dispel the myth that in private practice they took on the task of purifying their clients and other lawyers. That should help clear the air for a more accurate evaluation of the pros and cons of America's heavy reliance on lawyers.

Now we can move on to the track record of lawyer-statesmen in public office, and the question of whether we can rely on their civic virtue to assure that they will not abuse the unique powers we have trusted to them. This is part of a broader question: What is the role of lawyer-statesmen in today's American Rule of Law?

Chapter Fifteen

Lawyer-Statesmen and
the American Rule of Law

Daniel Webster (1782-1852) was the personification of the lawyer-statesman, the acknowledged leader of the American bar who argued (and won) many of the Supreme Court cases that shaped our constitutional law, while moving in and out of government repeatedly, returning to private practice between stints as a congressman, senator, and secretary of state for three presidents. In fact, Daniel took the lawyer-statesman title so literally that he was able to earn handsome legal fees from clients while they were profiting from his official actions as a statesman. This dexterity was possible because at the time, there were no enforceable conflict of interest rules for lawyer-statesmen. There was only the civic virtue extolled by Kronman, Glendon, Linowitz, and Cochran.

Throughout his government service, Webster maintained close ties with his business clients, who set up a private fund to supplement his government salary. He continued to advise his business clients and to argue important court cases for them even while serving in these high offices. Since many public offices were considered part-time jobs in the early years of the republic, this was not prohibited at the time. But Webster pushed the envelope much further. He received questionable off-the-books personal loans from Nicholas Biddle, head of the Bank of the United States, while he was openly supporting Biddle's interests on the Senate floor. By deception, he managed to remove those embarrassing loans from the bank's records. He pressured Biddle into paying him monthly retainers to cover his ongoing work for the bank in the Senate. Webster also used privileged Senate information to tip off his son Fletcher about impending government actions that would raise speculative values of western lands, which they then bought with help from Biddle and other business clients. As secretary of state, Webster sold ambassadorial and consular posts for cash.

It is a measure of the then-prevailing standards that Webster's conduct did not bring him censure or prosecution, although he did little to hide it, and he even complained openly in Senate speeches when Biddle fell behind schedule in his monthly retainer payments. This acceptance of Daniel Webster's misdeeds tells us much about the effectiveness of civic virtue as the lawyers' guiding light, for Webster was not an aberration, the one bad apple that spoiled the barrel—he was the undisputed leader, the role model for the lawyer-statesmen and the entire bar of his time. Indeed, Dean Kronman singles him out as such in *The Lost Lawyer:*

> In Daniel Webster's great speeches before the Supreme
> Court and on the floor of the Senate, it [the lawyer-
> statesman ideal] found a model to admire,...

Not surprisingly, there is no record of Daniel Webster attempting to purify a client.

Credit Mobilier

Virtue was still the watchword in 1872, when the government's worst financial scandal came to light, along with the evidence that it was driven by lawyer-statesmen, including one—James Garfield—who would go on to become the nation's 20th president.

Credit Mobilier was a construction company that the promoters of the Union Pacific Railroad organized to divert into their own pockets the exorbitant profits made by inflating the costs of building the line, which was highly subsidized by federal loans and land grants. The diversionary scheme, which impoverished the railroad in the process, required continuous Congressional support—especially the derailing of a proposed 1868 Congressional investigation which threatened to expose and unravel the corruption involved.

This was no problem for the head of Credit Mobilier, Oakes Ames, who happened to be a congressman from Massachusetts. He set about to bribe the members of Congress who controlled the fate of the 1868 investigation or were involved in creating other legislation relating to the Union Pacific line. Most of those congressmen were lawyers, including Garfield, who chaired the powerful House Appropriations Committee. The bribes took the form of $9 million worth of stock in Credit Mobilier, "sold" to key legislators at a price well below market value, under a sweetheart deal which allowed the purchase price to be covered by the healthy dividends without any cash outlay by the lawmakers. That was sweet enough to stop the Congressional investigation in its tracks.

The Credit Mobilier fraud kept on rolling until 1872, when Representative Ames got into a squabble with some of his greedy investors, who were callous enough to leak to the *New York Sun* documents telling the story of the 1868 wholesale bribery of Congress. The *Sun* published the documents under the headline, "HOW CREDIT MOBILIER BOUGHT ITS WAY THROUGH CONGRESS." Now Congress was forced to act. The House appointed a special five-man committee to investigate why it had not investigated Credit Mobilier four years earlier. The committee was chaired by Representative Luke Poland of Vermont, who, like the other four members, was a lawyer.

Garfield, called before the special House committee, gave an incoherent account of his dealings with Ames. Garfield denied ever subscribing to or receiving any Credit Mobilier shares, but after Ames contradicted that testimony and produced a cancelled dividend check, Garfield refused to testify in rebuttal, leaving Ames's version unchallenged. Apparently Garfield was confident that if he maintained his silence and thus facilitated the cover-up, the investigating committee of fellow lawyer-statesmen would not treat him harshly.

As Garfield biographer Professor Allan Peskin puts it, the special House committee "condemned Ames for bribing congressmen but exonerated the congressmen of taking bribes." *The American Heritage History of Congress* appraises the Poland committee's work succinctly: "Anxious to sweep the mess out of sight as quickly as possible, the committee accepted the confused and contradictory testimony, whitewashed many who were patently guilty, and fastened all the blame on two scapegoats," Republican Representative Oakes Ames, the instigator, and Representative James Brooks, the Democratic leader of the House, who (in apparent recognition of his leadership position) had received more shares than anyone else. In the end, the House refused to expel Ames or Brooks, and settled for a vote of censure against them, which was the only punishment imposed on anyone involved in the Credit Mobilier scandal.

As in the case of Daniel Webster, the significant point is not the wrong done by one lawyer, or a few lawyers. It is the high-level lawyer-statesmen as a group conspiring to cover up their complicity in the blatant theft of government funds. The Credit Mobilier scandal was the handiwork of an army of bribe-taking and whitewashing lawyers who controlled the entire Congress in 1872. Mercifully, Oakes Ames was a shovel manufacturer, not a lawyer. But somehow he managed to buy lawyer-statesmen by the dozen, despite the civic virtue attributed to them in some quarters today.

Those who claim that lawyers' standards have been lowered by the "more openly commercial culture" of the twenty-first century, and who long for the golden age when an "older sense of values" guided lawyers, should consider whether a Representative James Garfield could walk away from a Credit Mobilier scam today and go on to be elected to the White House.

Teapot Dome

When James Garfield began his term as president in 1881, the nation was well into the gilded age, and the robber barons controlled both Wall Street and the "independent" Wall Street lawyers whom they retained. While Professor Glendon prudently excludes the robber barons' lawyers from her golden age of lawyer virtue, neither her book nor those of Kronman or Linowitz explain how virtue was reborn in 1920. By that time, Warren Harding of Ohio had been elected president and was preparing to place his political cronies (known as the "Ohio Gang") in key government offices, led by his campaign manager, the exquisitely corrupt lawyer-statesman Harry Daugherty, as attorney general. The stage was being set for the massive thievery that would brand the Harding administration as the most corrupt in our history. The featured act was to be the second great lawyer-driven government financial scandal: Teapot Dome, the worthy successor to Credit Mobilier.

Teapot Dome was a 10,000-acre oil field on public land in Wyoming, so named because it was overlooked by a boulder shaped like a teapot. Along with fields located on public lands in California, its oil was reserved for emergency use by the U.S. Navy. These reserves remained under the jurisdiction of the Navy Department until 1921, when lawyer-statesman Albert Fall (former senator from New Mexico and now President Harding's secretary of the interior) persuaded the secretary of the navy, lawyer-statesman Edwin Denby, to transfer them to the Interior Department. Fall then proceeded to secretly lease the Teapot Dome field to oil magnate Harry Sinclair and the California fields to oil magnate Edward Doheny. Each of the oil magnates would later say that these leases were worth at least $100 million to them.

At that time, since competitive bidding was not required, these leases were not in themselves illegal. Only the inducements which Fall received from the oil magnates—a total value of $404,000—were illegal, but these bribes were artfully concealed, mostly in the form of improvements and additions (including livestock) to Fall's rundown New Mexico cattle ranch. When the *Wall Street Journal* ran a story about the secret Teapot Dome lease in 1922, the Senate Committee on Public Lands was called upon to investigate whether any bribery was involved. Although the Republicans had a controlling majority in the Senate, they thought so little of the prospects for exposing bribery that they turned control of the investigation over to the Public Lands Committee's most junior minority member, Senator Thomas J. Walsh (Democrat, Montana). The committee's chairman, Republican Senator Reed Smoot of Utah, took the precaution of stifling public interest by delaying public hearings until October 1923, some 18 months after the investigation resolution was adopted.

Senator Tom Walsh spent a frustrating year on the investigation without producing solid evidence of bribery. He was given a very small budget which precluded adequate staffing or travel, and he got no assistance from Harry Daugherty's Justice Department or any other Harding administration officials. Since Walsh was a former prosecutor, he did much of the investigation work himself. Secretary of the Interior Fall pursued a strategy of inundation, unloading thousands of pages of documents on the beleaguered Walsh. Most of these papers dealt with Fall's claim that drilling on private land adjacent to Teapot Dome was draining the Naval oil reserves, thus providing Fall with a patriotic reason for putting the field into production through the lease to Sinclair. Documents explaining the secret process of granting the leases were not forthcoming.

By October 1923, when the Senate public hearings began, Harding had died and had been succeeded by Vice President Calvin Coolidge; Fall had retired to his now-flourishing New Mexico ranch; and Tom Walsh, who had more committee assignments than any other senator, was beginning to regret his decision to head up the Teapot Dome investigation. Apart from the formidable obstacles which blocked access to the truth (including Attorney General Daugherty's harassing investigations of Walsh's activities), Walsh had to contend with anonymous threats directed against his daughter, who was told that she would be killed if the investigation continued.

The first day of the public hearings was devoted to technical testimony from geological experts about the drainage problem which supported Interior Secretary Fall's claim of patriotic motivation. Fall then testified for two days, and although he was evasive, Walsh was not able to confront him with evidence of bribery. At that point the media and the public largely lost interest in the hearings, which many regarded as Democrat Walsh's political mudslinging to discredit the Republican administration in the upcoming election campaign.

But Walsh's dogged pursuit of the truth finally exposed a chink in Albert Fall's armor. A $100,000 payoff to Fall from California oilman Doheny had been disguised as a loan from Edward McLean, publisher of the *Washington Post*, who had no connection with the oil leases. Walsh doubted that McLean had the money to make the loan, but he had been unable to question McLean, who was then sunning himself in Florida, claiming that ill health prevented him from testifying at the Washington hearings. When the hearings recessed in January 1924, Walsh decided to tap into his miniscule budget for a trip to Palm Beach, where he was able to put McLean under oath and take his deposition at the Breakers Hotel. When Walsh pressed him for details and documentation of the $100,000 transaction, McLean finally admitted that he had not made the loan. After that breakthrough, Walsh was able to trace the $100,000 payment from oilman Doheny to Fall. At last he had the smoking gun.

Walsh recalled Doheny to the witness chair, and in two days of dramatic public hearings which captivated the American public as no other governmental process had ever done, the Teapot Dome fraud unraveled. Whereas Fall had testified that the money had come from newspaperman McLean (and therefore had nothing to do with Teapot Dome), Doheny was forced to admit that his son had delivered $100,000 in currency to Fall "in a little black bag"—although Doheny insisted that he conducted much of his business in cash, and that the $100,000 was a personal loan to Fall which had nothing to do with the oil leases.

Typical of the media coverage was the *New Republic's* salute to Walsh: "A hard-boiled lawyer from the Montana copper country who, in the face of killing apathy and less passive hindrances…made one of the most brilliant, resourceful and persistent fights ever carried out against the private plundering of the public wealth." So it was that lawyer-statesman Tom Walsh painstakingly stamped out the template under which Congressional hearings run by lawyers would expose other great government scandals—notably Watergate.

Once Walsh's Palm Beach deposition pulled McLean's finger from the dike, Teapot Dome spilled out across the American landscape for the next six years. Here are a few of the 1924-1930 events that followed:

✦ After oilman Doheny's public admission of the $100,000 pay-off, Walsh decided to request President Calvin Coolidge to begin legal proceedings to cancel all of Albert Fall's fraudulent Teapot Dome and California oil leases. Normally Walsh would have requested the attorney general to take those steps, but he knew that this would be a waste of time with the corrupt Harry Daugherty still holding that office.

✦ The president, lawyer-statesman Calvin Coolidge, learned of Walsh's intentions, and before any public request, he decided to act himself. Instead of turning to the dishonest attorney general, he announced that he would appoint special prosecutors—one from each party—to void the leases and handle all the other court proceedings relating to the Teapot Dome scandal. Coolidge chose Republican Philadelphia attorney Owen Roberts (later a Supreme Court justice) and Ohio Democrat Atlee Pomerene (a former senator). To avoid any further obstruction by Daugherty's compromised Justice Department, Coolidge assigned Treasury Department Secret Service investigators to assist the special prosecutors.

✦ Facing an election in November 1924, Coolidge dispensed with the two remaining Harding cabinet officers involved in Teapot Dome: Navy Secretary Edwin Denby and Attorney General Harry Daugherty. Lawyer-statesman

Denby was unable to satisfactorily explain his role in the secret handover of the Naval oil reserves to Interior Secretary Fall which opened the way for the Teapot Dome scandal. Daugherty was not directly involved in Fall's thievery, but he provided the legal cover which long shielded Fall from exposure and prosecution. He also was known to be selling protection from prosecution to bootleggers and other crooks through his bagman, Jesse Smith, who committed suicide when evidence of this monumental corruption emerged. At the urgent request of prominent members of his own party, Coolidge forced Daugherty's resignation in March of 1924, a few weeks after oilman Doheny's admission of the $100,000 payment to Fall.

✦ Coolidge gained political popularity from his strong corrective moves in reaction to Walsh's Teapot Dome revelations. Despite the Democrats' flaunting of Teapot Dome as a typically corrupt Republican operation, Coolidge— helped by a prosperous economy—easily defeated his Democratic opponent, fellow lawyer-statesman John W. Davis, in the 1924 presidential election.

✦ The special prosecutors were busy for the next six years with the aftermath of Teapot Dome, facing dozens of high-powered defense lawyers, and carrying the added burdens of a cold evidentiary trail and many uncooperative and "unhealthy" witnesses. In that era, wealthy litigants were much more likely to escape or minimize accountability than today, as epitomized by this definition in Ambrose Bierce's 1911 *The Devil's Dictionary*: "*impunity* (n.): wealth." Roberts and Pomerene were unable to convict Sinclair or Doheny of bribery, but they were successful in most of the cases they filed, winning the civil suits to cancel the Teapot Dome and California Naval leases, which were finally declared fraudulent by the Supreme Court in 1927. Albert Fall's criminal trial for bribery was delayed until 1929 by his failing health. He was convicted, sentenced to a year in prison, and fined $100,000, making him the first American cabinet officer to be imprisoned for his actions in office. By that time he had lost his ranch and was unable to pay the fine. Oil magnate Harry Sinclair, who refused to testify before the Walsh committee, was sentenced to a total of nine months in prison for contempt.

✦ Two other Supreme Court decisions relating to Teapot Dome solidified the power of Congressional committees to compel witnesses to testify and produce their records, when the broad subject of the committee hearings relates to potential legislation. The first, *McGrain v. Daugherty*, arose out of the Congressional resolution which confirmed the special prosecutors (Roberts and Pomerene) appointed by President Coolidge. That resolution also established a special Senate committee to investigate Attorney General Daugherty's failure to prosecute Fall and his co-conspirators. The Supreme Court decision upheld the power of that Senate committee to compel production of Daugherty's Ohio bank accounts. The second decision, *Sinclair v. United States*, upheld the power of the Walsh committee to compel oilman Harry Sinclair to testify about his dealings with Fall. Both decisions laid the foundation for what today is the routine procedure of compelling witnesses to testify before Congressional committees.

Senator McCarthy v. the U.S. Army

Tom Walsh had only the print media to spur public interest in his Teapot Dome hearings. A later lawyer-statesman, Senator Joseph McCarthy (Republican, Wisconsin), gained fame by heading a Senate investigating committee in the 1950s, when black-and-white television had become available to most Americans. Perhaps McCarthy would have fared better in Walsh's era, for it was his demeanor during a 36-day television showdown in 1954 that exposed him as a demagogue and led to his downfall.

In 1950, Senator McCarthy made a speech in Wheeling, West Virginia, in which he charged that President Harry Truman's State Department was harboring traitorous Communists. He thundered:

> I have here in my hand a list of 205—a list of names that
> were made known to the secretary of state as being members
> of the Communist Party and who nevertheless are still
> working and shaping policy in the State Department.

Although advance copies of the Wheeling speech distributed to the press gave the number of Communists as 205, McCarthy later specified the number as 57. Whether it was 205 or only 57, that was enough Communists at policy levels in the State Department to shock the American public and gain McCarthy the media spotlight. The problem was that he never made any list public, and as it turned out he had no useful information about Communists actually serving in meaningful government positions.

At first, in the atmosphere of the nation's deep concern about the Cold War and the Soviet nuclear threat, McCarthy received wide public support. He appeared patriotic and appealingly plain-spoken. Then the Republicans gained control of the Senate in the 1952 election, leading to McCarthy's appointment as chairman of the Senate Government Operations Committee and of its Permanent Subcommittee on Investigations—a made-to-order vehicle for McCarthy's ongoing hunt for Communists in government. Now a staple of nightly television news, his mistakes were magnified accordingly. And one of his biggest mistakes was selecting New York lawyer Roy Cohn as his committee counsel.

Cohn was the poster boy for what became known as *McCarthyism*, loosely defined as determining guilt by association and abusing governmental power by smearing the reputations of people against whom there was no reliable evidence of wrongdoing. McCarthy labored to find and expose real Communists without publishing his "list," staying in the headlines by impugning the loyalty of such national heroes as President Dwight Eisenhower and former secretary of state George Marshall. Cohn hired a friend, David Schine, as a committee investigator, and the two of them traipsed around the world in search of evidence to support McCarthy's charges. When Schine was drafted into the Army in 1953, Army officials complained that Cohn was interfering with Schine's military service by using the leverage of his committee post to seek special treatment for his friend. That brought the Army's charges and McCarthy's counter-charges to live nationwide television in May of 1954— the soap opera that became known as the Army-McCarthy hearings.

With his scowling countenance dominating the hearings, McCarthy used every opportunity to browbeat witnesses, and public opinion began to turn against him. The climax was reached on June 9, 1954, on the 30th day of the hearings, when Boston lawyer Joseph Welch, representing the Army, challenged Roy Cohn to deliver to the attorney general McCarthy's list of 130 alleged subversives working in defense plants "before the sun goes down." This prompted McCarthy to charge that a young lawyer in Welch's firm had been a member of the National Lawyer's Guild, which Attorney General Brownell was then seeking to have designated as a Communist front organization.

Welch and Cohn had agreed that this subject would not be aired in the hearings because the Guild's Communist-front designation was then being litigated, but McCarthy bulldozed that agreement aside and smeared the young lawyer's name on nationwide television. That opened McCarthy to a body blow from the mild-mannered Welch:

> Let us not assassinate this lad further, Senator.... You've
> done enough. Have you no sense of decency, sir, at long
> last? Have you left no sense of decency?

The spontaneous applause which greeted Welch's rebuke was the beginning of the end for McCarthy. Later in the hearings, Senator Stuart Symington (Democrat, Missouri) seemed to speak for the majority of viewers when he said to McCarthy, "Senator, the American people have had a look at you now for six weeks. You're not fooling anyone, either."

Although the official results of the Army-McCarthy hearings were inconclusive, they marked the end of McCarthy's influence. The hearings had transformed him from a fearless patriot to the worst advertisement for anti-Communism. A few months later, on December 2, 1954, he was formally censured by a 67-to-22 vote of his fellow senators for his wild and unsupportable charges, which were found to be "contrary to senatorial ethics and tended to bring the Senate into dishonor and disrepute, to obstruct the constitutional processes of the Senate, and to impair its dignity." He was never a serious factor after that unusual Senatorial condemnation. Alcohol consumption became his major activity, and in 1957 he died at the age of 48.

The public was transfixed by the unprecedented spectacle of a powerful lawyer-statesman being brought down by another lawyer who was not wielding governmental authority. But that black-and-white television epic was child's play compared to the next major lawyer-statesmen confrontation, which was broadcast in living color 20 years later under the title of Watergate.

Watergate

In Chapter 6 we reviewed the sequence of events that began with the Watergate burglary and ended with President Richard Nixon's resignation. Here we will note the roles that lawyer-statesmen played in the drama which kept more than 70 million Americans glued to their television sets in 1973-1974. Nixon himself was a lawyer, as were nearly all those who conspired with him to cover up the Watergate fiasco. When the carnage was over, former attorney general John Mitchell went to prison, as did three major White House lawyers (Charles Colson, John Dean, and John Ehrlichman), as well as lower-level lawyers Egil Krogh, Gordon Liddy, and Donald Segretti.

The Senate Watergate Committee, known officially as the Select Committee on Presidential Campaign Activities, chaired by Sam Ervin (Democrat, North Carolina), was composed of seven senators, all of whom were lawyers. They were assisted by staffs of lawyers, headed by Georgetown Law Professor Sam

Dash for the majority Democrats and Fred Thompson of Tennessee for the Republican minority.

As noted by a leading historian of the legal profession, University of Wisconsin Law Professor Marc Galanter:

> The Watergate crisis (1972-1974) accelerated the decline
> of public confidence in elites and, in particular, discredited
> lawyers who figured so prominently among the Watergate
> villains, but at the same time it revived allegiance to the
> Rule of Law. The resolution of the crisis inspired apprecia-
> tion that "the system worked."

The fact that the lawyer-driven crisis was resolved by other lawyers was not lost on the public. It was as though the self-sealing fuel tanks of the World War II combat planes had been deployed again, this time to repair the damage done by the Watergate bullets. In addition to the lawyer-statesmen of the Senate Watergate Committee, those who used the legal system to thwart Nixon's obstruction of justice became heroes, especially U.S. District Judge John Sirica, Special Prosecutor Archibald Cox, and the two Nixon appointees who resigned rather than carry out Nixon's illegal orders, Attorney General Elliot Richardson and Deputy Attorney General William Ruckleshaus.

The final victory of the Rule of Law came in the court-like setting of the House Judiciary Committee, whose 38 members—every one a lawyer—were called upon to consider impeachment of the president. It seemed that the whole power of the Government of Laws was placed in the hands of the previously unheralded chairman, Peter Rodino (Democrat, New Jersey). *Time* magazine described the scene presided over by Rodino:

> When his committee faced its final act of judgment, the
> country was treated to a surprise: a group of nation-
> ally obscure and generally underrated Congressmen
> and Congresswomen rose to the occasion. Often with
> eloquence and poise, they faced the television cameras and
> demonstrated their mastery of complex detail, their dedi-
> cation to duty, and their conscientious search for solutions
> that would best serve the public interest.

When it was over, lawyer-statesman Peter Rodino had achieved his goal: adoption of an article of impeachment for obstruction of justice by a vote of 27 to 11, with six Republicans joining in the majority, making it clear that amidst the maelstrom of a constitutional crisis, the system—the Rule of Law—had transcended party politics.

The American Rule of Law Today

What do Daniel Webster, Credit Mobilier, Teapot Dome, Army-McCarthy, and Watergate tell us about the lawyer-statesmen and the American Rule of Law?

Since the nation's beginning, neither attainment of high public office nor admission to the bar have guaranteed integrity or civic virtue. Two of the last three lawyer-presidents prior to 2008, Richard Nixon and Bill Clinton, engaged in obstruction of justice, and the third, Gerald Ford, was never able to overcome the negative public reaction to his pardon of Nixon a month after taking office, despite the great pains Ford took (even testifying before a Congressional committee) to demonstrate that he was motivated only by the best interests of the country. But it is significant that their conduct was not condoned by their fellow lawyer-statesmen or the public. Leading lawyer-statesmen of earlier generations (e.g., Daniel Webster and James Garfield) got away with corrupt activities for which they would be prosecuted or driven from office today. In the prime years of the golden age envisioned by Kronman, Glendon, and Linowitz—the 1920s—lawyer-statesmen serving as attorney general, secretary of the interior, and secretary of the navy, were busy turning Teapot Dome into a timeless symbol of massive corruption.

American lawyer-statesmen have played an indispensable role in building the Government of Laws envisioned in the Constitution, which has evolved into what we now call the American Rule of Law. They conceived the unique role of law and lawyers in American democracy, and made it work by breathing life into Separation of Powers with Checks and Balances. But in private practice, they did not engage in any significant attempts at client purification, since it is neither desired nor expected by clients, even if we assume it is feasible for any lawyers to undertake that function in the absence of a statute compelling all lawyers to do so.

Strictly enforced ethical rules—and sometimes statutes imposing affirmative duties—are needed to assure virtuous conduct by lawyers, especially the lawyer-statesmen who have such vast and unique powers under the American Government of Laws. "Trust but verify," as President Ronald Reagan put it. If the Rule of Law has evolved to the point where lawyers should be called upon to purify their clients by assuming responsibility for preventing fraud, that function will not spring from civic virtue, tradition, or mythology. It will have to be imposed upon lawyers by statute, as was done to a degree in the Public Company Accounting Reform and Investor Protection Act of 2002 (Sarbanes-Oxley). Otherwise clients will shop around from one comparable law firm to another until they find one that will perform legal services without attempting purification.

The Rule of Law in the United States is heavily dependent on Separation of Powers with Checks and Balances, including the Checks and Balances of lawyer-vs.-lawyer, which at critical times produced a James Madison to checkmate a Patrick Henry, an Abraham Lincoln to save the Union from a disastrous James Buchanan, a Tom Walsh to expose an Albert Fall, a Joe Welch to unmask a Joe McCarthy, and a phalanx of dedicated lawyer-statesmen in the Senate, the House, and the special prosecutor's office to thwart the cadre of law-breaking lawyer-statesmen in the Nixon White House.

Today's law firms, which hire business managers, raid their rivals for personnel, advertise and compete for business, and publish their financial results in *The American Lawyer*, certainly *appear* to be more commercial than their pre-1960 counterparts. In 1960 the largest firms had 200 lawyers, compared to the two thousand or more in today's mega-firms. That altered appearance is a natural consequence of the globalization of business and its extensive regulation by government agencies, whose rules are written by lawyers and ultimately are enforced in the courts. It is also altered by the greatly expanded role of in-house company lawyers in the selection and direction of outside law firms. In both the business world and law practice, there is also much greater transparency—and, as in the sausage factory, transparency does not always present a more attractive tableau. Law practice has always been a hybrid means of livelihood—part business, part profession, and part public service, whether purposeful or unconsciously as an automatic exercise in the everyday Citizens' Checks and Balances.

The pre-1960 lawyers practiced at a time when their activities were screened from public view, and their role in the business world was far less prominent or demanding than it is in 2010. Behind the tweedy façade of the pre-1960s law firm (which created the illusion of being above the commercial scramble), its partners ran their practice as a hybrid of a business, a profession, and a public service, just as is done today. The explosive growth of pro bono and cause lawyering, which were barely specks on the horizon before 1960, demands that today's lawyers become far more deeply involved in public-interest functions than did previous generations.

Therefore, I suggest that despite the sometimes chaotic appearance of our legal system in 2010, we are much closer now to a golden age of the American Rule of Law than we were in the 1920s. Law practice in 2010 has a transparency and accountability which it lacked in the eras designated as the golden age by the myth-makers. Before Teapot Dome, the lawyer-statesmen (like Webster and Garfield) and the ordinary lawyers performed their legal chores largely in secrecy. In the seemingly less commercial pre-1960 atmosphere, the "older values" of lawyers often were not strong enough to prevent their participation in the fraud and corruption that they were called upon to deal with behind closed doors. Those closed doors protected the values held by the least virtuous of the lawyers, and shielded all lawyers from accountability to the public.

Today American lawyers know that in addition to keeping the Government of Laws functioning, they can make society more just and improve life on this planet through their lawyering, both in government service and in private practice. If there was a kernel of truth in Rufus Choate's nineteenth-century vision of the everyday lawyer as a statesman, it has ripened into a vast orchard in the twenty-first century. Ordinary American lawyers are performing more of the statesman's role each year, and getting better at it all the time. They are being trained for it in law school, in law firms, in government and corporate legal departments, and in post-admission education, on a scale which could not have been imagined by the most starry-eyed idealists of the mythical pre-1960 golden age.

A glance at the curriculum of Arizona State University's law school (now called the Sandra Day O'Connor College of Law) confirms this. In addition to the traditional courses like torts, contracts, criminal and civil procedure, today's students participate in "student-run pro bono groups and specialized law education projects" such as the Advocacy Program for Battered Women, the Black Mesa Trust Legal Project (to preserve the water resources of the Navajo and Hopi people), the Elder Law Project, the Homeless Legal Assistance Project, and more than a dozen others. This is typical of the nationwide law school experience.

The Bottom Line: Accountability to the People

A major factor in the stability of the American Rule of Law is the direct accountability of lawyers and the legal system to the American people. It was not until the public became involved (as in Teapot Dome, Army-McCarthy, and Watergate) that the self-sealing gas tanks, the Checks and Balances, gave the Rule of Law the upper hand over tyrannical power. Broad coverage of these events by a free and vibrant press is a vital factor in the public's involvement. Despite Tocqueville's effusive praise of the "legal spirit" in America, in its first 160 years (1789-1949) the legal system was not nearly as accessible, and did not afford anything like the Citizens' Checks and Balances which we enjoy today.

So the people, fully informed by the media, are a vital organ of Separation of Powers with Checks and Balances and the American Rule of Law. In fact, the people are the bottom line. George Washington University Law Professor Jeffrey Rosen, in his 2006 book, *The Most Democratic Branch: How the Courts Serve America*, makes the vital point that "courts for most of American history have tended to reflect the constitutional views of majorities," and that the judicial branch could not have achieved and maintained its co-equal status without broad public support. NYU Law Professor Barry Friedman's 2009 book, *The Will of the People: How Public Opinion Has Influenced the Supreme Court and Shaped the Meaning of the Constitution*, further documents this historical theme, and concludes that "the Supreme Court exercises the power it has precisely because that is the will of the people."

Legal commentator Jeffrey Toobin, in his 2007 book, *The Nine: Inside the Secret World of the Supreme Court*, focuses on the crucial swing-vote role of Justice Sandra Day O'Connor during the Rehnquist era:

> ...for O'Connor there was little difference between a judi-
> cial and a political philosophy. She had an uncanny ear for
> American public opinion, and she kept her rulings closely
> tethered to what most people wanted or at least would
> accept.... No justice ever succeeded more in putting her
> stamp on the law of a generation.

Rosen, Friedman, and Toobin reconfirm the credo of Archibald Cox: *Ultimately, only public support makes the Constitution and the Rule of Law work.*

On his third try behind closed doors, President Richard Nixon found an acting attorney general who agreed to fire Special Prosecutor Cox and thus challenge the American Rule of Law. But by the next day, the crescendo of the people's automobile horns responding to the Pennsylvania Avenue placards, "HONK TO IMPEACH," drowned out the desperate president's orders and brought the most powerful person in the free world to account—in court.

As we have seen, the American Rule of Law was put to a severe test in *Bush v. Gore*. The Supreme Court was able to maintain the confidence of the public even though it departed from precedent and its five conservative justices handed the presidency to the candidate whom the majority of voters had rejected. In that 2000 decision, the Rehnquist court made it clear that their ruling rested on the very narrow grounds presented in the Florida voting debacle, and that it was not to be considered a precedent for deciding future election disputes. But in January 2010, another 5-to-4 conservative majority decision put the Supreme Court at risk of losing public support in an area of much greater long-term significance: the ongoing problem of the funding of political campaigns.

In *Citizens United v. Federal Election Commission*, the majority overturned its 1990 decision in *Austin v. Michigan Chamber of Commerce*, which had upheld the restrictions on corporations' financial contributions to election campaigns. In the majority opinion, Justice Anthony Kennedy (now holding the swing vote) wrote:

> It has been noted that "*Austin* was a significant departure
> from First Amendment principles." We agree with that
> conclusion and hold that *stare decisis* does not compel the
> continued acceptance of *Austin*. The Government may
> regulate corporate political speech through disclaimer
> and disclosure requirements, but it may not suppress that
> speech altogether.

The specter of corporate treasuries being tapped to buy elections brought this response from President Obama:

> With its ruling today, the Supreme Court has given a green
> light to a new stampede of special interest money in our
> politics. It is a major victory for big oil, Wall Street banks,
> health insurance companies and the other powerful interests
> that marshal their power every day in Washington to drown
> out the voices of everyday Americans.... That's why I am
> instructing my Administration to get to work immediately
> with Congress on this issue. We are going to talk with bipar-
> tisan Congressional leaders to develop a forceful response to
> this decision. The public interest requires nothing less.

As this book goes to press early in 2010, it remains to be seen how this conflict will play out. Since the disclaimer and disclosure requirements of the campaign finance laws were left in place, candidates heavily financed by corporate contributions might find it a mixed blessing to be labeled "the rep-resentative of Goldman Sachs" or "the senator from Exxon." The legislation sought by President Obama may also play a role in determining how revolutionary the *Citizens United* decision turns out to be.

If in fact the *Citizens United* decision enables large corporations to control the outcome of elections, the Supreme Court will likely find itself well out of the range of public acceptance. But don't bet against the court's ability to depart from *stare decisis* (the following of precedent) by finding another provision of the Founding Lawyers' Constitution to distinguish (and bury) the *Citizens United* decision. As we have seen, that Constitution is flexible enough to enable the justices to do what is best for the country when push comes to shove.

———

I've been preaching the Rule of Law (sometimes under the label of the Government of Laws) since the first chapter. Now it's time to try to define it.

Chapter Sixteen

Defining the Rule of Law

How do you define the Rule of Law? Well, to coin a phrase, how do you catch a moonbeam in a jar?

The problem is that the Rule of Law is not really a rule, or a collection of rules. It is more of a philosophical/political concept, an idea, like "justice" or "law and order." St. John's Law Professor Brian Tamanaha writes that in view of the "rampant divergence of understandings, the Rule of Law is analogous to the notion of the 'good,' in the sense that everyone is for it, but have contrasting convictions about what it is." And German legal scholar Rainer Grote concludes that the Rule of Law "belongs to the category of open-ended concepts which are subject to permanent debate."

In a 1976 paper, Lord Widgery, then the Lord Chief Justice of England, defined the Rule of Law simply as "the general supremacy of law over anarchy." He went on to say that "although the Rule of Law demands the support of every citizen, it is the lawyers who must ensure that it works" and that the lawyers "cannot do this unless they are accessible to those who need the protection of the law, be it as civil litigants or defendants in a criminal charge." Therefore, a nation fails in its duty to provide that access "unless and until we have removed all the obstacles which separate the courts from the litigants who require their services."

Three decades after Lord Widgery's paper, the low priority assigned to access to justice in the English legal system has created a new obstacle: ridiculously high court fees caused by England's insistence that the courts be self-financing rather than a taxpayer-financed public service. In a 2008 article,

Frances Gibb, Legal Editor of the *London Times*, points out that court filing fees for civil cases were nominal up to the 1990s, when the government policy to make the civil courts self-sustaining was adopted. She writes:

> So court fees began to rise, culminating this year [2008] in a massive increase of about 2,500 percent. For local authorities bringing [childrens'] care cases it meant a rise in fees from £150 to £4,500. The increases hit all civil and family courts, where people bring and contest claims for accidents, breaches of contract or for maintenance after divorce.

I hope I have made it clear that the purpose of this book is to demonstrate that apart from the United States, the courts in the world's developed democracies are separated from the civil litigants who require their services by government-created obstacles, with that obstruction process usually aided and abetted by the legal profession, which regards the existing limited-access system as a sacrosanct profit center. There are important projects under way throughout the world which address much broader aspects of the Rule of Law than my focus on access to civil justice. In many countries, safety and human rights are at greater risk from governmental tyranny than from the inability to file civil lawsuits. Since justice itself is an unfamiliar concept in many nations, the process of installing the Rule of Law there must begin at a rudimentary level. Nevertheless, the worldwide interest in the Rule of Law creates the opportunity for citizens of the developed democracies to gain access to their own courts for the first time, and for Americans to appreciate and reinforce the broad access which they now enjoy.

The laudable efforts to define, refine, and propagate the Rule of Law throughout the world started in 1990 with the American Bar Association (ABA) Central European and Eurasian Law Initiative, providing technical legal assistance to the nations emerging from the Soviet Union dictatorship. The ABA's Rule of Law Initiative, now supported by the International Bar Association and other legal organizations, continues to train judges and lawyers in more than 40 nations. Its initial focus was on creating the elements of a legal system in nations with as lawless a history as Trujillo's Dominican Republic, where talk of independent judges, fixed rules, and challenges to governmental authority would be met with laughter, if not capital punishment. In 2007, the ABA broadened its undertaking by launching the World Justice Project, which seeks to unite the legal profession with many other disciplines to advance the Rule of Law globally.

The World Justice Project is developing a Rule-of-Law Index, to determine how well various nations (including the United States and other developed democracies) are adhering to the Rule of Law. That index holds the potential for awakening the citizens of the other developed democracies to the fact that in the category of access to their civil courts, they stand at the level of Trujillo's peons.

The World Justice Project has not officially defined the Rule of Law, but it has published four "universal principles" which serve as a working definition:

1. A system of self-government in which all persons, including the government, are accountable under the law;

2. A system based on fair, publicized, broadly understood and stable laws;

3. A robust and accessible process in which rights and responsibilities based in law are enforced impartially;

4. Diverse, competent, independent and ethical lawyers and judges.

From the standpoint of this book, the key word is "accessible." In my opinion, no nation apart from the United States can claim to comply with the third principle, not even those which impartially enforce legal rights and responsibilities through a robust process. If they continue to deny most of their citizens access to the courts, robust processes and impartiality of enforcement are meaningless except to the privileged few who have access. Learned Hand, one of America's most revered judges, put it this way:

> If we are to keep our democracy, there must be one
> commandment: Thou shalt not ration justice.

Therefore, I suggest that any meaningful definition of the Rule of Law should include a specific access clause along the following lines:

> **ACCESS TO COURTS. Since the Rule of Law requires
> that all citizens have equal access to the courts in order
> to enforce legal rights and responsibilities, each nation
> undertaking to follow the Rule of Law must refrain from
> erecting or maintaining obstructions to equal access. Such
> unacceptable obstructions include imposition of prohibi-
> tive court filing fees; prohibiting lawyers from entering
> into contingent percentage fee agreements; and shifting
> of the winner's legal costs, fees, and expenses to the loser,
> except in cases where the loser has engaged in litigation
> abuse.**

This access clause is also required if any sense is to be made of the first principle's call for a system "in which all persons and entities, including the government, are accountable under the law." Obviously, litigants like Oliver Brown, James Meredith, Elsie Parrish, Ralph Nader, Mayola Williams, and Don McCusker could not hold accountable the persons or entities who were depriving them of their rights without the access that is provided only by the American legal system.

The most comprehensive definition of the Rule of Law I have found is the one presented by Lord Bingham of Cornhill in delivering the 2006 Sir David Williams Lecture hosted by the Centre for Public Law at Cambridge University. At that time Lord Bingham was England's Senior Lord of Appeal in Ordinary, the counterpart of the U.S. Supreme Court's chief justice. He was moved to compose this definition by section 1 of the Constitutional Reform Act 2005, which provides that the act does not adversely affect "the existing constitutional principle of the rule of law," but does not explain what that principle actually means. Lord Bingham began the lecture with his under-standing of that existing principle:

> ...all persons and authorities within the state, whether
> public or private, should be bound by and entitled to the
> benefit of laws publicly and prospectively promulgated and
> publicly administered in the courts.

Using that principle as the foundation, Lord Bingham formulates eight sub-rules to flesh out the true meaning of the Rule of Law. Those sub-rules are a more elaborate and detailed presentation of the general points in the above-quoted World Justice Project's four universal principles, with some additional points, such as the need for separation of governmental powers, and a require-ment that the state must comply with its obligations under international law. Of special interest to our inquiry is Lord Bingham's number five:

> My fifth sub-rule is that means must be provided for
> resolving, without prohibitive cost or inordinate delay, bona
> fide civil disputes which the parties themselves are unable to
> resolve. It would seem to be an obvious corollary of the prin-
> ciple that everyone is bound by and entitled to the benefit of
> the law that people should be able, in the last resort, to go to
> court to have their rights and liabilities determined.

Lord Bingham states that the effect of this sub-rule is "to recognize the right of unimpeded access to a court as a basic right, protected by our own domestic law." He goes on to question whether it is possible for the English people to achieve that broad access, in view of the virtual disappearance of Legal Aid from civil cases. Nevertheless, he closes the discussion of sub-rule 5 by sticking to his guns, stating that the "Rule of Law plainly requires that legal redress should be an affordable commodity."

It is interesting that Lord Bingham uses the term "unimpeded access." With so much ground to cover in a lecture, he could not undertake a detailed analysis of what is now impeding access to the English courts. Clearly, the impediment—the "obstacle" in Lord Widgery's earlier formulation, the obstruction that caused Lord Devlin to observe that "for the ordinary citizen, a lawsuit is quite out of the question"—is the English insistence on Loser Pays and prohibition of workable contingency fees. Hence the need for our suggested access clause.

It bears repeating that each nation can work out its own method of achieving unimpeded access by simply removing the impediments in a manner which does not require revolutionary change. There is no need for the other developed democracies to mimic any American governmental structures (such as Separation of Powers with Checks and Balances) or American legal devices like class actions, punitive damages, or jury trials. Nor do other nations need to reach the same legal results or decisions as in the United States, since those decisions will reflect each nation's cultural consensus. But no developed democracy can claim that government-imposed obstruction of access to the courts is consistent with the Rule of Law.

Britain and the other developed democracies need to take a close look at the impediments, the obstructions, which are depriving most of their citizens of access to their courts, especially the Loser Pays rule which automatically turns the entire middle class into losers. They need to ask these questions:

+ Whose interests are the obstructions serving?

+ Why are those obstructions needed?

+ If we removed the obstructions, are our judges and lawyers so incompetent that we would be unable to prevent the inundation of our legal system by frivolous lawsuits?

Such a self-examination, if conducted with vigor, is likely to echo the sagacious conclusion reached by cartoonist Walt Kelly's Pogo: "We have met the enemy, and he is us."

––––––––––

Harvard Law Professor Alan Dershowitz is one of the most incisive critics of the American legal system. His scholarship and advocacy lend added significance to these words he wrote in *Taking Liberties:*

Even in European countries that have written constitutions, the courts have considerably less power to enforce their provisions than do our courts. Indeed, the legal profession in general has far less influence on the lives of Europeans than it does on ours....

All in all, I heartily recommend a trip abroad as a remedy for the peculiar American ailment—to which I am often subject—of gleefully knocking our lawyers, our courts, and our penchant for suing each other. As I think about returning home, I offer an enthusiastic two and a half cheers for the American legal system, with all its imperfections.

As we have seen, the crucial accomplishments of American lawyers in establishing the Government of Laws and developing the American Rule of Law have created a much broader role for the legal system than exists in other nations. Despite the many imperfections which Professor Dershowitz and other knowledgeable critics have exposed, all Americans should recognize and cherish the unique gift of access to justice which they enjoy because of the work of the Founding Lawyers and their successors.

We should also recall the words of the seldom-sung second stanza of "America the Beautiful" written by Katharine Lee Bates in 1893:

America! America!
God mend thine every flaw
Confirm thy soul
In self-control
Thy liberty in law!

Endnotes

Chapter One

Page 9: The pecuniary loss limitation originated in *Blake v. Midland Railway* (1852), 18 Queen's Bench Reports 93.

Page 11: The Jesus Galindez FBI file of 478 pages was supplied to the author on May 3, 2007, with the notation that "an estimated additional 14,100 pages of documents on this subject have not yet been processed."

Page 12: The USAID definition of the Rule of Law is from the Government Accountability Office (GAO) report, "Rule of Law Funding Worldwide for Fiscal Years 1993-1998," June 1999, p. 13.

Page 13: The term "Rule of Law" was coined by Oxford Law Professor Albert V. Dicey in his 1885 treatise on English Constitutional Law (see Dicey 1885). Dicey was alarmed by the rapid development of administrative agencies in Continental nations, fearing it would give too much unbridled power to government officials. He focused on the Rule of Law as a bulwark against collectivism and governmental tyranny. For an analysis of Dicey's views and influence, see Horwitz 1992, volume 2, pp. 221-230.

Chapter 2

Page 15: The Confederation Congress, officially styled in the Articles of Confederation as "the United States in Congress Assembled," was the governing body of the United States of America from March 1, 1781 to March 4, 1789, when it was replaced as the legislature by the Congress of the United States which was created by Article I of the new Constitution. The Confederation had neither an executive nor a judicial branch.

Page 15: The John Hancock quotation is from Kaminski and Leffler 1999, p. 188.

Page 17: Hamilton gave his date of birth as either 1755 or 1757 at various times during his life, but most historians fix it at 1755, making him 32 years old in 1787.

Page 18: While there is no evidence that Madison practiced law privately, his extensive scholarship in public law and his service in the Virginia attorney general's office qualify him as one of America's lawyer-statesmen. He was so designated by Chief Justice William Rehnquist in his definitive article, "The Lawyer-Statesman in American History" (Rehnquist 1986), as well as in Berkin 2002, p.31; Kane 1993, p. 18; and Linowitz 1994, p. 9

Page 19: For an account of how "republic" and "democracy" grew together in the nation's early years, see Farber and Sherry 2005, pp. 18-19.

Page 19: The John Adams "government of law" quotation is from the Massachusetts Constitution, Bill of Rights, Article XXX (1780).

Page 19: The John Adams quotation on corruption of the legislature is from Adams 1787, vol. 1, preface, paragraph 6.

Page 20: The David McCulloch quotation is from McCulloch 2001, p. 375.

Page 20: The John Adams quotation "that the laws alone can govern" is from Adams 1787, vol. 1, letter XXIII, p. 91.

Page 21: George Washington's "high ground" quotation is from his letter of May 18, 1786 to John Jay, reproduced in Fitzpatrick 1938, vol. 28, pp. 431-432.

Page 21: Fruitful sources on the Constitutional Convention include Amar 2005, Berkin 2002, Bowen 1966, Ellis 2007, Farrand 1911, Madison 1987, Warren 1928, Wood 1969, and Yates 1821.

Page 21: The Virginia Plan is sometimes called the Randolph Plan, since Governor Edmund Randolph formally introduced it, but most historians agree that it was largely Madison's work. Madison himself modestly credited it to the entire seven-man Virginia delegation.

Page 22: The Virginia Plan specified one representative for each 40,000 inhabitants, but at the very end of the Convention, with the Constitution already agreed, the number was changed to 30,000 at the request of George Washington to make the House more representative of the American people.

Page 22: The number of the 55 delegates described as lawyers varies from one historian to another, although all place the total over 30. My total of 34 "lawyers" includes those who were lawyers, judges, or legal scholars, regardless of their other sources of income. Historians giving the total as 34 include Bowen 1966, p. 63; Chernow 2004, p. 167; and McDonald 1986, p. 220.

Page 23: The Luther Martin quotation is from Bowen 1966, p. 140.

Page 23: A full discussion of the unreported New Jersey Supreme Court decision in *Holmes v. Walton* will be found in Hamburger 2008, pp. 407-422.

Page 24: The Preamble did not mention the Rule of Law, as that term did not come into usage until the nineteenth century, but immediately following the primary Constitutional purpose of forming a more perfect union came the phrase "to establish justice," the eighteenth-century equivalent of the Rule of Law.

Page 25: The Congressional resolution authorizing the Philadelphia convention is reproduced at *Report of Proceedings in Congress, February 21, 1787*, accessible at http://avalon.law.yale.edu/18th_century/const04.asp.

Page 26: Madison's deft deployment of the breached-treaty principle is discussed in Amar 2005, pp. 31-32, and in Labunski 2006, p. 16.

Page 27: Massachusetts and New Hampshire had ratified their state constitutions by popular vote, but all the others, as well as the Articles of Confederation, had been ratified by the state legislatures.

Page 29: It is generally accepted that of the 85 Federalist Papers, Hamilton authored fifty-one, Madison twenty-nine, and Jay five. (Jay's ability to contribute was hampered by illness.) A comprehensive study of their contributions, and the close cooperation between Hamilton and Madison throughout the process of creating and ratifying the Constitution, will be found in Meyerson 2008.

Chapter 3

Page 31: The 1985 Rehnquist speech was published in Rehnquist 1986, and the quotation is from page 553. Rehnquist was an associate justice from 1971 to 1986, when he became chief justice. His 1986 article is the earliest writing I found which uses the term "lawyer-statesman," and he appears to be originating it when he writes that "I shall call them lawyer-statesmen" (p. 537). The only earlier reference I found was in the title of the 1916 book, *Abraham Lincoln, the Lawyer-Statesman* by John T. Richards. The Rehnquist article was mainly a lament for the demise of the lawyer-statesman's extraordinary writing and speaking skills, a loss that he ascribes to changes in political campaigns and in the nature of law practice, which no longer nurture those skills to the same extent. He did not touch upon the unique role of the lawyer-statesmen in creating the Constitution or making it work, although he did praise them in general for "steering the ship of state" through dangerous shoals.

Page 33: The Obama quotation is from Obama 2006, p. 107.

Page 33: The Madison quotations and other details of his work on the Constitution will be found in volume 3 of the definitive biography, Brant 1941.

Page 35: The Amar quotation is from Amar 2005, p. 63.

Page 35: The Breyer quotation is from Breyer 2007, p. 55.

Page 36: The Cooke quotation is from Cooke 1973, p. 141.

Page 36: The Burgess quotation is from Burgess 1890, vol. 1, p. 105.

Page 38: The Rakove quotation is from Rakove 1996, p. 130.

Page 38: The Ellis quotations are from Ellis 2007, pp. 103, 106, and 117.

Page 38: The Chernow quotation is from Chernow 2004, p. 246.

Page 39: The Madison quotation is from his letter of September 15, 1821 to Thomas Ritchie, also quoted in Warren 1928, p. 800. (The full text of the letter will be found in the James Madison papers at the Library of Congress, Series 1, Microfilm Reel 19.)

Page 39: Details of the ratification proceedings in Pennsylvania, Massachusetts, Virginia, and New York are from Bowen 1966, pp. 273-310; Elliot 1861; Ferling 2003, pp. 298-304; Labunski 2006, pp. 67-119; Rakove 1990, pp. 70-79; and Rutland 1983, pp. 49-253.

Page 40: The Wilson quotation is from Wilson 1787, p.4.

Page 41: The Rutland quotation is from Rutland 1983, p. 66.

Page 45: The Congressional resolution authorizing the Philadelphia convention is reproduced at *Report of Proceedings in Congress, February 21, 1787*, accessible at http://avalon.law.yale.edu/18th_century/const04.asp.

Page 47: The Hamilton quotation is from his letter of May 19, 1788 to Madison, reprinted in Kaminski and Leffler 1999, pp. 230-231.

Page 48: The Ellis quotation is from Ellis 2007, p. 3.

Page 49: The Cox quotation is from Cox 1987, p. 38.

Page 50: For various versions of the Bill of Rights considered by Congress, and the detailed history of its passage, see Labunski 2006, pp. 178-241.

Page 52: The Hoffer quotations are from Hoffer 1998, pp. 132-136.

Page 53: The Adams "child Independence" quotation is from McCulloch 2001, p. 62.

Page 54: The Hoffer quotation is from Hoffer 1990, p. 64.

Page 55: The Hoffer quotation is from Hoffer 1998, p. 145.

Page 56: The quotations about John Adams are from McCulloch 2001, pp. 126-127.

Page 57: The Hoffer quotations about Dickinson's common law fixation and Jefferson's equitable remedies are from Hoffer 1990, pp. 66-68, 73.

Page 58: The Rakove quotations are from Rakove 2009, p. 30.

Page 58: The Schwartz quotations are from Schwartz 1974, pp. 2, 4.

Page 61: The Bowen quotations are from Bowen 1966, pp. 71 and 204.

Chapter 4

Page 63: The Chernow quotation is from Chernow 2004, p. 270.

Page 64: The Wood quotation is from Wood 2006, p. 48.

Page 64: George Washington's dedication to the Constitution and the principles he followed in launching and shaping the national government are detailed in Phelps 1993, and the quotations are from pages viii, 152, and 192. Similar conclusions are found in Higginbotham 2002 at pp. 67-68.

Page 64: The John Adams quotation is from Charles Francis Adams 1856, vol. VIII, pp. 486-487.

Page 65: Madison's role as Washington's prime minister is detailed in Leibiger 1999, Chapter 4.

Page 66: The O'Connor quotations are from O'Connor 2003, pp. 65-67.

Page 68: George Washington's quest to define and establish a unique American national character is described in detail in Spalding and Garrity 1996, especially in Chapter 2, "Establishing the National Character."

Page 68: The Phelps quotations are from Phelps 1993, pp. 152 and 192.

Page 68: The Higginbotham quotation is from Higginbotham 2002, pp. 67-68.

Page 68: The Leibiger quotation is from Leibiger 1999, p. 121.

Page 68: The quotation from Washington's farewell message is from Spalding and Garrity 1996, p. 188.

Page 68: The Marshall quotation is from Marshall 2000, pp. 467-468.

Page 68: The Ellis quotation is from Ellis 2004, p. 190.

Page 68: The Winik quotation is from Winik 2007, p.83.

Page 69: The Madison quotation is from Twohig 1987, vol. 10, p. 351.

Page 70: The Horwitz quotation is from Horwitz 1992, vol. 2, p. 193.

Page 71: The Smith quotation is from Smith 1996, p. 2.

Page 71: The state supreme courts' exercise of judicial review during the Confederation period is documented in Friedman 2009, pp. 19-43; Hamburger 2008, pp. 1-20; and Wood 1969, pp.453-463.

Page 74: *Marbury v. Madison,* 5 U.S. (1 Cranch) 137 (1803); *Stuart v. Laird,* 5 U.S. (1 Cranch) 299 (1803). For current views of these two decisions, see Ackerman 2005; Burns 2009; Ely 1980; Friedman 2009; Hamburger 2008; Nelson 2000; Sloan and McKean 2009; Wolfe 1994; and Wood 2009.

Page 76: The Smith quotation is from Smith 1996, pp. 325-326.

Page 76: The Nelson quotation is from Nelson 2000, p. 59.

Page 77: The Marshall quotation is from Johnson 1974, vol. 7, p. 270.

Page 77: The Cooke quotation is from Cooke 1973, p. 145.

Page 77: The Cox quotation is from Cox 1987, p. 43.

Page 77: The Tocqueville quotation is from Tocqueville 1835, p. 122.

Page 78: The Marshall Court's major post-*Marbury* decisions include *Fletcher v. Peck,* 6 Cranch 87 (1810); *Martin v. Hunter's Lessee,* 1 Wheaton 304 (1816); *McCulloch v. Maryland,* 4 Wheaton 316 (1819); *Trustees of Dartmouth College v. Woodward,* 4 Wheaton 518 (1819); *Cohens v. Virginia,* 6 Wheaton 264 (1821); and *Gibbons v. Ogden,* 9 Wheaton 1 (1824).

Page 78: The Cox quotation is from Cox 1987, p. 67.

Page 78: The Tocqueville quotation is from Tocqueville 1835, p. 315.

Page 78: For a twenty-first century analysis of the role of politics in Marshall's judicial career and the reasons for his greatness, see Balkin 2002.

Page 81: On Buchanan's collusion with Taney on the Dred Scott decision, see Farber 2003, p. 178; Finkelman 1997, pp.46-47; and Goodwin 2005, p. 189.

Page 81: The Taney Court's Dred Scott decision is *Scott v. Sandford,* 60 U.S. 393 (1857).

Page 82: The Finkelman quotation is from Finkelman 2004 in Gross ed. 2004, p. 135.

Page 83: John Marshall's views on the inevitability of armed conflict over slavery are documented and discussed in Hobson 1996, p. 164 and p. 236, note 44.

Page 83: The Goodwin quotation is from Goodwin 2005, p. xv.

Page 85: The McPherson quotation is from McPherson 2008, p. 108.

Page 86: The Farber quotations are from Farber 2003, pp.196, 199, and 200. Similar conclusions were reached by James F. Simon in Simon 2006, pp. 285-286, where he also notes the positive views expressed by Supreme Court justices Felix Frankfurter and Sandra Day O'Connor about Lincoln's balancing of national security interests against civil liberties.

Chapter 5

Page 89: The *Slaughter-House Cases* are reported at 83 U.S. 36 (1873). The *Civil Rights Cases* are reported at 109 U.S. 3 (1883).

Page 89: The Gillman quotation is from Tomlins 2005, p. 145.

Page 90: *Plessy v. Ferguson* is reported at 163 U.S. 537 (1896).

Page 91: The Schlesinger quotation is from Schlesinger 1958, p. 3.

Page 92: On Frankfurter's influence, see Irons 1982, pp. 8-9.

Page 92: The quotations about Frankfurter's power are from Parrish 1981, pp. 220-221.

Page 93: The major cases holding New Deal legislation unconstitutional are *Schechter Poultry Corp. v. U.S.*, 295 U.S. 495 (1935), invalidating the N.R.A.; *U.S. v. Butler et al.*, 297 U.S. 1 (1936), ending the Agricultural Adjustment Act; *Railroad Retirement Board v. Alton Railroad Co.*, 295 U.S. 330 (1935), terminating the Railroad Retirement Pension Act; *Louisville Joint Stock Land Bank v. Radford*, 295 U.S. 555 (1935), overturning the Frazier-Lemke Mortgage Act; *Carter v. Carter Coal Co.*, 298 U.S. 238 (1936), invalidating the Guffey Bituminous Coal Act; and *Ashton v. Cameron County District*, 298 U.S. 513 (1936), ending the Municipal Bankruptcy Act.

Page 96: The Lamneck quotation is from his radio address in the House of Representatives, March 4, 1937.

Page 97: The U.S. Supreme Court decisions dealing with state minimum-wage statutes are reported at *Adkins v. Children's Hospital*, 261 U.S. 525 (1923); *Morehead ex rel. New York v. Tipaldo*, 298 U.S. 602 (1936); and *West Coast Hotel Co. v. Parrish*, 300 U.S. 379 (1937).

Page 97: The Hughes quotations are from *West Coast Hotel Co. v. Parrish*, 300 U.S. 379, p. 391. The excerpts from the dissenting opinion written by Justice Sutherland are from 300 U.S. 379, pp. 401-402.

Page 98; The Wagner Act was upheld in *National Labor Relations Board v. Jones & Laughlin*, 301 U.S. 1 (1937).

Page 99: The Social Security Act of 1935 was upheld in *Helvering v. Davis*, 301 U.S. 619 (1937).

Page 99: The Senate Judiciary Committee report was published as Senate Report 711, 75th Congress, 1st session.

Page 100: Senator Joe Robinson died of a heart attack on July 14, 1937, during the final phase of the Court-packing bill's consideration by Congress.

Page 100: The Leuchtenburg quotation is from Leuchtenburg 1995, p. 163.

Page 101: The Roberts memorandum in response to Frankfurter was published in volume 104 of the *University of Pennsylvania Law Review* (December 1955), pp. 314-315.

Page 104: The Ickes quotations are from Ickes 1954. The diary entry for 5/22/37, *Hughes played bad hand*, is at p. 145. The diary entry for 6/17/37, *Hughes engineering the Van Devanter resignation*, is at p. 153.

Page 104: The Ickes quotation is from Ickes 1948, p. 31.

Page 104: The Hughes quotations are from Hughes 1973, pp. 303-311.

Page 104: The Pusey quotation on Van Devanter's retirement is from Pusey 1951, vol. 2, p. 761.

Page 104: The Wheeler quotation is from Pusey 1951, vol. 2, p. 755.

Page 106: The Alsop and Catledge quotation is from Alsop and Catledge 1938, p. 147.

Page 107: The Leuchtenburg quotation is from Leuchtenburg 1963, p. 235.

Page 107: The Smith quotation is from Smith 2007, p. 389.

Chapter 6

Page 110: The steel seizure case, *Youngstown Sheet & Tube Co. v. Sawyer*, is reported at 343 U.S. 579 (1952).

Page 111: The Rehnquist quotations are from Rehnquist 2002, pp. 189 and 192.

Page 112: *Plessy v. Ferguson* is reported at 163 U.S. 537 (1896).

Page 114: The Kluger quotation is from Kluger 2004, p. 662.

Page 115: In addition to Thurgood Marshall, these NAACP Legal Defense Fund lawyers participated in the reargument: Robert L. Carter, Spottswood W. Robinson III, Louis L. Redding, and Jack Greenberg. Other LDF lawyers who participated in writing the briefs were George E. C. Hayes, William R. Ming Jr., Constance Baker Motley, James M. Nabrit Jr., Charles S. Scott, Frank D. Reeves,

Harold R. Boulware, Oliver W. Hill, George M. Johnson, Loren Miller, Arthur D. Shores, and A.T. Walden.

Page 115: The Newton quotation is from Newton 2006, p. 311.

Page 116: *Brown v. Board of Education of Topeka* is reported at 347 U.S. 483 (1954). Another case, *Bolling v. Sharpe*, which was originally joined with the four cases decided under the *Brown* title, challenged school segregation in the District of Columbia. Since the Fourteenth Amendment applies only to the states, *Bolling* was decided separately by the Court. Immediately following the *Brown* decision, Chief Justice Warren delivered a unanimous opinion holding that "it would be unthinkable that the same Constitution would impose a lesser duty on the Federal Government" which was responsible for the District of Columbia laws and was subject to the Fifth Amendment's requirement of due process of law. *Bolling v. Sharpe*, 347 U.S. 497 (1954).

Page 117: The Warren quotation is from Warren 1977, p. 3.

Page 118: The Warren quotation is from Warren 1977, p. 4.

Page 118: The decision on implementation of the 1954 *Brown* decision, often called *Brown II*, is reported at *Brown v. Board of Education of Topeka*, 349 U.S. 294 (1955).

Page 120: President Kennedy's speech of September 30, 1962, is available at www.jfklibrary.org/Speech/JFK.

Page 120: The Patterson quotation is from Patterson 2006.

Page 121: The Ogletree quotation is from Ogletree 2008.

Page 121: The Bass quotations are from Bass 1981, p. 17.

Page 122: The Bass quotations are from Bass 1981, p. 82. Robert F. Kennedy Jr. wrote a biography of Judge Johnson (Kennedy 1978).

Page 124: Judge Sirica's decision ordering production of the nine tapes is reported at *In re Grand Jury Subpoena Duces Tecum to Nixon*, 360 F. Supp 1 (D.D.C., 1973).

Page 124: The appellate decision affirming Judge Sirica's order is reported at *Nixon v. Sirica*, 487 F. 2d 700 (D.C. Circ. 1973).

Page 126: The Cox quotation is from Cox 1987, p 24.

Page 126: Judge Sirica's decision ordering production of the 64 tapes is reported at *United States v. Mitchell*, 377 F.Supp. 1326 (D.D.C., 1974).

Page 126: The Supreme Court's decision ordering production of the 64 tapes is reported at *United States v. Nixon*, 418 U.S. 683 (1974).

Page 128: The Cox quotation is from Cox 1987, p 25.

Chapter 7

Page 130: The two Florida Supreme Court decisions are: *Palm Beach County Canvassing Board v. Harris*, 772 So. 2d 1220 (2000), and *Palm Beach County Canvassing Board v. Harris*, 772 So. 2d 1273 (2000). The three U.S. Supreme Court decisions are: *Bush v. Palm Beach County Canvassing Board*, 531 U.S. 70 (2000); *Bush v. Gore*, 531 U.S. 1046 (2000); and *Bush v. Gore*, 531 U.S. 98 (2000).

Page 131: The empowerment of the state legislature to choose its own slate of electors is found in Title 3 of the U.S. Code: "§2. *Failure to make choice on prescribed day*. Whenever any State has held an election for the purpose of choosing electors, and has failed to make a choice on the day prescribed by law, the electors may be appointed on a subsequent day in such a manner as the legislature of such State may direct."

Page 133: The Safe Harbor provision of the Electoral Count Act is found at Title 3 of the U.S. Code, §5, *Determination of controversy as to appointment of electors.*

Page 134: Professor Sunstein's potential scenario is from Sunstein and Epstein eds. 2001, pp. 216-217, where he writes that "things would have gotten extremely messy." Professor Gillman's potential scenario is from Gillman 2001, pp. 191-195. Judge Posner's potential scenario is from Posner 2001, pp. 249-250.

Page 146: In Kritzer 2005, Professor Herbert Kritzer reproduces the results of polls by Gallup, Pew, GSS, and other organizations measuring public opinion before and after the 2000 Supreme Court decision in *Bush v. Gore*. The September 2009 Gallup Poll results are from www.gallup.com/Poll/122897.

Page 147: The first Breyer quotation is from Breyer 1998, p. 58.

Page 147: The second Breyer quotation is from Breyer 2006, p. 16.

Page 148: The Gore quotation is from his concession speech of December 13, 2000, widely carried in the media and reproduced in Brinkley 2001, p. 311.

Page 148: The Kluger quotations are from Kluger 2004, pp. xii and 52-53.

Page 149: The Burns quotation is from Burns 2009, p. 228.

Page 149: The Hoffer quotations are from Hoffer 2010, pp. 21 and 128.

Chapter 8

Page 155: The Tocqueville quotation about judicial review is from Tocqueville 1835, p. 116.

Page 155: The Tocqueville quotation about the influence of lawyers is from Tocqueville 1835, p. 303.

Page 155: The Tocqueville quotation about the legal spirit is from Tocqueville 1835, p. 311.

Page 155: The Tocqueville quotation about the law as leveler is from Tocqueville 1835, p. 276.

Page 155: The Tocqueville quotation about the civil jury is from Tocqueville 1835, p. 318.

Page 156: The Commager quotation on the importance of law and lawyers in the U.S. is from Commager 1950, p. 20.

Page 156: The Commager quotation on the comparative influence of lawyers is from Commager 1950, p. 364. Commager expressed similar views in his later book, *Commager on Tocqueville* (1993).

Page 156: The Reeves interview with Justice Potter Stewart is from Reeves 1982, pp. 98-99.

Page 156: The Reeves quotation about "forced fairness" is from Reeves 1982, pp. 104-105.

Page 157: The Reeves interview with Justice G. Mennen Williams is from Reeves 1982, p. 151.

Page 157: The Ellis quotation is from Ellis 2007, p. 125.

Page 157: The Obama quotation is from Obama 2006, p, 110.

Page 158: The Souter quotation is from *Ortiz v. Fibreboard Corp.*, 527 U.S. 815 at 847 (1999).

Page 159: The Warren quotation is from Newton 2006, p. 512.

Page 159: The Witt quotation is from Witt 2007, p. 3.

Page 159: The Schwartz quotation is from Schwartz 1976, p. 2.

Page 161: The Solomons quotation is from "All you need is the bare minimum" by Edward Solomons, *London Times,* July 3, 2007.

Page 161: In 2008, the hourly rate for partners in large London solicitors firms was reported to range from £600 to £1,400 ($960 to $2,240); see "Are top lawyers worth their huge fees?" in the *London Sunday Times,* July 13, 2008.

Page 162: The *Daily Mirror* House of Lords decision is reported in *Campbell v. MGN Limited,* [2004] UKHL 22.

Page 162: The Devlin quotation is from Devlin 1979, p. 69.

Page 163: The *London Times* story about the pensioners appeared in the Banking and Finance section on July 7, 2006.

Page 164: The Tocqueville quotations are from Tocqueville 1958, pp. 91, 98, and 110.

Page 164: The Bentham quotation is from Bentham 1843, vol. 6, p. 101.

Page 165: *Arcambel v. Wiseman* is reported at 3 U.S. 306 (1796).

Page 165: The Kritzer quotation is from Kritzer 2001, p. 1946. This comprehensive law review article summarizes many comparative studies of the effects of the English Rule and the American Rule through the year 2000.

Page 165: The Warren quotation is from *Fleischmann Distilling Corp. v. Maier Brewing Co.*, 386 U.S. 714 at page 718.

Page 167: The Mikva quotation is from McGrory 1995.

Page 168: The Woolf quotation about the problem of costs is from Woolf 1995, Chapter 25, paragraph 1.

Page 168: The Woolf quotation about the arguments against the Loser Pays Rule is from Woolf 1995, Chapter 25, paragraph 15.

Page 168: The Woolf quotation about the phenomenon of the nuisance action is from Woolf 1995, Chapter 35, paragraph 21.

Page 169: The Woolf quotations are from Woolf 1996, Chapter 7, paragraphs 2 and 3.

Page 169: The Devlin quotations are from Devlin 1979, p. 69.

Chapter 9

Page 183: The *Wall Street Journal* article on the McDonald's coffee-spill case, "A Matter of Degree," was published in the September 1, 1994 edition, p.1.

Page 183: The quotation from Judge Robert Scott's decision is from the Transcript of Proceedings, September 14, 1994, *Liebeck v. McDonald's*, Second Judicial District Court, County of Bernalillo, State of New Mexico, case number CV-93-02419.

Page 184: Further details of the *Liebeck* case and the manner in which the media was led to distort its meaning will be found in Haltom and McCann 2004, Chapter 6 of which is devoted to the *Liebeck* case, and in Koenig and Rustad 2001, pp. 6-8. The 2004 study by the British government's Better Regulation Task Force reaching the same conclusion about this media distortion will be found in Arculus and Graham 2004, pp. 12-16.

Page 185: The Rhode quotation is from Rhode 2004, pp. 28-29. For details of the fabricated "frivolous" lawsuits and the truth about other urban legends, see the website *www.snopes.com/legal/lawsuits. asp*. Some of these fabrications were noted in the 2004 study by the British government's Better Regulation Task Force; see Arculus and Graham 2004, pp. 12-16.

Page 185: The role of tobacco companies in restricting access to the courts under the guise of "tort reform" is documented in Mencimer 2007, Chapter 2. Details of tobacco and other such corporate media campaigns are documented in Haltom and McCann 2004. Contrary views espousing the need for limiting access to the courts will be found in Crier 2002, Howard 1994, Howard 2001, Howard 2002, Huber 1988, Huber and Litan 1991, Olson 1991, and Olson 2003.

Page 186: The Nader quotation is from Nader 2004, pp. 46-47.

Page 187: The power of American courts to impose fee-shifting and other monetary penalties on those who abuse the litigation system was affirmed by the U.S. Supreme Court in *Chambers v. NASCO, Inc.*, 501 U.S. 32 (1991).

Page 188: The pre-dated panties case is reported at *Vargas v. Peltz*, 901 F.Supp. 1572 (S.D. Fla., West Palm Beach Div., 1995). This decision cites many other cases in which the courts imposed sanctions for litigation abuse and fraud on the court. Like the Peltz case, most of those which resulted in sanctions against the plaintiffs were brought by people who could not afford large legal fees and therefore could not have been deterred by fee-shifting.

Page 189: Joseph's Top Ten list is in Joseph 2000, pp. 52-53.

Page 189: The Jackson quotations are from Jackson 2009 a, pp. 187-190. In addition to the Final Report (Jackson 2009 a), Lord Justice Jackson published a much longer Preliminary Report (Jackson 2009) in May 2009, which contains most of the evidence and data he gathered for his review.

Page 190: The Federal Judicial Center survey results are from Rauma and Willging 2005, pp. 3-4 and 13-15. In response to the question, "Is there a problem with groundless litigation in federal civil cases on your docket?" the judges responded as follows: no problem, 15%; very small problem, 38%; small problem, 32%; moderate problem, 12%; large problem, 2%; very large problem, 1%. As to the need to modify Rule 11 to increase its effectiveness in deterring groundless filings, 13% of the judges responded affirmatively.

Chapter 10

Page 193: Further details of the Athens Piaggio crash and its aftermath will be found in my 2005 book, *The Deadly Sins of Aristotle Onassis.*

Page 200: The Greenslade quotation is from Greenslade 1992, pp.48-49.

Page 200: The Abrams quotations are from *Author's Guild Bulletin,* Fall 2006, pp. 28-29.

Page 205: The Gibb quotation is from the *London Times* of April 17, 2007.

Page 205: The Oldham quotation is from the article, "Woolf reforms and cost-cutting have led to acute shortages and a 'deficient' system," by Frances Gibb in the *London Times,* April 16, 2009.

Page 205: The Parker quotation is from Parker 1999, p. 33.

Page 205: The Lord Spens story is from the *Daily Telegraph,* June 7, 1999.

Page 207: The Lord Spens ATE premium story is from Zander 2002, fn 96.

Page 208: The Jackson quotation about the CFA-ATE regime is from Jackson 2009 a, p. 325, paragraph 3.8.

Page 208: The Middleton quotation is from Middleton 1997, paragraph 5.49.

Page 208: The Cook quotation is from Cook 2001, p. 465.

Page 209: The Civil Justice Council quotations are from Moorhead and Hurst 2008, pp. 6-12, 35-36.

Page 209: Other pre-2010 sources favoring contingency fees for England are Arculus and Graham 2004, p. 19; Peysner 2001, p. 8; Slapper and Kelly 2006, p. 142; and Zander 2002.

Page 210: Jackson's comments on contingency fees are from Jackson 2009 a, Part 12, pp. 125-133. His recommendations for the use of contingency fees are from Jackson 2009 a, p. 133, paragraph 5.1, and p. 464, paragraph 14.

Page 210: Jackson's recommendations for one-way cost-shifting in personal injury cases are from Jackson 2009 a, p. 193, paragraph 6.1, and p. 464, paragraph 19.

Page 210: Jackson's recommendations for one-way cost-shifting in defamation cases are from Jackson 2009 a, p. 329, paragraph 7.1. His comments regarding use of one-way cost-shifting in other categories of cases are from Jackson 2009 a, p. xvii, paragraph 2.7.

Page 210: The Gibb quotation is from Gibb, May 2009.

Chapter 11

Page 219: The Morton Mintz story appeared in the *Washington Post* of Sunday, February 5, 1967, page 1. A similar story by Sidney Zion appeared on the front page of the *New York Times* on the same date.

Page 219: The Appellate Division decision upholding the finding of no collusion in the Gillen deposition is reported at *Nader v. General Motors Corp.,* 292 N.Y.S. 2d 345 (App. Div. 1967).

Page 220: Justice Brust's constitutional right of privacy decision is reported at *Nader v. General Motors Corp.,* 292 N.Y.S. 2d 514 (Sup. Ct., Special Term 1968).

Page 221: The Appellate Division decision is reported at *Nader v. General Motors Corp.,* 298 N.Y.S. 2d 137 (App. Div. 1969).

Page 221: The Court of Appeals decision is reported at *Nader v. General Motors Corp.,* 25 N.Y. 2d 560, 307 N.Y.S. 2d 647 (1970).

Page 222: The *New York Times* editorial appeared in the edition of August 17, 1970.

Page 222: The *Newsweek* quotation is from the edition of August 24, 1970.

Page 222: The Prosser quotation is from Prosser 1971, p. 816.

Page 222: The Spock case is reported at *Spock v. United States,* 464 F. Supp. 510 (SDNY 1978). The Jackie Onassis photographer harassment case is reported at *Galetta v. Onassis,* 353 F. Supp. 196 (SDNY 1972).

Page 223: In my 1980 book, *Lawsuit,* I wrote about *Nader v. GM* in more detail. I included the results of a survey I conducted to determine how other legal systems were likely to have treated the case if Nader had been able to bring it to trial. The opinions of lawyers, judges, and scholars in Britain, Canada, France, Belgium, Netherlands, West Germany, Spain, Portugal, Norway, Japan, Israel, and Mexico are summarized at pp. 112-118 of *Lawsuit.*

Chapter 12

Page 226: The Choate speech, "The Position and Functions of the American Bar, as an Element of Conservatism in the State" is from Choate 1879, p. 133. From the context of the speech it is clear that Choate used the word "conservatism" in the sense of conserving, preserving, or maintaining the American system of government. The quotation about all lawyers being statesmen appears at p. 154. The quotation about law practice as "almost a department of government" appears at p. 136.

Page 226: The Matthews quotation is from Matthews 1980, p. 151.

Page 226: The Witt quotation is from Witt 2007, p. 3.

Page 226: The Schwartz quotation is from Schwartz 1976, p. 2.

Page 226: The Kagan quotations are from Kagan 2001, pp. 5 and 16.

Page 227: The Posner quotation is from Posner 2001, pp 205-206.

Page 228: The Kagan quotations are from Kagan 2001, pp. 3 and 14.

Page 228: The Carrington quotation is from Carrington 1999, pp. 63-64.

Page 228: The Hoffer quotation is from Hoffer 2010, p. xiii.

Page 229: The George Washington quotation is from his letter of August 15, 1786 to John Jay.

Page 230: The Gawalt quotation is from Gawalt 1984, p. vii.

Page 230: The Shays's Rebellion quotation is from Thomas Grover's list of grievances underlying the rebellion, in Minot 1810, pp. 84-86, reprinted in *Annals of America,* vol. 3, p. 62.

Page 230: For a definitive collection and analysis of lawyer jokes, see Galanter 2005.

Page 232: For details of the work of the Southern Poverty Law Center, see Dees and Fiffer 2001.

Page 232: The quotations about the Washington Legal Foundation were taken from its website, http://www.wlf.org, in March 2010. For descriptions of other cause-lawyering organizations, see Sarat & Scheingold 2001 and Sarat & Scheingold 2006.

Page 232: The Hoffman quotation about Ralph Nader is from Hoffman 1973, p. 194.

Page 232: Examples of major firms devoting as much as 7,000 hours to a single pro bono client will be found in *The American Lawyer,* July 2008, at pp.120-121.

Page 233: Professor Rhode's position is summarized in Rhode 2004, Chapter 8, "A Roadmap for Reform" (pp. 185-194).

Page 234: The Jefferson quotation is from Washington 1853, vol. iii, p. 71.

Page 235: The *National Review* quotation is from England 1991.

Page 236: For a history of the American Association for Justice, see Jacobson and White 2004.

Page 236: For an example of the services performed by the Center for Constitutional Litigation PC, see *Jones v. Halliburton,* 583 F.3d 228 (5th Cir. 2009), in which it was held that claims by an employee of a government contractor that she was gang-raped, falsely imprisoned, and otherwise mistreated in Iraq were not subject to arbitration under the terms of her employment contract, and therefore her civil action would be heard in open court.

Page 237: The lobbying activities of cigarette manufacturers and the U.S. Chamber of Commerce are documented in Mencimer 2006.

Page 242: The two main state court decisions in the *Williams* tobacco litigation are *Williams v. Philip Morris, Inc.*, 43 P.3d 824 (Or. App. 2002), and *Williams v. Philip Morris, Inc.*, 127 P.3d 1165 (Or. 2006). The main U.S. Supreme Court decision is *Williams v. Philip Morris, Inc.*, 549 U.S. 346 (2007). The final U.S. Supreme Court dismissal was reported at 129 S.Ct. 1436 (Mar. 31, 2009).

Chapter 13

Page 247: The statistics on British prime ministers are based on those who considered themselves lawyers according to their official biographies. The total would be somewhat higher if all those who had some connection with the barristers' Inns of Court, honorary or otherwise, were included.

Page 247: The *Washington Post* quotation is from Eggen 2009.

Page 248: The Miller quotations are from Miller 1995, pp. 3 and 29.

Page 248: The Supreme Court found that "Congress is predominantly a lawyers' body" in *Callanan v. U.S.*, 364 U.S. 587, 594 (1961).

Page 248: The statistics on lawyers as a percentage of Congress, state governors, and state legislators are from Miller 1995, pp. 31 and 57-63. The Congressional Research Service reported on February 4, 2010, in "Membership of the 111th Congress: A Profile" that 57 of the 100 Senators and 168 of the 435 House Members held law degrees.

Page 248: The statistics for Britain and other nations are from Miller 1995, p. 60, Table 3, which shows Britain at 16 percent for the 30-year period 1945-1974, and West Germany at 5 percent from 1969 to 1983.

Page 248: The Lincoln quotation is from Gross 2004, p. 147.

Page 249: The Friedman quotation is from Friedman 2005, p. 495.

Page 250: The Miller Government of Laws quotation is from Miller 1995, p. 25. The Miller "lawyer's world" quotation is from Miller 1995, p. 28. The Miller quotation on the lawyers' decision-making process is from Miller 1995, p. 55. The Miller legislative drafting quotation is from Miller 1995, p. 42.

Page 250: The Bryce quotation is from Bryce 1913, volume 1, chapter 24, paragraph 651.

Page 251: For detailed studies of the methods used to make students think like lawyers, see Mertz 2007 and Schauer 2009. The views of other scholars and commentators on the teaching of "thinking like a lawyer" are collected in Miller 1995, p. 171.

Page 251: The Frankfurter quotation is from Frankfurter 1948, p. 747.

Page 251: The McCloy quotations are from McCloy 1958, p. 171.

Page 252: The Zimmerman description of Elihu Root as secretary of war is from Zimmerman 2002, Chapter 4.

Page 253: The story of the U.S. Army Air Forces' use of lawyers in its wartime Operations Analysis Division is told in Leach 1965.

Page 254: The Miller quotation on lawyers' preoccupation with procedure is from Miller 1995, p. 23.

Page 254: The Miller quotation about the lawyer's incrementalist approach is from Miller, 1995, p. 15.

Page 254: The Ellis quotation about the lawyer's evolutionary approach is from Ellis 2007, p. 18.

Page 255: The Levi quotation is from Levi 1949, p. 104.

Chapter 14

Page 258: Kronman's "crisis" references are from Kronman 1993, pp. 1-2.

Page 258: Kronman's "old-fashioned name" reference is from Kronman 1993, p. 3.

Page 258: Kronman's "explosive growth" reference is from Kronman 1993, p. 4.

Page 259: Kronman's "early nineteenth-century bar" reference is from Kronman 1993, p. 12.

Page 259: Kronman's definition of the lawyer-statesman is from Kronman 1993, pp. 14-15.

Page 259: Kronman's "trait of character" reference is from Kronman 1993, p. 15.

Page 259: Kronman's reference to the limitations of lawyers in the past is from Kronman 1993, p. 5.

Page 260: Glendon's "crisis" references are from Glendon 1994, pp. 3 and 6.

Page 260: Glendon's "golden age" reference is from Glendon 1994, p. 28. For a comprehensive study of lawyers' golden ages, see Galanter 1996.

Page 261: Glendon's "wise counselor" and "lawyer-statesman" references are from Glendon 1994, p. 35 and footnote 47, p. 298.

Page 261: Glendon's choice of the Wall Street firms is from Glendon 1994, pp. 36-37.

Page 262: Glendon's condemnation of the earlier Wall Street lawyers is from Glendon 1994, p. 57.

Page 262: Glendon's quotation of the Elihu Root "damned fool" statement is from Glendon 1994, p. 37.

Page 263: The full Root statement appears on pages 132-133 of the first volume of Jessup's biography, *Elihu Root* (Jessup 1938). Jessup identifies the Havemeyers as "lords of the sugar trust" in Jessup 1938, p. 132.

Page 263: Glendon's second Root quotation is from Glendon 1994, pp. 75-76.

Page 264: Glendon's citation of the Harbaugh biography of John W. Davis is from Glendon 1994, p. 52.

Page 264: The quotation about Davis's indifference to corporate policy is from Harbaugh 1973, pp. 263-264.

Page 264: Linowitz's reference to the changes in the legal profession during the past half century is from Linowitz 1994, p. 18.

Page 264: Linowitz's admiration for the lawyer-statesmen is from Linowitz 1994, p. 9.

Page 264: Linowitz's description of lawyers' non-pecuniary satisfactions is from Linowitz 1994, p. 67.

Page 264: Linowitz's nostalgia for the "independent" Wall Street lawyers is from Linowitz 1994, p. 228.

Page 265: Linowitz's Elihu Root quotation is from Linowitz 1994, p. 4.

Page 265: It may be useful here to review the authorities cited and quoted in the Kronman, Glendon, and Linowitz books pertaining to the history of the American lawyer-statesmen and their relationship to client purification.

Kronman cites the 1986 article by the late Chief Justice William H. Rehnquist, *The Lawyer-Statesman in American History*, as authority for the proposition that the lawyer-statesmen had "been regarded by their contemporaries as models to be copied and admired" (Kronman 1993, p. 11). Kronman uses the Rehnquist article as a starting point for his thesis that the lawyer-statesmen purified their clients. However, the qualities of the early American lawyer-statesmen praised by Rehnquist relate entirely to their statecraft and language skills, not to their private law practices. The Rehnquist article makes no reference to anything that could possibly be described as client purification.

Kronman cites the 1964 book by Erwin O. Smigel, then chairman of the Sociology Department at New York University, *The Wall Street Lawyer: Professional Organization Man?* Smigel was able to interview 188 lawyers from 18 Wall Street law firms only by agreeing to maintain complete anonymity and forego access to documents. His primary goal was to study the large law firm as a bureaucracy, in tune with sociology's then-current preoccupation with the individual as a cog in a business machine—"the Organization Man." He concluded that the main function of the Wall Street lawyers was "to maintain the status quo for their large corporate clients" (Smigel 1964, p. 342). Kronman states that Smigel found a pattern indicating that lesser partners of lawyer-statesmen were inspired and uplifted by the latter (Kronman 1993, p. 283). However, the Smigel book does not contain a single example of client purification, nor do any of the sources cited by Smigel.

Glendon also cites Smigel 1964, stating that Smigel "had concluded that corporate lawyers then possessed enough independence to permit them to serve not only as advisers but also, at least 'sometimes,' as 'conscience' to big business" (Glendon 1994, p. 75). She removes Smigel as a source of evidence of client purification by adding, "Smigel did not try to determine, however, how often lawyers actually exercised that independence" (Glendon 1994, p. 303, note 33*)*.

As noted in the text, Glendon and Linowitz used the attenuated Elihu Root "damned fool" anecdote as the basis for claiming that Root and his contemporaries actually purified clients. Linowitz does not provide any source reference. Glendon cites as her source "Gerald W. Gawalt, 'Introduction,' in *The New High Priests,* p. 4" (Glendon 1994, p. 298, note 49). Professor Robert F. Cochran Jr., a supporter of Glendon's thesis, cites Glendon's Gawalt citation as his source for the Root anecdote (Cochran 1996, p. 715, fn. 52).

Gerald W. Gawalt served as the editor of *The New High Priests,* a collection of articles by Gawalt and other contributors (Gawalt 1984). The incomplete Root anecdote appears in Gawalt 1984 at page 4, in the article contributed by Wayne K. Hobson, "Symbol of the New Profession: Emergence of the Large Law Firm, 1870-1915." Hobson's Root quotation is part of a paragraph relating to several different subjects, followed by footnote 8. In that footnote (at page 22) Hobson cites these sources: "Philip C. Jessup, *Elihu Root,* 2 vols. (New York, 1938), 1:133; notes on a conversation with Elihu Root, May 4, 1930, Philip C. Jessup Papers, Box 243, Library of Congress." On the chance that the notes of Jessup's 1930 conversation with Root might have referred to the "damned fool" statement, I obtained a copy of those notes from the Library of Congress and found no such reference. I also consulted Professor Hobson, who confirmed that his citation of the 1930 notes in the Library of Congress box referred to Root's claim that he was "a lawyer for corporate clients rather than a corporation lawyer," which Hobson had mentioned in the sentence preceding the "damned fool" statement. Hobson also confirmed that his sole source for the "damned fool" statement was the published Jessup biography.

Martin Mayer collaborated with Linowitz in writing *The Betrayed Profession* (Linowitz 1994). In his closing chapter, Linowitz mentions the two-part *Harper's Magazine* article by Mayer, "The Wall Street Lawyers," the second part of which was entitled "Keepers of the Corporate Conscience" (Mayer 1956). Linowitz used that title to pose the question, "Who today would make such a claim?" (Linowitz 1994, p. 228). The Mayer article in *Harper's Magazine,* which was written under the same conditions of anonymity as those imposed on Smigel, contains no examples of client purification, with or without identifying the firms involved. Indeed, Mayer closes his article with his only examples of client counseling, both of them occurring during the alleged golden age, and both negative: the 1955 advice of an "important" Wall Street law firm which used questionable artifices to open the way for sale of an insurance stock in New York that was not legally qualified, and the financial scandals of the 1920s which "could not have occurred without the willingness of lawyers to abandon their position of public trust, to regard themselves as servants of business rather than servants of the law" *(*Mayer 1956, Part II, p. 56).

Therefore, the 1956 Mayer article, like all the other sources cited by Kronman, Glendon, and Linowitz, provides no basis for any history of client purification.

Page 266: The biographies and collected papers of lawyer-statesmen I consulted are as follows: Acheson, 1969; Arnold, 1965; Bancroft, 1900; Beal, 1957; Beveridge, 1916; Bigelow, 1895; Brookhiser, 2003; Brownell, 1993; Cherny, 1985; Conrad, 1956; Dewey, 1986; Dumbauld, 1978; Field, 1898; Frank, 1991; Goebel, 1964; Harbaugh, 1973; Hill, 1906; Jessup, 1938; Johannsen, 1973; Lash, 1975; Leopold, 1954; Matthews, 1991; Mayer, 1964; McCullough, 2001; Morrison, 1964; Nevins, 1957; Niven, 1995; Parrish, 1981; Peskin, 1999; Philips, 1962; Remini, 1997; Schlesinger, 1957; Spiegel, 2002; Stimson and Bundy, 1948; Strong, 1914; Tuttle, 2002; Van Ee, 1986; Williams, 2002; Wroth and Zobel, 1995.

Page 266: The letter signed by Taft and Root opposing the Brandeis nomination appears at Mersky and Jacobstein 1977, vol. 2, p. 1226.

Page 267: The *Le Guen* litigation is described in great detail in Goebel 1964, vol. 2, pp. 48-94, and reported officially in *Le Guen v. Gouverneur et al,* 1 Johnson, *Cases* 436 (1800).

Page 267: The law firm and bar histories I consulted are as follows: Abel, 1989; Abel, 1997; Adams and Adams, 1956; Auerbach, 1976; Auerbach, 1940; Earle, 1963; Ellis and Clark, 1988; Ferguson, 1984; Friedman, 2005; Galanter, 1996; Galanter and Palay, 1991; Gilmore, 1977; Gross, 2004; Hoffman, 1973; Horwitz, 1992; Hurst, 1950; Katzman, 1995; Lisagor and Lipsius, 1988; McWhirter, 1998; Matthews, 1980; Mayer, 1956; Nelson, 1992; Rehnquist, 1986; Schlesinger, 1986; Schwartz, 1974; Shaffer and Shaffer, 1991; Smigel, 1964; Swaine, 1946; Taft, 1938; Vile, 2001; Warren, 1911.

Page 267: "*The Cravath System*" appears in volume 2 of Swaine (1946) beginning at page 1.

Page 267: The quotation about lawyers ignoring social and economic problems is from Swaine 1946, vol. 1, p. 667.

Page 268: The Frankfurter quotation is from Phillips 1962, pp. 66-67.

Page 268: The J.P. Morgan quotation is from Josephson 1962, p. 299.

Page 269: The Field quotation about Lord Brougham is from Field 1844, p. 345.

Page 269: The Field quotation about lawyers' moral duties is from Field 1884, vol. 1, pp. 298-299.

Page 270: Details of Jacob Sharp's bribery of the New York Board of Aldermen appear in Swaine 1946, vol 1, pp. 404-413.

Page 270: The story of the Erie Wars and the involvement of Field and other leading New York lawyers is from Josephson 1962, pp. 121-136, and Martin 1970, pp. 4-9.

Page 270: The Schlesinger quotation is from Schlesinger 1945, p. 502.

Page 271: The description of Field's role in the genesis of the Association of the Bar of the City of New York is from Martin 1970, pp. 97-103.

Page 271: The Field quotation is from Martin 1970, p. 97.

Page 272: Cochran's observation that Kronman and Glendon rejected rule-based ethics is from Cochran 1996, p. 709.

Page 272: Cochran's alignment with the call for a return to the exercise of virtues is from Cochran 1996, p. 707.

Page 272: Cochran's "thoughtful histories of the leaders" is from Cochran 1996, p. 709.

Page 272: Cochran's "independent judgment, moral and legal" is from Cochran 1996, p. 715.

Page 272: Cochran's conclusion is from Cochran 1996, p. 730.

Page 273: Cochran's "Virtues More Important Than Rules" is from Cochran 1996, p. 723.

Page 273: Judge Rakoff's call for rule-based ethics is from Rakoff 2004, pp. 4-6, 63.

Chapter 15

Page 275: The information about Daniel Webster's government career and law practice is based largely on the definitive biography, *Daniel Webster: The Man and his Time* by Robert Remini, professor of history emeritus at the University of Illinois (Remini 1997). Remini, a National Book Award winner, exhaustively researched the Webster Papers Project at Dartmouth College, as well as official government documents and the memoirs of John Quincy Adams, who was a contemporary of Webster.

Page 276: The Kronman quotation about Daniel Webster is from Kronman 1993, p. 21.

Page 277: The other four special House committee members were Nathaniel Banks of Massachusetts, George McCrary of Iowa, William Niblack of Indiana, and William Merrick of Maryland. Poland, McCrary, Ellis, and Merrick were former judges.

Page 277: The Peskin quotation is from Peskin 1978, p. 359.

Page 277: The American Heritage quotation is from Josephy 1975, p. 260.

Page 278: The history of the Senate Teapot Dome investigation is based on Bates 1999, Chapter 21.

Page 280: The *New Republic* quotation is from Anderson 1924, pp. 277-279.

Page 281: The U.S. Supreme Court decisions canceling Albert Fall's Naval oil leases are *Pan American Petroleum and Transport Company v. United States,* 273 U.S. 456 (1927), and *Mammoth Oil Company et al. v. United States,* 275 U.S. 13 (1927).

Page 282: The U.S. Supreme Court decisions compelling witnesses to testify before Congressional committees are *McGrain v. Daugherty,* 273 U.S. 135 (1927), and *Sinclair v. United States,* 279 U.S. 263 (1929).

Page 284: The other members of the Ervin Watergate Committee were: Ranking Member Howard Baker (Republican, Tennessee); Edward Gurney (Republican, Florida); Daniel Inouye (Democrat, Hawaii); Joseph Montoya (Democrat, New Mexico); Herman Talmadge (Democrat, Georgia); and Lowell Weicker (Republican, Connecticut).

Page 285: The Galanter Watergate quotation is from Galanter 2005, p. 7.

Page 285: The *Time* Rodino story is from "The Fateful Vote to Impeach" in the edition of August 5, 1974.

Page 289: The Rosen quotation is from Rosen 2006, p. xii.

Page 289: The Friedman quotation is from Friedman 2009, p. 15.

Page 289: The Toobin quotation is from Toobin 2007, p. 7.

Page 289: The Cox statement about public support is from Cox 1987, p. 25.

Page 290: The *Citizens United* decision is reported at *Citizens United v. Federal Election Commission,* 556 U.S. _____ (2010), 2010 WL 183856 (January 21, 2010).

Page 290: The *Austin* case is reported at *Austin v. Michigan Chamber of Commerce,* 494 U.S. 652 (1990).

Page 290: The statement of President Obama is from the White House press release of January 21, 2010.

Chapter 16

Page 291: The Tamanaha quotation is from Tamanaha 2004, p. 3.

Page 291: The Grote quotation is from Grote 1999, p. 1.

Page 291: The Lord Widgery quotation is from Schwartz 1976, pp. 433, 441-442.

Page 292: The article by Frances Gibb, "Self-financing legal cases are too high a price for society," appeared in the *London Times* edition of September 4, 2008.

Page 292: The website of the World Justice Project is www.abanet.org/wjp/ .

Page 293: The Learned Hand quotation is from his speech of February 16, 1951, to the Legal Aid Society in New York.

Page 294: Lord Bingham's lecture will be found at Bingham 2006. He elaborated on the theme of his lecture in a forthcoming book, *The Rule of Law,* to be published in 2010 by Allen Lane, London.

Page 294: The sub-rules composed by Lord Bingham of Cornhill are from Bingham 2006. The fifth sub-rule is discussed at Bingham 2006, pp. 20-22.

Page 296: The Dershowitz quotation is from Dershowitz 1988, p. 32.

Bibliography / Sources

Abel, Richard L. (1989). *American Lawyers*. New York: Oxford University Press.

———(1997). *Lawyers: A Critical Reader*. New York: The New Press.

Acheson, Dean (1969). *Present at the Creation*. New York: W.W. Norton.

Ackerman, Bruce (2005). *The Failure of the Founding Fathers: Jefferson, Marshall, and the Rise of Presidential Democracy*. Cambridge: Belknap Press of Harvard University Press.

Adams, Charles Francis, ed. (1856). *The Works of John Adams*. 10 volumes. Boston: Little, Brown.

Adams, Charles Francis Jr. and Henry Adams (1956). *Chapters of Erie*. Ithaca, N.Y.: Great Seal Books.

Adams, John (1787). *A Defence of the Constitutions of Government of the United States of America*. New York: Da Capo Press (unabridged republication, 3 volumes, 1971).

Alsop, Joseph, and Turner Catledge (1938). *The 168 Days*. Garden City: Doubleday.

Amar, Akhil Reed (2005). *America's Constitution: A Biography*. New York: Random House.

Anderson, Paul Y. (1924). "The Scandal in Oil," *The New Republic*, Feb. 6, 1924, pp. 277-279.

Arculus, David and Teresa Graham (2004). *Better Routes to Redress*. London: Better Regulation Task Force.

Arnold, Thurman W. (1965). *Fair Fights and Foul: A Dissenting Lawyer's Life*. New York: Harcourt, Brace & World.

Auerbach, Jerold S. (1976). *Unequal Justice: Lawyers and Social Change in Modern America*. New York: Oxford University Press.

Auerbach, Joseph S. (1940). *The Bar of Other Days*. New York: Harper.

Balkin, Jack (2002). *The Use that the Future Makes of the Past: John Marshall's Greatness and its Lessons for Today's Supreme Court Justices*. 43 William and Mary Law Review 1321.

Bancroft, Frederic (1900). *The Life of William H. Seward*. 2 vols. New York: Harper & Bros.

Banning, Lance (1995). *The Sacred Fire of Liberty: James Madison and the Founding of the Federal Republic*. Ithaca: Cornell University Press.

Bass, Jack (1981). *Unlikely Heroes*. New York: Simon and Schuster.

Bates, J. Leonard (1999). *Senator Thomas J. Walsh of Montana*. Urbana: University of Illinois Press.

Bawdon, Fiona, Michael Napier and Gordon Wignall (2001). *Conditional Fees: A Survival Guide*. London: The Law Society.

Beal, John R. (1957). *John Foster Dulles: a Biography*. New York: Harper.

Bentham, Jeremy (1843). *The Works of Jeremy Bentham*, vol. 6, *An Introductory View of the Rationale of Judicial Evidence*. Edinburgh: William Tait.

Berkin, Carol (2002). *A Brilliant Solution: Inventing the American Constitution*. New York: Harcourt.

Bernstein, R.B. (2009). *The Founding Fathers Reconsidered*. New York: Oxford University Press.

Beveridge, Albert J. (1916). *The Life of John Marshall*. 4 vols. Boston: Houghton Mifflin.

Bigelow, John (1895). *The Life of Samuel Tilden*. 2 vols. New York: Harper.

Bingham, Lord, of Cornhill (2006). The Sixth Sir David Williams Lecture, "The Rule of Law." Cambridge: Centre for Public Law, Cambridge University.

Bowen, Catherine Drinker (1966). *Miracle at Philadelphia: The Story of the Constitutional Convention, May to September, 1787*. Boston: Little Brown.

Brant, Irving (1941). *James Madison*. 6 vols. Indianapolis: Bobbs-Merrill.

Breyer, Stephen (1998). "The Work of the Supreme Court" in *Bulletin of the American Academy of Arts and Sciences* No. 52 (September-October 1998), p. 47.

———(2006). "Active Liberty: Interpreting our Democratic Constitution" in *Bulletin of the American Academy of Arts and Sciences* No. 59 (Summer 2006), p. 12.

———(2007). "Wise Constraints" in "The American Idea," *The Atlantic,* November 2007, p. 55.

Brinkley, Douglas ed. (2001). *36 Days: The Complete Chronicle of the 2000 Presidential Election Crisis.* New York: Times Books/Henry Holt.

Broadwater, Jeff (2006). *George Mason: Forgotten Founder.* Chapel Hill: University of North Carolina Press.

Brookhiser, Richard (2003). *Gentleman Revolutionary: Gouverneur Morris—The Rake Who Wrote the Constitution.* New York: Free Press.

Brownell, Herbert (1993). *Advising Ike: The Memoirs of Attorney General Herbert Brownell.* Lawrence: University Press of Kansas.

Bryce, James (1913). *The American Commonwealth.* 2 vols. New York: Macmillan.

Burgess, John W. (1890). *Political Science and Comparative Constitutional Law.* 2 vols. Boston: Ginn & Co.

Burns, James MacGregor (2009). *Packing the Court: The Rise of Judicial Power and the Coming Crisis of the Supreme Court.* New York: Penguin Press.

Carrington, Paul D. (1999). "Recent Efforts To Change Discovery Rules: Do They Advance The Purposes Of Discovery?" in *Controversies Surrounding Discovery and Its Effect on the Courts.* Washington D.C.: Pound Civil Justice Institute. (http://www.poundinstitute.org/images/1999ForumReport.PDF)

Chernow, Ron (2004). *Alexander Hamilton.* New York: Penguin Press.

Cherny, Robert W. (1985). *A Righteous Cause: The Life of William Jennings Bryan.* Boston: Little, Brown.

Choate, Rufus (1879). *Addresses and Orations of Rufus Choate.* Boston: Little Brown.

Cochran, Robert F. Jr. (1996). *Lawyers and Virtues: A Review Essay of Mary Ann Glendon's "A Nation Under Lawyers" and Anthony T. Kronman's "The Lost Lawyer."* 71 Notre Dame Law Review 707.

Commager, Henry Steele (1950). *The American Mind: An Interpretation of American Thought and Character Since the 1880's.* New Haven: Yale University Press.

———(1993). *Commager on Tocqueville.* Columbia: University of Missouri Press.

Conrad, Earl (1956). *Mr. Seward for the Defense.* New York: Rinehart.

Cook, Michael J. (2001). *Cook on Costs, 2001.* London: Butterworth's.

Cooke, Alistair (1973). *Alistair Cooke's America.* New York: Knopf.

Cox, Archibald (1987). *The Court and the Constitution.* Boston: Houghton Mifflin.

Crier, Catherine (2002). *The Case Against Lawyers.* New York: Broadway Books.

Dees, Morris, with Steve Fiffer (2001). *A Lawyer's Journey: The Morris Dees Story.* Chicago: American Bar Association.

Dellapenna, Joseph W. ed. (1997). *The Report of the ILEX Briefing Trip to Hong Kong, March 7-12, 1997.* Chicago: American Bar Association.

Dershowittz, Alan M. (1988). *Taking Liberties: A Decade of Hard Cases, Bad Laws, and Bum Raps.* Chicago: Contemporary Books.

Devlin, Lord Patrick (1979). *The Judge.* Chicago: University of Chicago Press.

Dewey, Frank L. (1986). *Thomas Jefferson, Lawyer.* Charlottesville: University Press of Virginia.

Dicey, Albert V. (1885). *Lectures Introductory to the Study of the Law of the Constitution.* London: Macmillan.

Dumbauld, Edward (1978). *Thomas Jefferson and the Law.* Norman: University of Oklahoma Press.

Earle, Walter K. (1963). *Mr. Shearman and Mr. Sterling and How They Grew.* New Haven: Yale University Press.

Eggen, Dan (2009). "Obama Stocks White House With Prominent Lawyers." *Washington Post,* January 30, 2009.

Elliot, Jonathan (1861). *The Debates in the Several State Conventions on the Adoption of the Federal Constitution, 2d edition.* 5 volumes. Philadelphia: J. B. Lippincott.

Ellis, Francis M. and Edward F. Clark, Jr. (1988). *A Brief History of Carter, Ledyard & Milburn.* Portsmouth NH: Peter E. Randall.

Ellis, Joseph J. (2004). *His Excellency: George Washington.* New York: Random House.

———(2007). *American Creation.* New York: Knopf.

Ely, John Hart (1980). *Democracy and Distrust: A Theory of Judicial Review.* Cambridge: Harvard University Press.

England, Robert Stowe (1991). "Can the American Bar Association declare independence?" New York: *National Review,* July 1991.

Farber, Daniel A. (2003). *Lincoln's Constitution.* Chicago: University of Chicago Press.

Farber, Daniel A. and Suzanna Sherry (2005). *A History of the American Constitution.* St. Paul: Thomson/West.

Farrand, Max, ed. (1911). *The Records of the Federal Convention of 1787.* 3 vols. New Haven: Yale University Press.

———(1913). *The Framing of the Constitution of the United States.* New Haven: Yale University Press.

Ferguson, Robert A. (1984). *Law and Lawyers in American Culture.* Cambridge: Harvard University Press.

Ferling, John (2003). *A Leap in the Dark: The Struggle to Create the American Republic.* New York: Oxford University Press.

Field, David Dudley (1844). "The Study and Practice of the Law," in *Democratic Review,* vol. XIV, p. 345.

———(1884). *Speeches, Arguments, and Miscellaneous Papers of David Dudley Field.* 3 vols. A.P. Sprague, ed. New York: D. Appleton & Co.

Field, Henry M. (1898). *The Life of David Dudley Field.* New York: C. Scribner's Sons.

Finkelman, Paul (1997). *Dred Scott v. Sandford: A Brief History with Documents.* Boston: Bedford Books.

———(2004). "Abraham Lincoln: Prairie Lawyer" in Gross ed. 2004, pp. 129-137.

Fitzpatrick, John C., ed. (1938). *The Writings of George Washington.* Washington D.C.: Government Printing Office.

Frank, John P. (1991). *Lincoln as a Lawyer.* Chicago: Americana House.

Frankfurter, Felix (1948). "Personal Ambitions of Judges," in 34 American Bar Association Journal 656.

Friedman, Barry (2009). *The Will of the People: How Public Opinion Has Influenced the Supreme Court and Shaped the Meaning of the Constitution.* New York: Farrar, Straus and Giroux.

Friedman, Lawrence M. (2005). *A History of American Law, 3d ed.* New York: Simon & Schuster.

Galanter, Marc (1996). *Lawyers in the Mist: The Golden Age of Legal Nostalgia,* 100 Dickinson Law Review 549.

———(2005). *Lowering the Bar: Lawyer Jokes and Legal Culture.* Madison: University of Wisconsin Press.

Galanter, Marc and Thomas M. Palay (1991). *Tournament of Lawyers: The Transformation of the Big Law Firm.* Chicago: University of Chicago Press.

Gawalt, Gerard W., ed. (1984). *The New High Priests: Lawyers in Post-Civil War America.* Westport: Greenwood Press.

Gibb, Frances (2008). "Self-financing legal cases are too high a price for society" in the *London Times,* September 4, 2008.

———(April 2009). "Woolf reforms and cost-cutting have led to acute shortages and a deficient system" in the *London Times,* April 16, 2009.

———(May 2009). "Let's be civil and stop Loser Pays" in the *London Times,* May 13, 2009.

Gillman, Howard (2001). *The Votes that Counted: How the Court Decided the 2000 Presidential Election.* Chicago: University of Chicago Press.

Gilmore, Grant (1977). *The Ages of American Law.* New Haven: Yale University Press.

Glendon, Mary Ann (1994). *A Nation Under Lawyers: How the Crisis in the Legal Profession is Transforming American Society.* New York: Farrar, Straus and Giroux.

Goebel, Julius Jr., ed. (1964). *The Law Practice of Alexander Hamilton: Documents and Commentary.* 5 vols. New York: Columbia University Press.

Goodwin, Doris Kearns (2005). *Team of Rivals: The Political Genius of Abraham Lincoln.* New York: Simon & Schuster.

Greenslade, Roy (1992). *Maxwell.* New York: Carol.

Gross, Norman, ed. (2004). *America's Lawyer-Presidents: From Law Offices to Oval Office.* Evanston: Northwestern University Press.

Grote, Rainer (1999). "Rule of Law, Rechtsstaat and Etat de Droit" in *Constitutionalism, Universalism, and Democracy—A Comparative Analysis,* edited by Christian Starck. Baden-Baden: Nomos Verlagsgesellschaft.

Haltom, William and Michael McCann (2004). *Distorting the Law: Politics, Media, and the Litigation Crisis.* Chicago: University of Chicago Press.

Hamburger, Philip (2008). *Law and Judicial Duty.* Cambridge: Harvard University Press.

Harbaugh, William (1973). *Lawyer's Lawyer: The Life of John W. Davis.* New York: Oxford University Press.

Higginbotham, Don (2002). *George Washington: Uniting a Nation*. Lanham: Rowman and Littlefield.

Hill, Frederick T. (1906). *Lincoln the Lawyer*. New York: Century Co.

Hobson, Charles F. (1996). *The Great Chief Justice: John Marshall and the Rule of Law*. Lawrence: University Press of Kansas.

Hobson, Wayne K. (1984). "Symbol of the New Profession: Emergence of the Large Law Firm, 1870-1915" in Gawalt 1984, pp. 3-27.

Hoffer, Peter Charles (1990). *The Law's Conscience: Equitable Constitutionalism in America*. Chapel Hill: University of North Carolina Press.

———(1998). *Law and People in Colonial America, 2nd edtion*. Baltimore: Johns Hopkins University Press.

———(2010). *A Nation of Laws: America's Imperfect Pursuit of Justice*. Lawrence: University Press of Kansas.

Hoffman, Paul (1973). *Lions in the Street: The Inside Story of the Great Wall Street Law Firms*. New York: Saturday Review Press.

Horwitz, Morton J. (1992). *The Transformation of American Law*. 2 vols. New York: Oxford University Press.

Howard, Philip K. (1994). *The Death of Common Sense: How Law is Suffocating America*. New York: Warner Books.

———(2001). *The Lost Art of Drawing the Line: How Fairness Went Too Far*. New York: Random House.

———(2002). *The Collapse of the Common Good: How America's Lawsuit Culture Undermines our Freedom*. New York: Ballantine.

Huber, Peter W. (1988). *Liability*. New York: Basic Books.

Huber, Peter W. and Robert E. Litan, eds. (1991). *The Liability Maze: The Impact of Liability Law on Safety and Innovation*. Washington: Brookings Institution.

Hughes, Charles Evans (1973). *The Autobiographical Notes of Charles Evans Hughes*. Cambridge: Harvard University Press.

Hurst, James W. (1950). *The Growth of American Law: the Law Makers*. Boston: Little Brown.

Ickes, Harold L. (1948). "My 12 Years with FDR," part 5, published in *The Saturday Evening Post*, July 33, 1948, p. 31.

———(1954). *The Secret Diary of Harold L. Ickes*, vol. II, *The Inside Struggle, 1936-1939*. New York: Simon and Schuster.

Irons, Peter H. (1982). *The New Deal Lawyers*. Princeton: Princeton University Press.

Jackson, Lord Justice Rupert (2009). *Review of Civil Litigation Costs: Preliminary Report*. 2 vols. London: Royal Courts of Justice.

———(2009 a). *Review of Civil Litigation Costs: Final Report*. London: Royal Courts of Justice.

Jacobson, Richard S. and Jeffrey R. White (2004). *David v. Goliath: ATLA and the Fight for Everyday Justice*. Washington D.C.: American Association for Justice.

Jessup, Philip C. (1938). *Elihu Root*. 2 vols. New York: Dodd, Mead & Co.

Johannsen, Robert W. (1973). *Stephen A. Douglas*. New York: Oxford University Press.

Johnson, Herbert A. ed. (1974). *The Papers of John Marshall*. Chapel Hill: University of North Carolina Press.

Joseph, Gregory P. (2000). *Sanctions: The Federal Law of Litigation Abuse, 3rd ed*. Charlottesville: Lexis Law Publishing.

Josephson, Matthew (1962). *The Robber Barons: The Great American Capitalists, 1861-1901*. New York: Harcourt, Brace & World.

Josephy, Alvin M. Jr. (1975). *The American Heritage History of the United States*. New York: American Heritage Publishing Company.

Kagan, Robert A. (2001). *Adversarial Legalism: The American Way of Law*. Cambridge: Harvard University Press.

Kaminski, John P. and Richard Leffler, ed. (1999). *Creating the Constitution*. Acton: Copley Publishing Group.

Kane, Joseph Nathan, ed. (1993). *Facts About the Presidents*. New York: H.W. Wilson Co.

Katzman, Robert A., ed. (1995). *The Law Firm and the Public Good*. Washington: Brookings Institution.

Kennedy, Robert F. Jr. (1978). *Judge Frank M. Johnson, Jr*. New York: Putnam.

Kluger, Richard (2004). *Simple Justice: The History of Brown v. Board of Education and Black America's Struggle for Equality*. New York: Vintage (Random House).

Koenig, Thomas H. and Michael L. Rustad (2001). *In Defense of Tort Law.* New York: New York University Press.

Kritzer, Herbert M. (2001). "Lawyer Fees and Lawyer Behavior in Litigation: What Does the Empirical Literature Really Say?" 80 Texas Law Review 1943.

———ed. (2002). *Legal Systems of the World: a Political, Social, and Cultural Encyclopedia.* 4 vols. Santa Barbara: ABC-CLIO.

———(2004). *Risks, Reputations, and Rewards: Contingency Fee Legal Practice in the United States.* Stanford: Stanford Law and Politics.

———(2005). "The American Public's Assessment of the Rehnquist Court." *Judicature* (November/December 2005), pp. 168-176.

———(2005 a). " 'Loser Pays' Doesn't." *Legal Affairs* (November/December 2005), pp. 24-25.

Kronman, Anthony T. (1993). *The Lost Lawyer: Failing Ideals of the Legal Profession.* Cambridge: Belknap Press of Harvard University Press.

Labunski, Richard (2006). *James Madison and the Struggle for the Bill of Rights.* New York: Oxford University Press.

Lash, Joseph P. (1975). *From the Diaries of Felix Frankfurter.* New York: W.W. Norton.

Leach, W. Barton (1965). "Meeting Ground of Law and Science in War: Operations Analysis in the USAAF, 1942-1945," in *Lex et Scientia* 2 (July-September 1965), p. 163.

Leibiger, Stuart (1999). *Founding Friendship: George Washington, James Madison, and the Creation of the American Republic.* Charlottesville: University Press of Virginia.

Leopold, Richard W. (1954). *Elihu Root and the Conservative Tradition.* Boston: Little Brown & Co.

Leuchtenburg, William E. (1963). *Franklin D. Roosevelt and the New Deal.* New York: Harper & Row.

———(1995). *The Supreme Court Reborn: The Constitutional Revolution in the Age of Roosevelt.* New York: Oxford University Press.

Levi, Edward H. (1949). *An Introduction to Legal Reasoning.* Chicago: University of Chicago Press.

Linowitz, Sol M. (1994). *The Betrayed Profession: Lawyering at the End of the Twentieth Century.* New York: Scribner.

Lisagor, Nancy, and Frank Lipsius (1988). *A Law Unto Itself: the Untold Story of the Law Firm of Sullivan & Cromwell.* New York: Morrow.

Llewellyn, Karl N. (2008). *The Bramble Bush.* New York: Oxford University Press.

Madison, James (1987). *Notes of Debates in the Federal Convention of 1787.* New York: W.W. Norton.

Marshall, John (2000). *The Life of George Washington.* Indianapolis: Liberty Fund.

Martin, George (1970). *Causes and Conflicts: The Centennial History of the Association of the Bar of the City of New York, 1870-1970.* Boston: Houghton Mifflin.

Matthews, Elizabeth W. (1991). *Lincoln as a Lawyer: An Annotated Bibliography.* Carbondale: Southern Illinois University Press.

Matthews, Jean V. (1980). *Rufus Choate: The Law and Civic Virtue.* Philadelphia: Temple University Press.

Mayer, Martin (1956). "The Wall Street Lawyers," Part I, "The Elite Corps of American Business," *Harper's Magazine,* January 1956, pp. 31-37; Part II, "Keepers of the Business Conscience," *Harper's Magazine,* February 1956, pp. 50-56.

———(1964). *Emory Buckner: A Biography.* New York: Harper & Row.

McCloy, John J. (1958). "The Extracurricular Lawyer" in 15 Washington & Lee Law Review 171.

McCullough, David G. (2001). *John Adams.* New York: Simon & Schuster.

McDonald, Forest (1985). *Novus Ordo Seclorum: The Intellectual Origins of the Constitution.* Lawrence: The University Press of Kansas.

McGrory, Mary (1995). "Putting People in Their Place," *Washington Post,* March 7, 1995.

McPherson, James M. (2008). *Tried by War: Abraham Lincoln as Commander in Chief.* New York: The Penguin Press.

McWhirter, Darien A. (1998). *The Legal 100: A Ranking of the Individuals who Have Most Influenced the Law.* New York: Carol.

Mencimer, Stephanie (2006). *Blocking the Courthouse Door: How the Republican Party and its Corporate Allies are Taking Away Your Right to Sue.* New York: Free Press.

Mersky, Roy. M. and J. Myron Jacobstein, eds. (1977). *The Supreme Court of the United States: hearings and reports of successful and unsuccessful nominations of Supreme Court Justices by the Senate Judiciary Committee.* Buffalo: W.S. Hein.

Mertz, Elizabeth (2007). *The Language of Law School: Learning to "Think Like a Lawyer."* New York: Oxford University Press.

Meyerson, Michael I. (2008). *Liberty's Blueprint: How Madison and Hamilton Wrote the Federalist Papers, Defined the Constitution, and Made Democracy Safe for the World.* New York: Basic Books.

Middleton, Sir Peter (1997). *Review of Civil Justice and Legal Aid.* London: Her Majesty's Stationery Office.

Miller, Mark C. (1995). *The High Priests of American Politics: The Role of Lawyers in American Political Institutions.* Knoxville: The University of Tennessee Press.

Minot, George R. (1810). *The History of the Insurrection in Massachusetts in the Year 1786 and the Rebellion Consequent Thereon, 2nd ed.* Boston: James W. Burditt & Co.

Moorhead, Richard and Peter Hurst (2008). *Contingency Fees: A Study of Their Operation in the United States of America.* London: Civil Justice Council.

Morison, Elting E. (1964). *Turmoil and Tradition: A Study of the Life and Times of Henry L. Stimson.* New York: Atheneum.

Nader, Ralph (1965). *Unsafe at Any Speed: The Designed-In Dangers of the American Automobile.* New York: Grossman Publishers.

———(2004). *The Good Fight: Declare your Independence & Close the Democracy Gap.* New York: HarperCollins.

Nelson, Robert L., David M. Trubeck and Rayman L. Solomon, eds. (1992). *Lawyers' Ideals/Lawyers' Practices.* Ithaca: Cornell University Press.

Nelson, William E. (2000). *Marbury v. Madison: The Origins and Legacy of Judicial Review.* Lawrence: University Press of Kansas.

Nevins, Allan (1957). *Hamilton Fish: The Inner History of the Grant Administration.* New York: F. Ungar Publishing Co.

Newton, Jim (2006). *Earl Warren and the Nation He Made.* New York: Riverhead Books.

Niven, John (1995). *Salmon P. Chase: a Biography.* New York: Oxford University Press.

Obama, Barack (2006). *The Audacity of Hope: Thoughts on Reclaiming the American Dream.* New York: Crown Publishers.

O'Connor, Sandra Day (2003). *The Majesty of the Law: Reflections of a Supreme Court Justice.* New York: Random House.

Ogletree, Charles J., Jr. (2008). "Social Justice Lawyering: The Rule and the Limits of Law." Chicago: American Bar Association Section of Litigation, *Litigation Update,* July 16, 2008.

Olson, Walter K. (1991). *The Litigation Explosion: What Happened When America Unleashed the Lawsuit.* New York: Truman Talley/Dutton.

———(2003). *The Rule of Lawyers: How the New Litigation Elite Threatens America's Rule of Law.* New York: Truman Talley/St. Martin's.

Parker, Christine (1999). *Just Lawyers: Regulation and Access to Justice.* London: Oxford University Press.

Parrish, Michael E. (1981). *Felix Frankfurter and His Times: The Reform Years.* New York: Free Press.

Partington, Martin (2006). *An Introduction to the English Legal System (3rd ed.).* Oxford: Oxford University Press.

Patterson, Orlando (2006). "The Last Race Problem," *New York Times Op-Ed Page,* December 30, 2006.

Peskin, Allan (1999). *Garfield: a Biography.* Kent, Ohio: Kent State University Press.

Peysner, John (2001). *A Revolution by Degrees: From Costs to Financing and the End of the Indemnity Principle.* Nottingham: Centre for Legal Research, Nottingham Law School.

Phelps, Glenn A. (1993). *George Washington & American Constitutionalism.* Lawrence: University Press of Kansas.

Philips, Harlan B. (1962). *Felix Frankfurter Reminisces.* New York: Anchor Books.

Posner, Richard A. (2001). *Breaking the Deadlock: the 2000 Election, the Constitution, and the Courts.* Princeton: Princeton University Press.

Prosser, William L. (1971). *Handbook of the Law of Torts,* 4th ed. St. Paul: West Publishing Co.

Pusey, Merlo J. (1951). *Charles Evans Hughes.* 2 vols. New York: Macmillan.

Rakoff, Jed S. (2004). *Is the Ethical Lawyer an Endangered Species?* LITIGATION, Vol. 30, No. 3 (Spring 2004). Chicago: American Bar Association.

Rakove, Jack N. (1990). *James Madison and the Creation of the American Republic.* New York: HarperCollins.

———(1996). *Original Meanings: Politics and Ideas in the Making of the Constitution.* New York: Random House.

———(2009). *The Annotated U.S. Constitution and Declaration of Independence.* Cambridge: Belknap Press of Harvard University Press.

Rauma, David and Thomas E. Willging (2005). *Report of a Survey of United States District Judges' Experience and Views Concerning Rule 11, Federal Rules of Civil Procedure.* Washington, D.C.: Federal Judicial Center.

Reeves, Richard (1982). *American Journey: Traveling with Tocqueville in Search of Democracy in America.* New York: Simon and Schuster.

Rehnquist, William H. (1986). "The Lawyer-Statesman in American History." 9 Harvard Journal of Law & Public Policy 537.

———(2002). *The Supreme Court.* New York: Vintage (Random House).

Remini, Robert V. (1997). *Daniel Webster: the Man and his Time.* New York: W.W. Norton.

Rhode, Deborah L. (2004). *Access to Justice.* New York: Oxford University Press.

Richards, John T. (1916). *Abraham Lincoln, the Lawyer-Statesman.* Boston: Houghton Mifflin.

Rosen, Jeffrey (2006). *The Most Democratic Branch: How the Courts Serve America.* New York: Oxford University Press.

Rutland, Robert Allen (1983). *The Ordeal of the Constitution: The Antifederalists and the Ratification Struggle of 1787-1788.* Boston: Northeastern University Press.

Sandbach, James (2004). *No Win, No Fee, No Chance: CAB Evidence on the Challenges Facing Access to Injury Compensation.* London: Citizens Advice Bureau.

Sarat, Austin, and Stuart Scheingold (2001). *Cause Lawyering and the State in a Global Era.* New York: Oxford University Press.

———(2006). *Cause Lawyers and Social Movements.* Stanford: Stanford University Press.

Schauer, Frederick (2009). *Thinking Like a Lawyer: A New Introduction to Legal Reasoning.* Cambridge: Harvard University Press.

Schlesinger, Arthur M. Jr. (1945). *The Age of Jackson.* Boston: Little, Brown.

———(1957). *The Age of Roosevelt.* 3 vols. Boston: Houghton Mifflin.

———(1958). *The Coming of the New Deal.* Boston: Houghton Mifflin.

———(1986). *The Cycles of American History.* Boston: Houghton Mifflin.

Schwartz, Bernard (1974). *The Law in America: A History.* New York: McGraw-Hill.

———(1976). Ed., *American Law: The Third Century,* New York: New York University School of Law.

Shaffer, Thomas L. and Mary L. Shaffer (1991). *American Lawyers & Their Communities: Ethics in the Legal Profession.* Notre Dame: University of Notre Dame Press.

Simon, James F. (2006). *Lincoln and Chief Justice Taney: Slavery, Secession, and the President's War Powers.* New York: Simon & Schuster.

Slapper, Gary and David Kelly (2006). *The English Legal System (6ᵗʰ ed.).* Abingdon: Routledge-Cavendish.

Sloan, Cliff and David McKean (2009). *The Great Decision: Jefferson, Adams, Marshall, and the Battle for the Supreme Court.* New York: PublicAffairs.

Smigel, Erwin O. (1964) *The Wall Street Lawyer.* Bloomington: Indiana University Press.

Smith, Jean Edward (1996). *John Marshall: Definer of a Nation.* New York: Henry Holt.

———(2007). *FDR.* New York: Random House.

Spalding, Matthew, and Patrick J. Garrity (1996). *A Sacred Union of Citizens: George Washington's Farewell Address and the American Character.* Lanham: Rowman & Littlefield.

Spiegel, Allen D. (2002). *A. Lincoln, Esquire: A Shrewd, Sophisticated Lawyer in His Time.* Macon: Mercer University Press.

Stimson, Henry L. and McGeorge Bundy (1948). *On Active Duty in Peace and War.* New York: Harper.

Strong, Theron G. (1914). *Landmarks of a Lawyer's Lifetime.* New York: Dodd, Mead.

Sunstein, Cass R. (2001). "Order Without Law" in Sunstein and Epstein eds. (2001), *The Vote: Bush, Gore & the Supreme Court.* Chicago: University of Chicago Press.

Sunstein, Cass R. and Richard A. Epstein eds. (2001). *The Vote: Bush, Gore & the Supreme Court.* Chicago: University of Chicago Press.

Swaine, Robert T. (1946). *The Cravath Firm and its Predecessors, 1819-1947.* 3 vols. New York: privately printed.

Taft, Henry (1938). *A Century and a Half at the New York Bar: Being the annals of a law firm and sketches of its members, with brief references to collateral events of historical interest.* New York: privately printed.

Tamanaha, Brian Z. (2004). *On the Rule of Law: History, Politics, Theory.* Cambridge: Cambridge University Press.

Tocqueville, Alexis de (1835). *Democracy in America.* London: Penguin Group (2003 Bevan translation).

———(1958). *Journeys to England and Ireland.* (Edited by J.P. Mayer.) New Haven: Yale University Press.

Tomlins, Christopher, ed. (2005). *The United States Supreme Court: The Pursuit of Justice.* Boston: Houghton Mifflin.

Toobin, Jeffrey (2007). *The Nine: Inside the Secret World of the Supreme Court.* New York: Doubleday.

Tuttle, Charles H. (2002). *Life Stories of a Celebrated Lawyer: The Memoirs of Charles H. Tuttle, Esq.* Clinton Corners: College Avenue Press.

Twohig, Dorothy et al., eds. (1987). *The Papers of George Washington: Presidential Series.* Charlottesville: University Press of Virginia.

Van Ee, Daun (1986). *David Dudley Field and the Reconstruction of the Law.* New York: Garland.

Vile, John R., ed. (2001). *Great American Lawyers: an Encyclopedia.* 2 vols. Santa Barbara: ABC-CLIO.

Warren, Charles (1911). *A History of the American Bar.* Boston: Little Brown.

———(1928). *The Making of the Constitution.* Boston: Little Brown.

Warren, Earl (1977). *The Memoirs of Earl Warren.* New York: Doubleday.

Washington, H. A., ed. (1853). *The Writings of Thomas Jefferson.* Washington, D.C.: United States Congress.

Whiting, William (1863). *The War Powers of the President, and the Legislative Powers of Congress in Relation to Rebellion, Treason, and Slavery,* 7th ed. Boston: J.L. Storey.

Wicker, Tom (2006). *Shooting Star: The Brief Arc of Joe McCarthy.* Orlando: Harcourt.

Williams, Frank J. (2002). *Judging Lincoln.* Carbondale: Southern Illinois University Press.

Wilson, James (1787). *Speech of October 6, 1787. Pennsylvlania Packet,* October 10, 1787, reprinted at http://www.constitution.org/afp/jwilson0.htm.

Winik, Jay (2007). *The Great Upheaval: America and the Birth of the Modern World, 1788-1800.* New York: HarperCollins.

Witt, John Fabian (2007). *Patriots and Cosmopolitans: Hidden Histories of American Law.* Cambridge: Harvard University Press.

Wolfe, Christopher (1994). *The Rise of Modern Judicial Review: From Constitutional Interpretation to Judge-Made Law.* Lanham: Rowman & Littlefield Publishers.

Wood, Gordon S. (1969). *The Creation of the American Republic, 1776-1787.* Chapel Hill: University of North Carolina Press.

———(1979). *The Confederation and the Constitution: The Critical Issues.* Lanham: University Press of America.

———(2006). *Revolutionary Characters: What Made the Founders Different.* New York: Penguin Press.

———(2009). *Empire of Liberty: A History of the Early Republic, 1789-1815.* New York: Oxford University Press.

Woolf, Lord Harry (1995). *Interim Report on Access to Justice.* London: Her Majesty's Stationery Office.

———(1996). *Final Report on Access to Justice.* London: Her Majesty's Stationery Office.

Wroth, L. Kinvin and Hiller B. Zobel, eds. (1965). *Legal Papers of John Adams.* 3 vols. Cambridge: The Belknap Press of Harvard University Press.

Yates, Robert (1821). *Secret Proceedings and Debates of the Convention.* Albany: Websters and Skinner.

Zander, Michael (2002). *Will the Revolution in the Funding of Civil Litigation in England Eventually Lead to Contingency Fees?* 52 DePaul Law Review 259.

Zimmerman, Warren (2002). *First Great Triumph: How Five Americans Made Their Country a World Power.* New York: Farrar, Straus & Giroux.

Index

AAJ. *See* American Association for Justice

ABA. *See* American Bar Association

Abrams, Floyd, 200

Access to Justice Act 1999, 168

Acheson, Dean, 92, 252, 266

Actors Equity, 171

Adams, John, 13, 18, 19, 33, 40, 49, 52-59, 64, 65, 69-72, 255, 265, 297, 299

Adams, John Quincy, 69, 252, 310

Adams, Samuel, 40, 59

Adkins v. Children's Hospital, 102

Alger, Horatio, 159

Alien and Sedition Acts, 73

Allen, Terry, 135

Alsop, Joseph, 106

Amar, Akhil Reed, 35

American Association for Justice, 236, 237

American Bar Association, 234-236, 266, 292, 314, 315, 319

American Civil Liberties Union, 231

American Idol, 159

Americans with Disabilities Act, 166

Annapolis Convention, 16, 17

apartheid, 122

Apprentice, The, 159

Arcambel v. Wiseman, 165, 303

Arculus, David, 304, 305

Aristotle, 20, 259

Arizona State University, 288

Army-McCarthy hearings, 283-288

Arnold, Thurman, 92

Articles of Confederation, 15-21, 25, 26, 32, 45, 50, 54, 61, 251, 298

Associated Press, 129

Attlee, Clement, 204, 247

Austin v. Michigan Chamber of Commerce, 289

Baigent, Michael, 161, 162

Baker, Howard, 125, 311

Baker, James III, 132, 225, 252

Baldwin, Abraham, 23, 59

Balkin, Jack, 300, 313

Bank of England, 67, 205, 207

Banks, Nathaniel, 310

Barkley, Alben, 94

Barrymore, John, 171

Bass, Jack, 121

Bates, Edward, 83

Bentham, Jerry, 164

Berle, Adolph, 92

Bernstein, Nahum, 173-181

Bill of Rights, 29, 42, 44, 48-51, 66-70, 76, 159, 233, 254, 299

Bingham, Lord, of Cornhill, 294, 311

Black, Hugo, 113, 118

Blair, Montgomery, 83

Blair, Tony, 163, 247

Blake v. Midland Railway, 9, 297

BOAC, 192

Boies, David, 132

Booth, Edwin, 171, 176

Booth, John Wilkes, 171

Bork, Robert, 126

"Boss" Tweed, 263, 270

Boston Red Sox, 159

Boston Tea Party, 42, 52

Bowen, Catherine Drinker, 60

Brandeis, Louis, 93, 97, 105, 266, 309

Brearly, David, 23

Breyer, Stephen, 35, 132, 133, 134, 147, 298, 303

British Overseas Airway Corporation. *See* BOAC

Brown v. Board of Education of Topeka, 113, 114, 115, 116, 118, 119, 120, 121, 122, 148, 166, 167, 302

Brown, Dan, 161

Brown, John, 121

Brown, Oliver, 119, 160, 166, 167, 207, 225, 229, 244

Brutus, 71, 72, 82

Buchanan, James, 69, 80, 83, 287

Burger, Warren, 122, 126

Burgess, John W., 36

Burns, James MacGregor, 148

Burton, Harold, 113

Bush v. Gore, 134, 146-149, 289, 302, 303

Bush, George W., 2, 129-145, 154, 185, 186, 235, 243

Bush, John Ellis ("Jeb"), 131, 136, 137

Butler, Pierce, 93

Butterfield, Alexander, 123, 127

Butterworth, Robert, 137

Caesar, Julius, 19, 36

Cagney, James, 171

Cardiff University, 209

Cardozo, Benjamin N., 93, 97, 105

Carrington, Paul D., 228

Carroll, Charles, 50, 59

CDA. *See* Compania Dominicana de Aviacion

Center for Constitutional Litigation, PC, 236, 306

CFAs. *See* Conditional Fee Agreements

Chandler, Raymond, 98

Chase, Salmon P., 83, 87, 265

Chase, Samuel, 73, 75

Cheney, Dick, 143

Chernow, Ron, 38, 63

Chicago Cubs, 159

Choate, Rufus, 225, 233, 258, 265, 288

Christina (yacht), 192, 199

Christopher, Warren, 225, 252

Cicero, 20

Citizens United v. Federal Election Commission, 289, 311

Ciudad Trujillo, 8, 10, 11

Civil Justice Council (England), 208, 209

Civil Rights Act of 1875, 89

Civil Rights Act of 1964, 119, 166

Civil Rights Revolution, 111, 120, 121

Civil War, 31, 82-91, 111, 230, 268

Clapper, Raymond, 100

Clark, Tom, 110, 113, 116, 118

Clean Air Act, 166

Cleveland, Grover, 89

Clinton, George, 47, 50, 255

Clinton, William J., 143, 286

Cochran, Robert F. Jr., 272-275, 309, 310

Code Napoleon, 9

Cohn, Roy, 283

College of New Jersey. *See* Princeton University

Columbia Law School, 8

Columbia University, 10, 17, 36, 92

Commager, Henry Steele, 156

Committee of Detail, 23, 24

Committee of Style and Arrangement, 24

Committee on Postponed Matters, 23

Committee to Reelect the President. *See* CREEP

Compania Dominicana de Aviacion, 7-11

Conditional Fee Agreements, 206-209

Confederacy, 83, 84

Confederate States of America. *See* Confederacy

Confederation Congress, 15-18, 25-29, 37, 45, 54, 254

Connecticut compromise, 22, 37

Connell, John, 171-182, 187

Constitutional Convention, 2, 21, 25, 29, 31, 35-38, 44-45, 66, 71, 79, 157, 252

Constitutional Reform Act 2005 (England), 163, 164, 294

Continental Congress, 18, 53-59

contingency fee, 201, 208, 210, 216, 243

Cook, Michael, 208

Cooke, Alistair, 36, 48, 77

Coolidge, Calvin, 279, 282

Corcoran, Tommy, 92, 104

cost-shifting. *See* fee-shifting

Court-packing bill, 95-106

Cox, Archibald, 49, 77, 78, 123-128, 256, 285, 289

CREEP, 123

Cushing, William, 75

Da Vinci Code, The, 161

Dana, Francis, 41, 59

dangling chad, 130

Daugherty, Harry, 278, 279

Davis, Jefferson, 83

Davis, John W., 110, 114, 115, 257, 263, 265, 308

de la Maza, Octavio, 11

Dean, John, 123, 124, 284

Declaration of Independence, 18, 19, 25, 26, 44, 52-54, 59, 76, 118, 234

Dees, Morris, 232

Defence of the Constitutions, 18

Democratic National Committee, 123

Dershowitz, Alan, 296

desegregation, 112-119, 167

Devlin, Lord Patrick, 162, 163, 169, 203, 295

Dewey, Thomas E., 114, 159, 217

Dickens, Charles, 200

Dickinson, John, 16, 23, 52-59, 254

Dilulio, John J. Jr., 149

dimpled chad, 130

Dominican Republic, 7-13, 292

Donovan, William ("Wild Bill"), 253, 256

Douglas, William, 92, 113

Dred Scott v. Sandford, 80-87, 103, 111, 300, 301, 304

Duane, James, 47, 53, 55, 59

Eastland, James, 118

ECA. *See* Electoral Count Act of 1887

Edmund Randolph, 23

Ehrlichman, John, 123, 284

Eisenhower, Dwight D., 10, 114, 119, 147, 283

Electoral College, 34, 88, 130-135, 141-144, 148

Electoral Commission, 88

Electoral Count Act of 1887, 131-147

Ellis, Joseph, 38, 48, 51, 68, 157, 254

Ellsworth, Oliver, 23, 50, 59, 66

Emancipation Proclamation, 85, 86

Emerson, John, 80

English Rule of Law, 160

Enron Corporation, 185, 257, 273

Ervin, Sam, 125, 284

European Court of Human Rights, 205

executive privilege, 122-127

Farber, Daniel, 86

FDR. *See* Roosevelt, Franklin Delano

Federal Rules of Civil Procedure, 186

Federalist Papers, The, 29-33, 37-41

fee-shifting, 164-169, 187-190, 199-202, 206, 207, 231-234, 304

Field, David Dudley Jr., 268, 270

Fillmore, Millard, 69

Finkelman, Paul, 82

Fish, Hamilton, 103, 265

Ford, Gerald R., 123, 286

Fortas, Abe, 92

Four Horsemen, 93-105, 109

Frank, Jerome, 92

Frankfurter, Felix, 92, 101, 109, 113, 118, 251-256, 266, 268, 300

Franklin, Benjamin, 19, 22, 32, 58, 59, 251

French Revolution, 20, 72, 254

Friedman, Barry, 289

Friedman, Lawrence M., 249

frivolous lawsuits, 181-190

Fugitive Slave Laws, 84

Fuller, Melville, 90

Galanter, Marc, 285, 306, 308, 309, 311, 315

Galindez, Jesus, 8-12, 297

Gallup News Service, 146

Gallup Poll, 146, 303

Gandhi, Mohandas, 256

GAO. *See* Government Accountability Office

Garfield, James, 266, 276-278, 286, 287

Gary, Elbert, 268

Gawalt, Gerald W., 309

Gerry, Elbridge, 40, 41

Gettysburg address, 85, 116

Gibb, Frances, 204, 210, 292, 305, 311

Gielgud, Sir John, 171

Gillman, Howard, 89, 134

Ginsburg, Ruth Bader, 132-134

Gladstone, William, 33

Glendon, Mary Ann, 258-278, 286

Goodwin, Doris Kearns, 83

Gore, Albert, 129-148, 154

Gorham, Nathaniel, 23, 41, 59

Government Accountability Office, 12

Government of Laws (not of men), 2, 3, 13, 51, 57, 59, 64, 65, 69-77, 83, 87, 91, 95, 101, 106, 120-128, 134, 149-154, 165, 226, 229, 237, 249, 285, 286, 290, 296, 307

Grant, Ulysses S., 89

Great Depression, 91

Greenbaum, Edward, 177

Greenslade, Roy, 200

Grier, Robert, 81

Grote, Rainer, 291

Gurney, Edward, 311

habeas corpus, suspension of, 84, 85, 86

Haldeman, H. R., 123

Hamburger, Philip, 298

Hamilton, Alexander, 1, 16-24, 28-38, 47-51, 59, 65, 67, 72, 73, 225, 257, 265, 267

Hancock, John, 15, 43, 50, 59, 297

Harbaugh, William H., 263, 264

Harding, Warren G., 102, 105, 278, 279

Harris, Katherine, 130, 132

Harrison, William Henry, 69

Harvard Law School, 212, 226, 237, 260

Hastert, Dennis, 139-145

Hayes, Rutherford B., 88

Hayes-Tilden, 131

HBHG (Holy Blood, Holy Grail), 161, 162

Hearst, William Randolph, 102

Henry, Patrick, 24, 43-52, 59, 60, 287

Higginbotham, Don, 68, 299

Hitler, Adolf, 95, 106, 119, 181

Hobson, Wayne K., 309

Hoffer, Peter Charles, 52-57, 149, 228

Holmes v. Walton, 23, 298

Holy Blood and the Holy Grail, The. See HBHG

Hoover, Herbert, 102, 103, 252

Hoover, J. Edgar, 197

Horwitz, Morton J., 69, 297

Houston, Charles, 112

Howard University Law School, 112

Howard, Philip K., 304

Huber, Peter W., 304

Hughes, Charles Evans, 102-107, 122, 252

Hughes, Howard, 191, 192, 219

Hunting, Roger Bryant, 177, 178

Hurst, Peter, 209

Ickes, Harold, 96, 104

Innes, James, 46, 59

Inouye, Daniel, 311

Internal Revenue Service, 197

Iraq War, 157, 254, 306

Jackson State College, 119

Jackson, Andrew, 78

Jackson, Lord Justice Rupert, 189, 208, 209, 210, 304

Jackson, Robert, 92, 110, 113

Jaworski, Leon, 126

Jay, John, 29, 47, 53, 55, 59, 65, 70, 252, 255, 297, 306

Jefferson, Thomas, 18, 19, 26, 31, 46-59, 65, 69, 72, 231, 233, 249, 252-256, 265

Jessup, Philip C., 262-265, 308, 309

JFK. *See* Kennedy, John F.

Jim Crow, 88-90, 111, 112, 119-122, 140

Johnson, Frank Jr., 121

Johnson, Hugh, 92

Johnson, Lyndon B., 89, 123, 215

Johnson, William, 24, 59

Joseph, Gregory, 188

judicial review, 35, 61, 71-78, 100, 127, 149, 155, 164, 300, 303

Judiciary Act of 1789, 66, 75, 94

Judiciary Act of 1801, 74

Judiciary Act of 1802, 74

Kagan, Robert A., 226

Kaminski, John P., 297

Kant, Immanuel, 259

Kelly, Walt, 295

Kennedy, Jacqueline. *See* Onassis, Jacqueline Kennedy

Kennedy, John F., 119, 120, 121, 123, 214, 253

Kennedy, Robert F., 213, 214, 256

Kiley, Richard, 173, 174, 175, 176

King, Martin Luther Jr., 119, 122

King, Rufus, 23, 24, 41, 59

King's College. *See* Columbia University

Kleindienst, Richard, 123

Kluger, Richard, 114, 148, 149, 301, 303

Knox, Henry, 65

Koenig, Thomas H., 304

Korean conflict, 109, 110

Kritzer, Herbert, 165, 303, 304

Kronman, Anthony T., 258-278, 286, 307-310

Lady Ghislaine (yacht), 199

Lamneck, Arthur, 95, 301

Landon, Alfred ("Alf"), 94

Lansing, John, 17, 47

Lay, Kenneth, 186

LDF. *See* Legal Defense Fund

Le Guen v. Gouverneur, 267

Leach, W. Barton, 253, 307

Lee, Richard Henry, 27, 55, 59, 60

Leffler, Richard, 297, 299

Legal Aid (England), 163, 204-207, 223, 295, 311

Legal Defense Fund (NAACP), 112-116, 166, 167, 238, 301

legal expense insurance, 163, 207

Legal Services Corporation (LSC), 232, 235

Leibiger, Stuart, 68, 299

Leigh, Richard, 161, 162

Leuchtenburg, William E., 100, 106, 301

Levi, Edward H., 255, 307

Levin, Joe, 232

lex loci delicti, 8

Liebeck v. McDonald's, 182-184, 243, 304

Lieberman, Joseph, 140, 141

Lincoln, Abraham, 69, 82-87, 95, 116, 118, 171, 225, 229, 247, 248, 252, 256, 266, 287, 298

Linowitz, Sol M., 225, 258, 264-278, 286

Litan, Robert E., 304
"Litigious Society, The", 158
Livingston, Robert, 19, 47, 59
Loser Pays, 160-168, 186-190, 203-210, 234, 295, 304
Louisiana Purchase, 82
LSC. *See* Legal Services Corporation
Mad magazine, 35, 74
Madison, James, 1, 16-51, 59, 61, 65-70, 75, 79, 154, 157, 252, 253, 264, 287, 297-300
Madonna, 9
Man of La Mancha, 173
Mandela, Nelson, 256
Marbury v. Madison, 74-78, 127
Marshall, Burke, 121
Marshall, John, 31, 46, 59, 68, 70, 75, 78, 83, 87, 88, 101, 107, 122-127, 149, 252, 253, 300
Marshall, Thurgood, 112, 115, 167, 231, 256, 301
Martin, Luther, 23, 298
Mason, George, 29, 44-46
Matthews, Jean V., 226, 306, 309
Maxwell, Robert, 199
Mayer, Martin, 309
Mayola Williams v. Philip Morris, 244
McCartney, Sir Paul, 161
McCloy, John J., 251, 252
McCrary, George, 310
McCulloch, David, 19, 56, 297
McCusker, Donald, 193-203, 223, 225, 294
McCusker, Helena, 195-198, 202
McDonald's coffee case. *See Liebeck v. McDonald's*
McGovern, George, 123
McGrain v. Daugherty, 282, 310
McGregor, Donald, 192-194
McKean, Thomas, 40, 60
McPherson, James M., 85, 300
McReynolds, James, 93, 105
Mehlhorn, Herb, 196
Mencimer, Stephanie, 304, 307
Meredith, James, 119, 154, 207, 244, 294
Merrick, William, 310
Mertz, Elizabeth, 307
Meyer, Johnny, 191
Middleton, Sir Peter, 208
Mikva, Abner J., 167
Miller, Mark C., 247-249, 254
Mills, Heather, 161

Minton, Sherman, 110, 113
Mintz, Morton, 219
Missouri Compromise, 81
Moley, Raymond, 92
Monroe, James, 45, 69, 252
Montoya, Joseph, 311
Montpelier, 17
Moore, Alfred, 75
Moorhead, Richard, 209
More, St. Thomas, 256
Morris, Gouverneur, 22-27, 49, 59-61, 66, 77, 265, 267
Murphy, Gerald, 11
NAACP, 111-113, 119, 166, 167, 231, 238, 301
NACCA. *See* National Association of Claimant's Compensation Attorneys
Nader v. General Motors, 211-223, 305
Nader, Ralph, 172, 185, 211-225, 232, 237, 244, 294
National Archives, 76, 215-218
National Association for the Advancement of Colored People. *See* NAACP
National Association of Claimant's Compensation Attorneys, 236
National Review, 235, 306
Nelson, William E., 76
New Deal, 91-106, 110-113, 252, 254, 301
New York Law Journal, 258
New York Times, 7, 98, 213, 221, 222, 260, 305
Newton, Jim, 115
Nicholas, George, 46, 60
Nixon, Richard M., 123-127, 219, 284-289
O'Connor, Sandra Day, 66, 132, 133, 256, 289
Obama, Barack H., 1, 3, 33, 157, 247, 290
Office of Strategic Services. *See* OSS
Ogletree, Charles J. Jr., 121, 302
Oldham, David, 205
Olson, Theodore, 132
Olson, Walter K., 304
Olympic Airways, 192-198, 202, 206, 207
Olympic Aviation, 192-195
Olympic Maritime, 192
Onassis, Alexander, 192-195, 225
Onassis, Aristotle, 177, 191-206, 223, 225, 273, 305
Onassis, Christina, 194-197
Onassis, Jacqueline Kennedy, 191-197, 222

Onassis, Nicholas, 192

OSS, 173, 253

Otis, James Jr., 53, 60

Paine, Thomas, 19, 30, 55, 59

Parker, Christine, 205

Parks, Gordon, 176

Parks, Rosa, 119

Parrish, Elsie, 96, 97, 101, 154, 207, 225, 244, 294

Parsons, Theophilus, 41, 60

Paterson, William, 50, 60, 75

Patterson, Orlando, 120

Pearl Harbor, 103

Pegler, Westbrook, 92

Peltz, Nelson, 188

Pendleton, Edmund, 45, 53, 60

Pennsylvania Packet & Daily Advertiser, 25, 28, 29

Peron, Evita, 9

Peron, Juan, 9

Peskin, Allan, 277

Peysner, John, 305

Phelps, Glenn, 64

Philadelphia Convention, 27, 29, 41, 45, 64

Philip Morris, 186, 237-244, 307

Piaggio (aircraft), 192-196, 206, 305

Pickering, Timothy, 65

Pierce, Franklin, 69

Pinckney, Charles, 30, 60

Pinckney, Charles Cotesworth, 30, 60

Plato, 20

Players Club, The, 171-181, 187

Plessy v. Ferguson, 90, 112-118, 166, 301

Polk, James K., 69

Posner, Richard, 134, 227

Pound, Roscoe, 237

Presidential Succession Act of 1947, 143

Princeton University, 17

pro bono, 53, 205, 232-235, 266, 287, 288

Progressive Era, 90

Prosser, William, 222

Public Justice, 236

Publius, 29, 72

Pusey, Merlo, 104, 301

Rakove, Jack N., 38, 58

Randolph, Edmund, 18, 21, 46, 60, 65

Reagan, Ronald, 181, 286

Reconstruction, 87, 88, 89, 268

Reed, Stanley, 92, 113, 115, 118

Reeves, Richard, 156

Rehnquist, William H., 31, 110, 126, 131, 132, 133, 289, 297

Reign of Terror, 20

Remini, Robert, 309, 310

Revolutionary War, 2, 17, 33, 45-49, 54-56, 65, 70, 72

Rhode, Deborah, 185

Richardson, Elliot, 123, 126, 285

Rives, Richard, 121

Robards, Jason, 171, 176

robber barons, 261, 263, 270, 278

Roberts, Owen, 93-105, 282

Robinson, Joe, 100

Rodino, Peter, 285

Rolls-Royce, 160, 164

Roosevelt, Franklin Delano, 91-111, 252, 253, 266

Roosevelt, Theodore, 267

Root, Elihu, 252, 257, 262-267, 272, 273

Rosen, Jeffrey, 288, 289

Rowland, Roland, 200

Ruckleshaus, William, 126, 285

Rule of Law (defined), 294-295

Rush, Benjamin, 39

Rustad, Michael L., 304

Rutland, Robert Allen, 41

Rutledge, John, 23, 53, 60, 70

Ryan, George, 143

SAG (Screen Actors Guild), 172

Sandra Day O'Connor College of Law, 288

Sarat, Austin, 306

Saturday Night Massacre, 126

Sawyer, Charles, 111

Sawyer, Raymond, 154

Scalia, Antonin, 132-133

Schechter Poultry Corp. v. United States, 93

Scheingold, Stuart, 306

Schlesinger, Arthur M., 91, 270

Schwartz, Bernard, 58, 159, 226

Scott, Dred, 80, 154

Screen Actors Guild. *See* SAG

separate-but-equal standard, 112-115

Separation of Powers with Checks and Balances, 13, 33, 35, 51, 64, 65, 78, 95-99, 106-107, 148-149, 154, 158, 164, 165, 224-226, 230, 235, 286-288, 295

Seward, William H., 83, 265

Shays's Rebellion, 16, 41, 42, 230, 306

Sherman, Roger, 19, 22, 23, 37, 50, 53, 59, 60, 61, 66

Simon, James F., 300

Simpson, O. J., 195

Singletary, Amos, 41, 42

Sirica, John J., 124-127, 285

Slapper, Gary, 305

slavery, 49, 60, 61, 79-90, 103, 118, 121-122, 300

Smigel, Erwin O., 308, 309

Smith, Caleb, 83

Smith, Jean Edward, 71, 76, 107

Smith, Jonathan, 42

Social Security Act of 1935, 99, 301

Socrates, 19, 46

Solomons, Edward, 161

Souter, David, 132, 133, 158

Spens, Lord Patrick, 205, 207

Spock, Dr. Benjamin, 222

Spy vs. Spy (comic strip), 35, 74

Stalin, Josef, 95

Stallone, Sylvester, 159

Stanton, Edwin, 83

Statute of Westminster, 160

Stennis, John, 125

Stevenson, Adlai, 92

Stewart, Potter, 156

Stimson, Henry, 252, 257, 266

Stone, Harlan Fiske, 93, 97, 105

Strong, Caleb, 41, 60, 66

Stuart v. Laird, 74, 75, 300

Sunday Times (of London), 303

Sunstein, Cass, 134

Sutherland, George, 93, 101, 105

Taft, William Howard, 90, 91, 266

Talmadge, Herman, 311

Tamanaha, Brian Z., 291

Taney, Roger, 78-87

Taylor, Zachary, 69

Teapot Dome, 103, 278, 279, 280, 281, 282, 286, 287, 288

Thatcher, Margaret, 247

Thomas, Clarence, 132

Thyssen-Bornemisza, Baroness (*nee* Fiona Campbell), 193

Tilden, Samuel, 88, 140, 141, 266

Times of London, The, 161, 163, 204, 210, 292

Tocqueville, Alexis, 77, 78, 154, 155, 156, 157, 164, 230, 288

Toobin, Jeffrey, 289

Tredwell, Thomas, 47

Trial Lawyers for Public Justice. *See* Public Justice

Trujillo, Rafael, 7-13, 48, 231, 234, 292, 293

Truman, Harry S, 109-111, 114, 154, 159, 282

Trump, Donald, 159

Tugwell, Rexford, 92

Turgot, Jacques, 20

Tuttle, Elbert, 121

Tweed, William Marcy. *See* "Boss" Tweed

Tyler, John (governor), 45

Tyler, John (president), 69

U.S. Chamber of Commerce, 190, 307, 311

Van Buren, Martin, 69

Van Devanter, Willis, 93, 99, 104, 105

Vining, John, 50, 60

Vinson, Fred, 110, 113, 114, 167

Virginia Declaration of Rights, 44

Virginia Plan, 21, 22, 44, 46, 298

Voter News Service, 129

Voting Rights Act of 1965, 119

Wagner Act, 98, 99, 301

Waite, Morrison, 89, 90

Wallace, George, 122

Wallace, Henry, 106

Walsh, Thomas, 287

Warren, Earl, 114-122, 147, 159, 165

Washington Legal Foundation, 232

Washington Post, 100, 219, 221, 247, 279, 305, 307

Washington, Bushrod, 46, 60, 75

Washington, George, 20-27, 32, 39, 45, 46, 50-54, 59-72, 86, 95, 154, 223, 229, 247, 251

Watergate Committee, 284-285

Watergate scandal, 123-128, 212, 280, 284-288

Weber, Max, 259

Webster, Daniel, 226, 252, 257, 265, 275-277, 286, 287

Weicker, Lowell, 311

Welch, Joseph, 283-287

Welles, Gideon, 83

West Coast Hotel Co. v. Parrish, 96-103

Wheeler, Burton, 104

White, Walter, 111

Williams, G. Mennen, 156

Williams, Jesse, 239-244
Williams, Mayola, 239-244, 294
Wilson, James, 22-26, 39-41, 52, 55, 59, 60, 70
Wilson, Woodrow, 8, 102, 105, 249, 266
Winik, Jay, 68
Winters, Roland, 174-179
Wisdom, John Minor, 121
Witt, John Fabian, 159, 226
Wood, Gordon, 63
Woolf, Lord Harry, 168, 169, 182, 184, 189, 203

World War II, 106, 110, 119, 158, 166, 173, 181, 193, 195, 234, 235, 285
WorldCom Corporation, 257
Wythe, George, 46, 60
Yale Law School, 258
Yates, Robert, 17, 47, 71
Zander, Michael, 305
Zimmerman, Warren, 252
Zion, Sidney, 305

About the Author

Stuart M. Speiser is the author of 56 volumes on law and economics. His legal works, several of them in their fourth editions, have been cited hundreds of times by the U.S. Supreme Court and other federal and state appellate courts throughout the country.

A World War II bomber pilot and later a commercial pilot, he helped to pioneer the plaintiff's side of air crash litigation, successfully representing victims of most of the major air disasters of the 20th Century, including claimants from dozens of foreign countries. He was the organizer of the Aviation Law Section of the American Association for Justice (the first such section in any bar association) and served as chairman for its first ten years (1955-1964).

He pioneered the use of economists as expert witnesses to appraise loss of earning power, and authored the definitive text on the subject. He represented plaintiffs in many famous cases, including Ralph Nader's suit against General Motors, the war of the Guccis, the Entebbe hijacking, the death of Roberto Clemente, the Pan Am Lockerbie bombing, the suit against the estate of Aristotle Onassis which revealed Onassis's complicity in his son's fatal airplane crash, and four of the nine cases which formed the basis for adoption of strict liability for injuries caused by defective products in the 1964 revision of the American Law Institute's *Restatement of Torts.*

He has testified on legal matters before Congressional committees and England's Law Commission, and has been called as the court's expert witness by federal judges.

For his work in spreading American legal principles to other nations, he was honored by creation of the Stuart Speiser Chair at England's Nottingham Law School. He is a member of the Honorary Board of Editors of the *Journal of Post Keynesian Economics,* and was awarded the James Smithson medal by the Smithsonian Institution for his art contributions to the National Air and Space Museum.

About the Pound Civil Justice Institute

The Pound Civil Justice Institute is a national legal "think tank" created by pioneering members of the trial bar and dedicated to ensuring access to justice for ordinary citizens. Through its activities, the Institute works to give lawyers, judges, legal educators and the public a balanced view of the issues affecting the U.S. civil justice system.

The Institute was established in 1956 as the Roscoe Pound-American Trial Lawyers Foundation by a group of lawyers to honor and build upon the work of Roscoe Pound (1870–1964). Pound served as Dean of the Harvard Law School from 1916 to 1936, and is acknowledged as the founder of sociological jurisprudence—an interdisciplinary approach to legal concepts in which the law is recognized as a dynamic system that is influenced by social conditions and that, in turn, influences society as a whole. For several years in the 1950s, Dean Pound edited the law journal of the National Association of Claimants' Compensation Attorneys (NACCA)—the precursor to the Association of Trial Lawyers of America (ATLA) and today's American Association for Justice (AAJ).

Throughout its history, the Pound Institute has tailored its activities to the changing needs of the judiciary and the legal academic community, with emphases on adding balance to the debates on the U.S. civil justice system and supporting the principle of judicial independence and the right to trial by jury in civil cases. These activities have included conferences; publications; grants for academic research; law school symposia for legal academics; recognition of achievements of law professors and students in the areas of health care law, environmental law, and teaching trial advocacy; and the annual Forum for State Appellate Court Judges—a full-day educational program open only to judges, which has been held since 1992 and is accredited by all state mandatory continuing legal education authorities.

The Pound Institute's work is supported by a roster of over 1,000 members—the Pound Fellows. Every member of the bar who is in good standing and who supports a strong American civil justice system is eligible to become a Pound Fellow. To inquire about becoming a Fellow, or supporting Pound in other ways, please contact the Institute.

 Pound Civil Justice Institute
777 Sixth Street, N.W., Suite 200
Washington DC 20001
Phone: 202-944-2841
info@poundinstitute.org
www.poundinstitute.org